Wake Up, Sleeping Beauty

1

MEGUMI
MORINO

CONTENTS

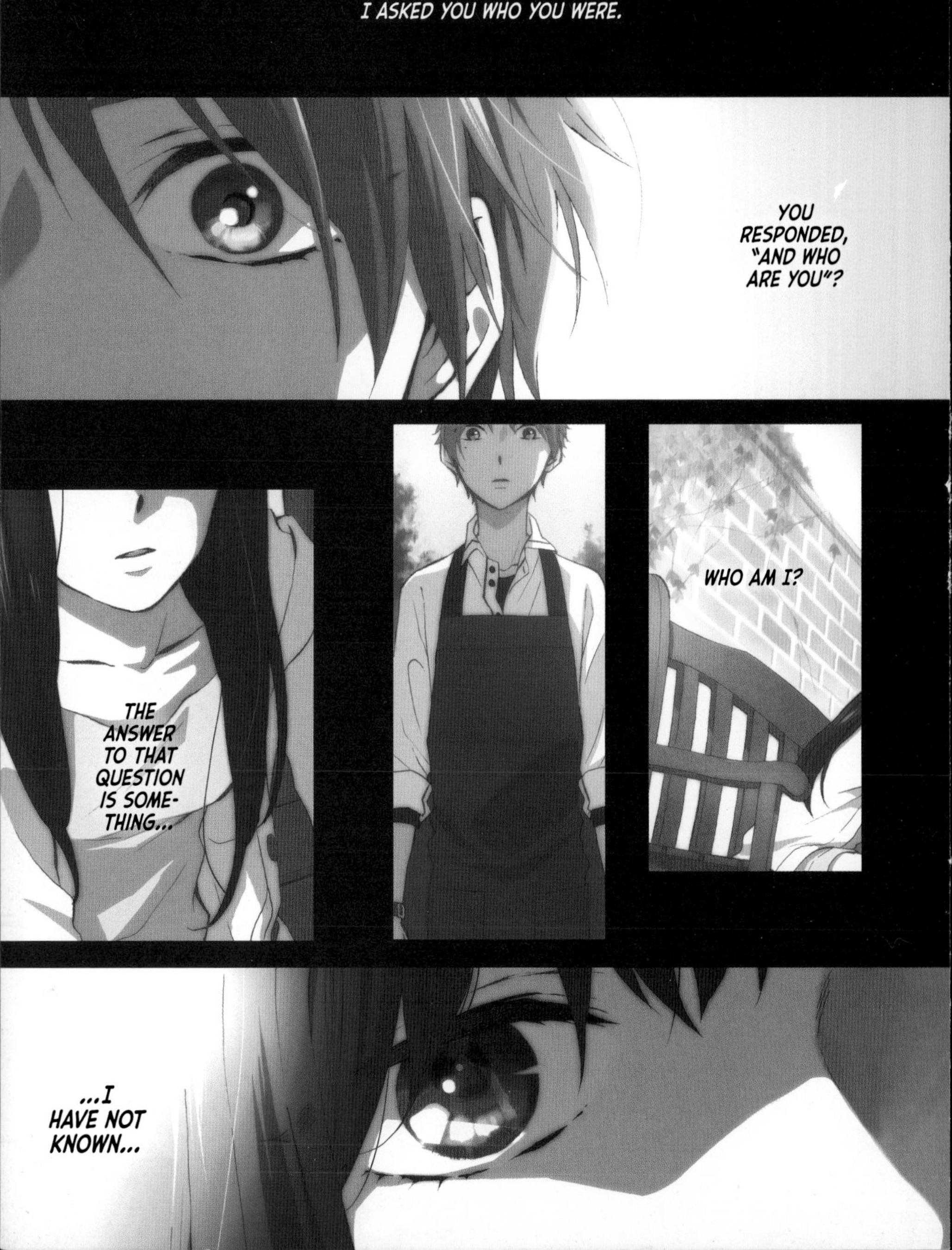
I ASKED YOU WHO YOU WERE.
YOU RESPONDED, "AND WHO ARE YOU"?
WHO AM I?
THE ANSWER TO THAT QUESTION IS SOME-THING...
...I HAVE NOT KNOWN...

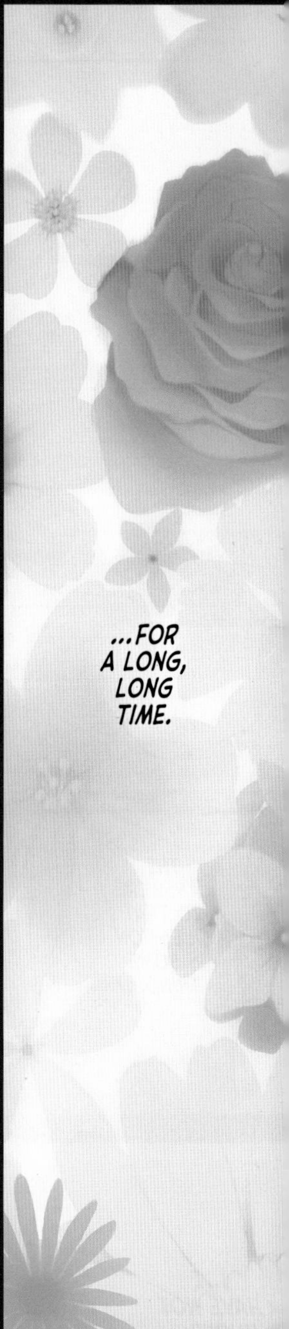
...FOR A LONG, LONG TIME.

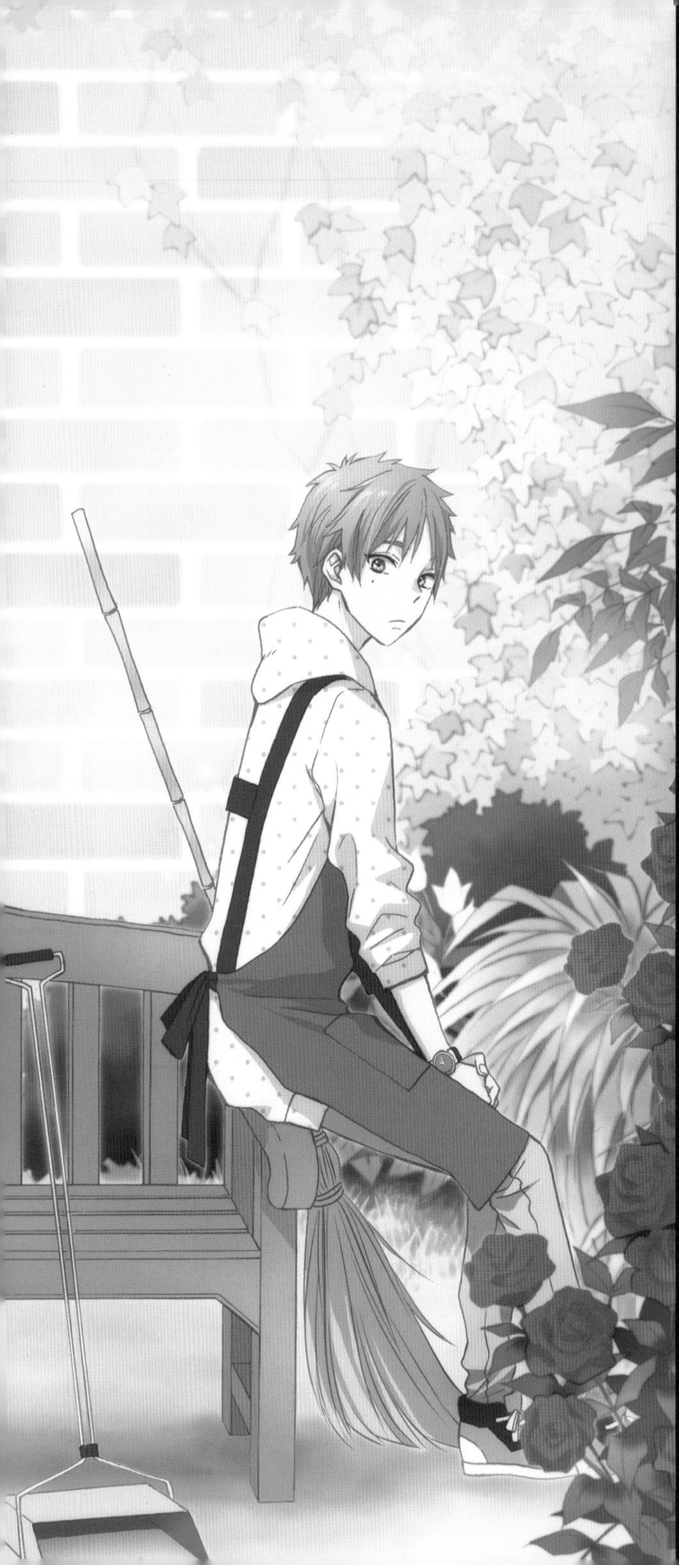

Chapter 1

I Like You

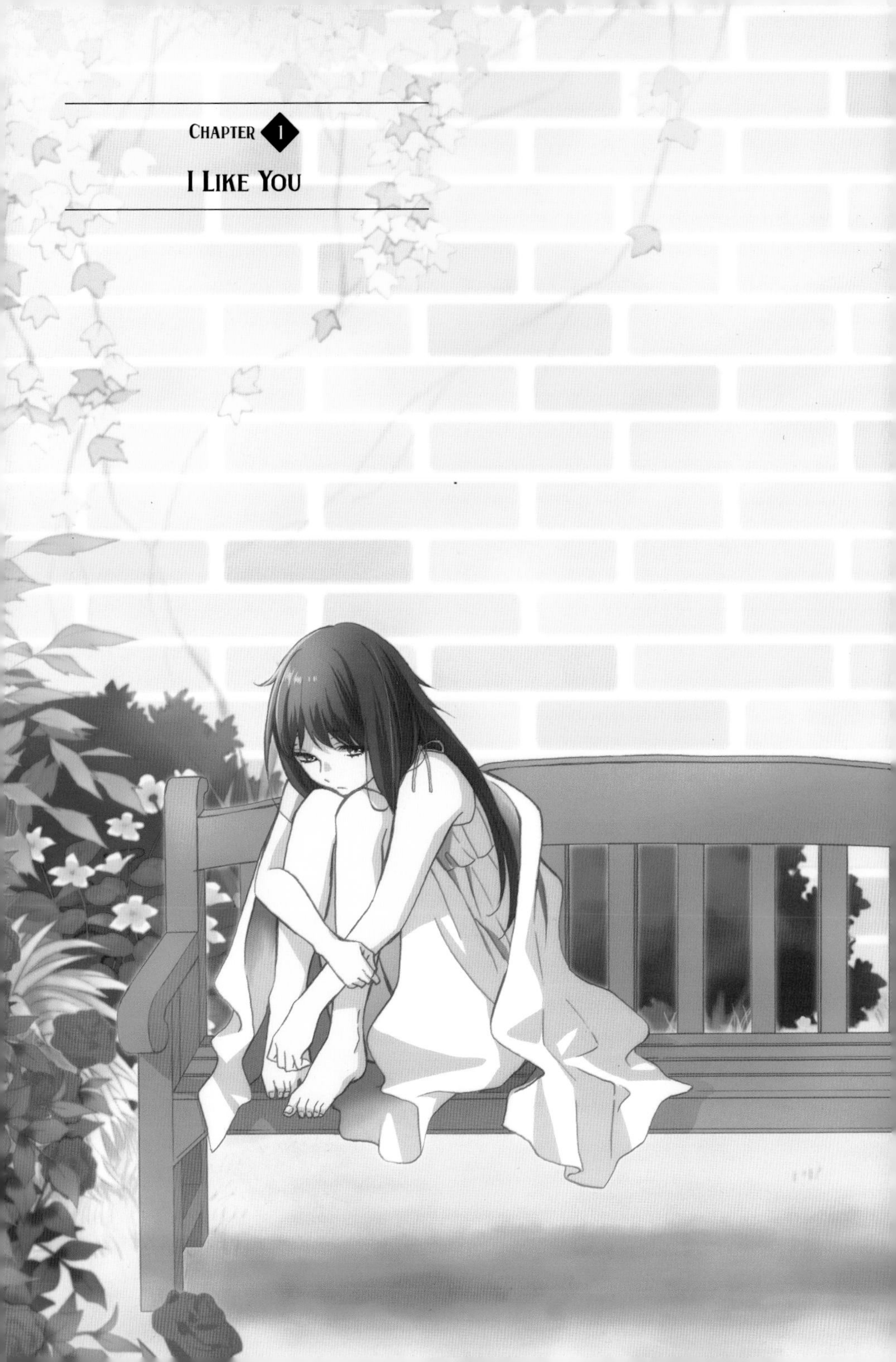

Wake Up, Sleeping Beauty

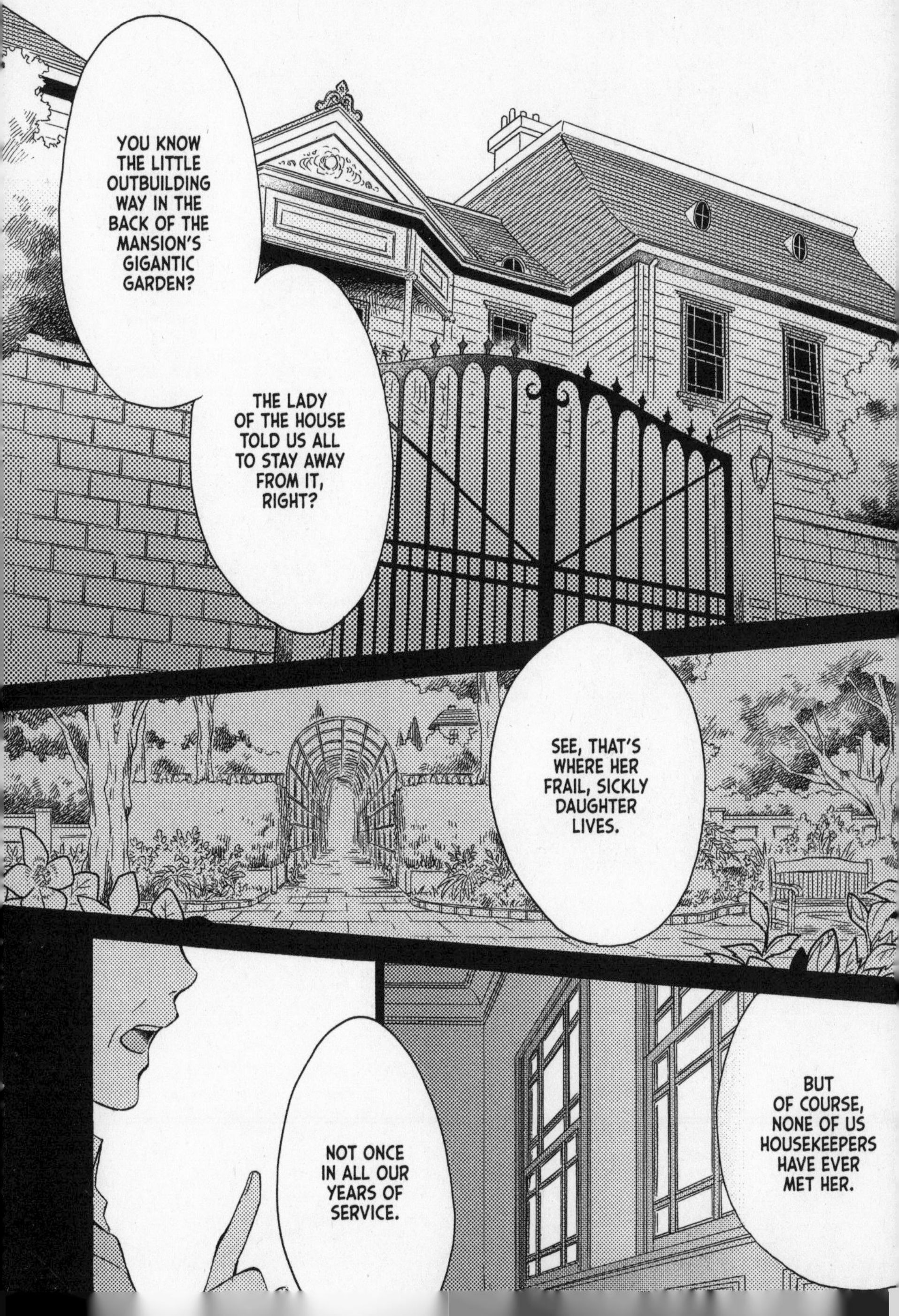
YOU KNOW THE LITTLE OUTBUILDING WAY IN THE BACK OF THE MANSION'S GIGANTIC GARDEN?
THE LADY OF THE HOUSE TOLD US ALL TO STAY AWAY FROM IT, RIGHT?
SEE, THAT'S WHERE HER FRAIL, SICKLY DAUGHTER LIVES.
BUT OF COURSE, NONE OF US HOUSEKEEPERS HAVE EVER MET HER.
NOT ONCE IN ALL OUR YEARS OF SERVICE.

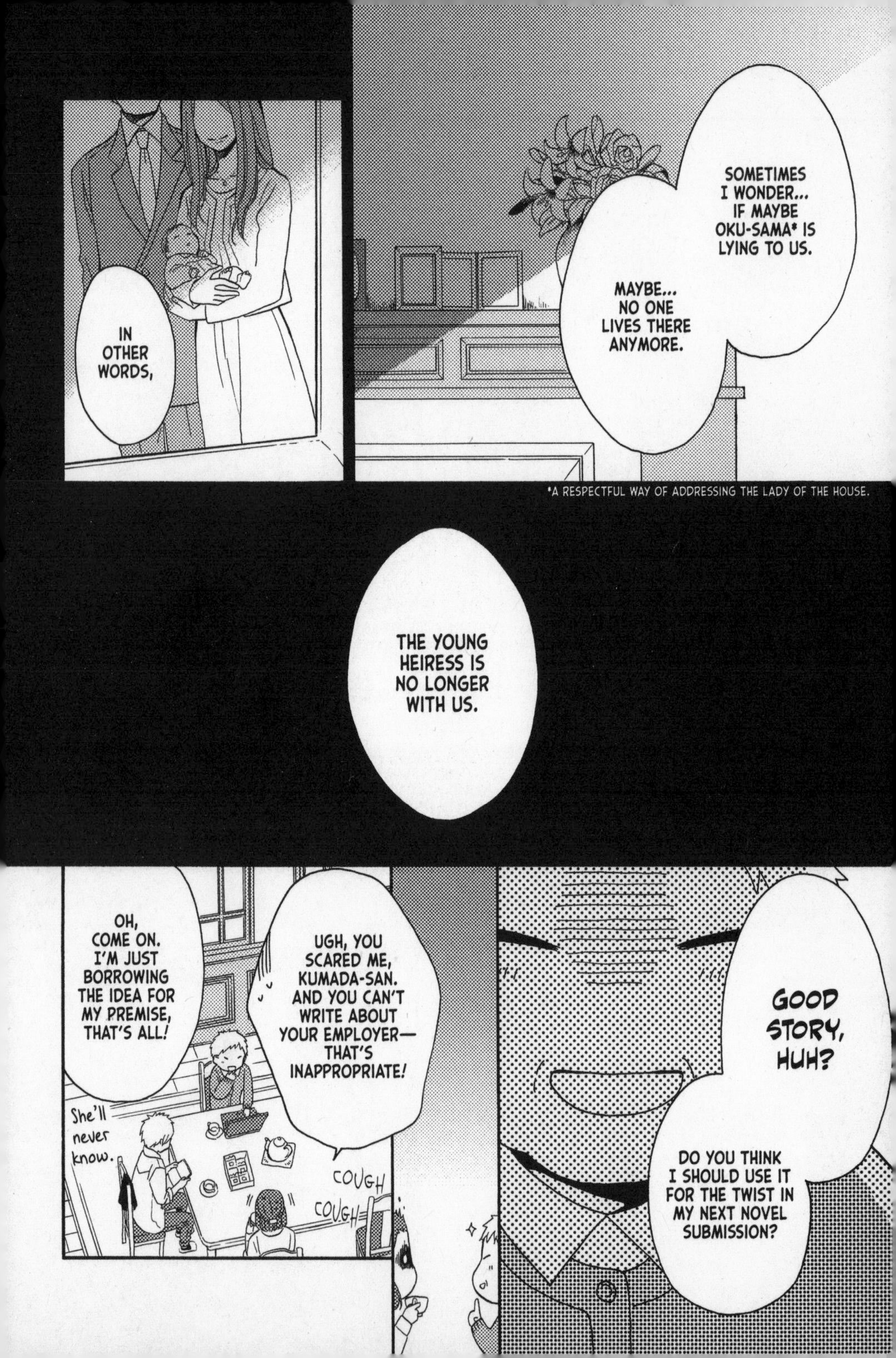
SOMETIMES I WONDER... IF MAYBE OKU-SAMA* IS LYING TO US.
MAYBE... NO ONE LIVES THERE ANYMORE.
IN OTHER WORDS,
THE YOUNG HEIRESS IS NO LONGER WITH US.
GOOD STORY, HUH?
DO YOU THINK I SHOULD USE IT FOR THE TWIST IN MY NEXT NOVEL SUBMISSION?
UGH, YOU SCARED ME, KUMADA-SAN. AND YOU CAN'T WRITE ABOUT YOUR EMPLOYER—THAT'S INAPPROPRIATE!
OH, COME ON. I'M JUST BORROWING THE IDEA FOR MY PREMISE, THAT'S ALL!
COUGH
COUGH
She'll never know.

*A RESPECTFUL WAY OF ADDRESSING THE LADY OF THE HOUSE.

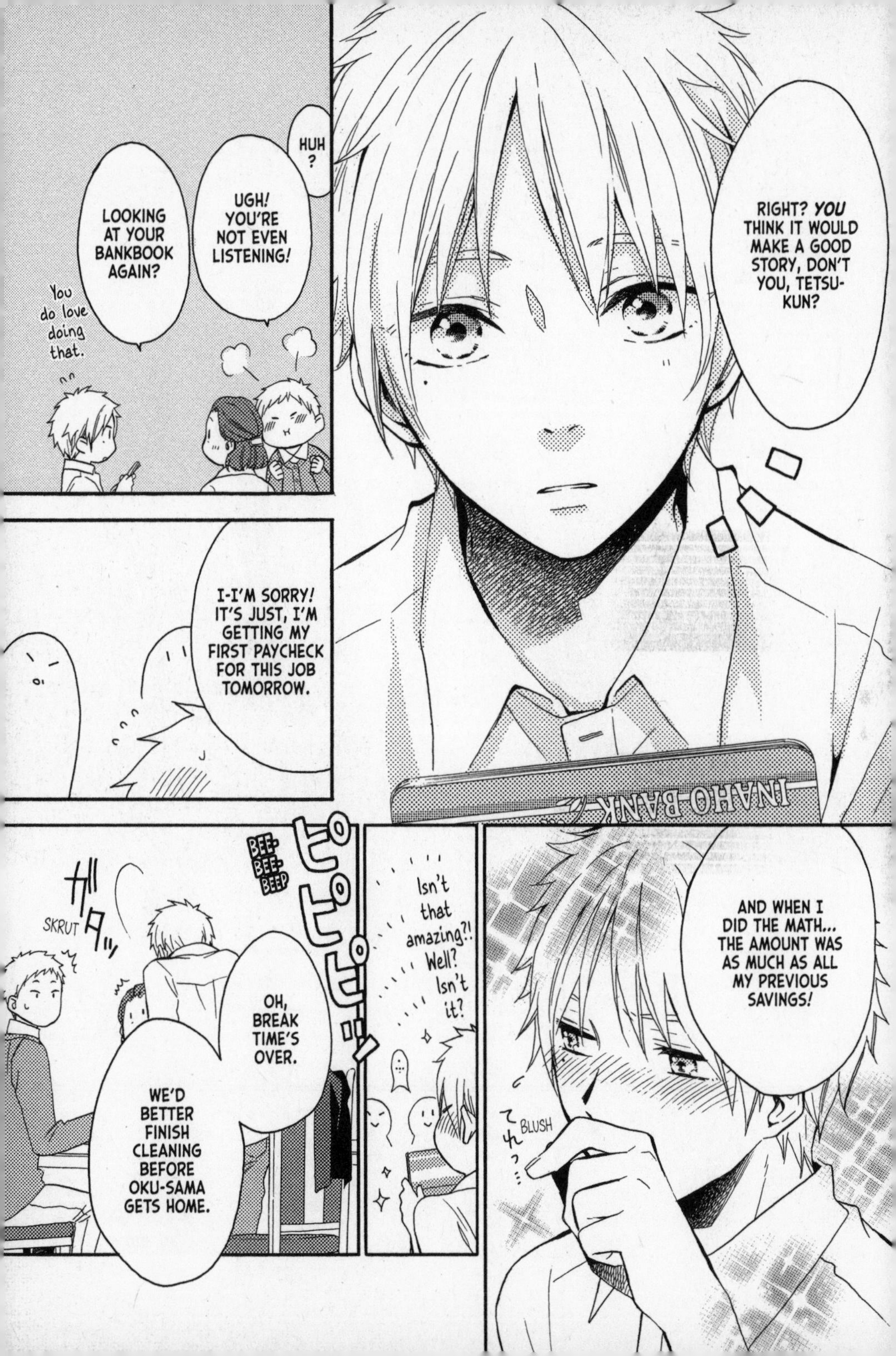
RIGHT? *YOU* THINK IT WOULD MAKE A GOOD STORY, DON'T YOU, TETSU-KUN?
INAHO BANK
HUH?
UGH! YOU'RE NOT EVEN LISTENING!
LOOKING AT YOUR BANKBOOK AGAIN?
You do love doing that.
I-I'M SORRY! IT'S JUST, I'M GETTING MY FIRST PAYCHECK FOR THIS JOB TOMORROW.
AND WHEN I DID THE MATH... THE AMOUNT WAS AS MUCH AS ALL MY PREVIOUS SAVINGS!
BLUSH
Isn't that amazing?! Well? Isn't it?
BEE-BEE-BEEP
OH, BREAK TIME'S OVER.
SKRUT
WE'D BETTER FINISH CLEANING BEFORE OKU-SAMA GETS HOME.

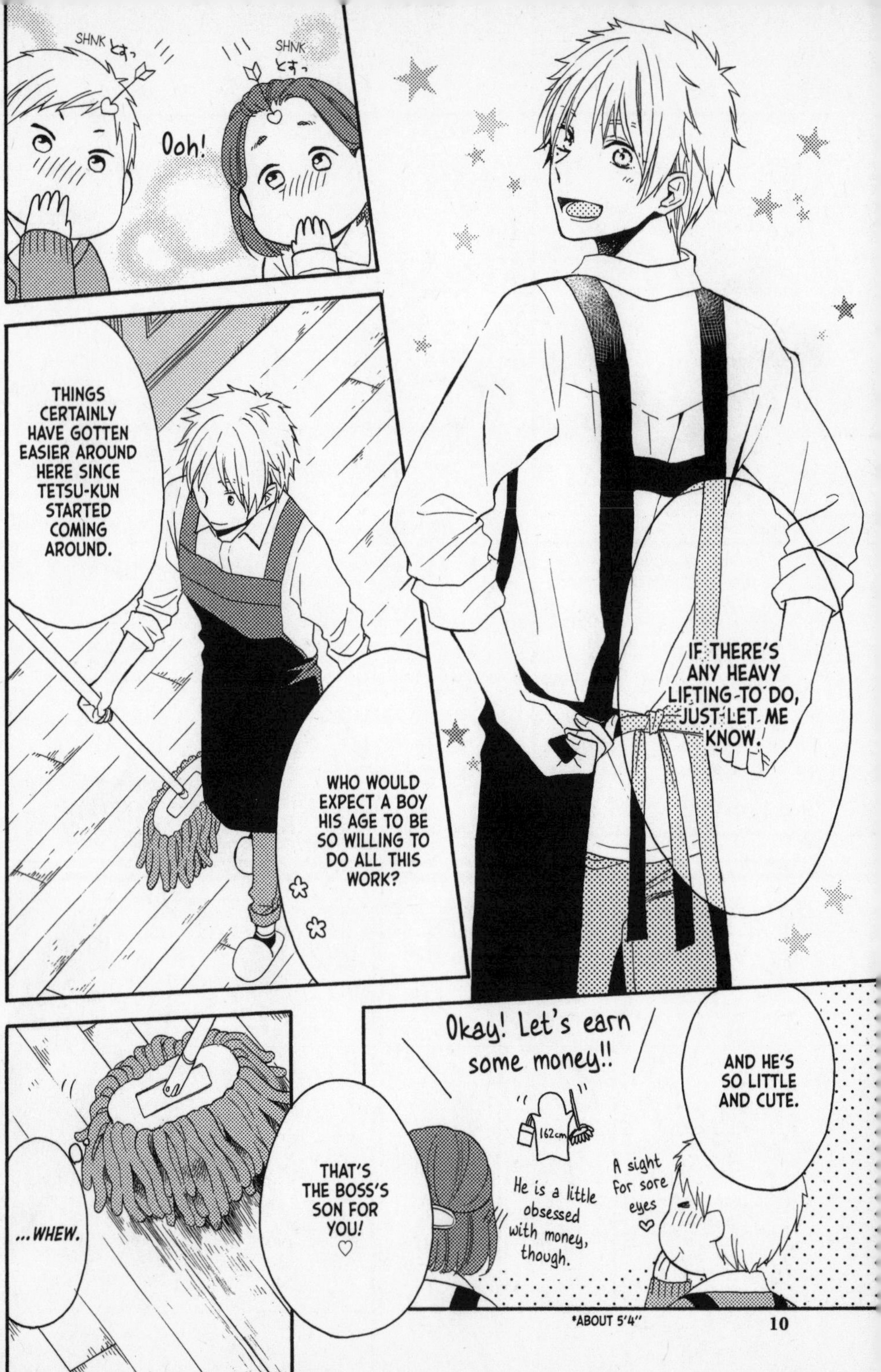
IF THERE'S ANY HEAVY LIFTING TO DO, JUST LET ME KNOW.
SHNK とすっ
Ooh!
SHNK とすっ
THINGS CERTAINLY HAVE GOTTEN EASIER AROUND HERE SINCE TETSU-KUN STARTED COMING AROUND.
WHO WOULD EXPECT A BOY HIS AGE TO BE SO WILLING TO DO ALL THIS WORK?
AND HE'S SO LITTLE AND CUTE.
Okay! Let's earn some money!!
162cm
A sight for sore eyes ♡
He is a little obsessed with money, though.
THAT'S THE BOSS'S SON FOR YOU! ♡
...WHEW.

*ABOUT 5'4"

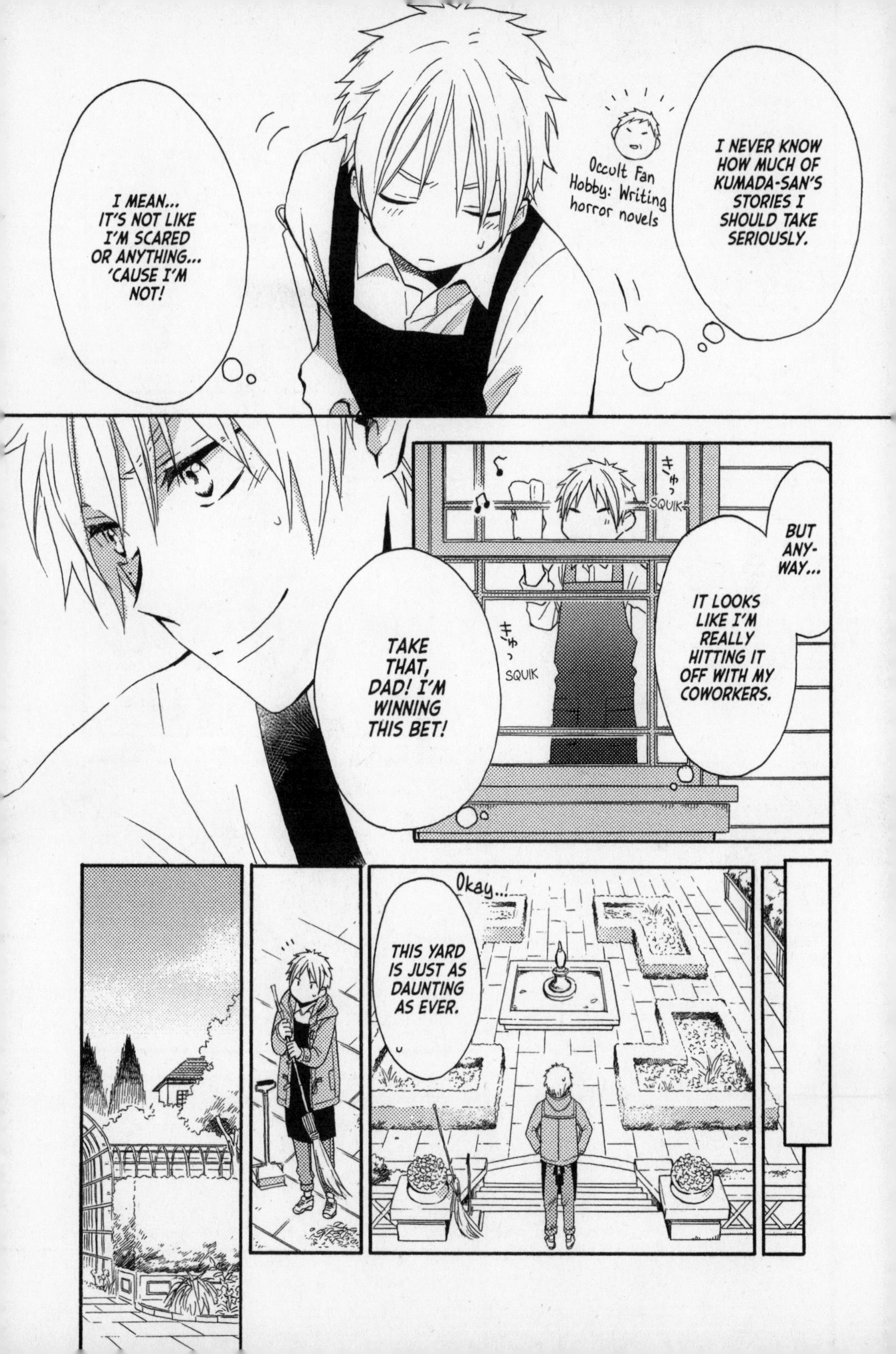
I NEVER KNOW HOW MUCH OF KUMADA-SAN'S STORIES I SHOULD TAKE SERIOUSLY.
Occult Fan
Hobby: Writing horror novels
I MEAN... IT'S NOT LIKE I'M SCARED OR ANYTHING... 'CAUSE I'M NOT!
きゅっ SQUIK
BUT ANY-WAY...
IT LOOKS LIKE I'M REALLY HITTING IT OFF WITH MY COWORKERS.
きゅっ SQUIK
TAKE THAT, DAD! I'M WINNING THIS BET!
Okay...
THIS YARD IS JUST AS DAUNTING AS EVER.

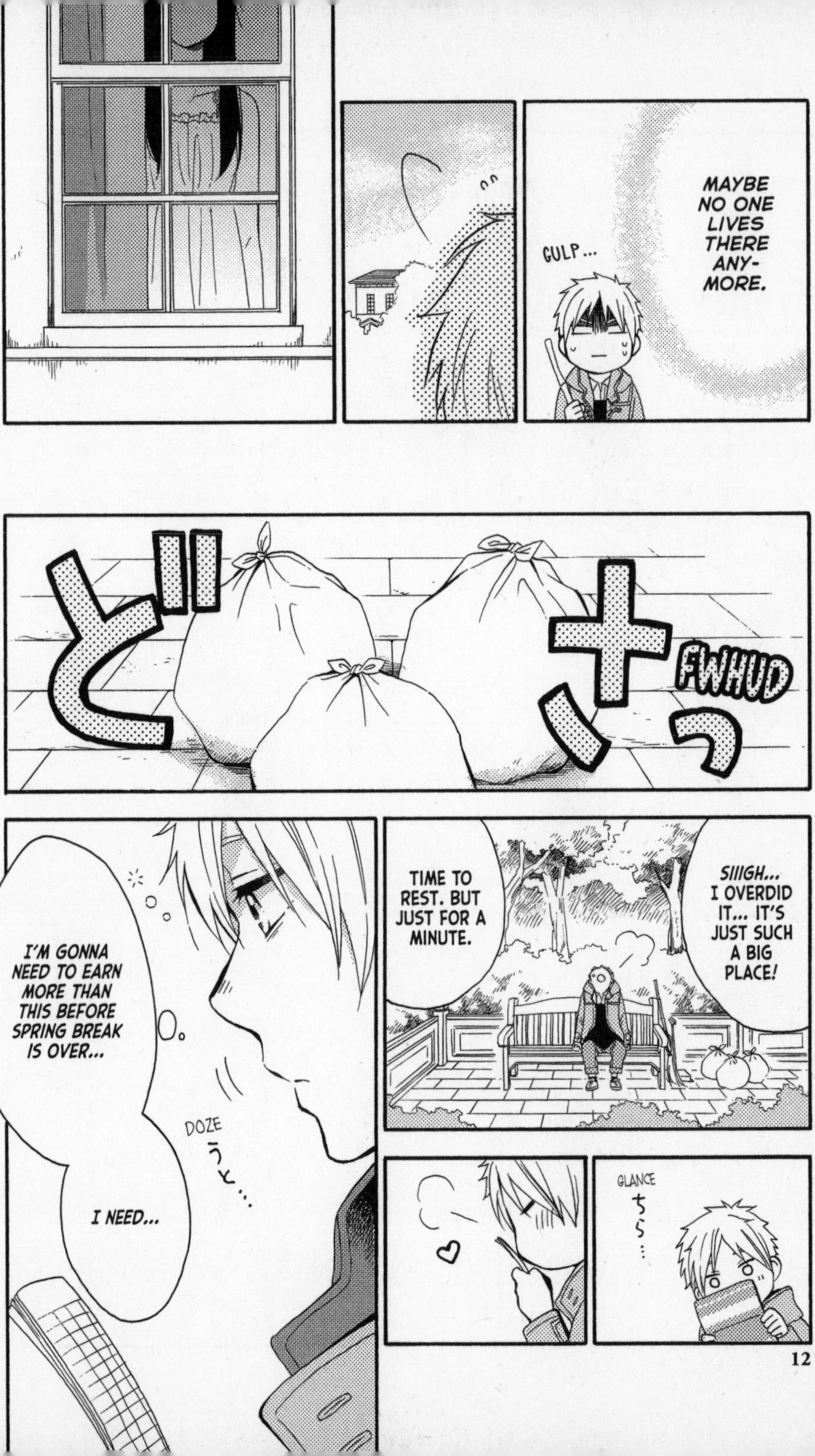
MAYBE NO ONE LIVES THERE ANY-MORE.
GULP...
どさっ
FWHUD
SIIIGH... I OVERDID IT... IT'S JUST SUCH A BIG PLACE!
TIME TO REST. BUT JUST FOR A MINUTE.
GLANCE
ちら…
I'M GONNA NEED TO EARN MORE THAN THIS BEFORE SPRING BREAK IS OVER...
DOZE
うと…
I NEED...

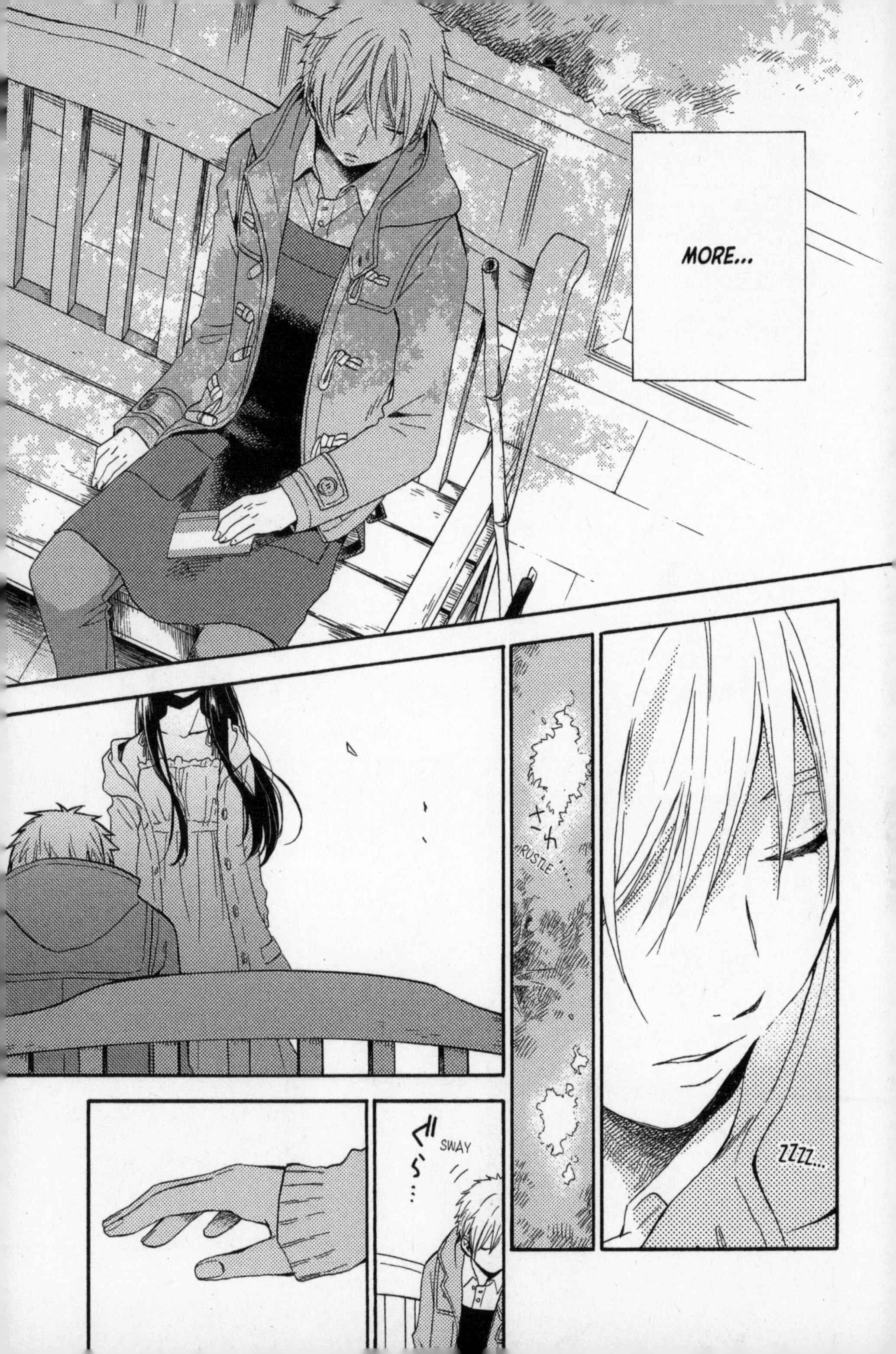
MORE...
ZZZZ...
RUSTLE...
ぐら…
SWAY

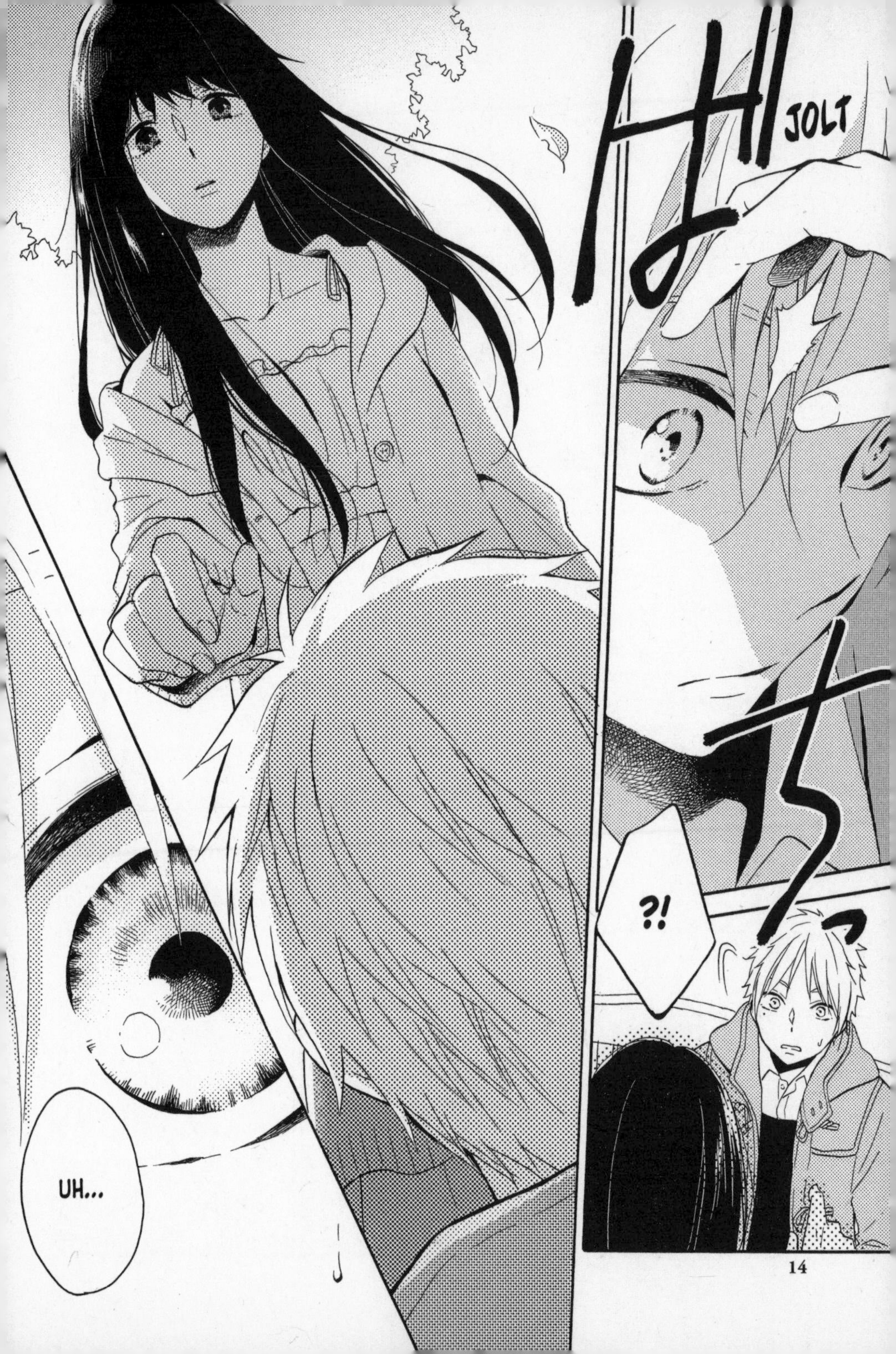
JOLT
?!
UH...

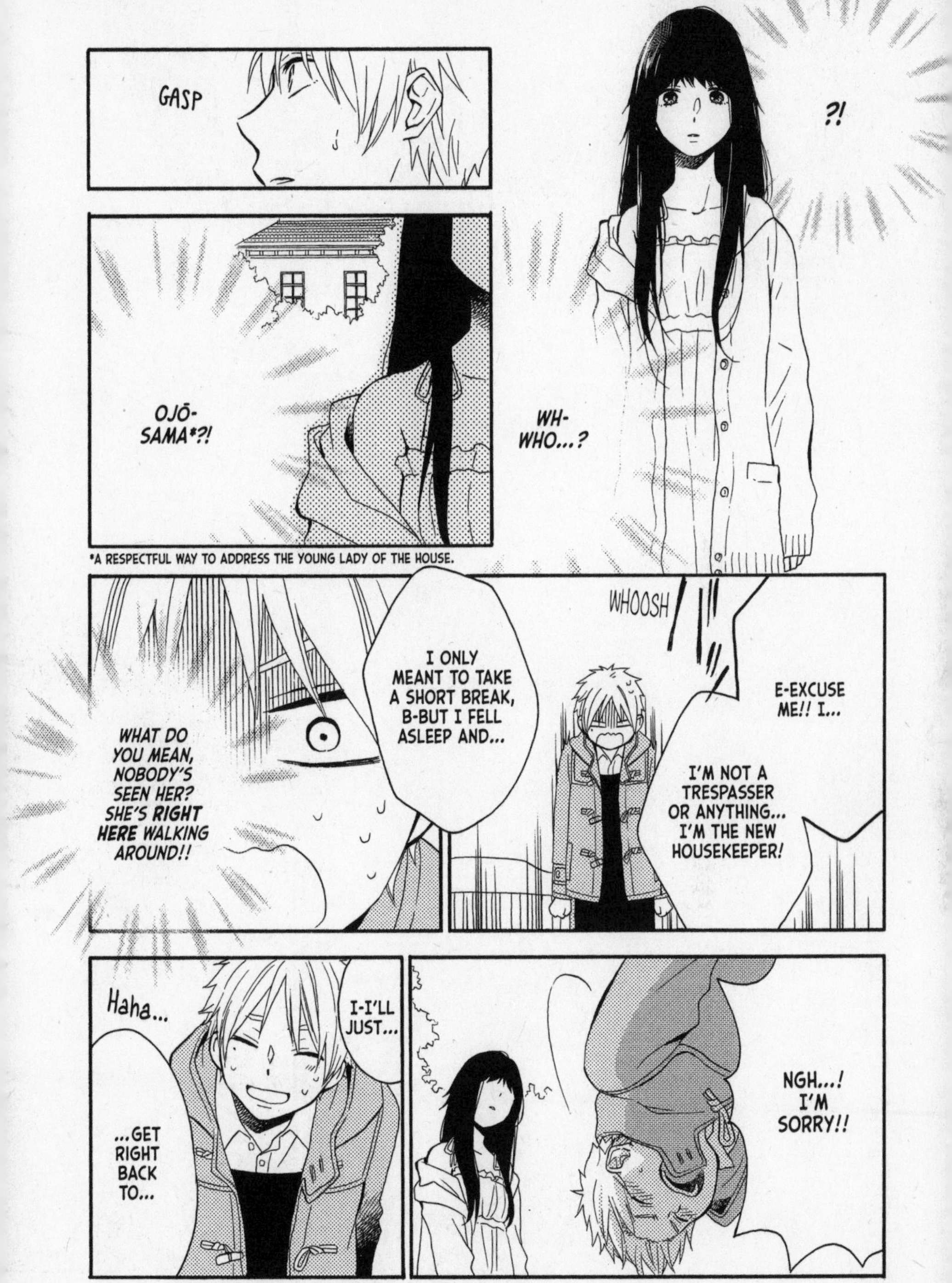
?!
WH-
WHO...?
GASP
OJŌ-
SAMA*?!
WHOOSH
E-EXCUSE ME!! I...
I'M NOT A TRESPASSER OR ANYTHING... I'M THE NEW HOUSEKEEPER!
I ONLY MEANT TO TAKE A SHORT BREAK, B-BUT I FELL ASLEEP AND...
WHAT DO YOU MEAN, NOBODY'S SEEN HER? SHE'S **RIGHT HERE** WALKING AROUND!!
NGH...! I'M SORRY!!
I-I'LL JUST...
Haha...
...GET RIGHT BACK TO...

*A RESPECTFUL WAY TO ADDRESS THE YOUNG LADY OF THE HOUSE.

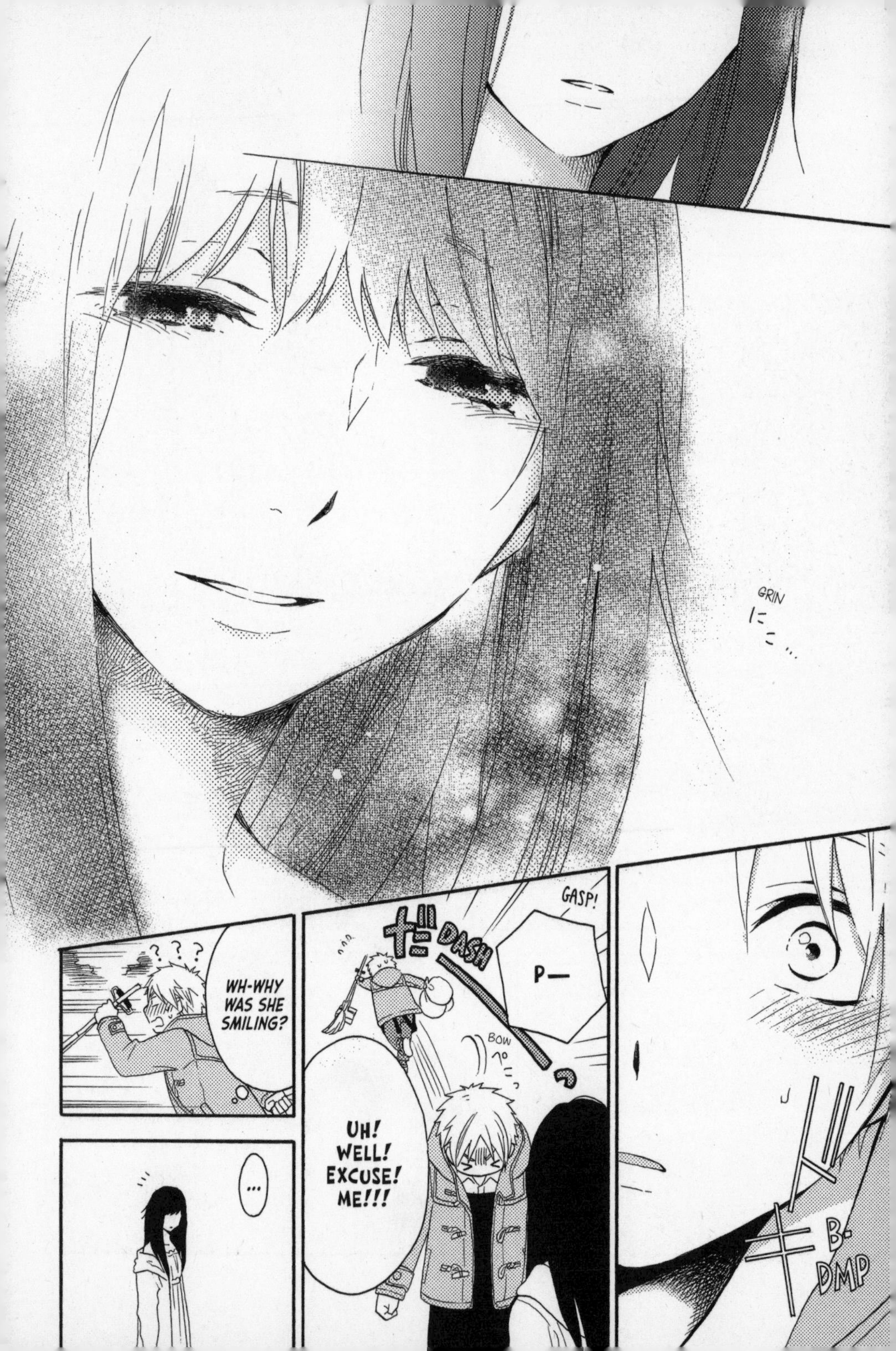
GRIN
B-
DMP
GASP!
P—
DASH
BOW
UH! WELL! EXCUSE! ME!!!
WH-WHY WAS SHE SMILING?
...

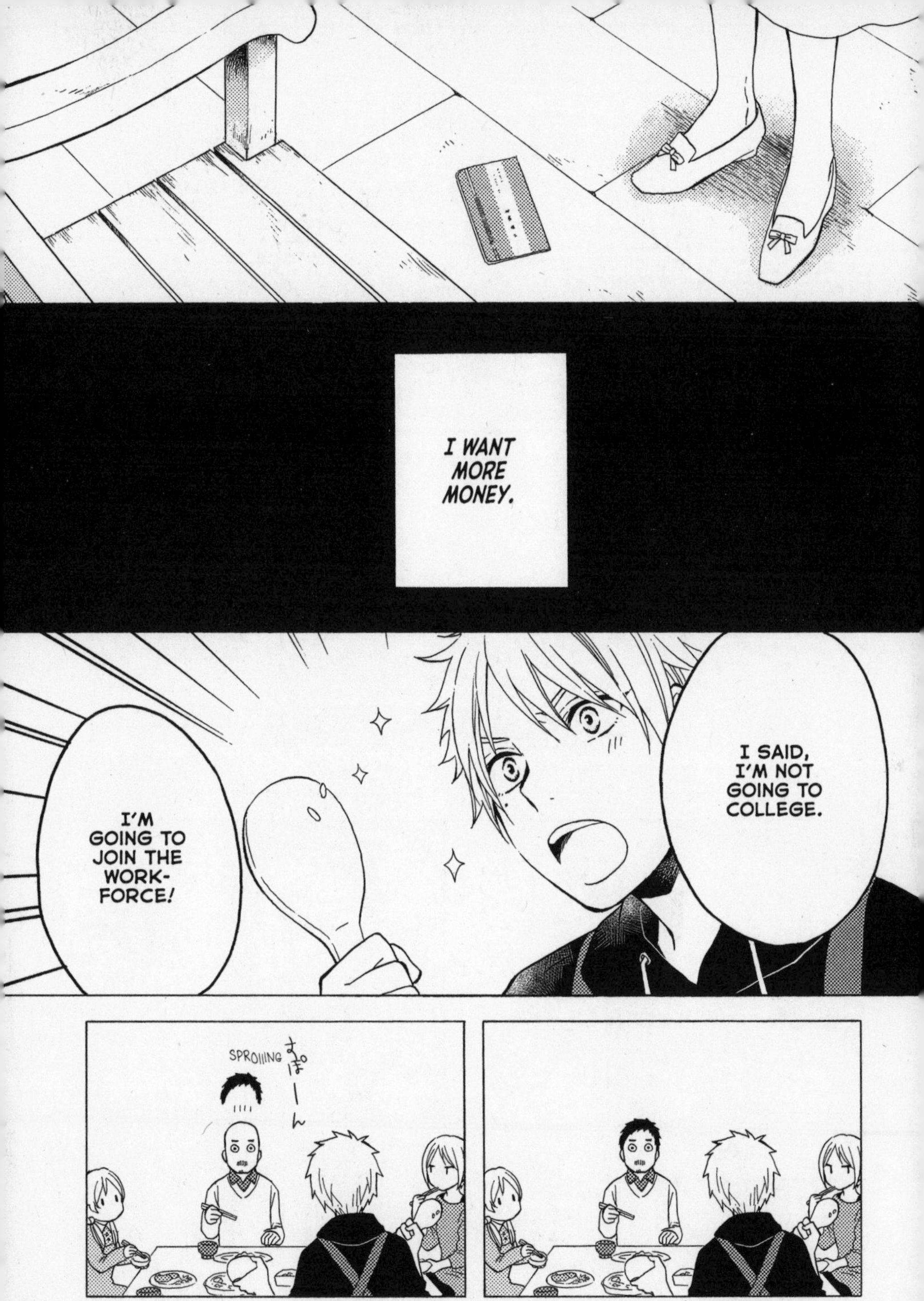
I WANT MORE MONEY.
I SAID, I'M NOT GOING TO COLLEGE.
I'M GOING TO JOIN THE WORK-FORCE!
SPROIIING
すぽーん

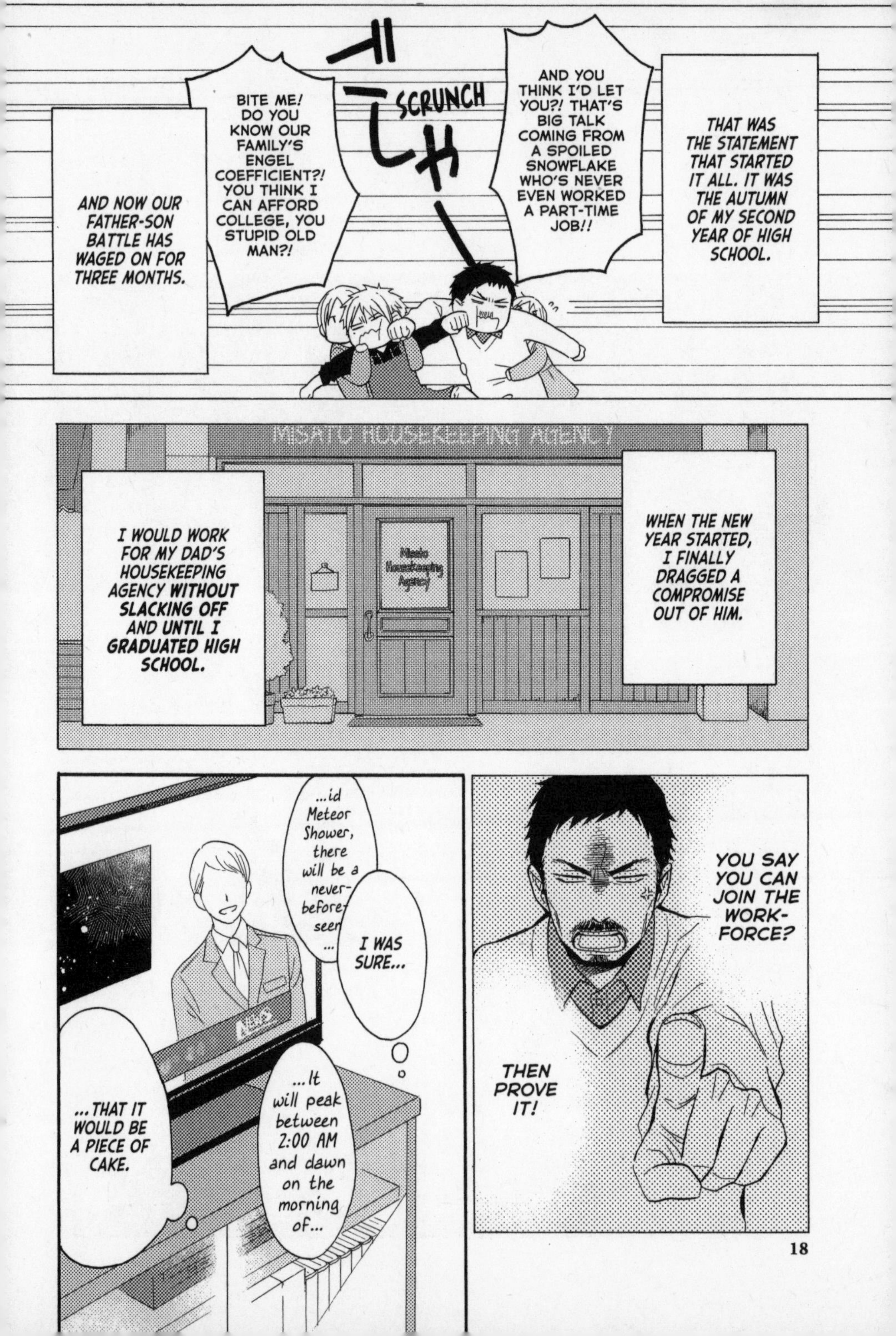
THAT WAS THE STATEMENT THAT STARTED IT ALL. IT WAS THE AUTUMN OF MY SECOND YEAR OF HIGH SCHOOL.
AND YOU THINK I'D LET YOU?! THAT'S BIG TALK COMING FROM A SPOILED SNOWFLAKE WHO'S NEVER EVEN WORKED A PART-TIME JOB!!
SCRUNCH
BITE ME! DO YOU KNOW OUR FAMILY'S ENGEL COEFFICIENT?! YOU THINK I CAN AFFORD COLLEGE, YOU STUPID OLD MAN?!
AND NOW OUR FATHER-SON BATTLE HAS WAGED ON FOR THREE MONTHS.
MISATO HOUSEKEEPING AGENCY
WHEN THE NEW YEAR STARTED, I FINALLY DRAGGED A COMPROMISE OUT OF HIM.
Misato Housekeeping Agency
I WOULD WORK FOR MY DAD'S HOUSEKEEPING AGENCY WITHOUT SLACKING OFF AND UNTIL I GRADUATED HIGH SCHOOL.
YOU SAY YOU CAN JOIN THE WORK-FORCE?
THEN PROVE IT!
...id Meteor Shower, there will be a never-before-seen...
I WAS SURE...
...It will peak between 2:00 AM and dawn on the morning of...
...THAT IT WOULD BE A PIECE OF CAKE.

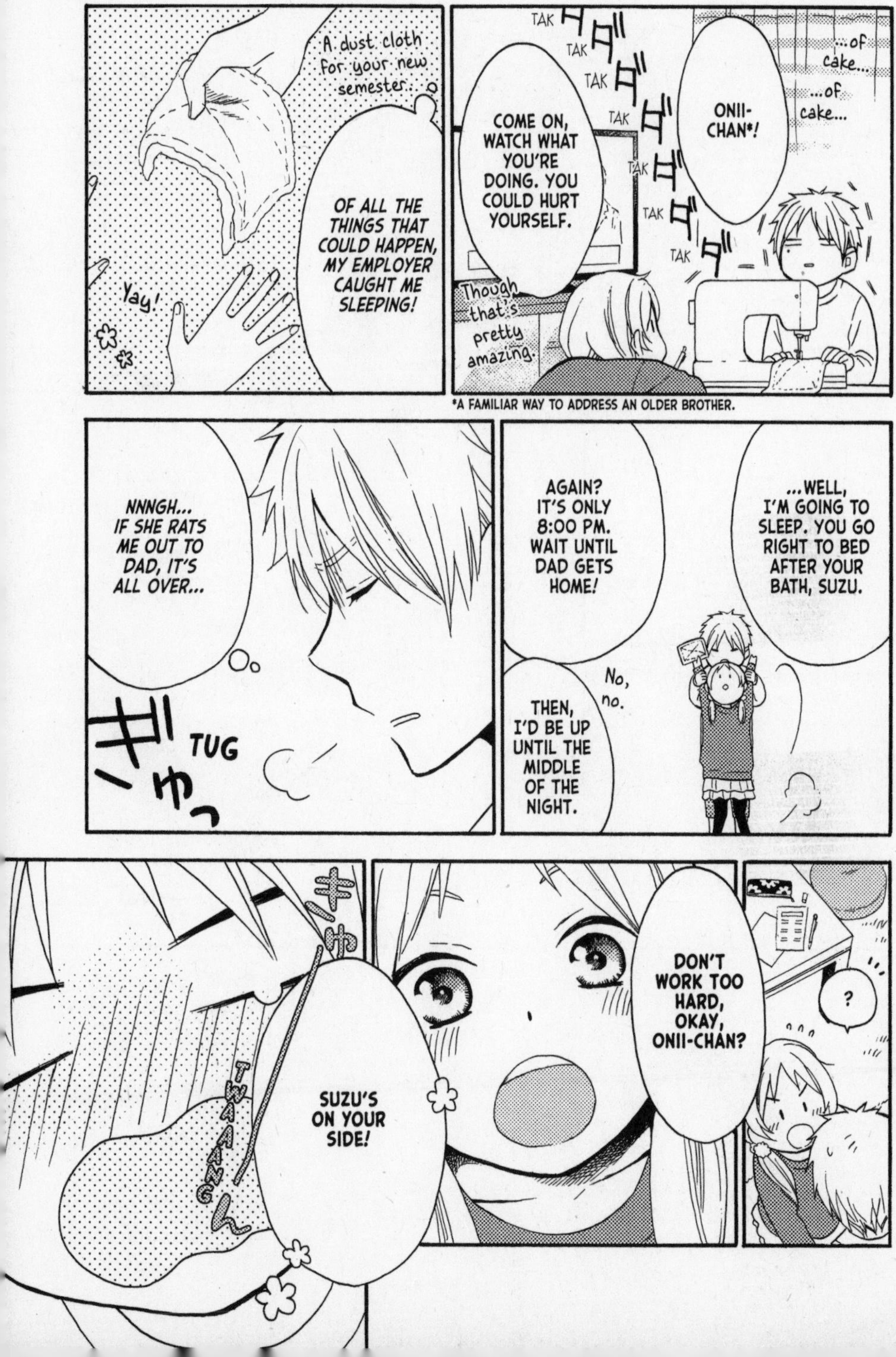
...of cake...
...of cake...
ONII-CHAN*!
TAK TAK TAK TAK TAK TAK TAK
COME ON, WATCH WHAT YOU'RE DOING. YOU COULD HURT YOURSELF.
Though that's pretty amazing.
A dust cloth for your new semester...
OF ALL THE THINGS THAT COULD HAPPEN, MY EMPLOYER CAUGHT ME SLEEPING!
Yay!
...WELL, I'M GOING TO SLEEP. YOU GO RIGHT TO BED AFTER YOUR BATH, SUZU.
AGAIN? IT'S ONLY 8:00 PM. WAIT UNTIL DAD GETS HOME!
No, no.
THEN, I'D BE UP UNTIL THE MIDDLE OF THE NIGHT.
NNNGH... IF SHE RATS ME OUT TO DAD, IT'S ALL OVER...
TUG
?
DON'T WORK TOO HARD, OKAY, ONII-CHAN?
SUZU'S ON YOUR SIDE!
TWAAANG

*A FAMILIAR WAY TO ADDRESS AN OLDER BROTHER.

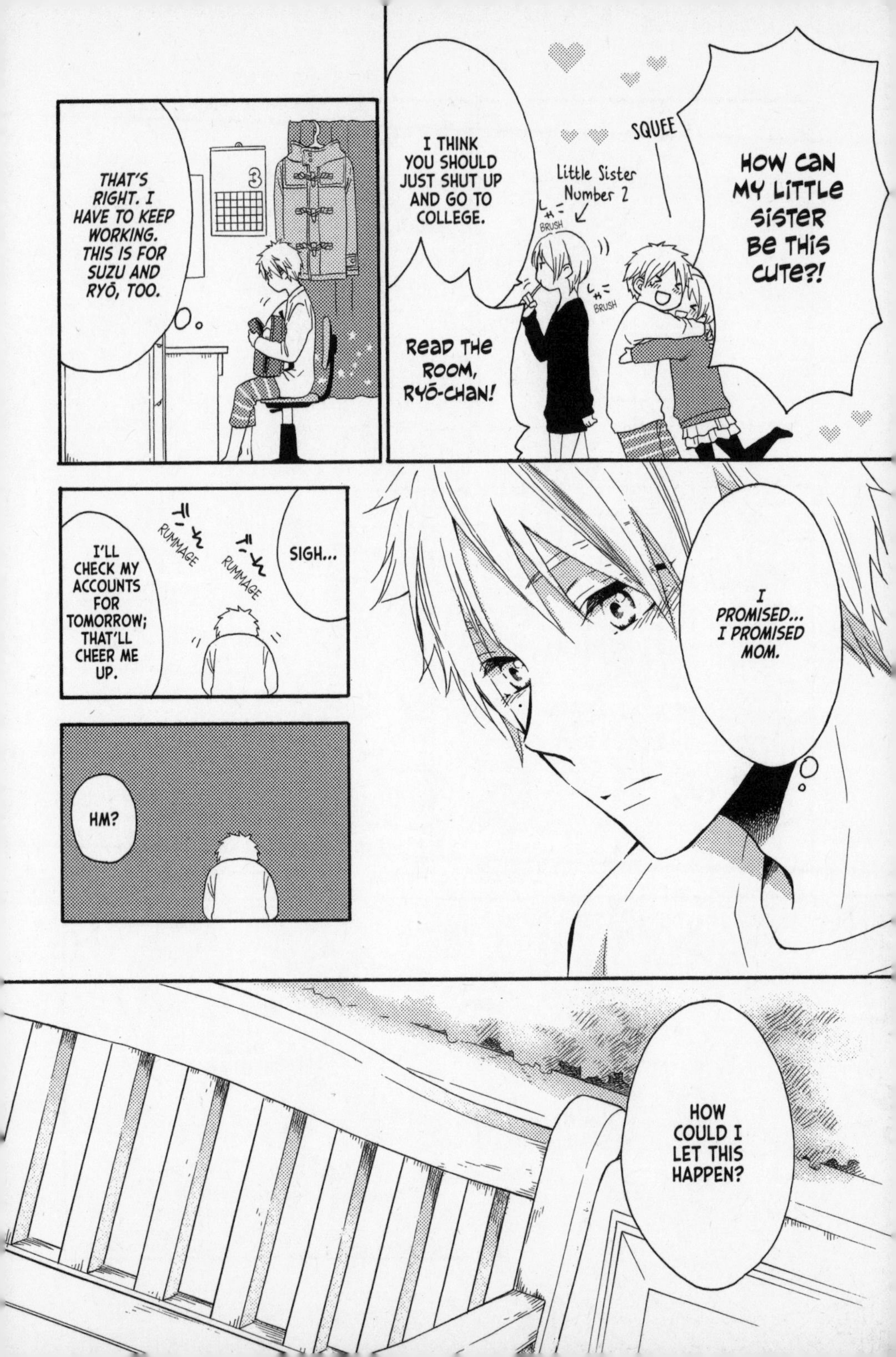
HOW CAN MY LITTLE SISTER BE THIS CUTE?!
SQUEE
Little Sister Number 2
BRUSH
BRUSH
I THINK YOU SHOULD JUST SHUT UP AND GO TO COLLEGE.
READ THE ROOM, RYŌ-CHAN!
THAT'S RIGHT. I HAVE TO KEEP WORKING. THIS IS FOR SUZU AND RYŌ, TOO.
I PROMISED... I PROMISED MOM.
SIGH...
RUMMAGE
RUMMAGE
I'LL CHECK MY ACCOUNTS FOR TOMORROW; THAT'LL CHEER ME UP.
HM?
HOW COULD I LET THIS HAPPEN?

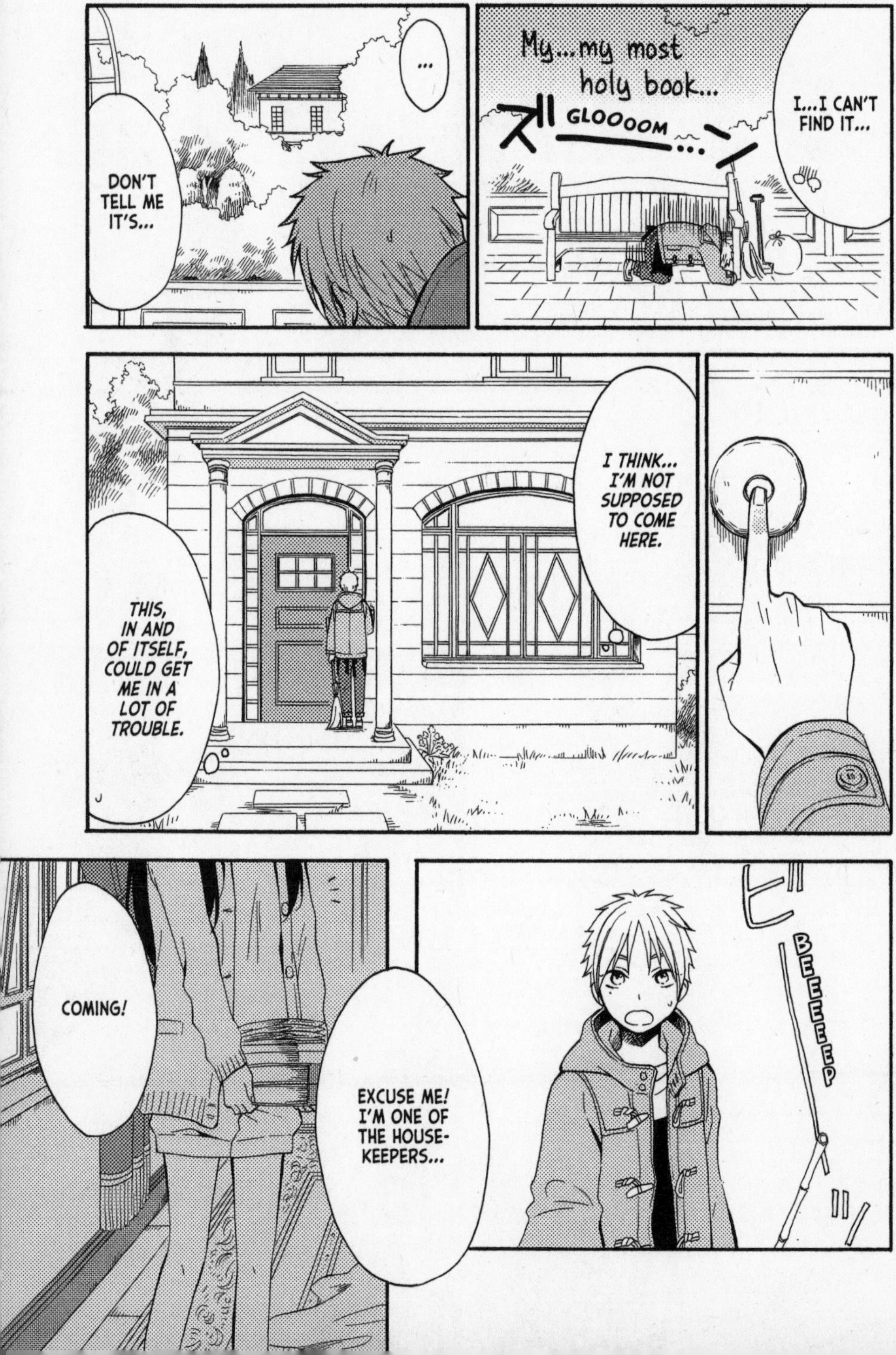

I...I CAN'T FIND IT...
My...my most holy book...
GLOOOOM...
...
DON'T TELL ME IT'S...
I THINK... I'M NOT SUPPOSED TO COME HERE.
THIS, IN AND OF ITSELF, COULD GET ME IN A LOT OF TROUBLE.
BEEEEEP
EXCUSE ME! I'M ONE OF THE HOUSE-KEEPERS...
COMING!

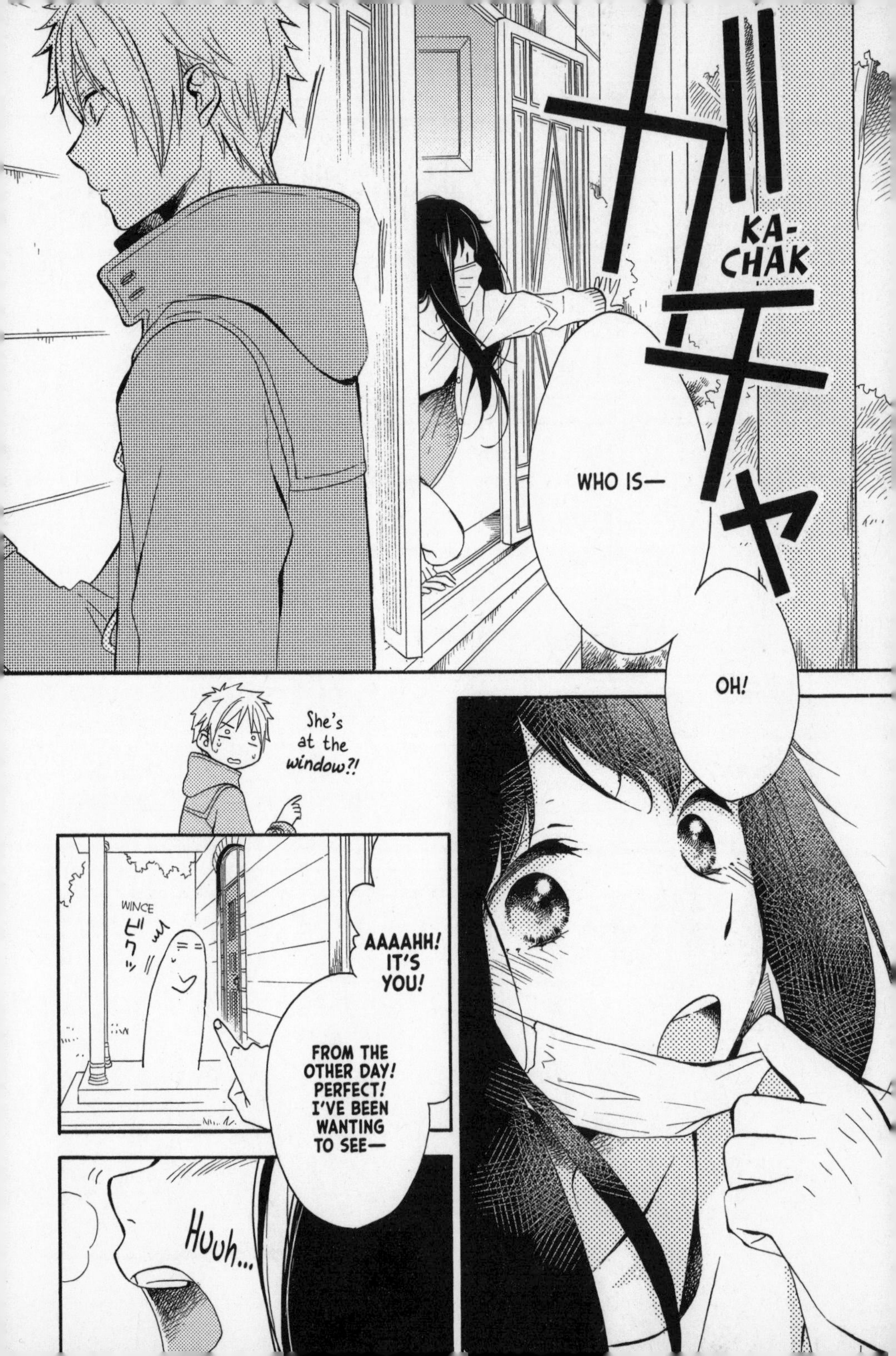
ガチャ
KA-CHAK
WHO IS—
OH!
AAAAHH! IT'S YOU!
FROM THE OTHER DAY! PERFECT! I'VE BEEN WANTING TO SEE—
She's at the window?!
ビクッ
WINCE
Huuh...

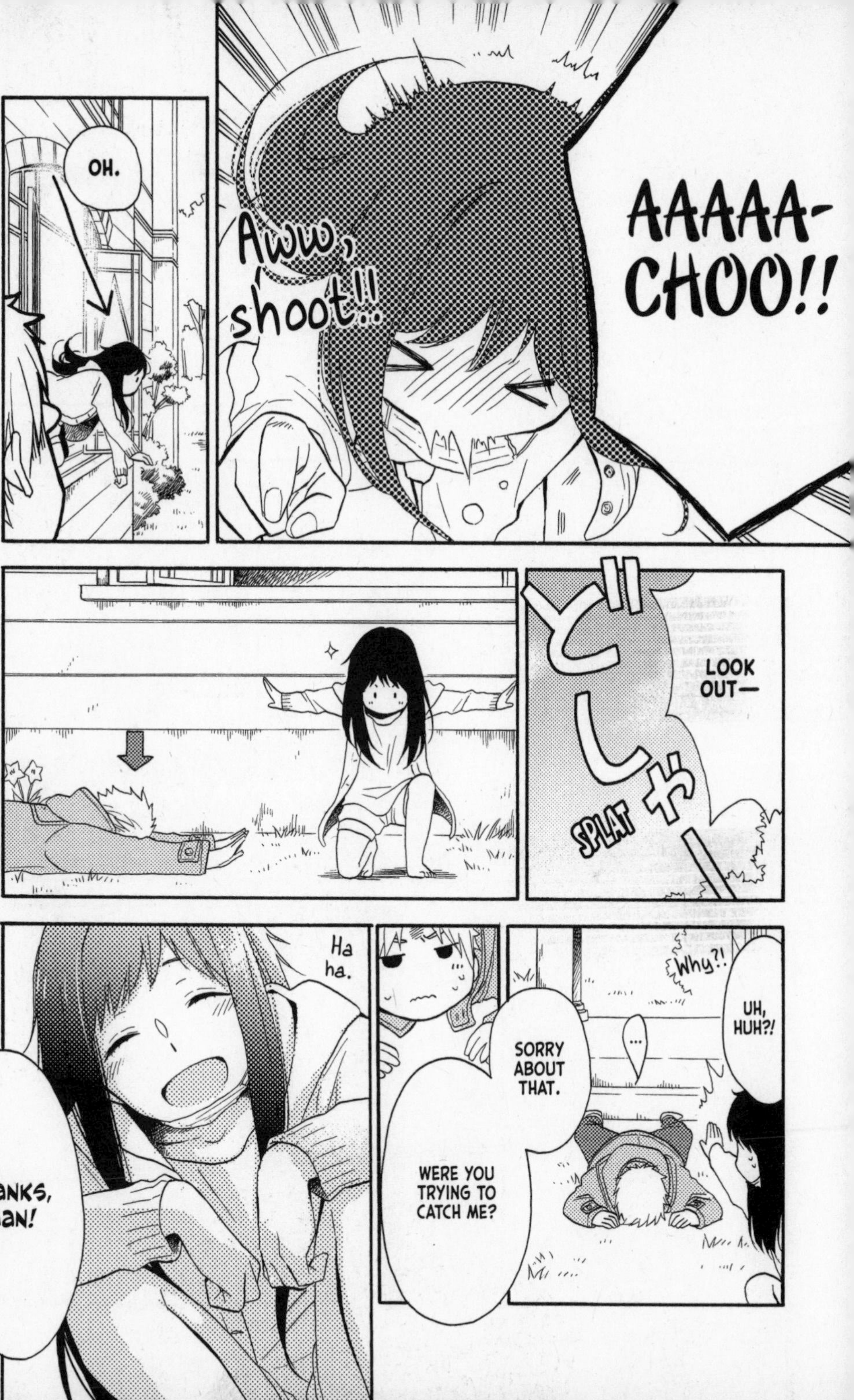
AAAAA-CHOO!!
Aww, shoot!!
OH.
LOOK OUT—
どしゃ
SPLAT
UH, HUH?!
Why?!
...
SORRY ABOUT THAT.
WERE YOU TRYING TO CATCH ME?
Ha ha.
THANKS, MAN!

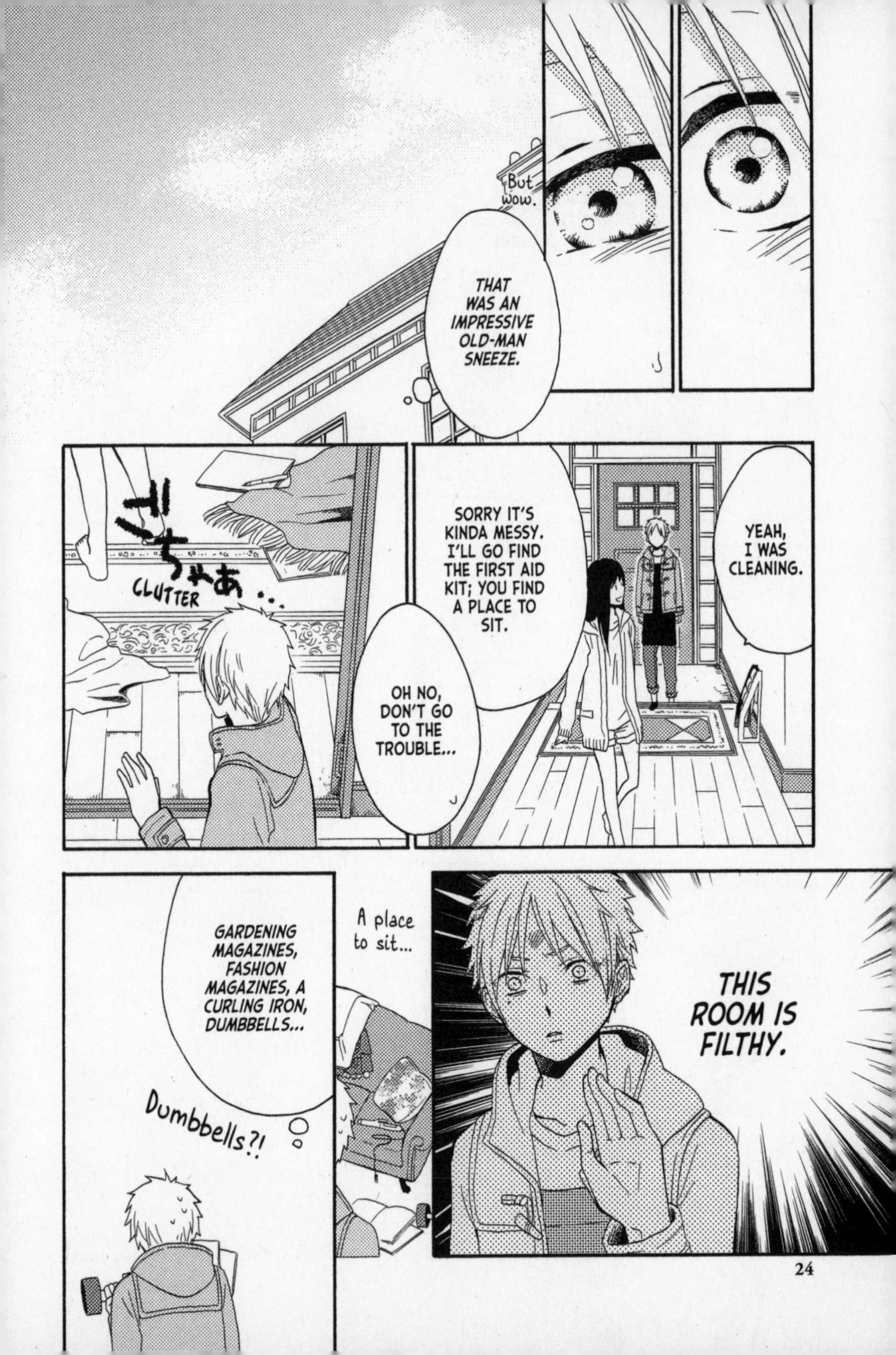
But wow.
THAT WAS AN IMPRESSIVE OLD-MAN SNEEZE.
YEAH, I WAS CLEANING.
SORRY IT'S KINDA MESSY. I'LL GO FIND THE FIRST AID KIT; YOU FIND A PLACE TO SIT.
OH NO, DON'T GO TO THE TROUBLE...
CLUTTER
THIS ROOM IS FILTHY.
A place to sit...
GARDENING MAGAZINES, FASHION MAGAZINES, A CURLING IRON, DUMBBELLS...
Dumbbells?!

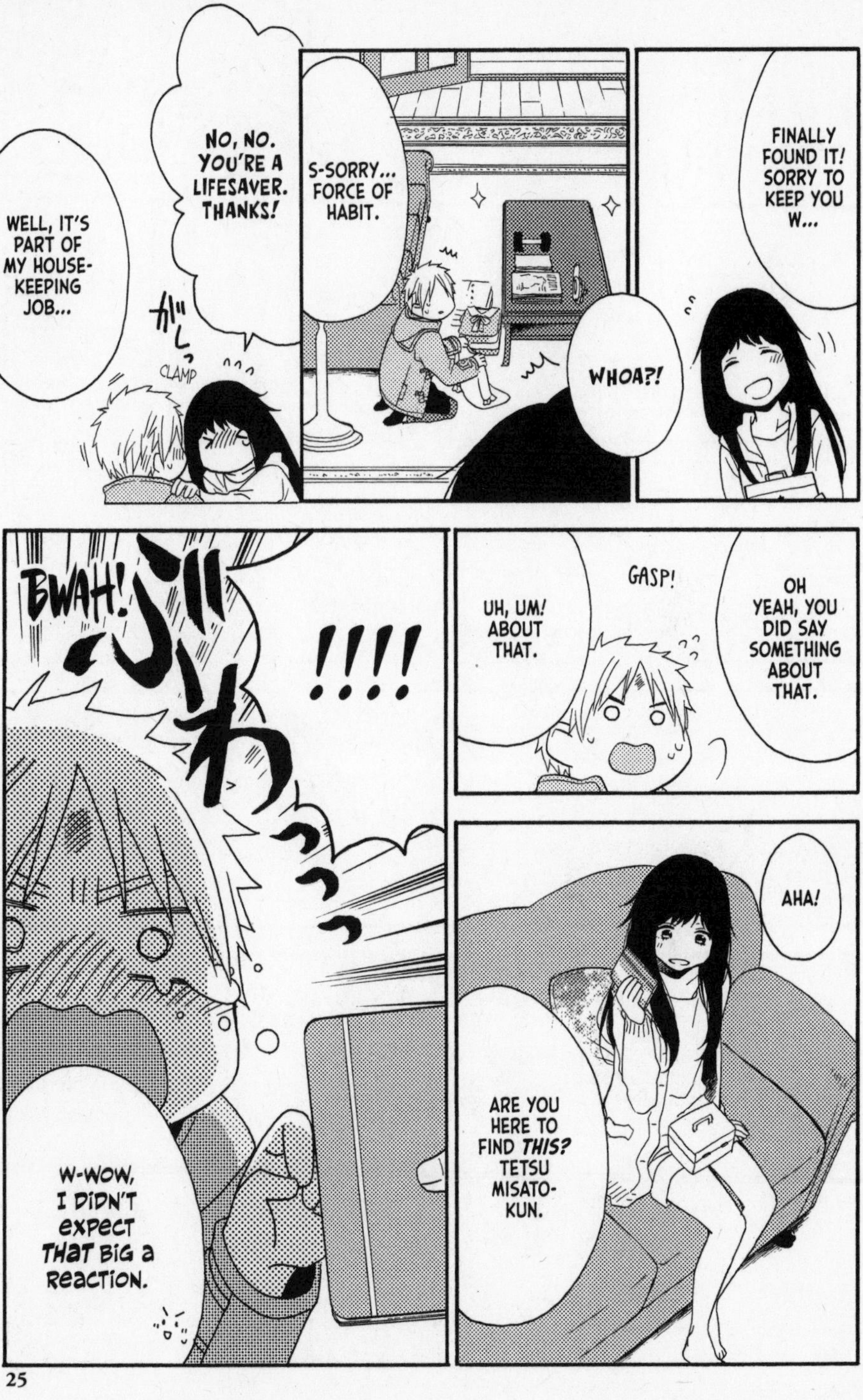
FINALLY FOUND IT! SORRY TO KEEP YOU W...
WHOA?!
S-SORRY... FORCE OF HABIT.
NO, NO. YOU'RE A LIFESAVER. THANKS!
WELL, IT'S PART OF MY HOUSE-KEEPING JOB...
CLAMP
OH YEAH, YOU DID SAY SOMETHING ABOUT THAT.
GASP!
UH, UM! ABOUT THAT.
AHA!
ARE YOU HERE TO FIND *THIS?* TETSU MISATO-KUN.
!!!!
BWAH!
W-WOW, I DIDN'T EXPECT *THAT* BIG a REaCTION.

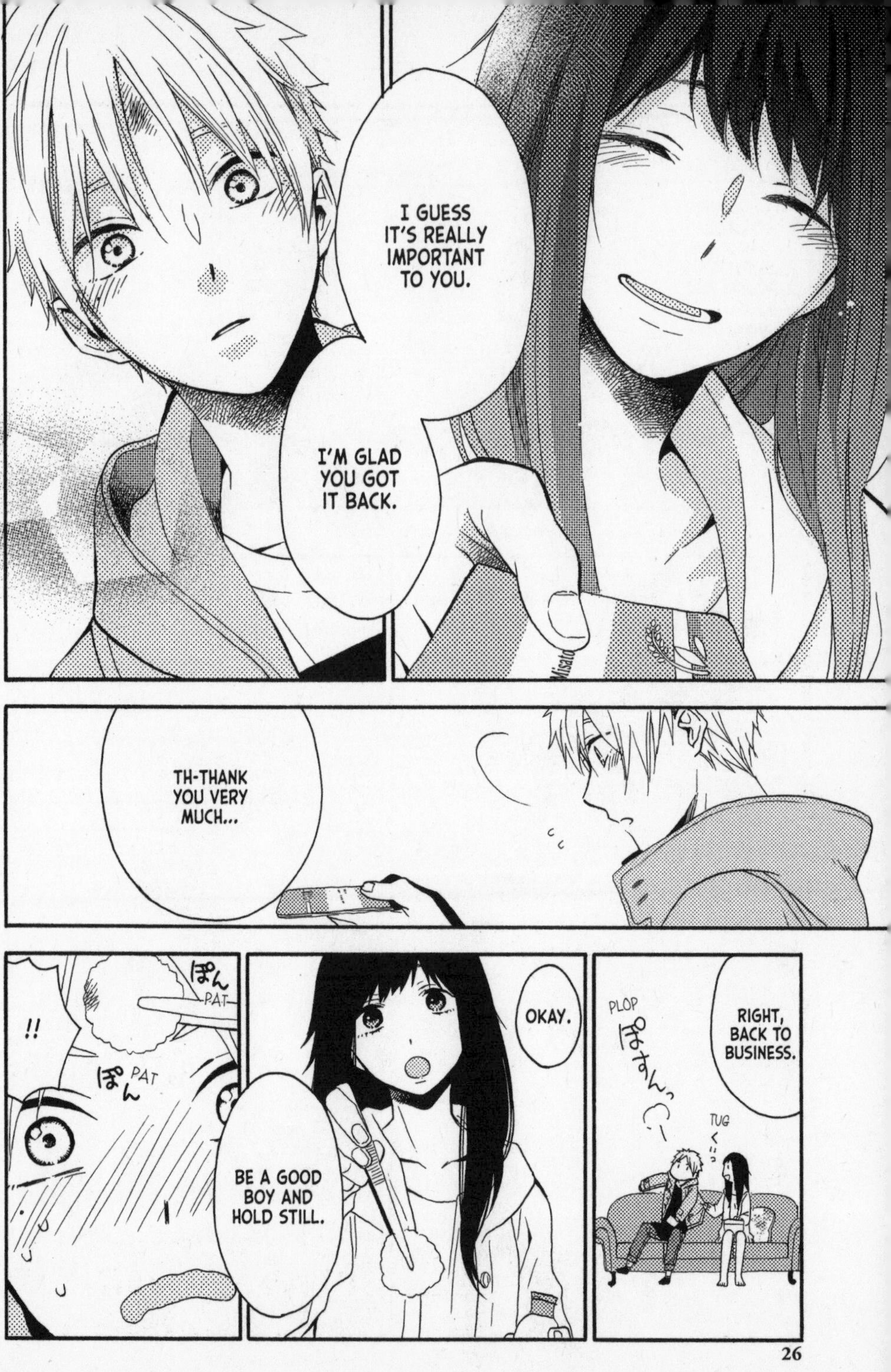

I GUESS IT'S REALLY IMPORTANT TO YOU.
I'M GLAD YOU GOT IT BACK.
TH-THANK YOU VERY MUCH...
RIGHT, BACK TO BUSINESS.
PLOP
ぽすん
TUG
OKAY.
BE A GOOD BOY AND HOLD STILL.
ぽん
PAT
ぽん
PAT
!!

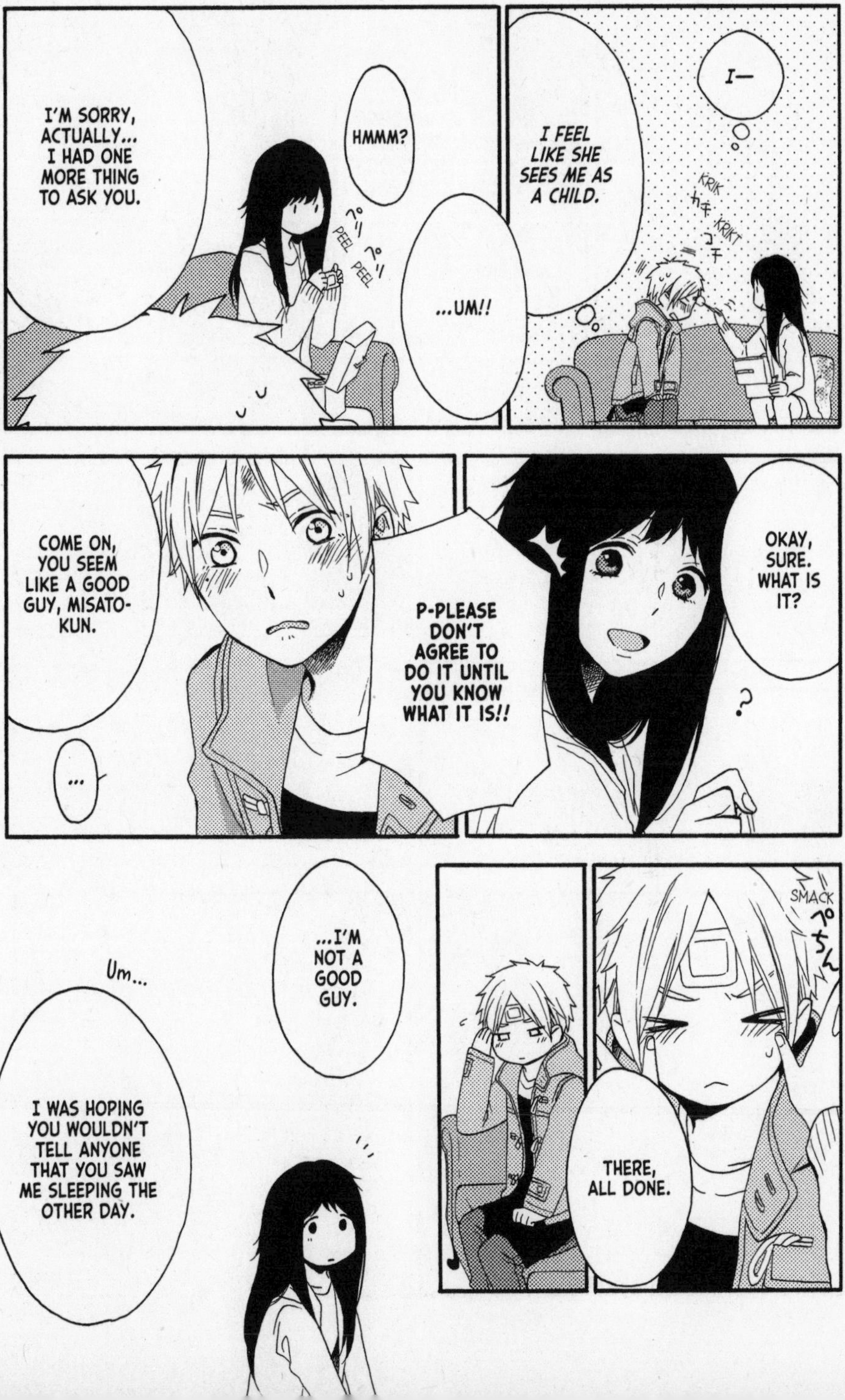
I—
I FEEL LIKE SHE SEES ME AS A CHILD.
KRIK
KRIKT
HMMM?
...UM!!
PEEL
PEEL
I'M SORRY, ACTUALLY... I HAD ONE MORE THING TO ASK YOU.
OKAY, SURE. WHAT IS IT?
P-PLEASE DON'T AGREE TO DO IT UNTIL YOU KNOW WHAT IT IS!!
COME ON, YOU SEEM LIKE A GOOD GUY, MISATO-KUN.
...
SMACK
THERE, ALL DONE.
...I'M NOT A GOOD GUY.
Um...
I WAS HOPING YOU WOULDN'T TELL ANYONE THAT YOU SAW ME SLEEPING THE OTHER DAY.

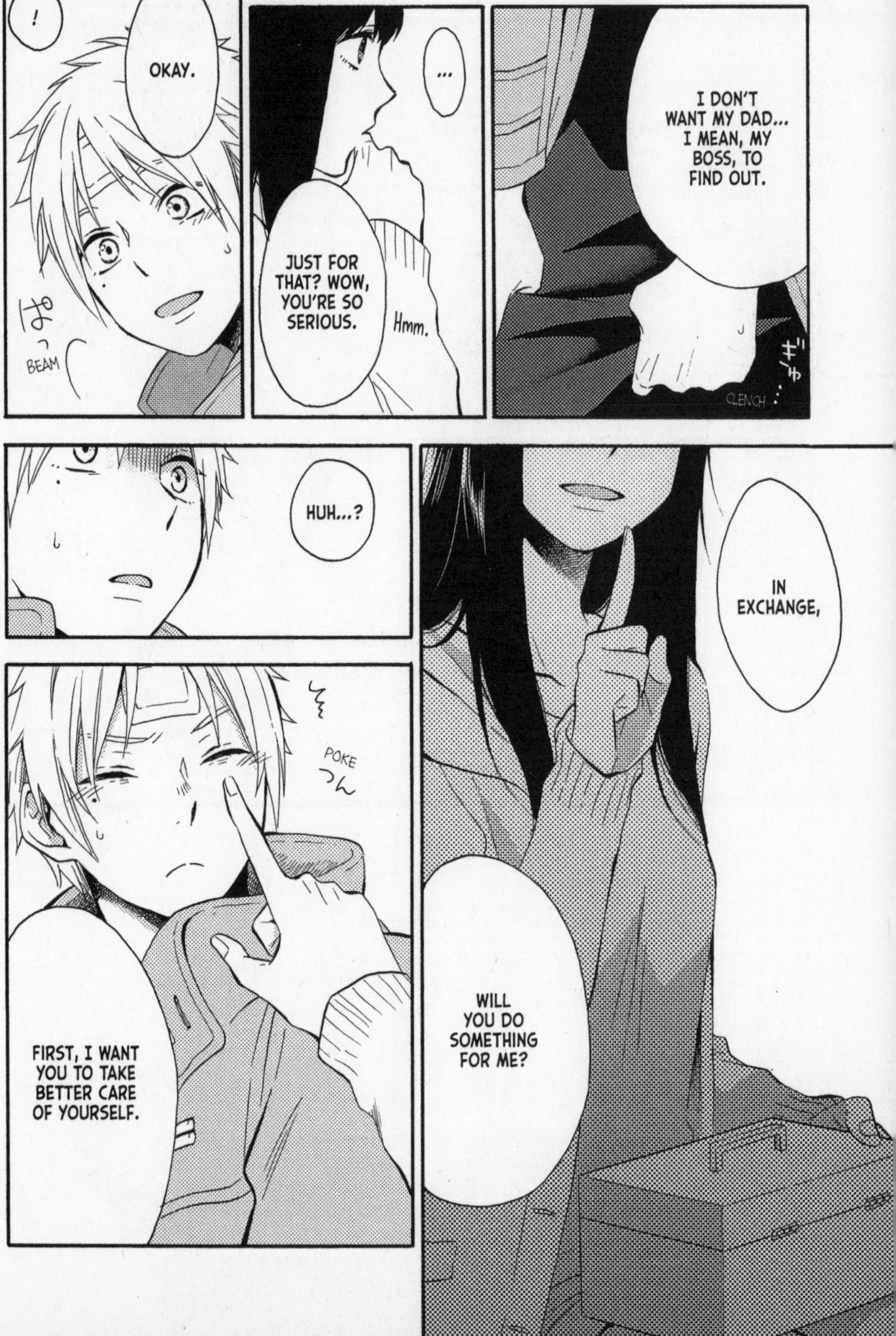
I DON'T WANT MY DAD... I MEAN, MY BOSS, TO FIND OUT.
ギュ…
CLENCH
...
Hmm.
JUST FOR THAT? WOW, YOU'RE SO SERIOUS.
OKAY.
!
ぱっ
BEAM
IN EXCHANGE,
WILL YOU DO SOMETHING FOR ME?
HUH...?
POKE
つん
FIRST, I WANT YOU TO TAKE BETTER CARE OF YOURSELF.

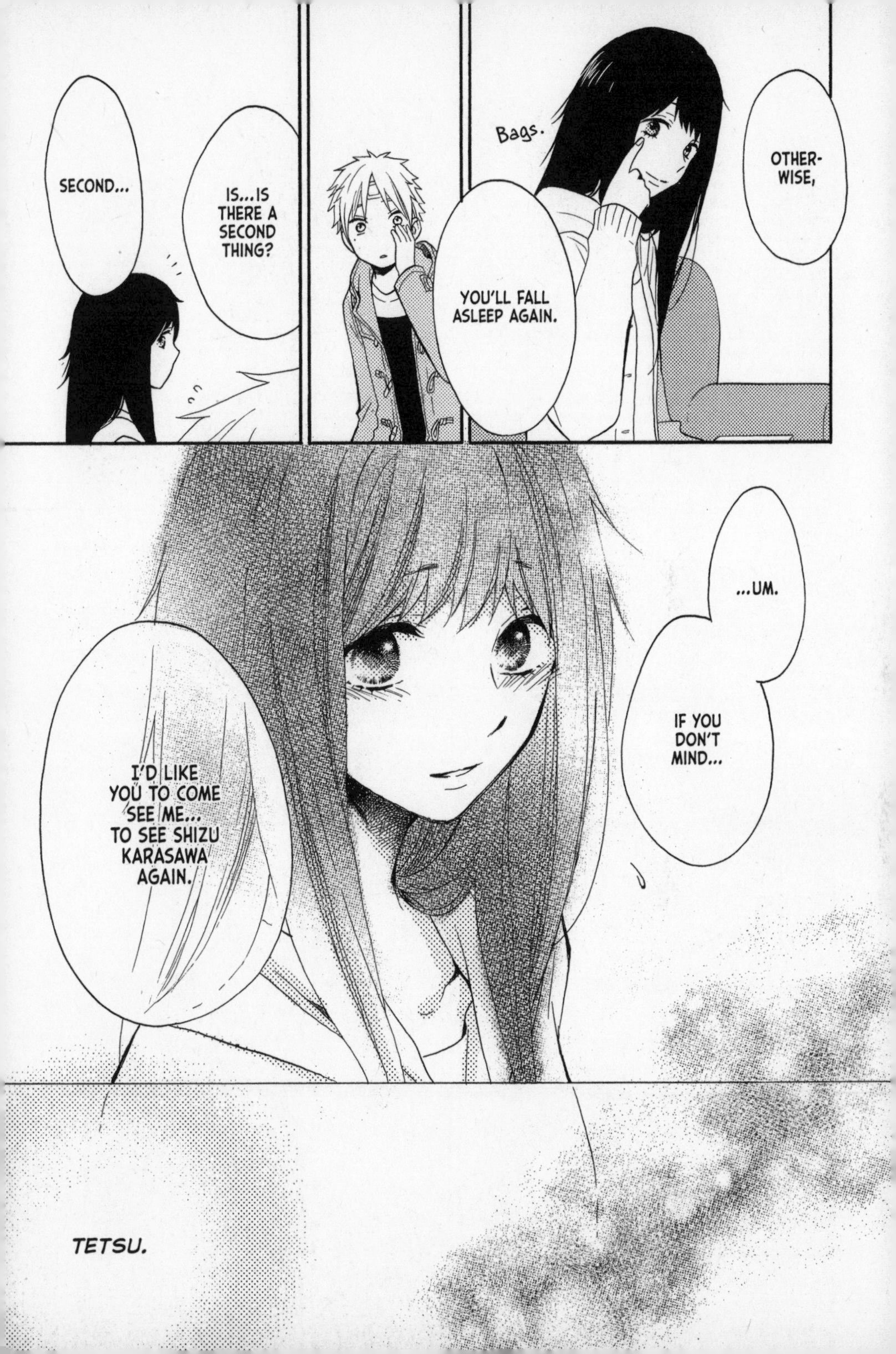
OTHER-WISE,
Bags.
YOU'LL FALL ASLEEP AGAIN.
IS...IS THERE A SECOND THING?
SECOND...
...UM.
IF YOU DON'T MIND...
I'D LIKE YOU TO COME SEE ME... TO SEE SHIZU KARASAWA AGAIN.
TETSU.

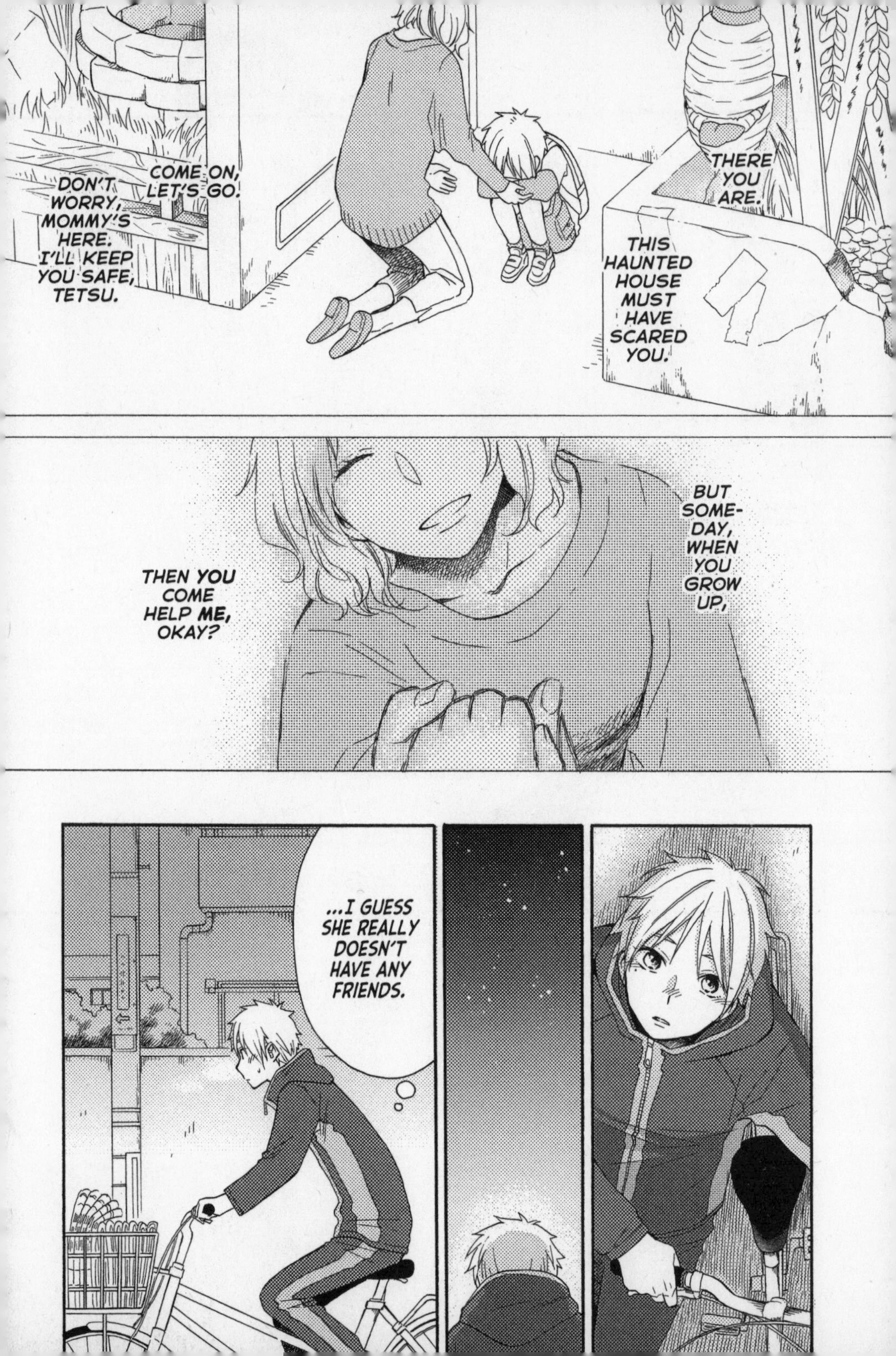
THERE YOU ARE.
THIS HAUNTED HOUSE MUST HAVE SCARED YOU.
COME ON, LET'S GO.
DON'T WORRY, MOMMY'S HERE. I'LL KEEP YOU SAFE, TETSU.
BUT SOME-DAY, WHEN YOU GROW UP,
THEN YOU COME HELP ME, OKAY?
...I GUESS SHE REALLY DOESN'T HAVE ANY FRIENDS.

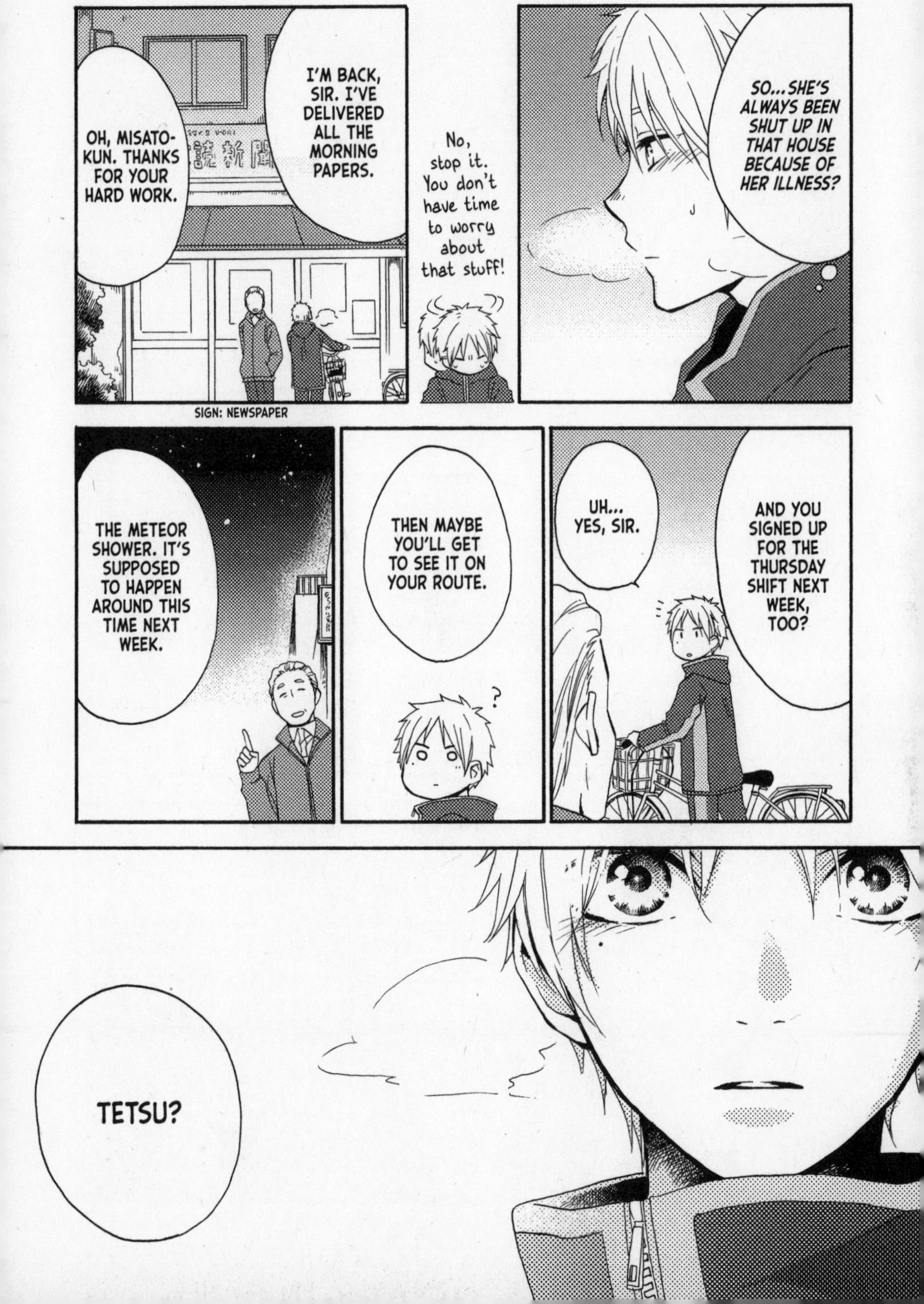
SO...SHE'S ALWAYS BEEN SHUT UP IN THAT HOUSE BECAUSE OF HER ILLNESS?
No, stop it. You don't have time to worry about that stuff!
I'M BACK, SIR. I'VE DELIVERED ALL THE MORNING PAPERS.
OH, MISATO-KUN. THANKS FOR YOUR HARD WORK.
SIGN: NEWSPAPER
AND YOU SIGNED UP FOR THE THURSDAY SHIFT NEXT WEEK, TOO?
UH... YES, SIR.
THEN MAYBE YOU'LL GET TO SEE IT ON YOUR ROUTE.
THE METEOR SHOWER. IT'S SUPPOSED TO HAPPEN AROUND THIS TIME NEXT WEEK.
TETSU?

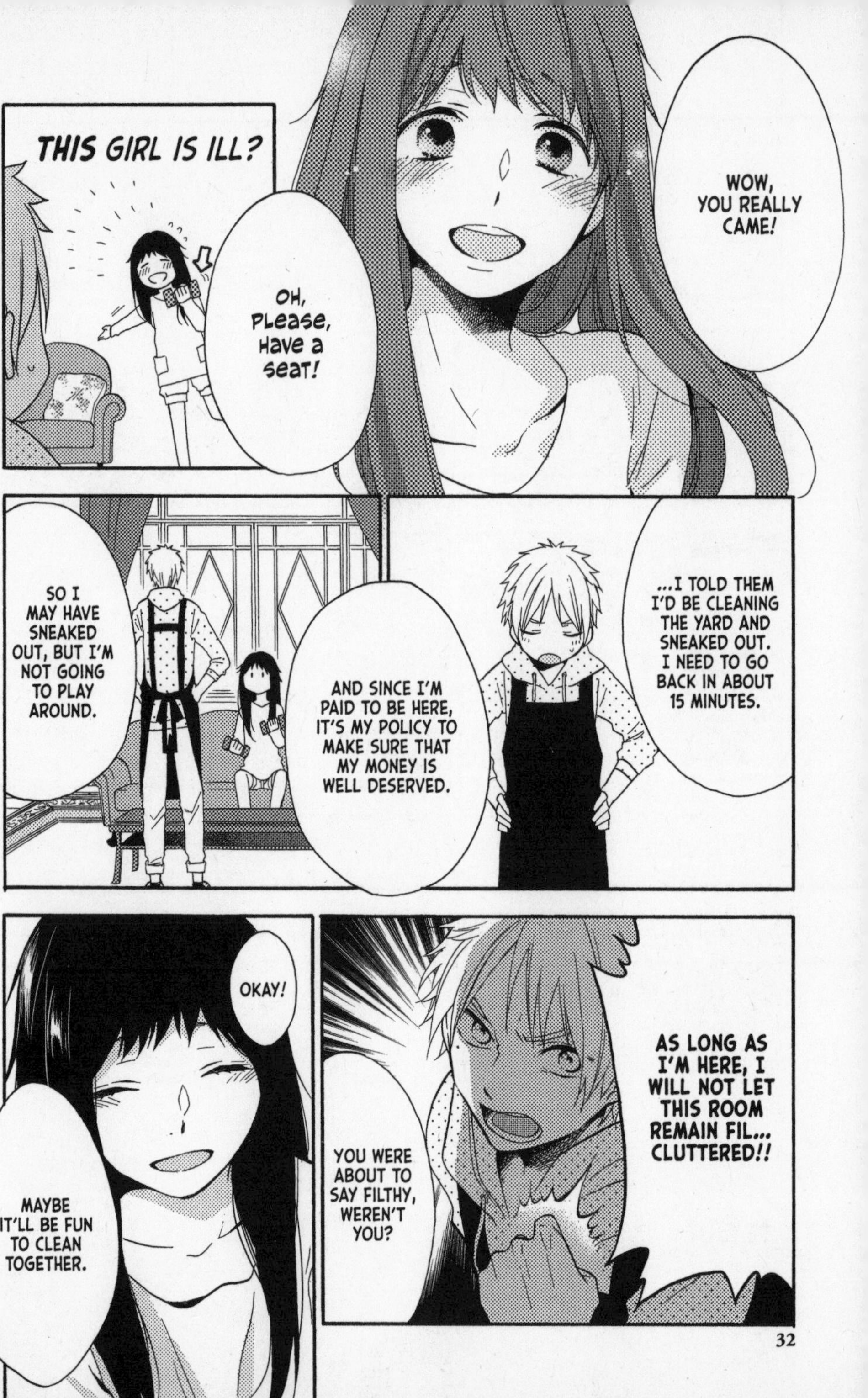
WOW, YOU REALLY CAME!
OH, PLEASE, HAVE A SEAT!
THIS GIRL IS ILL?
...I TOLD THEM I'D BE CLEANING THE YARD AND SNEAKED OUT. I NEED TO GO BACK IN ABOUT 15 MINUTES.
SO I MAY HAVE SNEAKED OUT, BUT I'M NOT GOING TO PLAY AROUND.
AND SINCE I'M PAID TO BE HERE, IT'S MY POLICY TO MAKE SURE THAT MY MONEY IS WELL DESERVED.
AS LONG AS I'M HERE, I WILL NOT LET THIS ROOM REMAIN FIL... CLUTTERED!!
YOU WERE ABOUT TO SAY FILTHY, WEREN'T YOU?
OKAY!
MAYBE IT'LL BE FUN TO CLEAN TOGETHER.

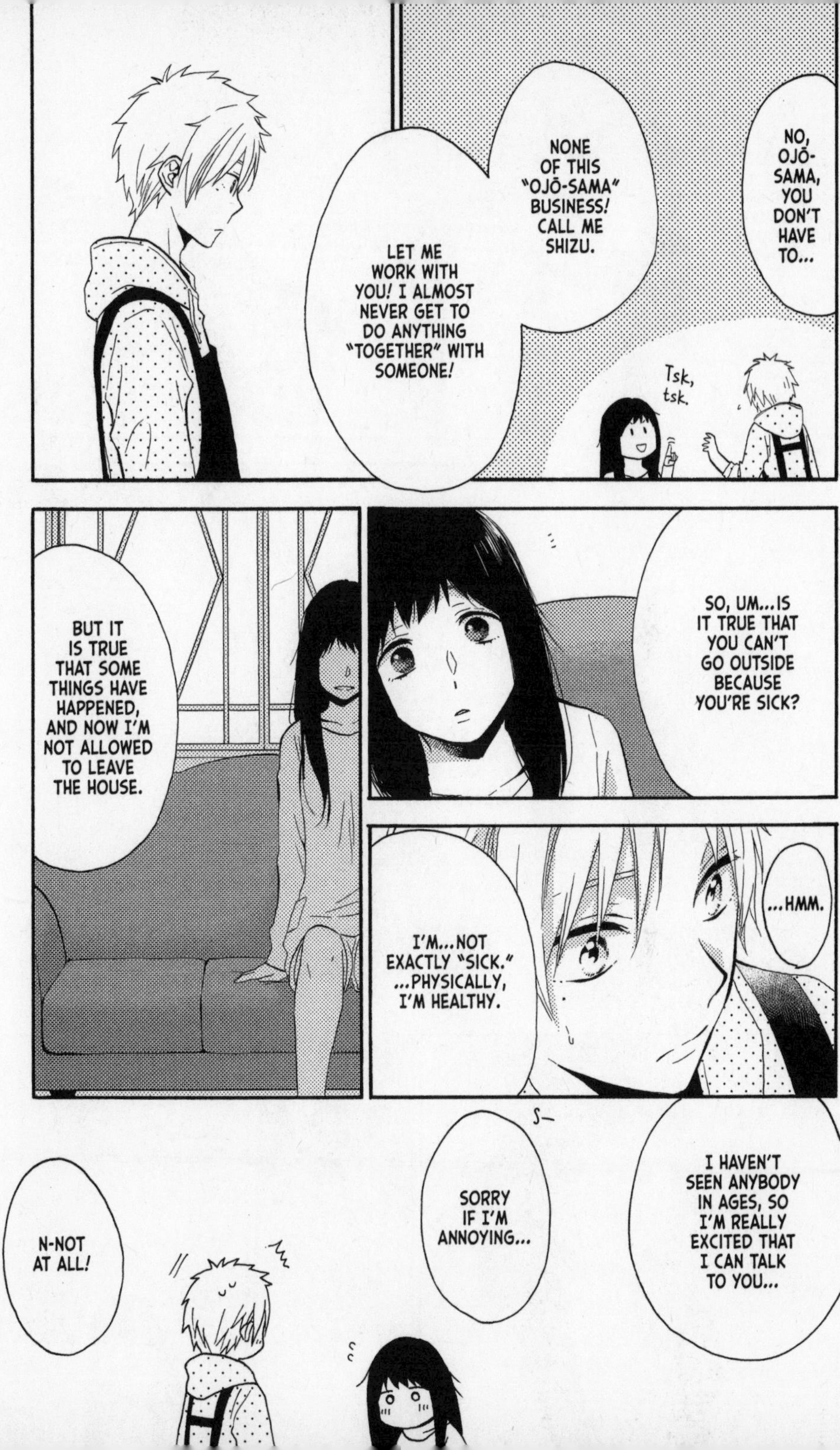
NO, OJŌ-SAMA, YOU DON'T HAVE TO...
NONE OF THIS "OJŌ-SAMA" BUSINESS! CALL ME SHIZU.
Tsk, tsk.
LET ME WORK WITH YOU! I ALMOST NEVER GET TO DO ANYTHING "TOGETHER" WITH SOMEONE!
SO, UM...IS IT TRUE THAT YOU CAN'T GO OUTSIDE BECAUSE YOU'RE SICK?
...HMM.
I'M...NOT EXACTLY "SICK." ...PHYSICALLY, I'M HEALTHY.
BUT IT IS TRUE THAT SOME THINGS HAVE HAPPENED, AND NOW I'M NOT ALLOWED TO LEAVE THE HOUSE.
I HAVEN'T SEEN ANYBODY IN AGES, SO I'M REALLY EXCITED THAT I CAN TALK TO YOU...
S—
SORRY IF I'M ANNOYING...
N-NOT AT ALL!

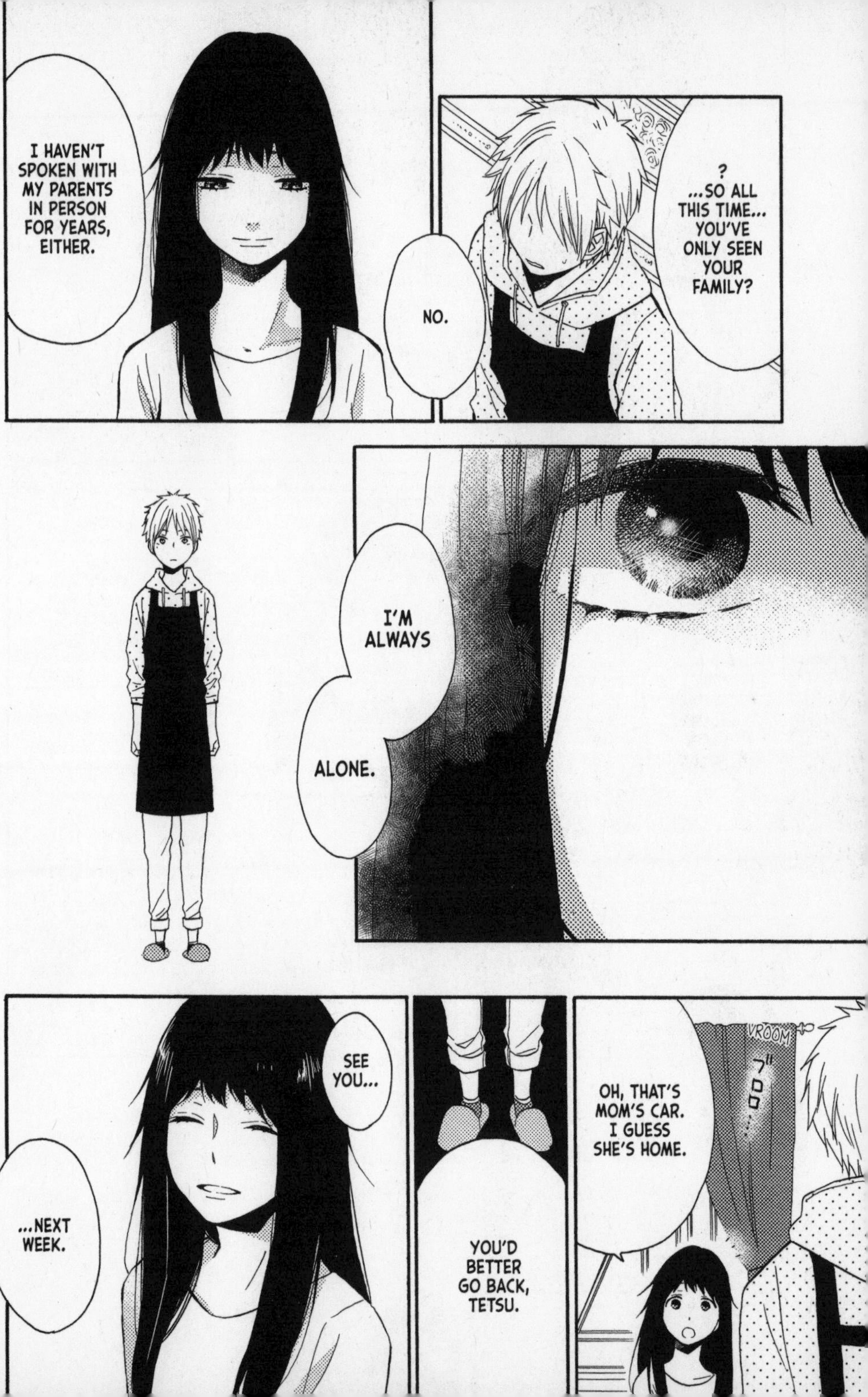
? ...SO ALL THIS TIME... YOU'VE ONLY SEEN YOUR FAMILY?
NO.
I HAVEN'T SPOKEN WITH MY PARENTS IN PERSON FOR YEARS, EITHER.
I'M ALWAYS
ALONE.
VROOM
ブロロ…
OH, THAT'S MOM'S CAR. I GUESS SHE'S HOME.
YOU'D BETTER GO BACK, TETSU.
SEE YOU...
...NEXT WEEK.

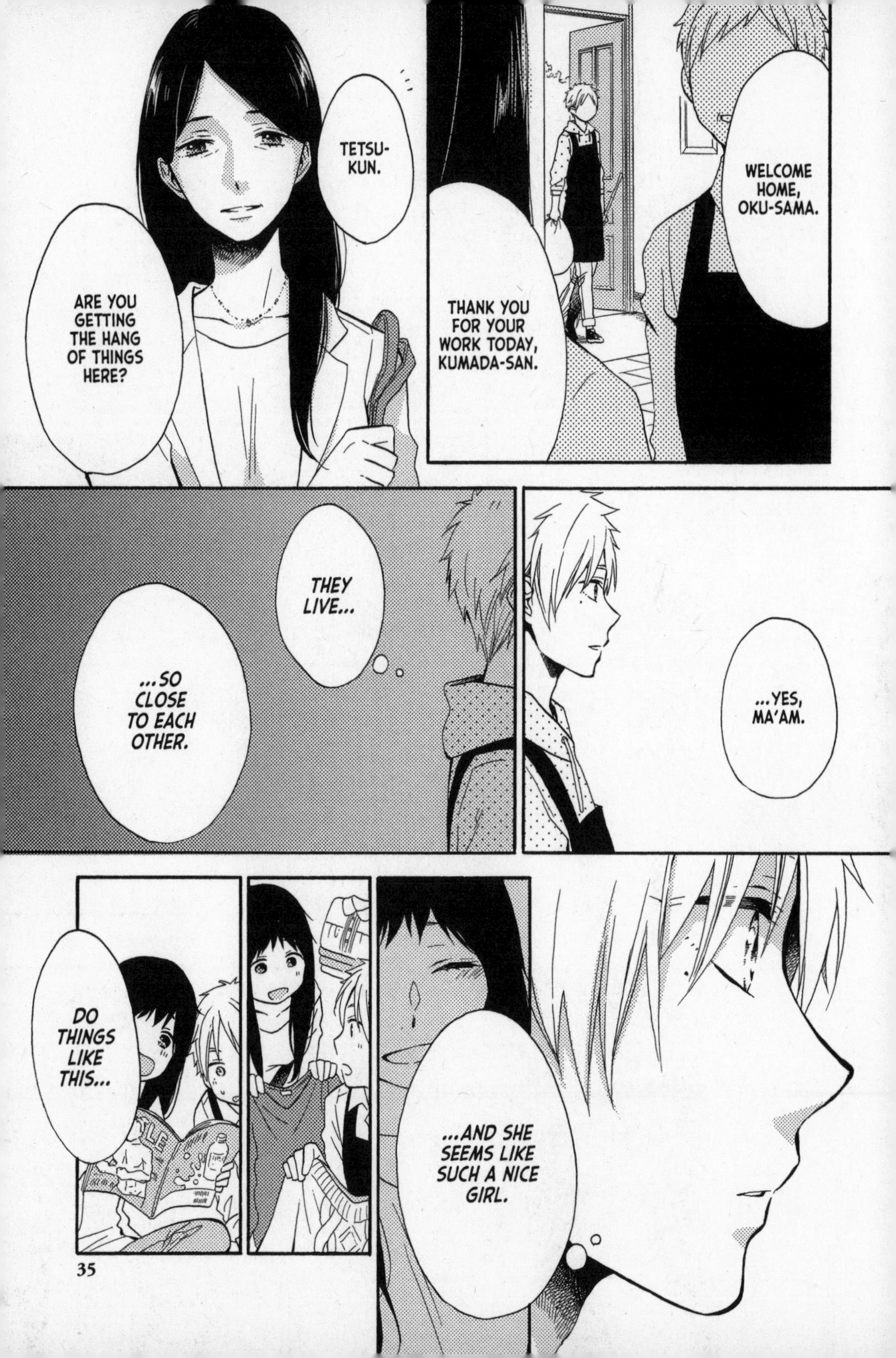
WELCOME HOME, OKU-SAMA.
THANK YOU FOR YOUR WORK TODAY, KUMADA-SAN.
TETSU-KUN.
ARE YOU GETTING THE HANG OF THINGS HERE?
...YES, MA'AM.
THEY LIVE...
...SO CLOSE TO EACH OTHER.
DO THINGS LIKE THIS...
...AND SHE SEEMS LIKE SUCH A NICE GIRL.

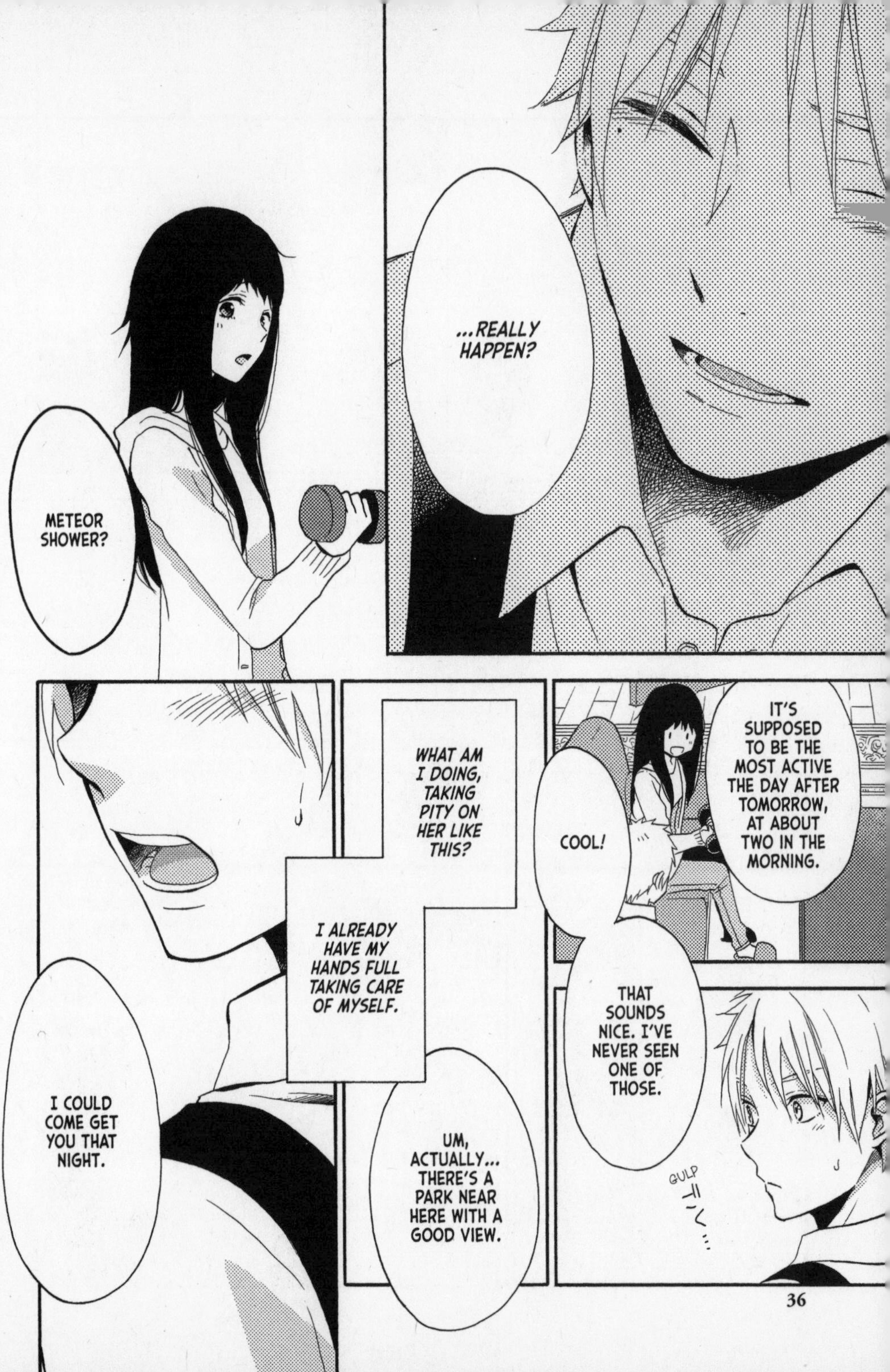
...REALLY HAPPEN?
METEOR SHOWER?
IT'S SUPPOSED TO BE THE MOST ACTIVE THE DAY AFTER TOMORROW, AT ABOUT TWO IN THE MORNING.
COOL!
THAT SOUNDS NICE. I'VE NEVER SEEN ONE OF THOSE.
GULP
WHAT AM I DOING, TAKING PITY ON HER LIKE THIS?
I ALREADY HAVE MY HANDS FULL TAKING CARE OF MYSELF.
UM, ACTUALLY... THERE'S A PARK NEAR HERE WITH A GOOD VIEW.
I COULD COME GET YOU THAT NIGHT.

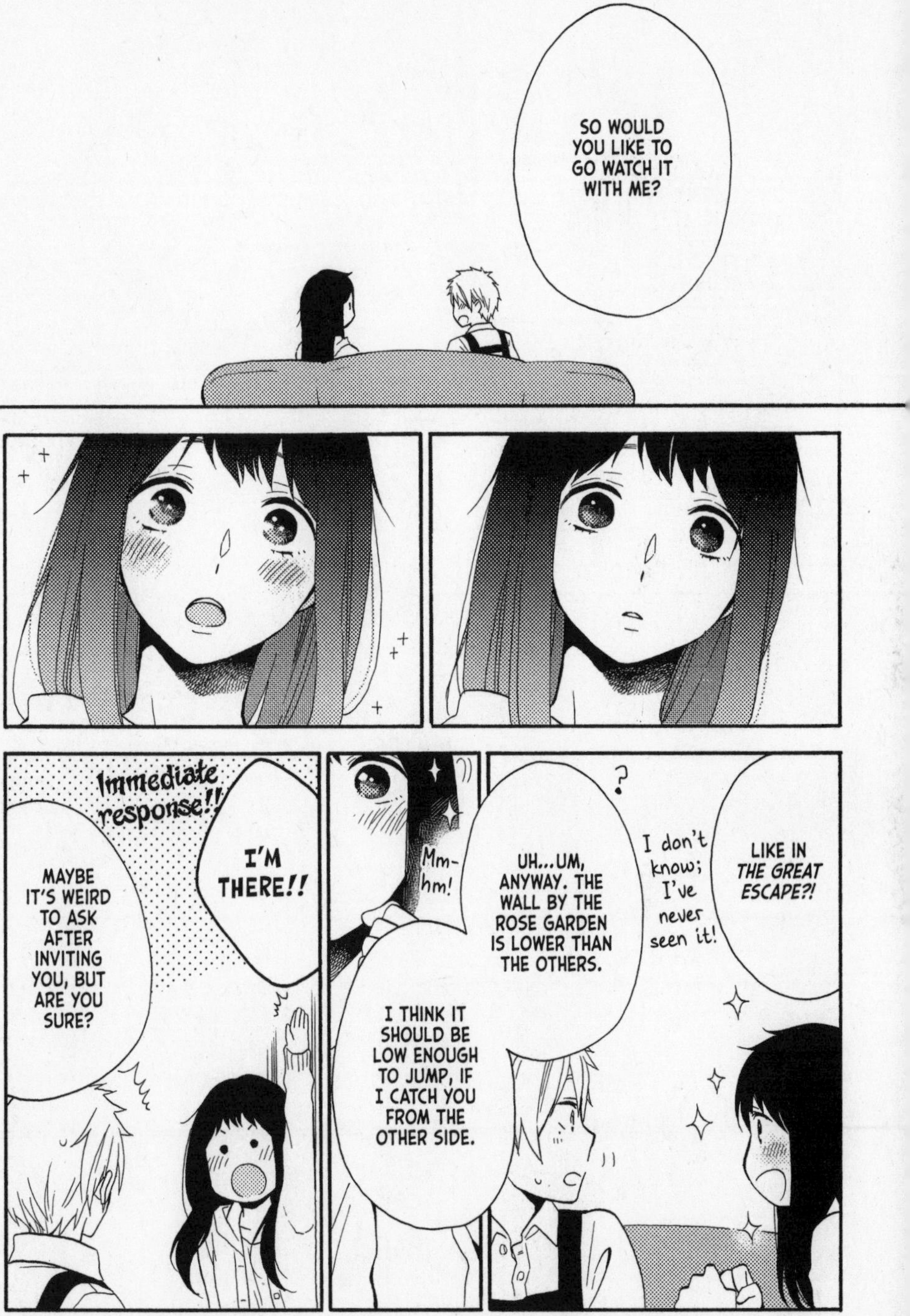
SO WOULD YOU LIKE TO GO WATCH IT WITH ME?
LIKE IN *THE GREAT ESCAPE?!*
I don't know; I've never seen it!
?
UH...UM, ANYWAY. THE WALL BY THE ROSE GARDEN IS LOWER THAN THE OTHERS.
I THINK IT SHOULD BE LOW ENOUGH TO JUMP, IF I CATCH YOU FROM THE OTHER SIDE.
Mm-hm!
I'M THERE!!
Immediate response!!
MAYBE IT'S WEIRD TO ASK AFTER INVITING YOU, BUT ARE YOU SURE?

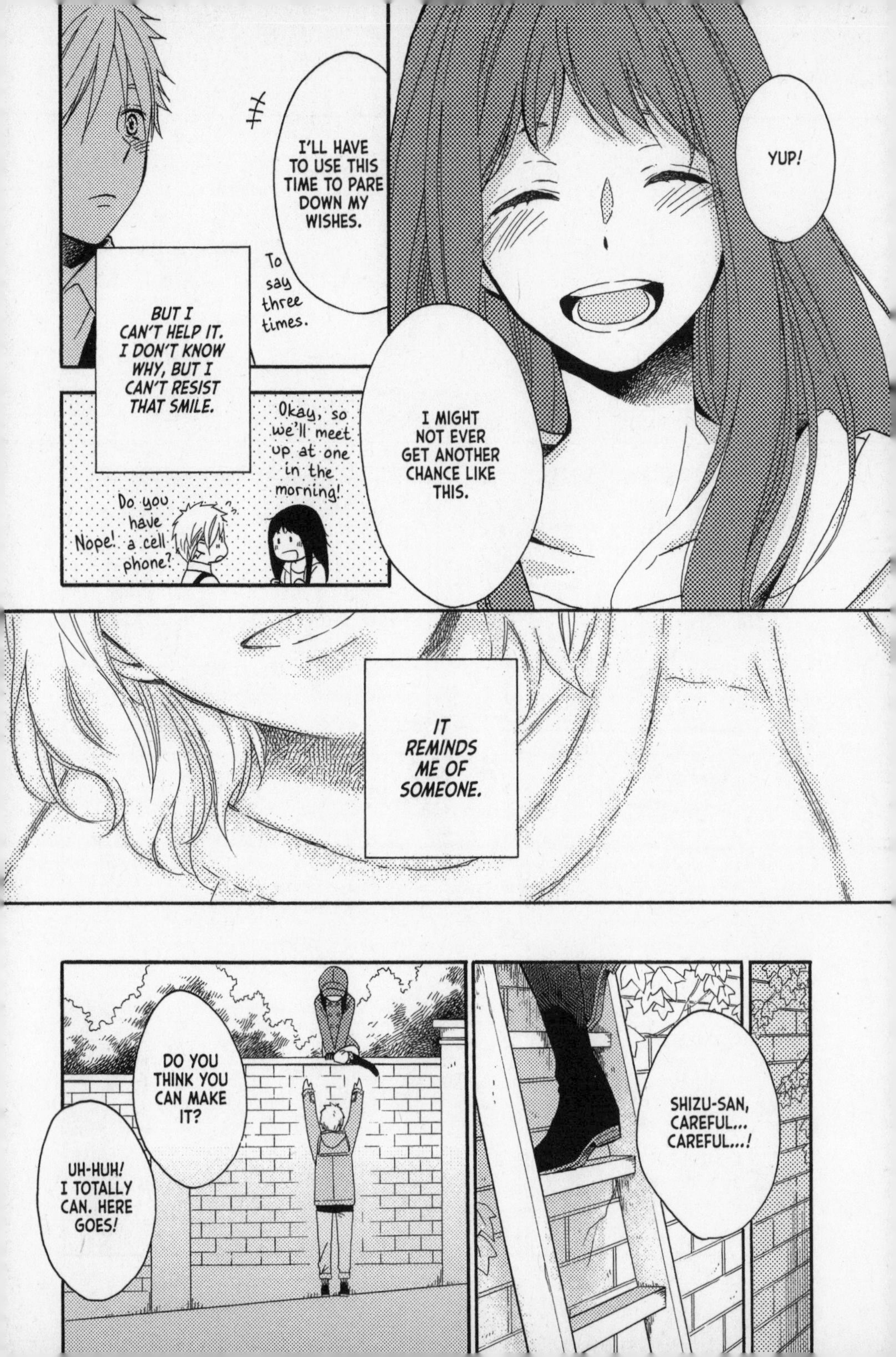
YUP!
I MIGHT NOT EVER GET ANOTHER CHANCE LIKE THIS.
I'LL HAVE TO USE THIS TIME TO PARE DOWN MY WISHES.
To say three times.
BUT I CAN'T HELP IT. I DON'T KNOW WHY, BUT I CAN'T RESIST THAT SMILE.
Okay, so we'll meet up at one in the morning!
Do you have a cell phone?
Nope!
IT REMINDS ME OF SOMEONE.
SHIZU-SAN, CAREFUL... CAREFUL...!
DO YOU THINK YOU CAN MAKE IT?
UH-HUH! I TOTALLY CAN. HERE GOES!

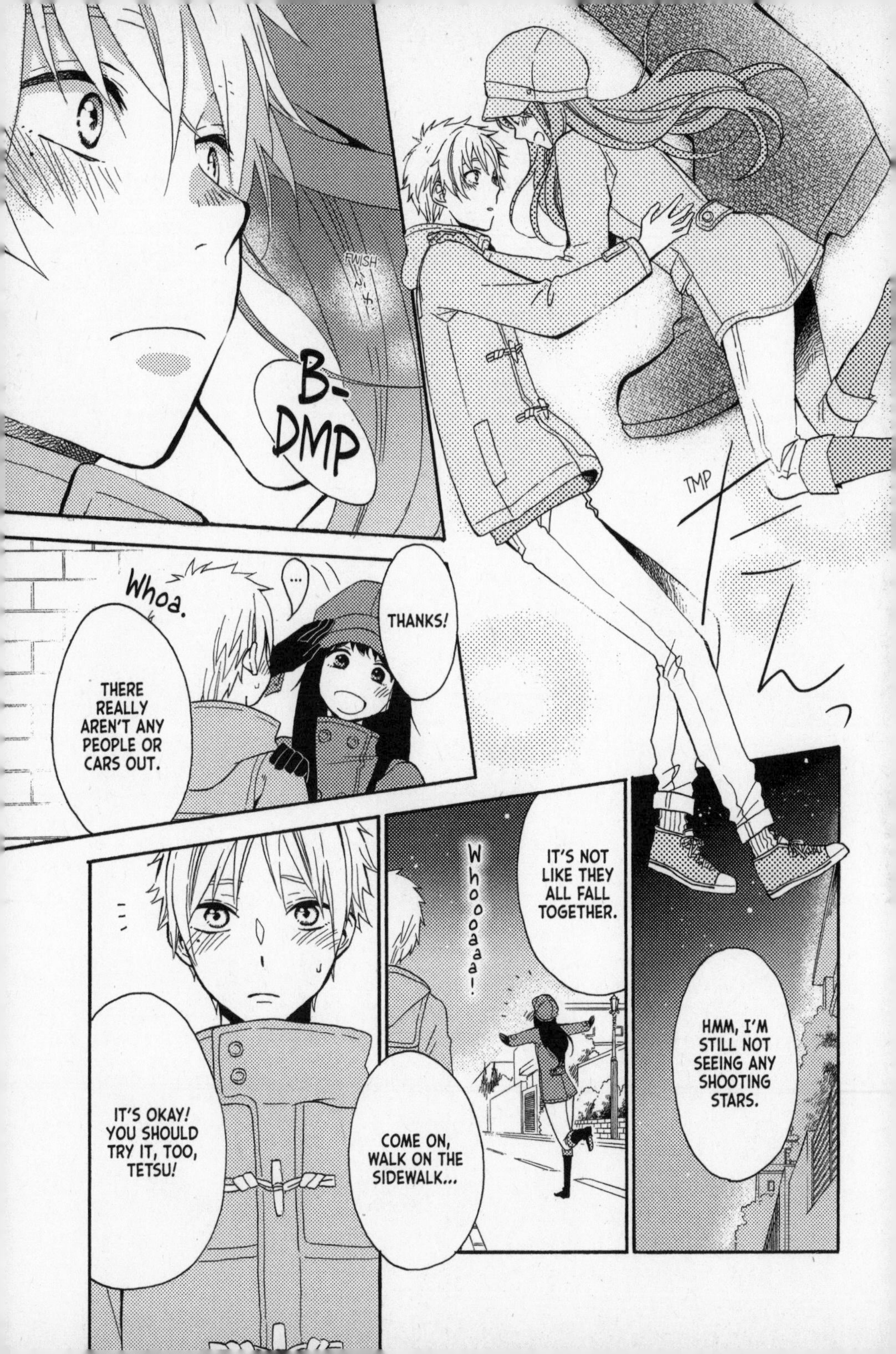
TMP
FWISH
B-DMP
THANKS!
...
Whoa.
THERE REALLY AREN'T ANY PEOPLE OR CARS OUT.
HMM, I'M STILL NOT SEEING ANY SHOOTING STARS.
IT'S NOT LIKE THEY ALL FALL TOGETHER.
Whoooaaa!
COME ON, WALK ON THE SIDEWALK...
IT'S OKAY! YOU SHOULD TRY IT, TOO, TETSU!

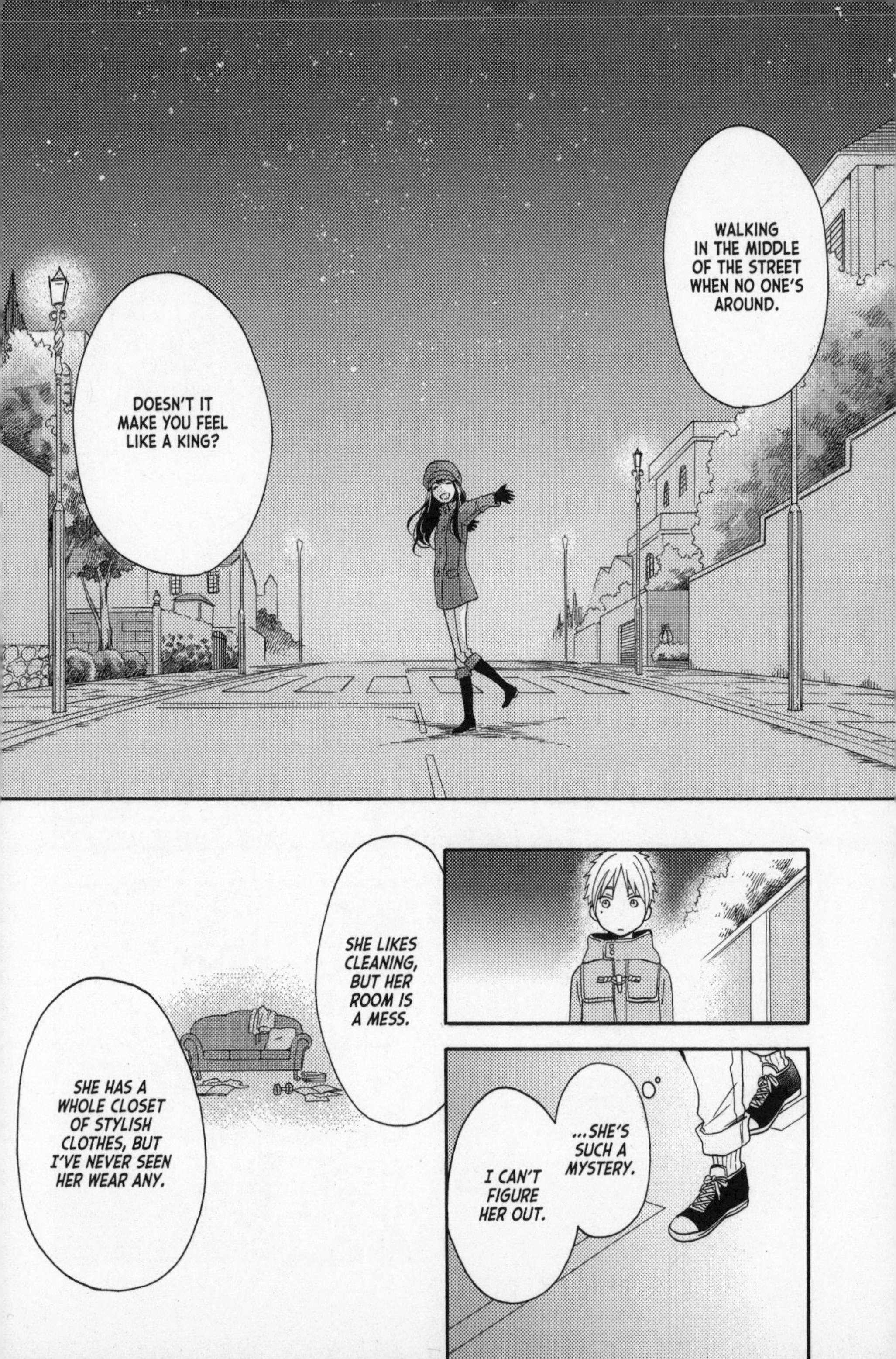
WALKING IN THE MIDDLE OF THE STREET WHEN NO ONE'S AROUND.
DOESN'T IT MAKE YOU FEEL LIKE A KING?
SHE LIKES CLEANING, BUT HER ROOM IS A MESS.
SHE HAS A WHOLE CLOSET OF STYLISH CLOTHES, BUT I'VE NEVER SEEN HER WEAR ANY.
...SHE'S SUCH A MYSTERY.
I CAN'T FIGURE HER OUT.

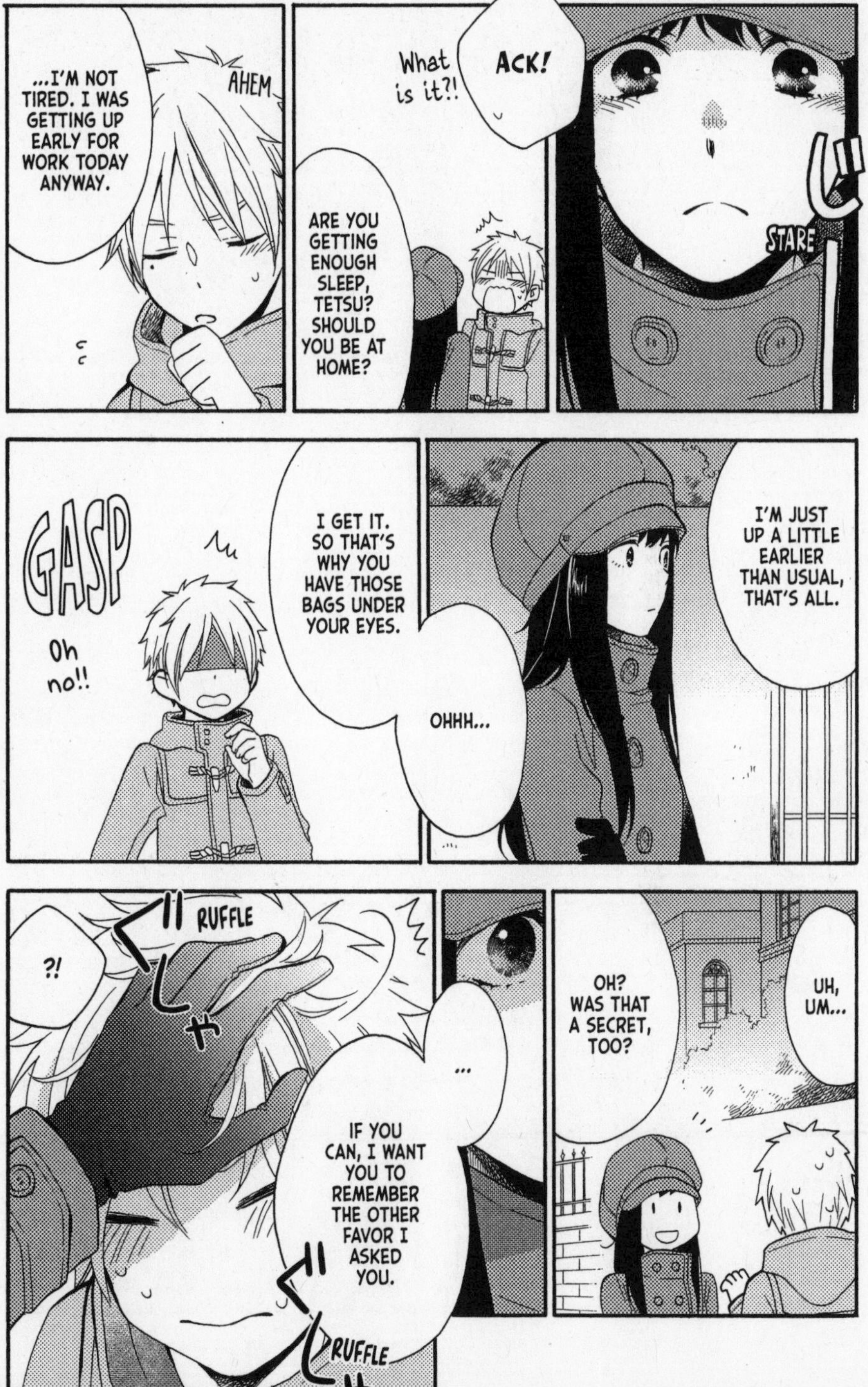
STARE
ACK!
What is it?!
ARE YOU GETTING ENOUGH SLEEP, TETSU? SHOULD YOU BE AT HOME?
AHEM
...I'M NOT TIRED. I WAS GETTING UP EARLY FOR WORK TODAY ANYWAY.
I'M JUST UP A LITTLE EARLIER THAN USUAL, THAT'S ALL.
OHHH...
I GET IT. SO THAT'S WHY YOU HAVE THOSE BAGS UNDER YOUR EYES.
GASP
Oh no!!
UH, UM...
OH? WAS THAT A SECRET, TOO?
...
IF YOU CAN, I WANT YOU TO REMEMBER THE OTHER FAVOR I ASKED YOU.
RUFFLE
?!
RUFFLE

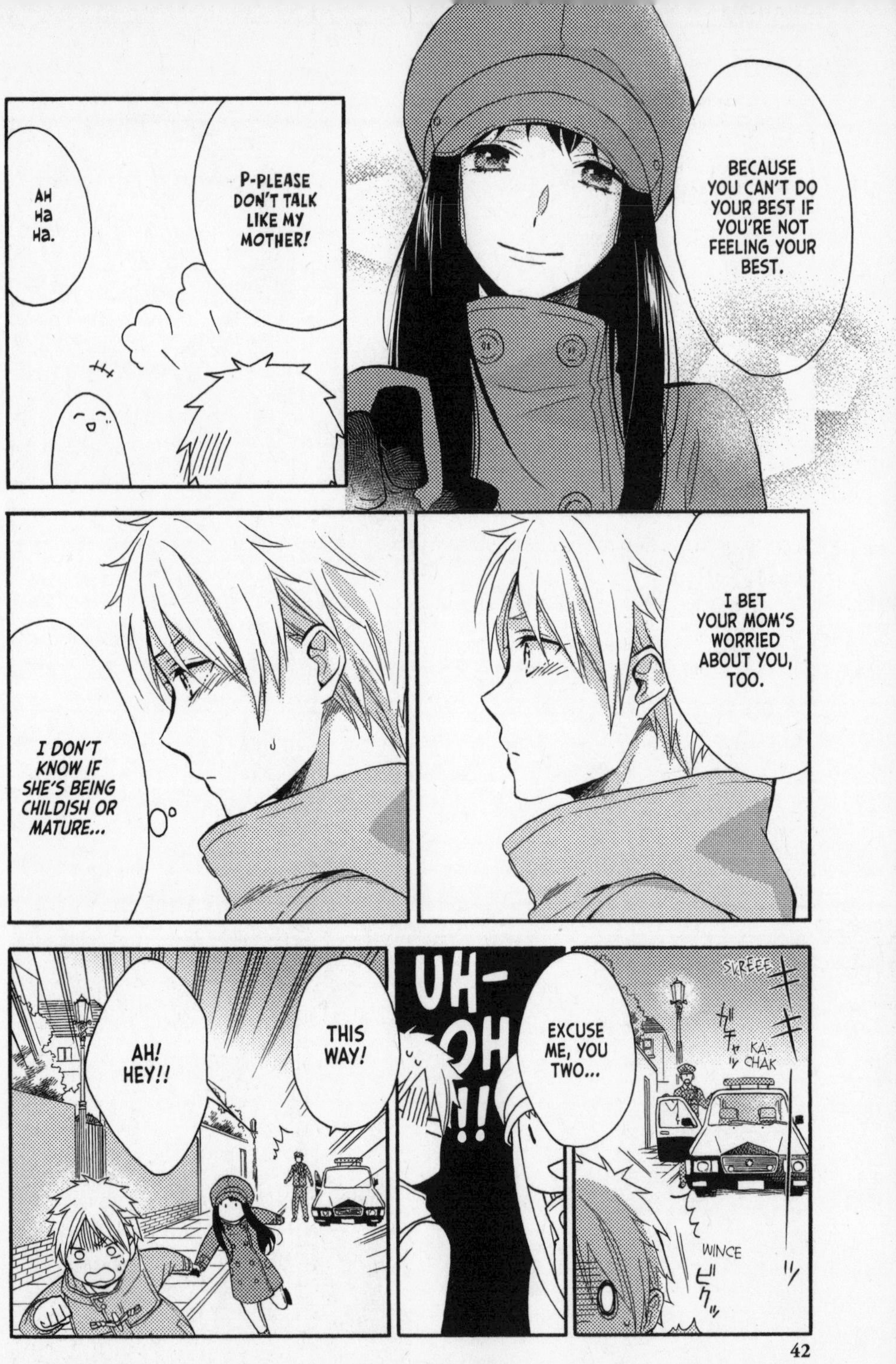
BECAUSE YOU CAN'T DO YOUR BEST IF YOU'RE NOT FEELING YOUR BEST.
P-PLEASE DON'T TALK LIKE MY MOTHER!
AH HA HA.
I BET YOUR MOM'S WORRIED ABOUT YOU, TOO.
I DON'T KNOW IF SHE'S BEING CHILDISH OR MATURE...
SKREEE
KA-CHAK
EXCUSE ME, YOU TWO...
WINCE
UH-OH!!
THIS WAY!
AH! HEY!!

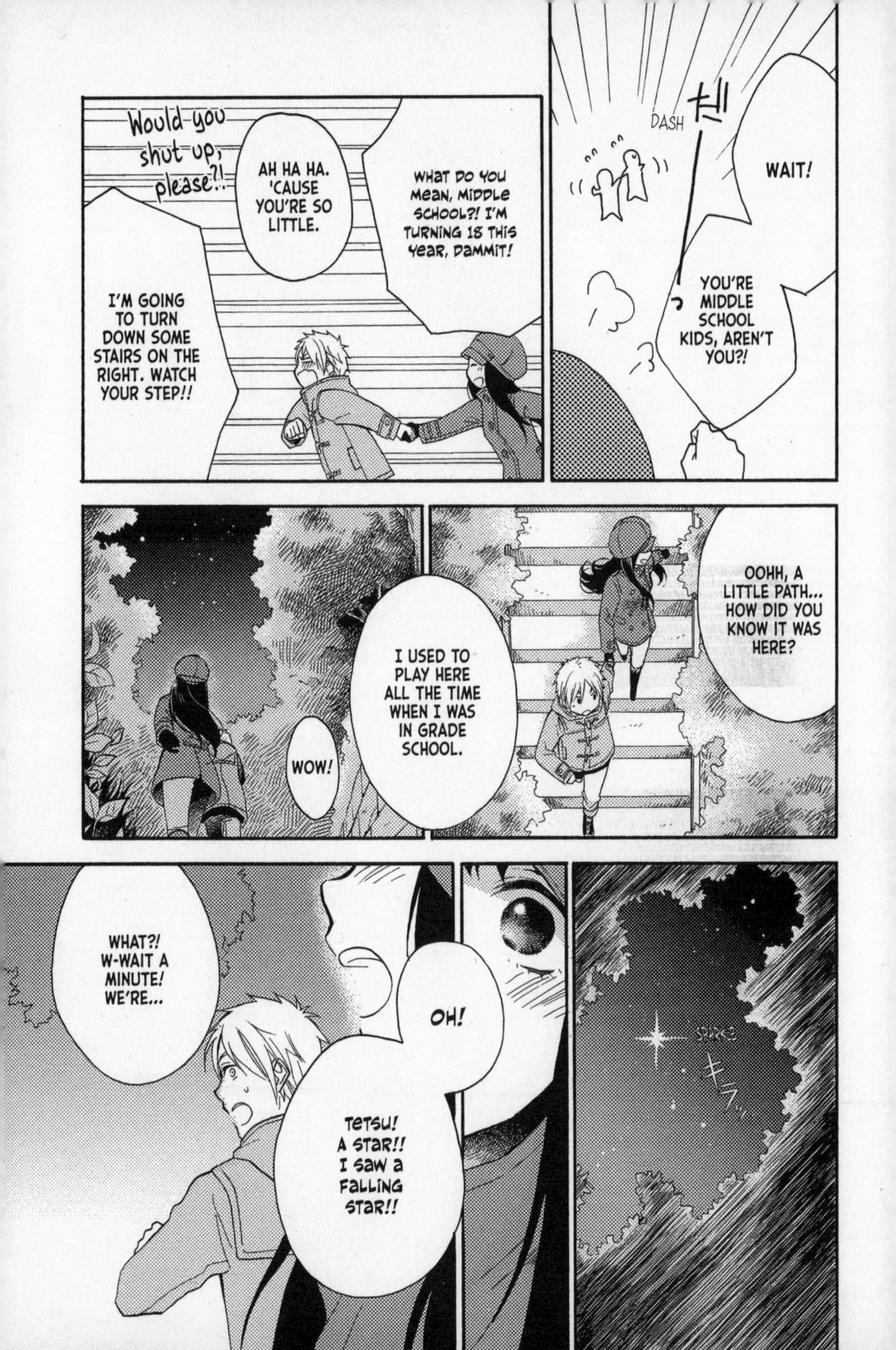
DASH
WAIT!
YOU'RE MIDDLE SCHOOL KIDS, AREN'T YOU?!
WHAT DO YOU MEAN, MIDDLE SCHOOL?! I'M TURNING 18 THIS YEAR, DAMMIT!
AH HA HA. 'CAUSE YOU'RE SO LITTLE.
Would you shut up, please?!
I'M GOING TO TURN DOWN SOME STAIRS ON THE RIGHT. WATCH YOUR STEP!!
OOHH, A LITTLE PATH... HOW DID YOU KNOW IT WAS HERE?
I USED TO PLAY HERE ALL THE TIME WHEN I WAS IN GRADE SCHOOL.
WOW!
SPARKLE
OH!
TETSU! A STAR!! I SAW A FALLING STAR!!
WHAT?! W-WAIT A MINUTE! WE'RE...

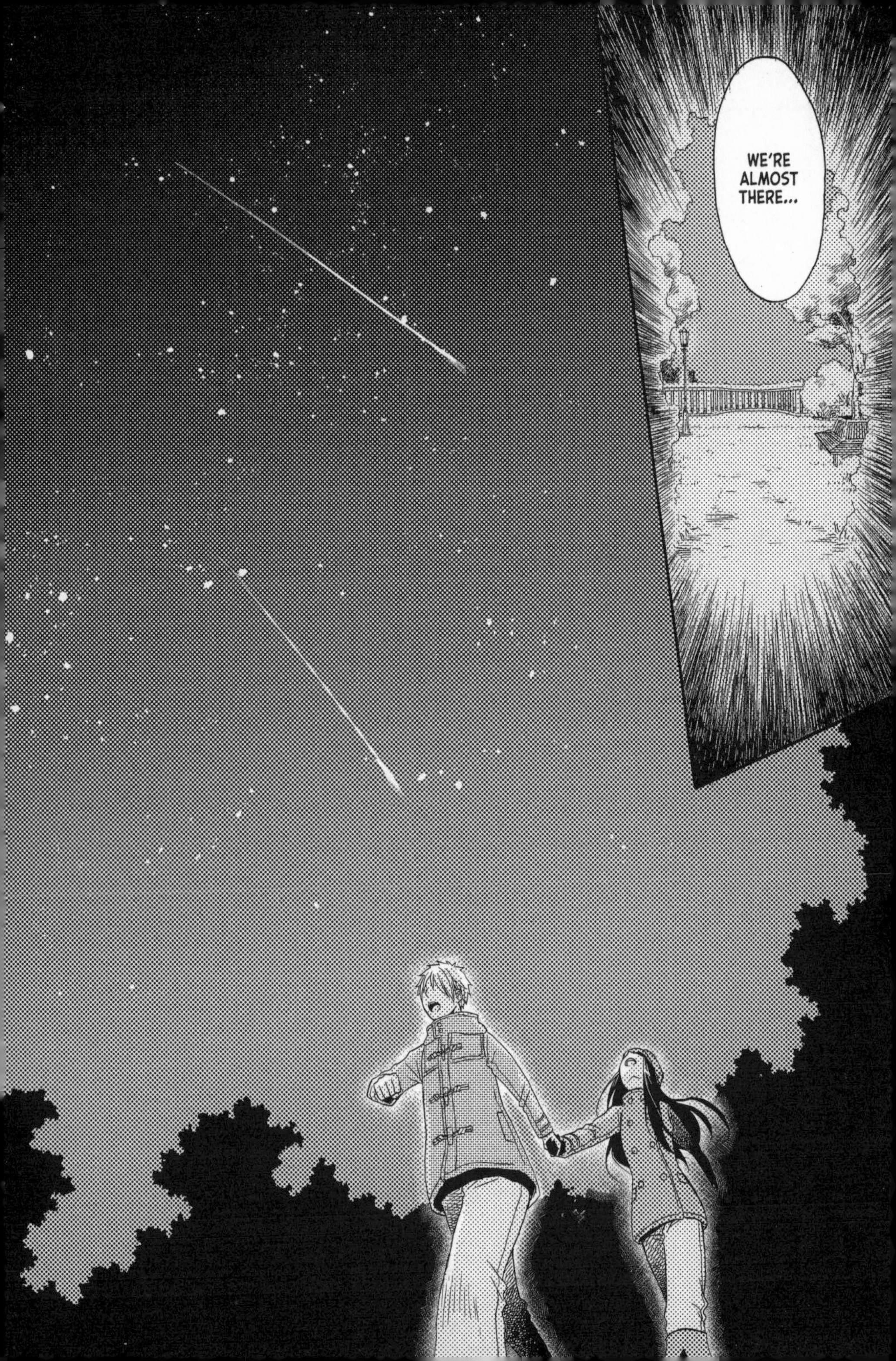
WE'RE ALMOST THERE...

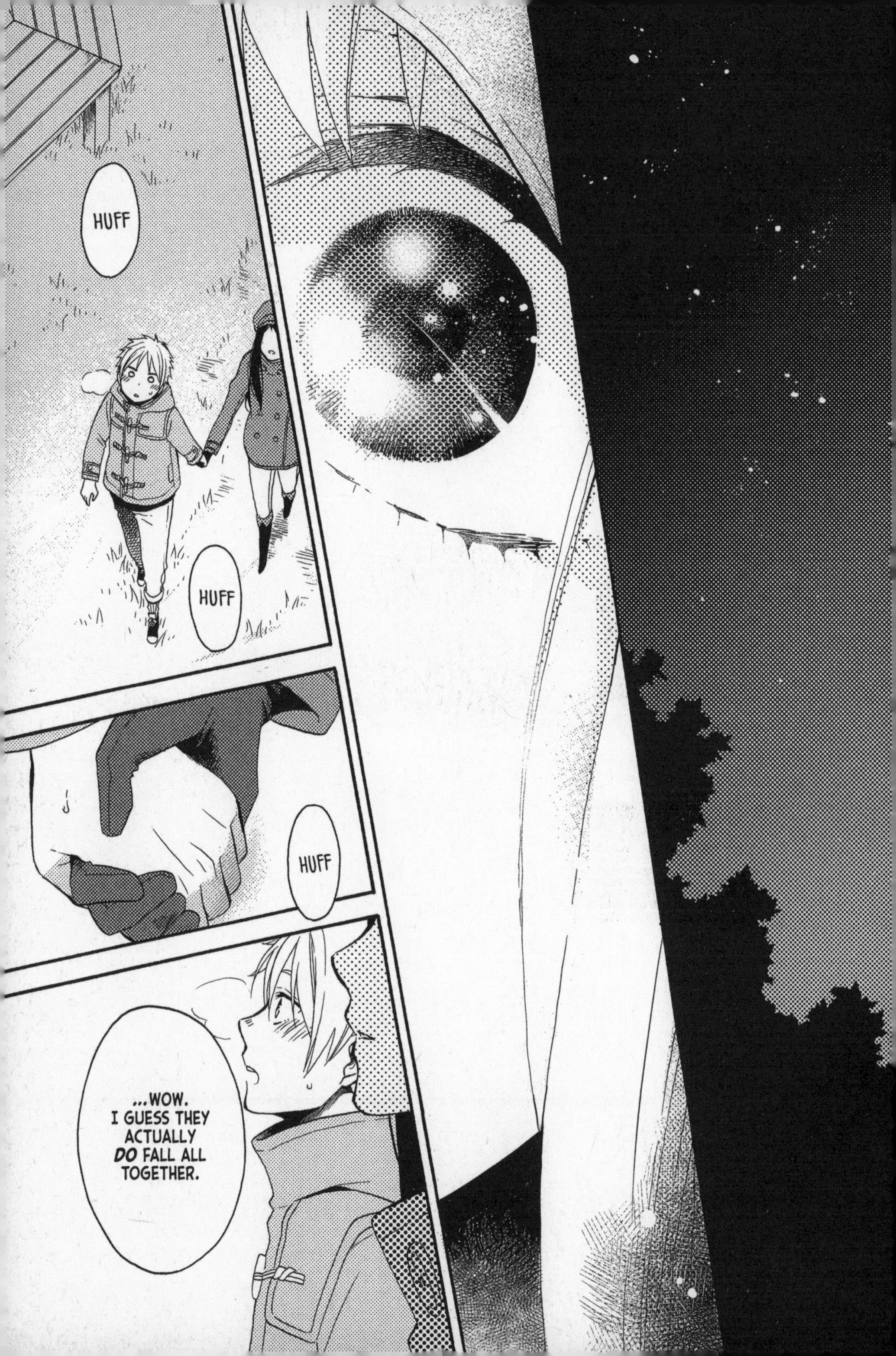
HUFF
HUFF
HUFF
...WOW. I GUESS THEY ACTUALLY *DO* FALL ALL TOGETHER.

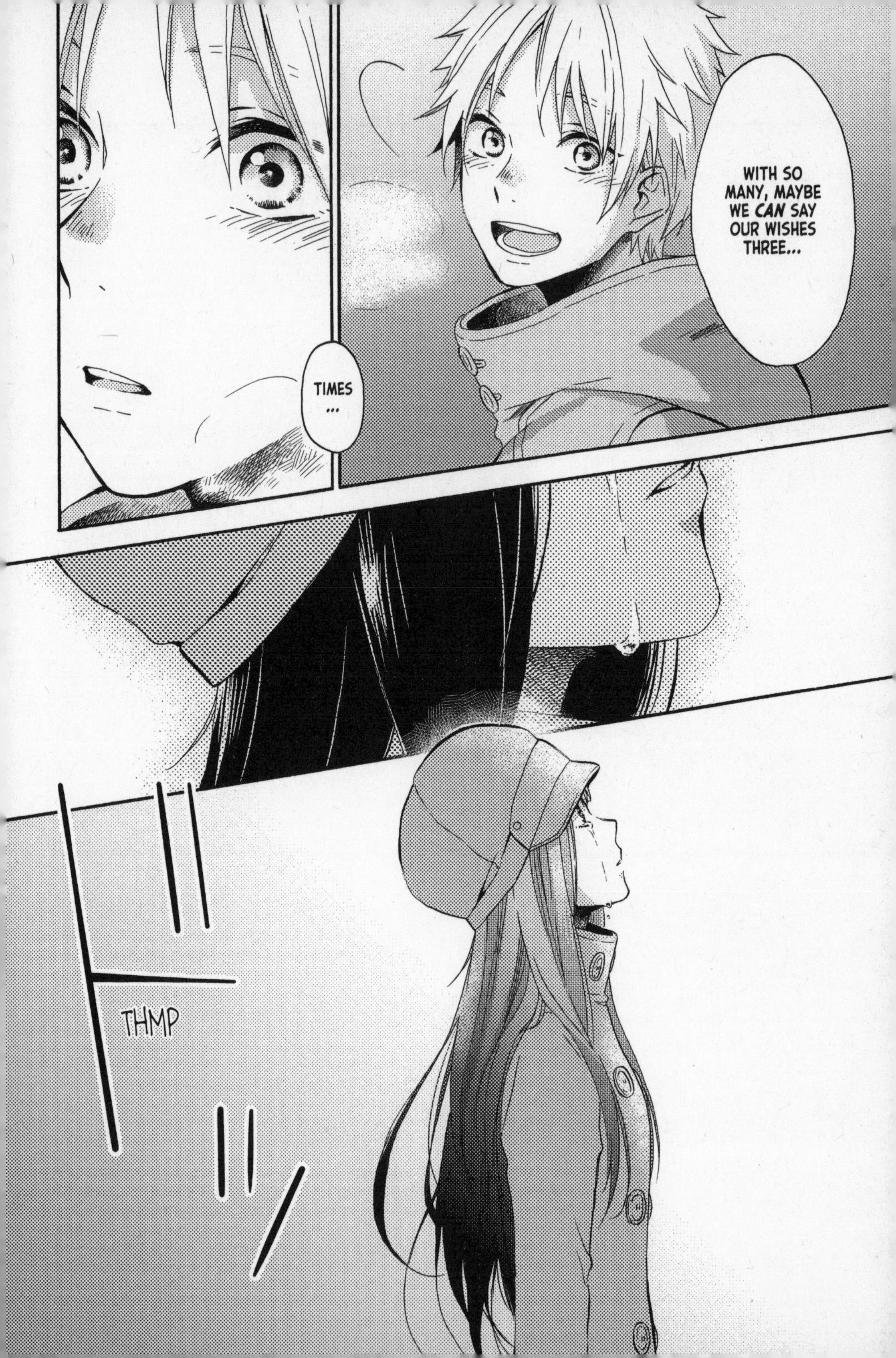
WITH SO MANY, MAYBE WE *CAN* SAY OUR WISHES THREE...
TIMES ...
THMP

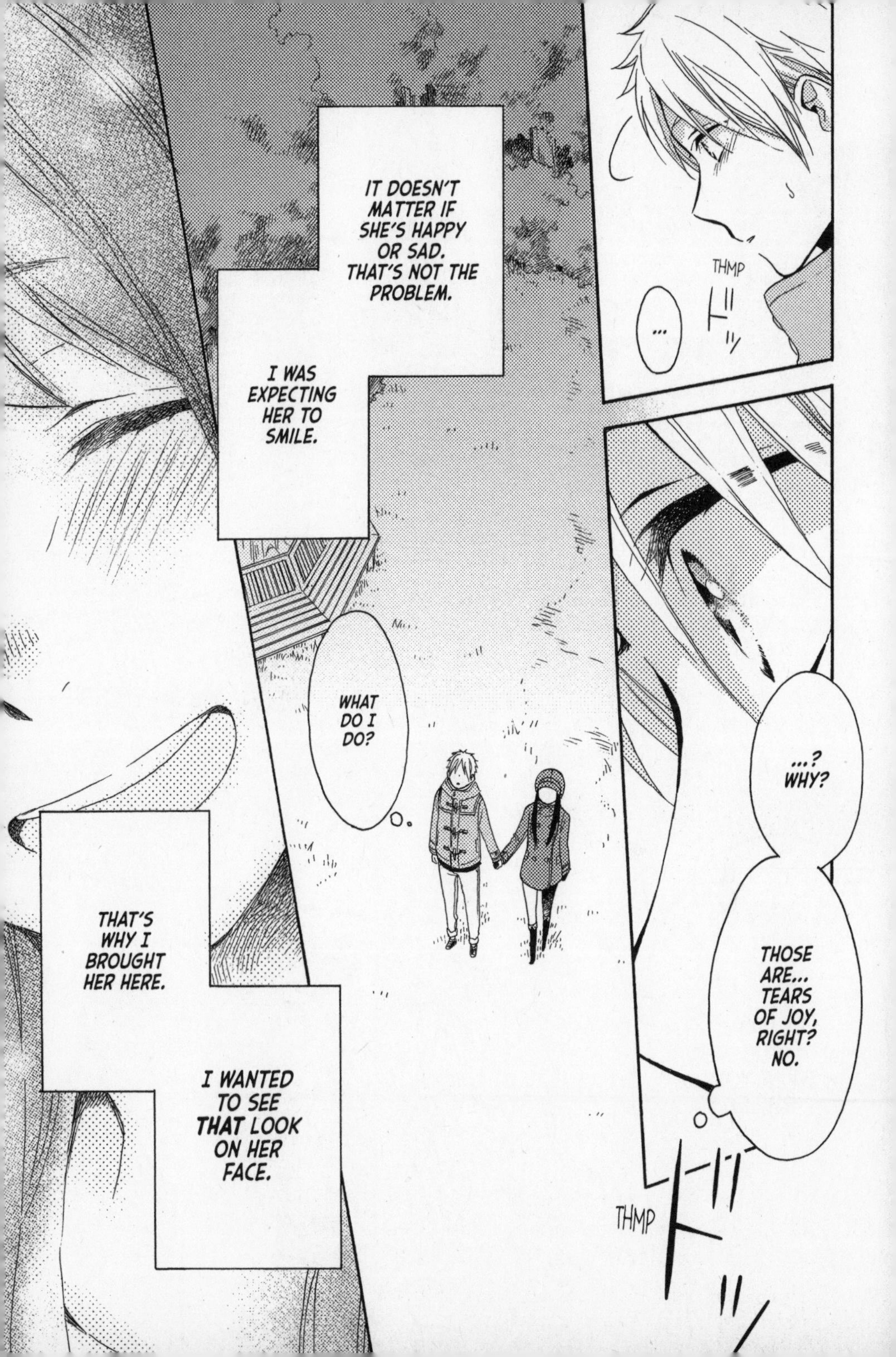
THMP
ドッ
...
...?
WHY?
THOSE ARE... TEARS OF JOY, RIGHT? NO.
THMP
IT DOESN'T MATTER IF SHE'S HAPPY OR SAD. THAT'S NOT THE PROBLEM.
I WAS EXPECTING HER TO SMILE.
WHAT DO I DO?
THAT'S WHY I BROUGHT HER HERE.
I WANTED TO SEE THAT LOOK ON HER FACE.

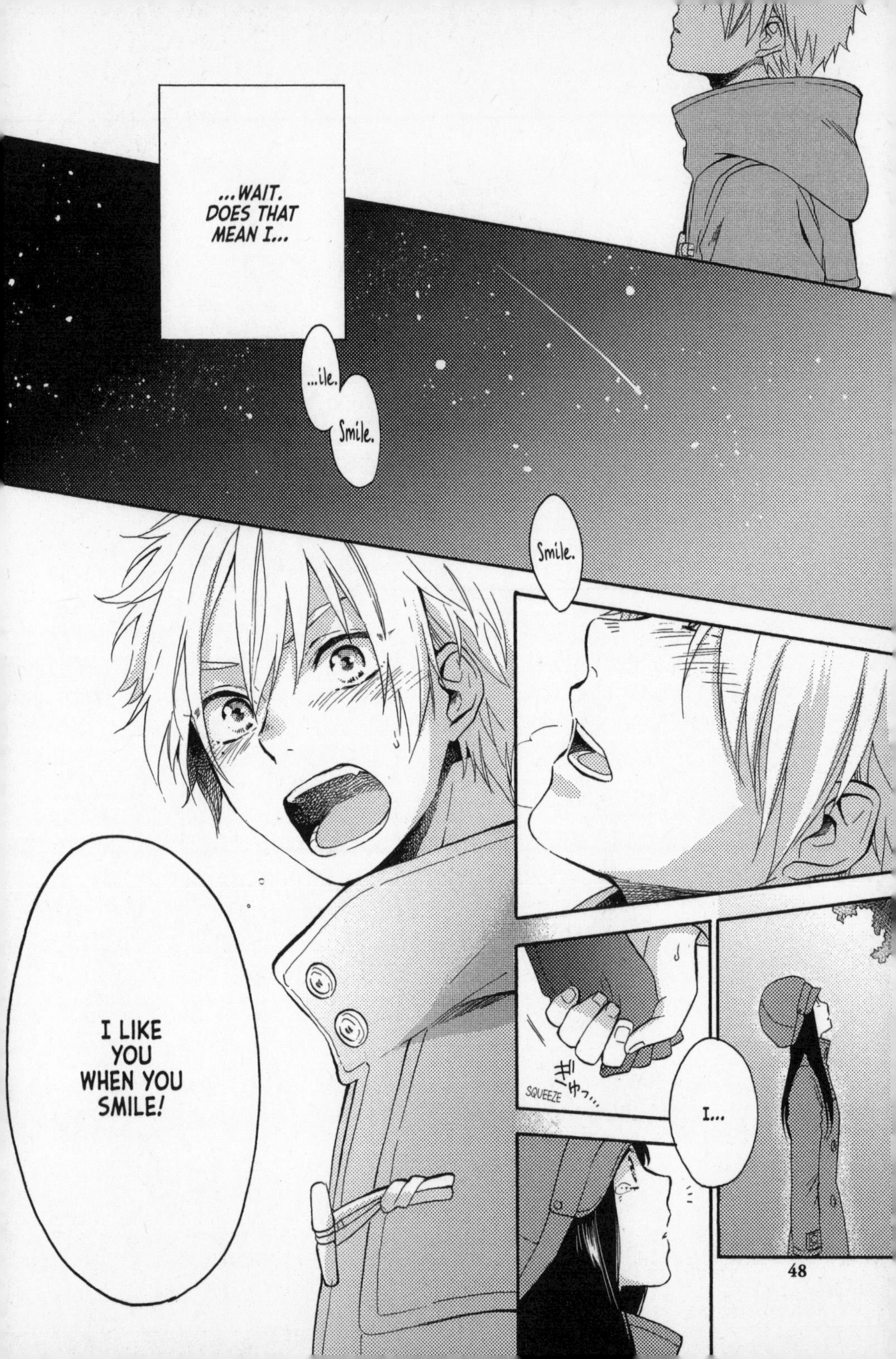
...WAIT. DOES THAT MEAN I...
...ile.
Smile.
Smile.
ぎゅっ...
SQUEEZE
I...
I LIKE YOU WHEN YOU SMILE!

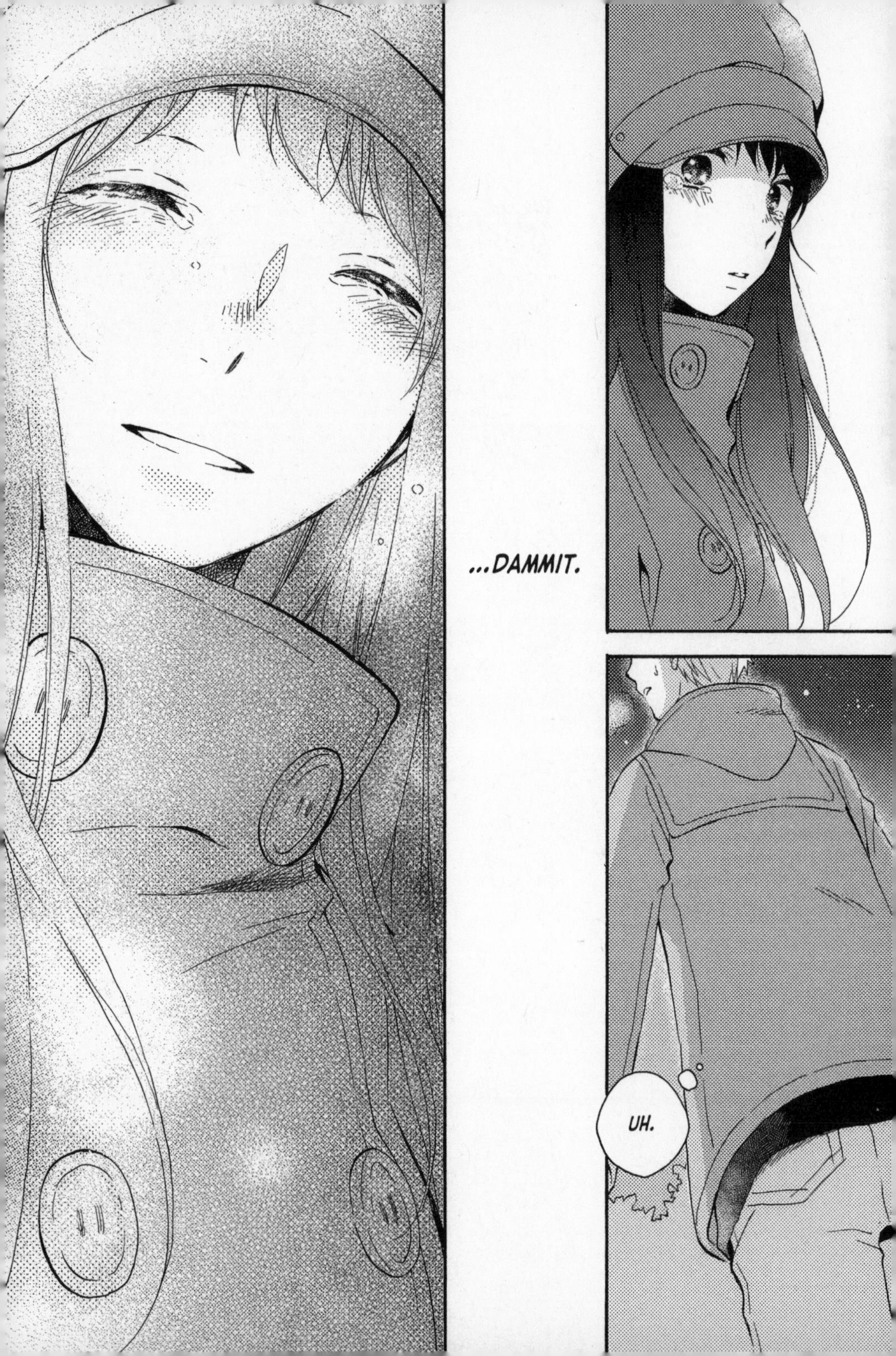
...DAMMIT.
UH.

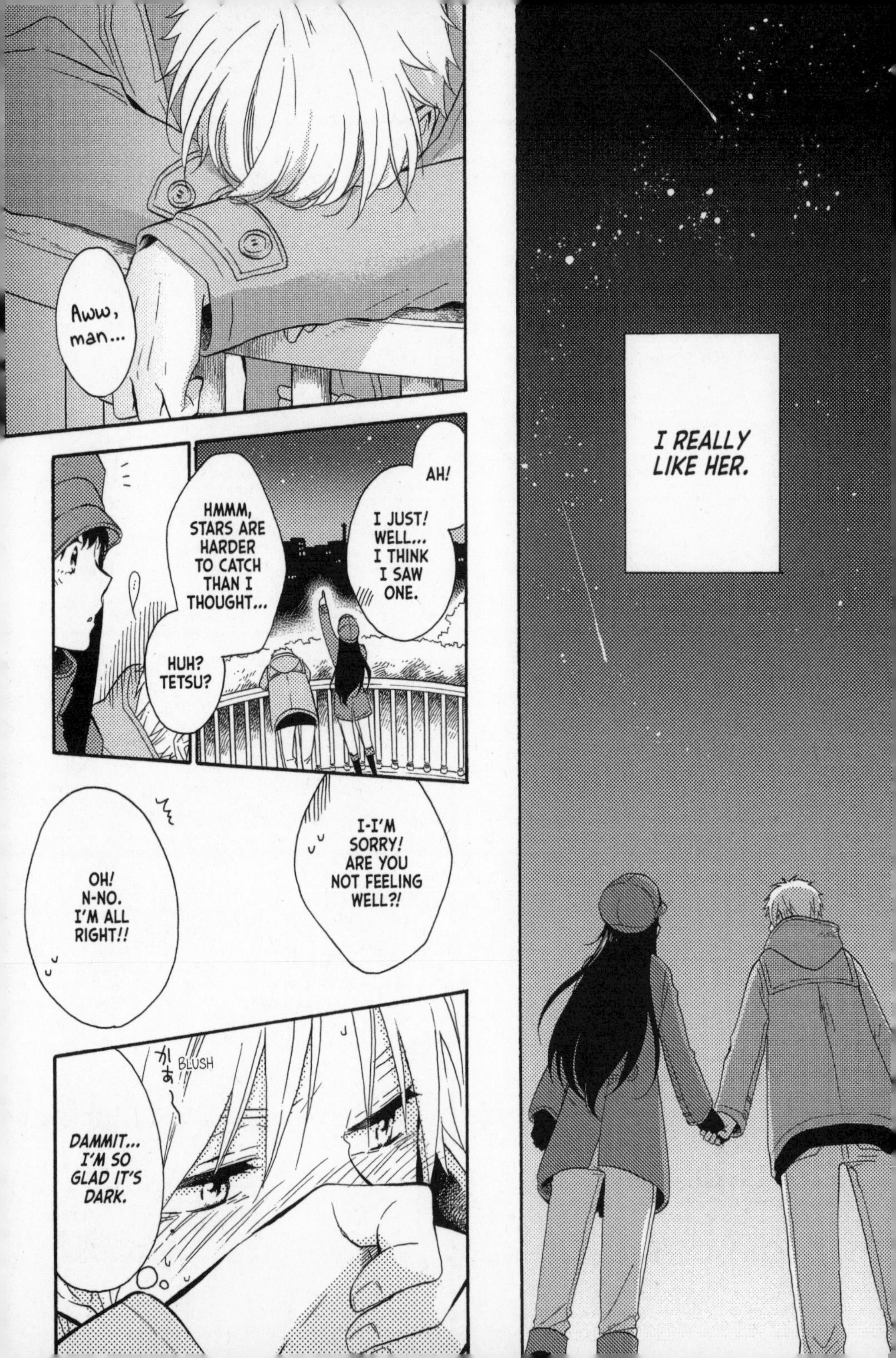
I REALLY LIKE HER.
Aww, man...
AH!
I JUST! WELL... I THINK I SAW ONE.
HMMM, STARS ARE HARDER TO CATCH THAN I THOUGHT...
HUH? TETSU?
I-I'M SORRY! ARE YOU NOT FEELING WELL?!
OH! N-NO. I'M ALL RIGHT!!
かぁ~ BLUSH
DAMMIT... I'M SO GLAD IT'S DARK.

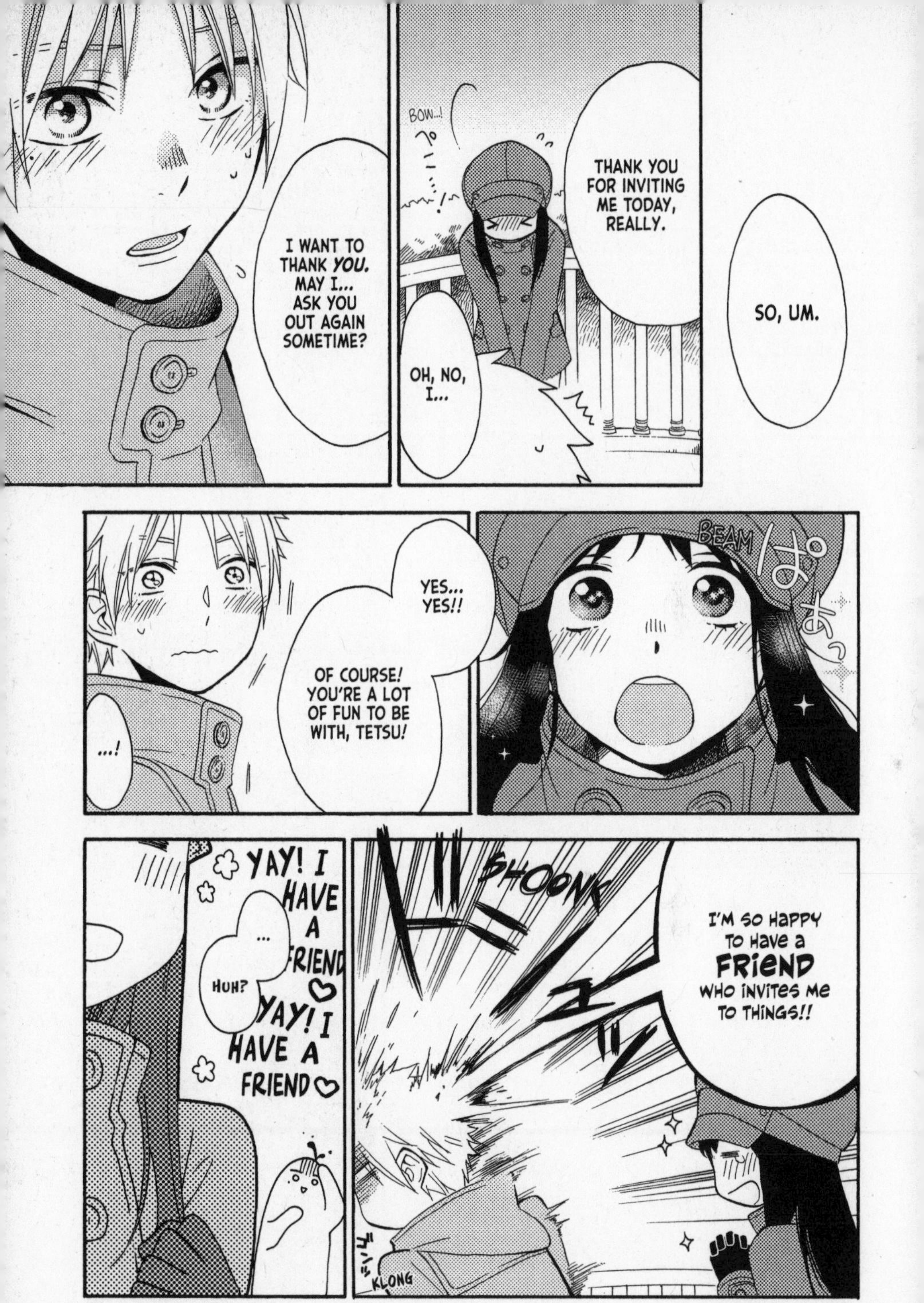
SO, UM.
THANK YOU FOR INVITING ME TODAY, REALLY.
BOW...!
OH, NO, I...
I WANT TO THANK *YOU.* MAY I... ASK YOU OUT AGAIN SOMETIME?
BEAM
YES... YES!!
OF COURSE! YOU'RE A LOT OF FUN TO BE WITH, TETSU!
...!
I'M SO HAPPY TO HAVE A **FRIEND** WHO INVITES ME TO THINGS!!
SHOONK
KLONG
YAY! I HAVE A FRIEND♡
YAY! I HAVE A FRIEND♡
...
HUH?

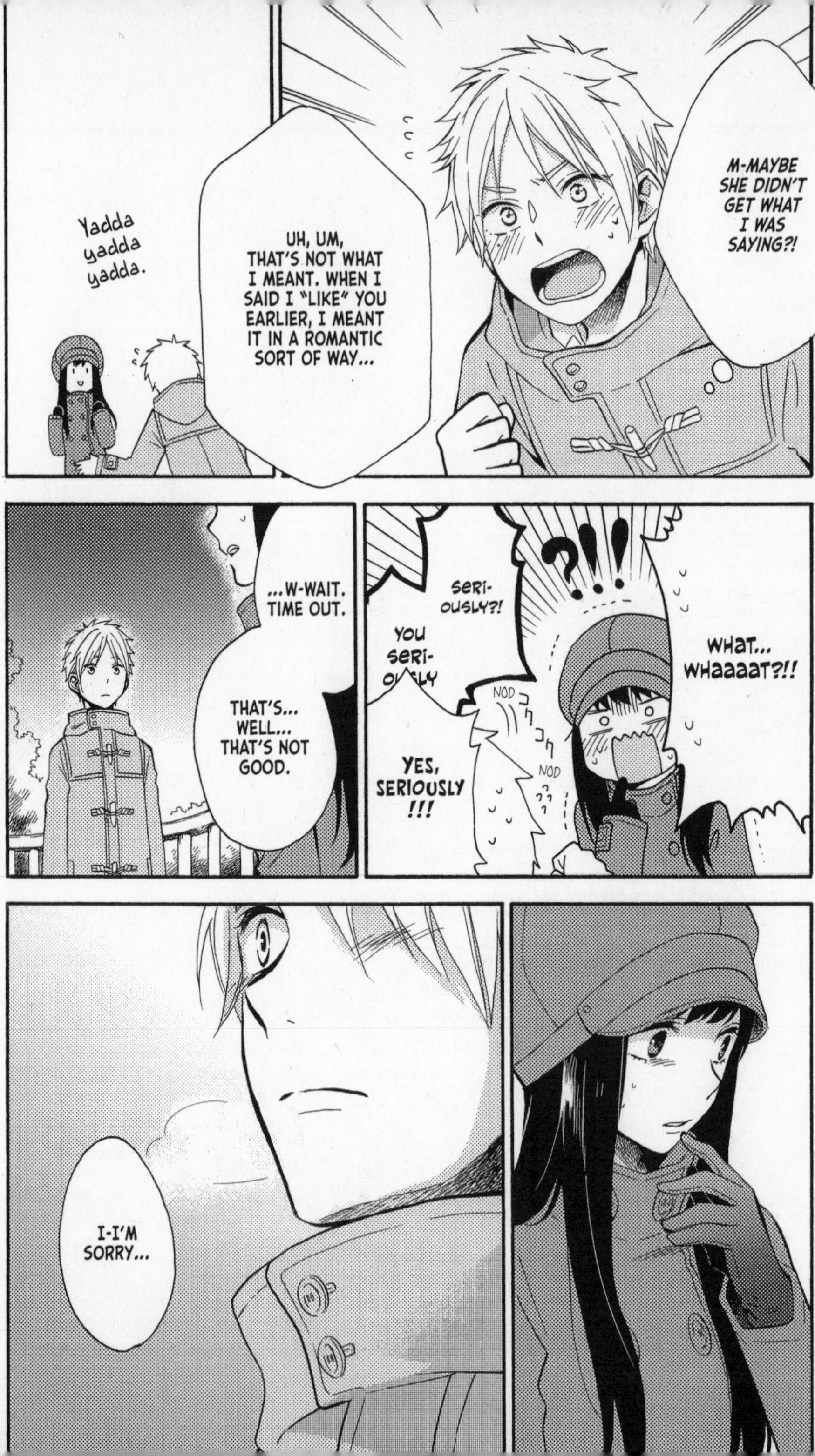
M-MAYBE SHE DIDN'T GET WHAT I WAS SAYING?!
UH, UM, THAT'S NOT WHAT I MEANT. WHEN I SAID I "LIKE" YOU EARLIER, I MEANT IT IN A ROMANTIC SORT OF WAY...
Yadda yadda yadda.
?!!
WHAT... WHAAAAT?!!
SERI-OUSLY?!
YOU SERI-OUSLY
NOD
NOD
YES, SERIOUSLY!!!
...W-WAIT. TIME OUT.
THAT'S... WELL... THAT'S NOT GOOD.
I-I'M SORRY...

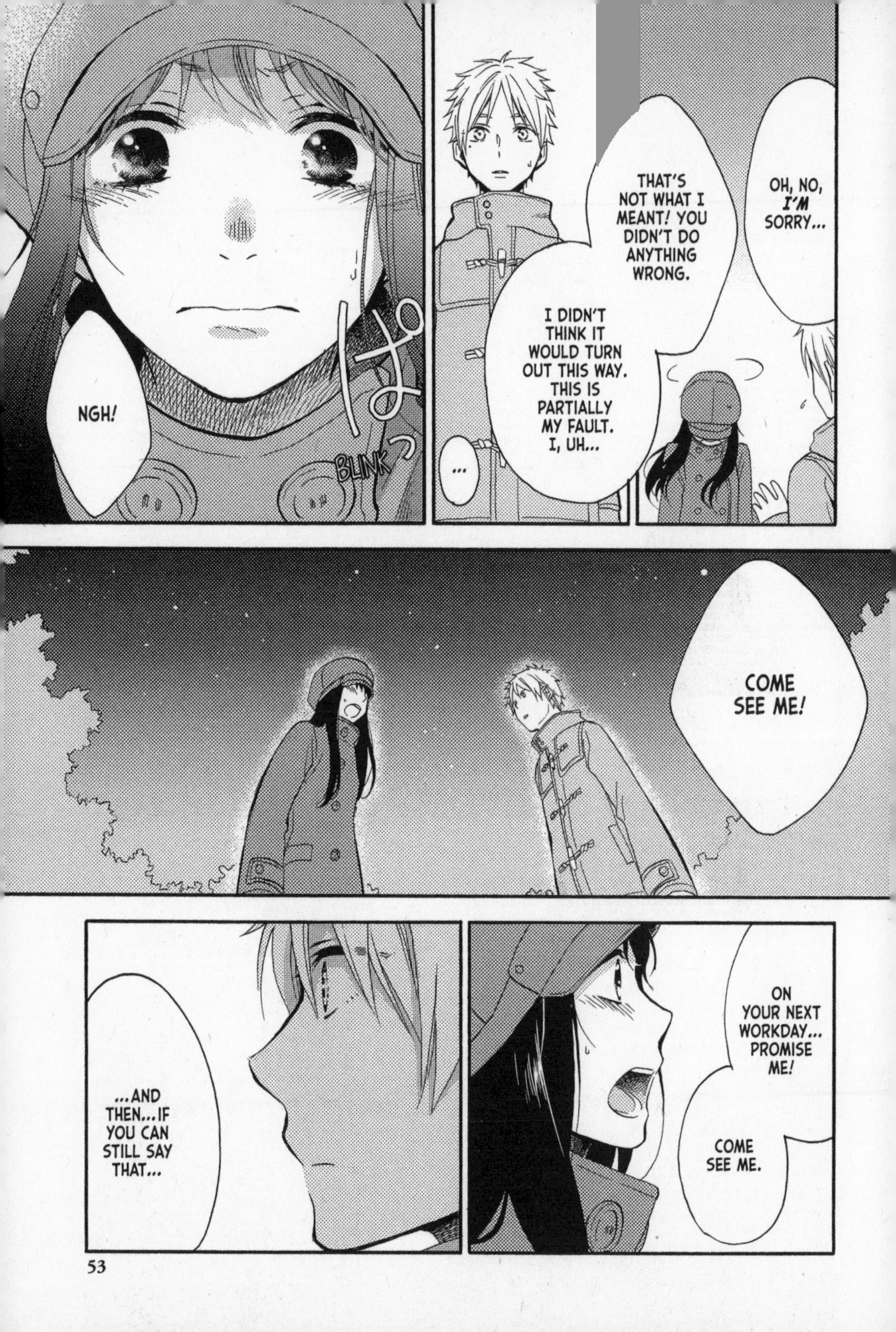
OH, NO, *I'M* SORRY...
THAT'S NOT WHAT I MEANT! YOU DIDN'T DO ANYTHING WRONG.
I DIDN'T THINK IT WOULD TURN OUT THIS WAY. THIS IS PARTIALLY MY FAULT. I, UH...
...
NGH!
BLINK
COME SEE ME!
ON YOUR NEXT WORKDAY... PROMISE ME!
COME SEE ME.
...AND THEN...IF YOU CAN STILL SAY THAT...

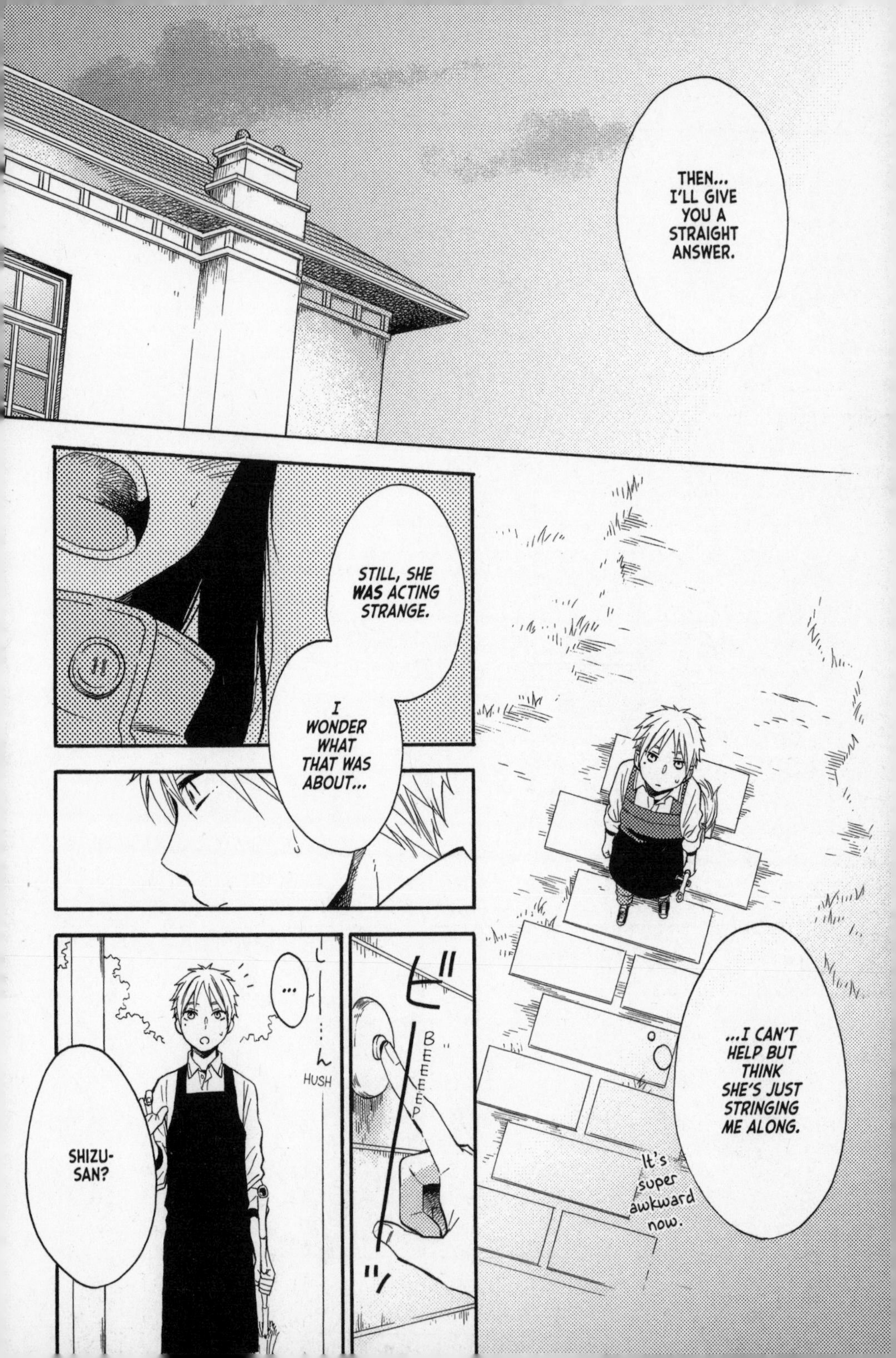
THEN... I'LL GIVE YOU A STRAIGHT ANSWER.
...I CAN'T HELP BUT THINK SHE'S JUST STRINGING ME ALONG.
It's super awkward now.
STILL, SHE WAS ACTING STRANGE.
I WONDER WHAT THAT WAS ABOUT...
ビーッ
BEEEEP
...
しーん
HUSH
SHIZU-SAN?

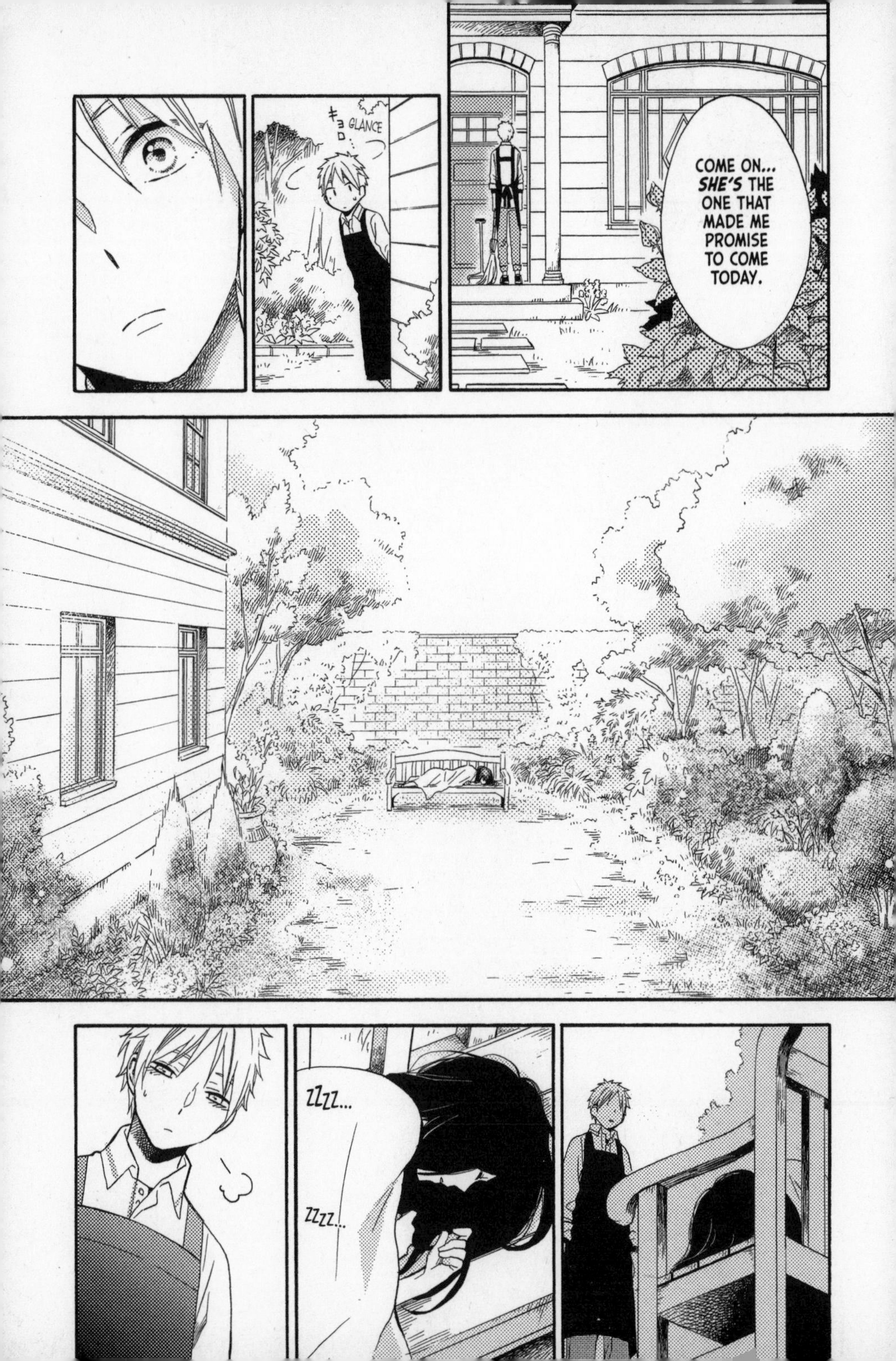
COME ON... SHE'S THE ONE THAT MADE ME PROMISE TO COME TODAY.
キョロ
GLANCE
ZZZZ...
ZZZZ...

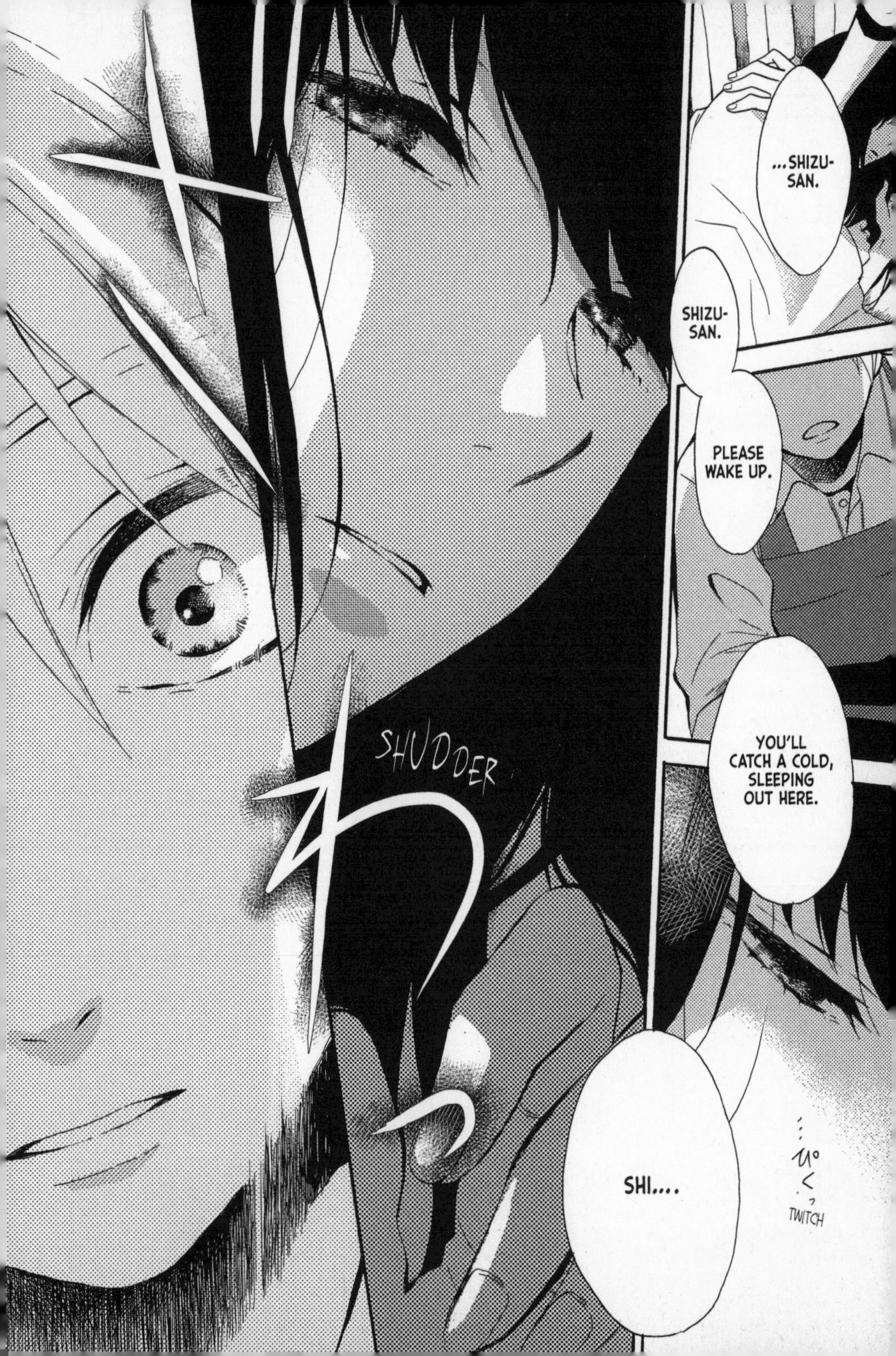

...SHIZU-SAN.
SHIZU-SAN.
PLEASE WAKE UP.
YOU'LL CATCH A COLD, SLEEPING OUT HERE.
SHUDDER
SHI....
…ぴく
TWITCH

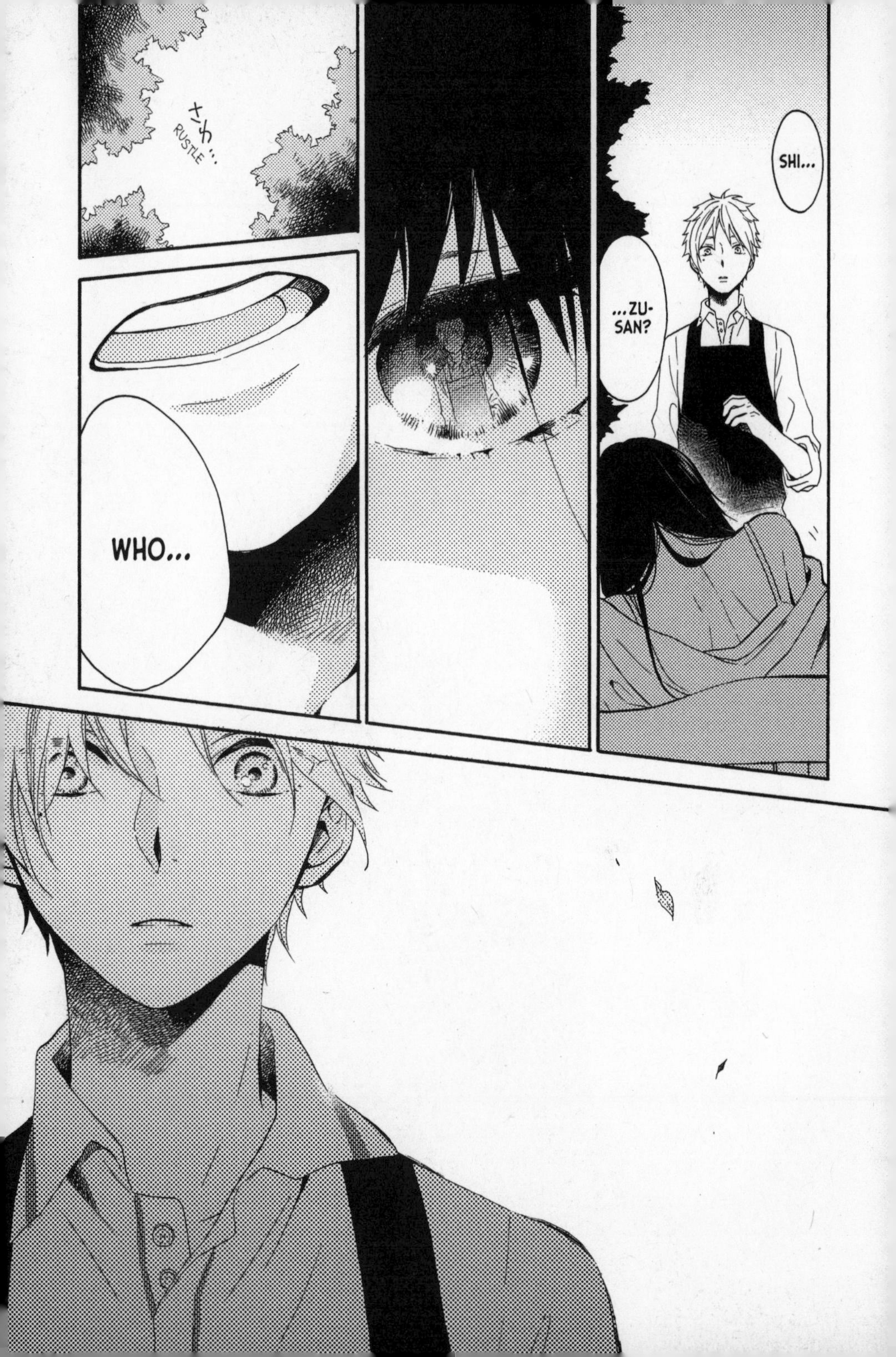
SHI...
...ZU-SAN?
さわ…
RUSTLE
WHO...

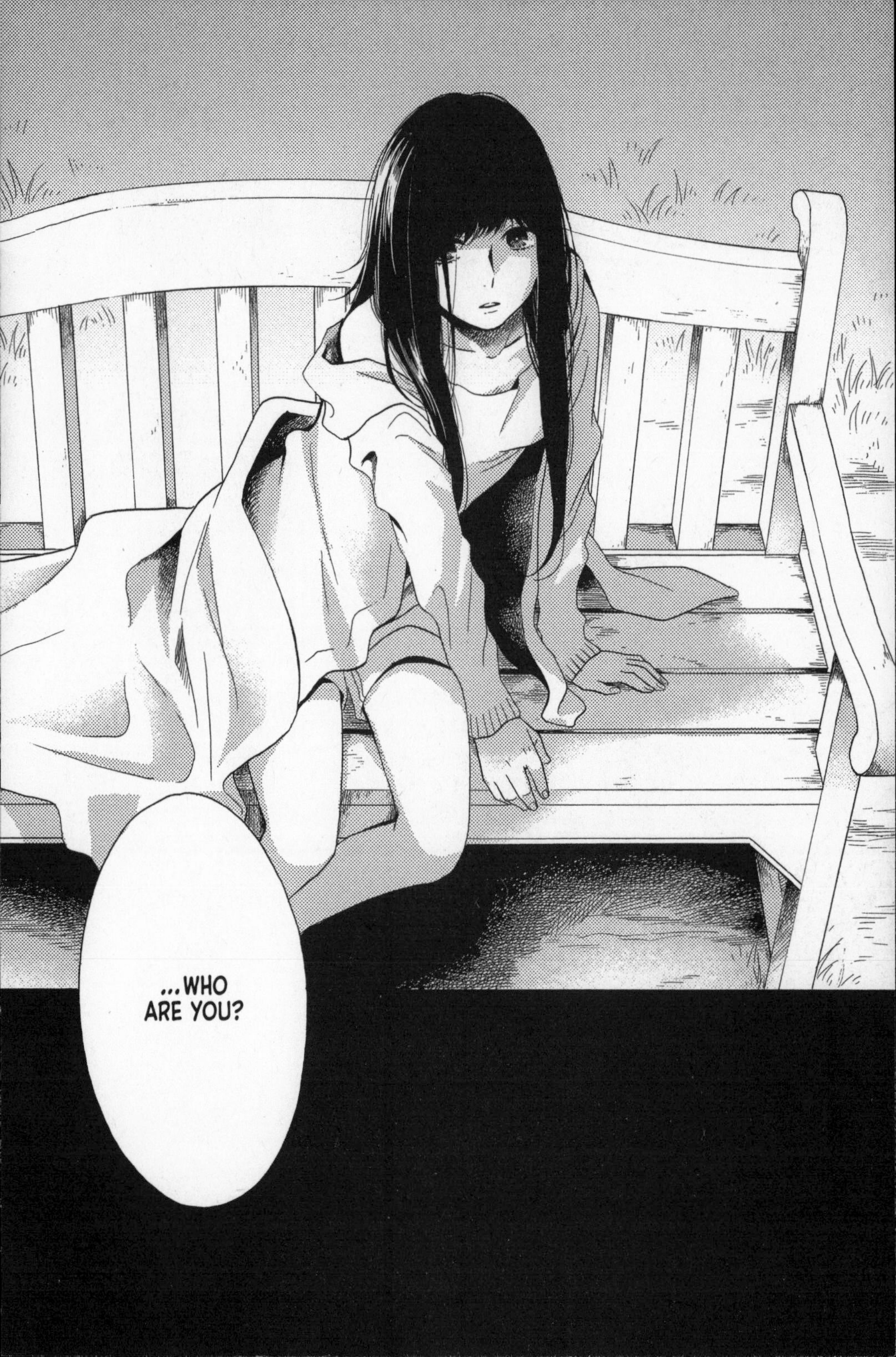
...WHO ARE YOU?

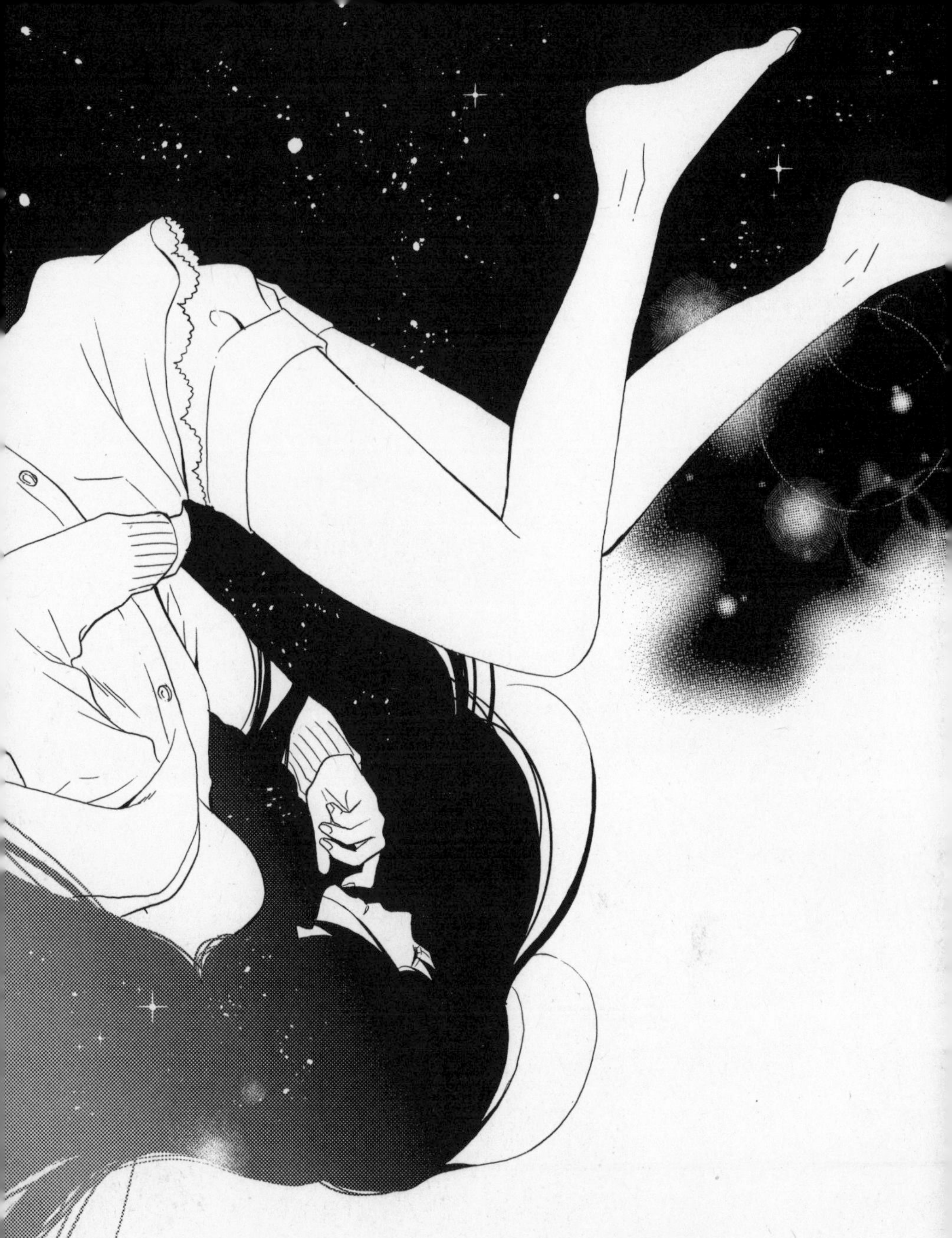

CHAPTER 2

WHO IS IN THE HAUNTED HOUSE?

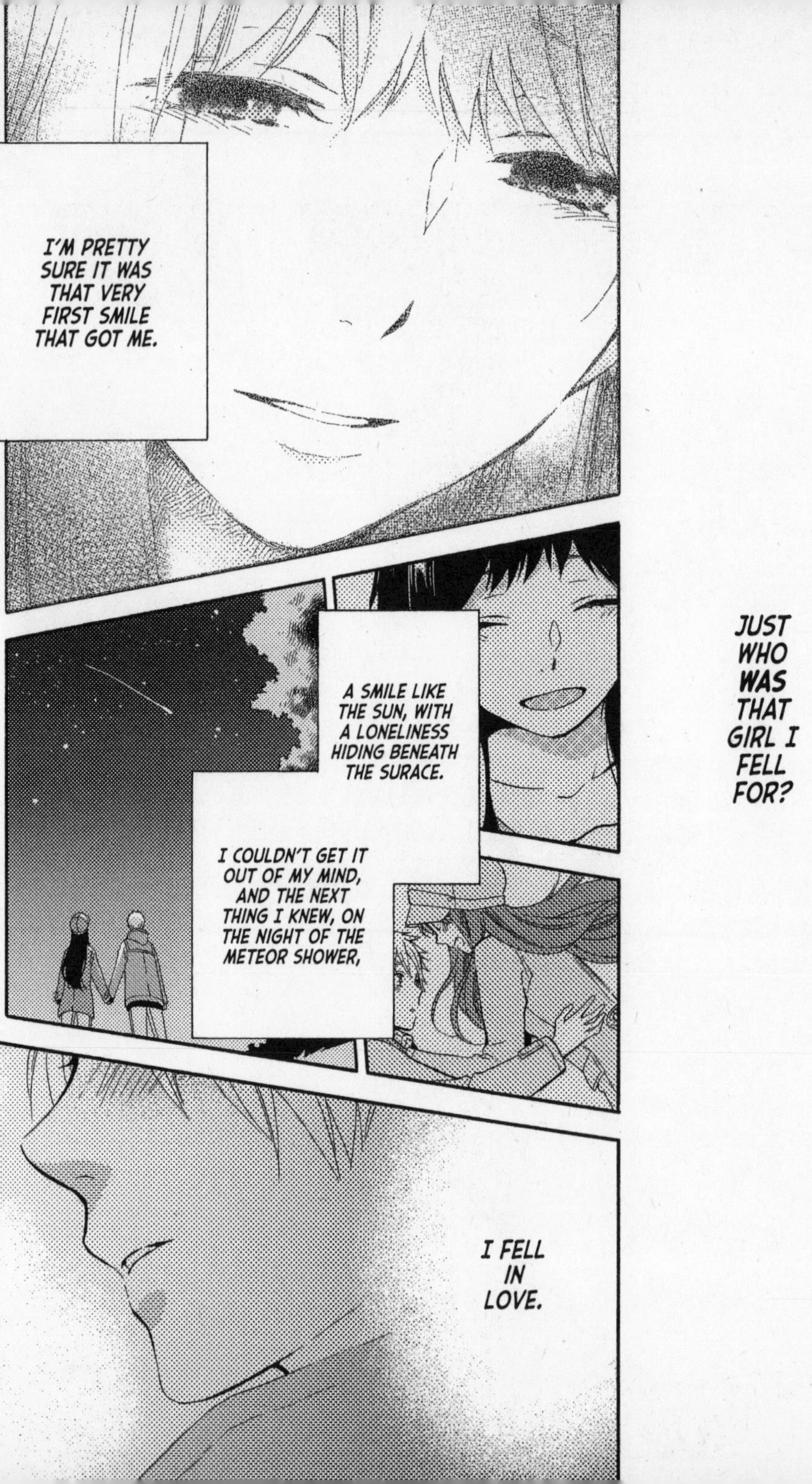
I'M PRETTY SURE IT WAS THAT VERY FIRST SMILE THAT GOT ME.
JUST WHO WAS THAT GIRL I FELL FOR?
A SMILE LIKE THE SUN, WITH A LONELINESS HIDING BENEATH THE SURACE.
I COULDN'T GET IT OUT OF MY MIND, AND THE NEXT THING I KNEW, ON THE NIGHT OF THE METEOR SHOWER,
I FELL IN LOVE.

OR...

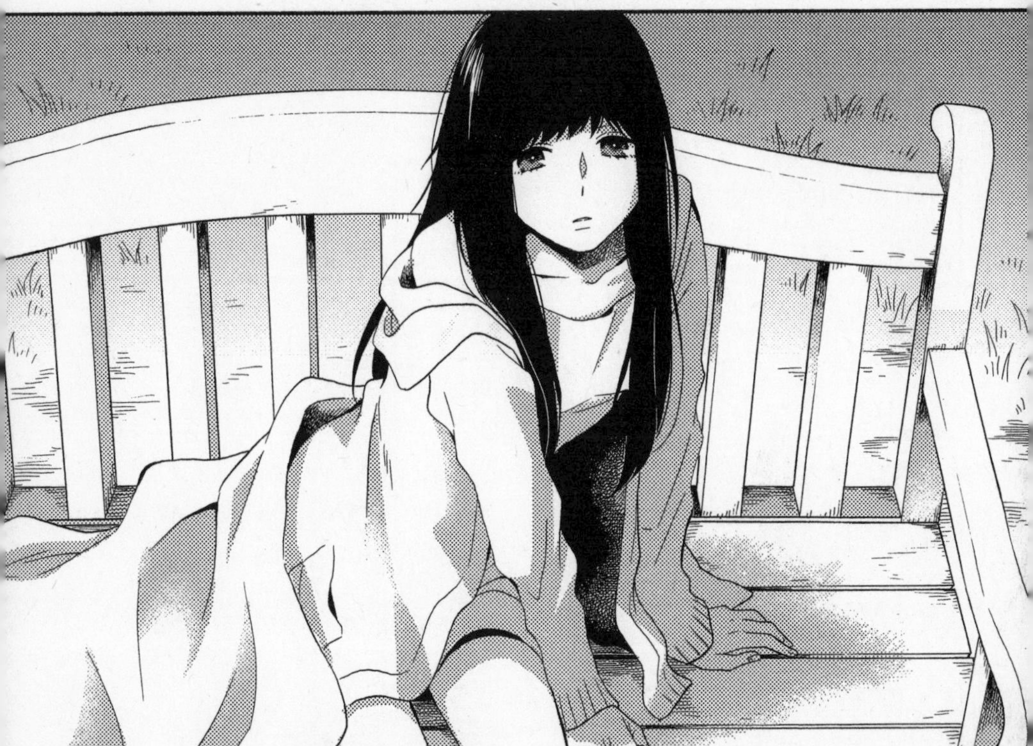

...SO I THOUGHT.

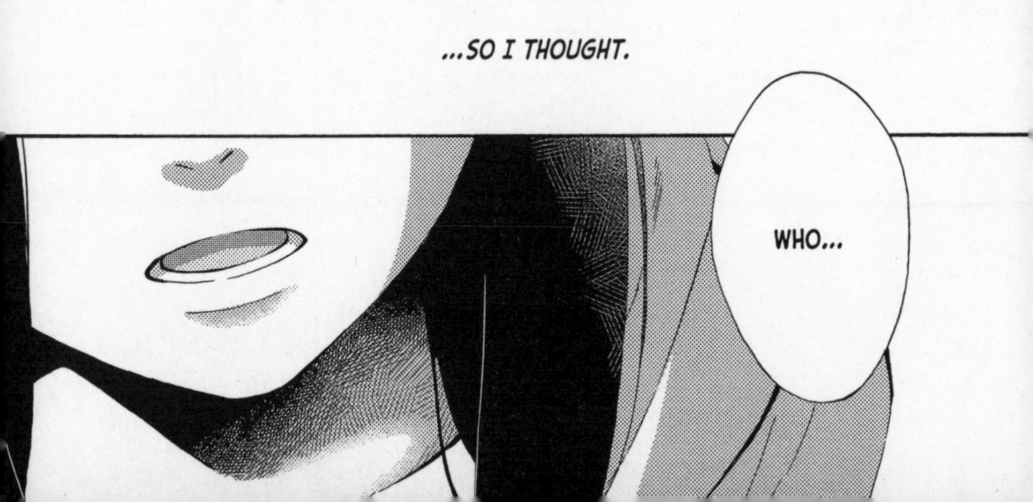
WHO...

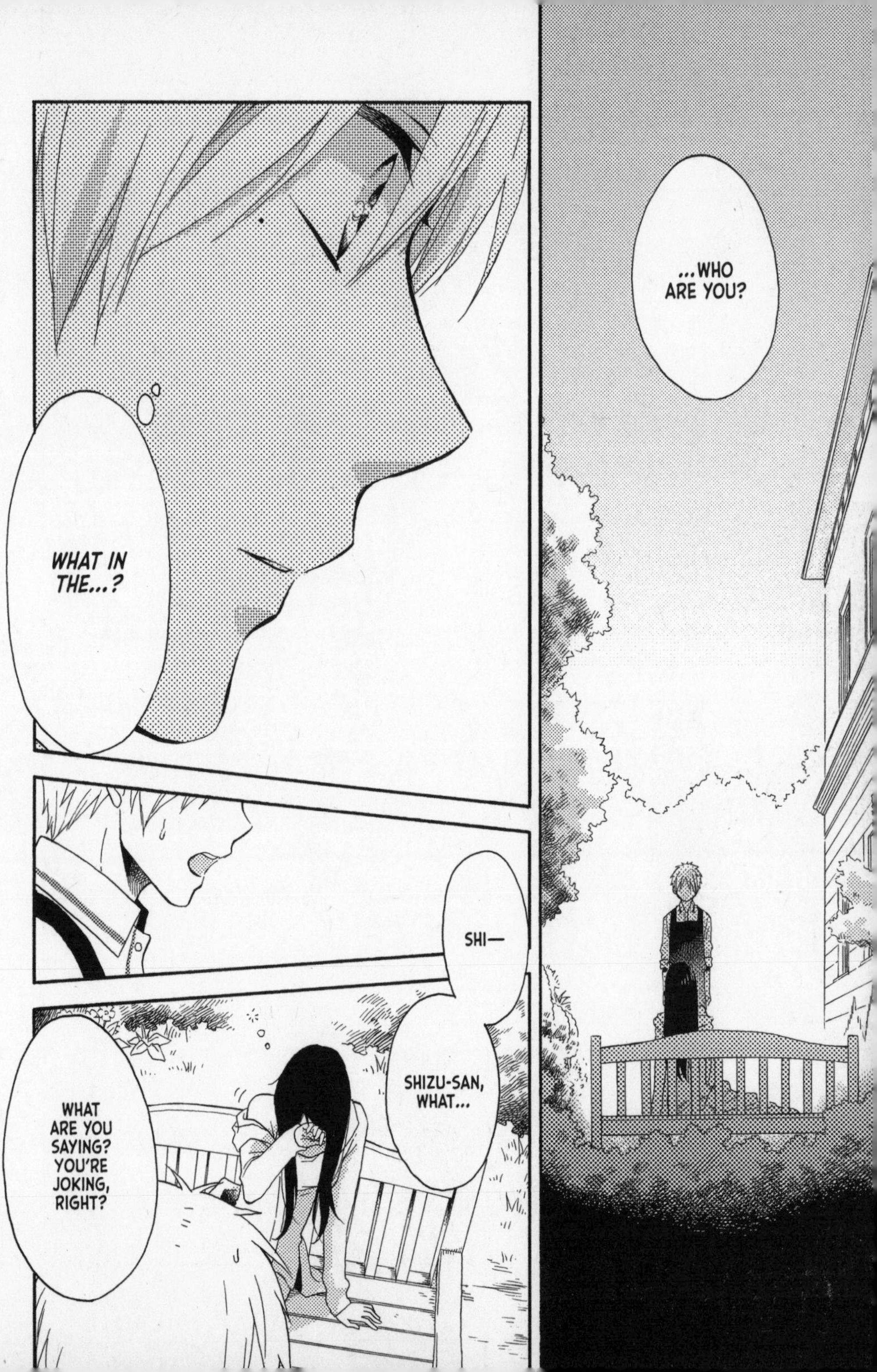
...WHO ARE YOU?
WHAT IN THE...?
SHI—
SHIZU-SAN, WHAT...
WHAT ARE YOU SAYING? YOU'RE JOKING, RIGHT?

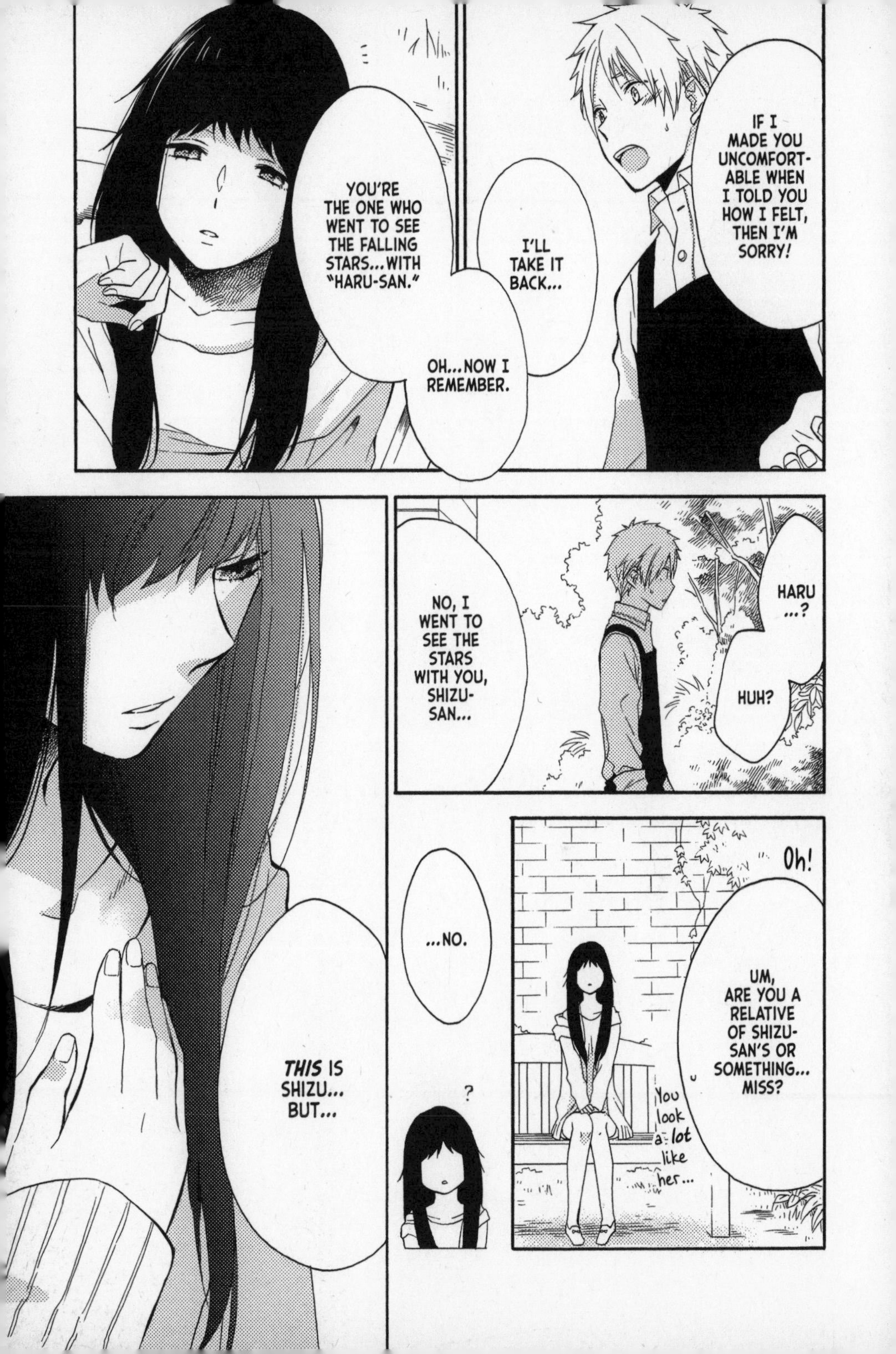
IF I MADE YOU UNCOMFORTABLE WHEN I TOLD YOU HOW I FELT, THEN I'M SORRY!
I'LL TAKE IT BACK...
OH...NOW I REMEMBER.
YOU'RE THE ONE WHO WENT TO SEE THE FALLING STARS...WITH "HARU-SAN."
HARU ...?
HUH?
NO, I WENT TO SEE THE STARS WITH YOU, SHIZU-SAN...
Oh!
UM, ARE YOU A RELATIVE OF SHIZU-SAN'S OR SOMETHING... MISS?
You look a lot like her...
...NO.
?
THIS IS SHIZU... BUT...

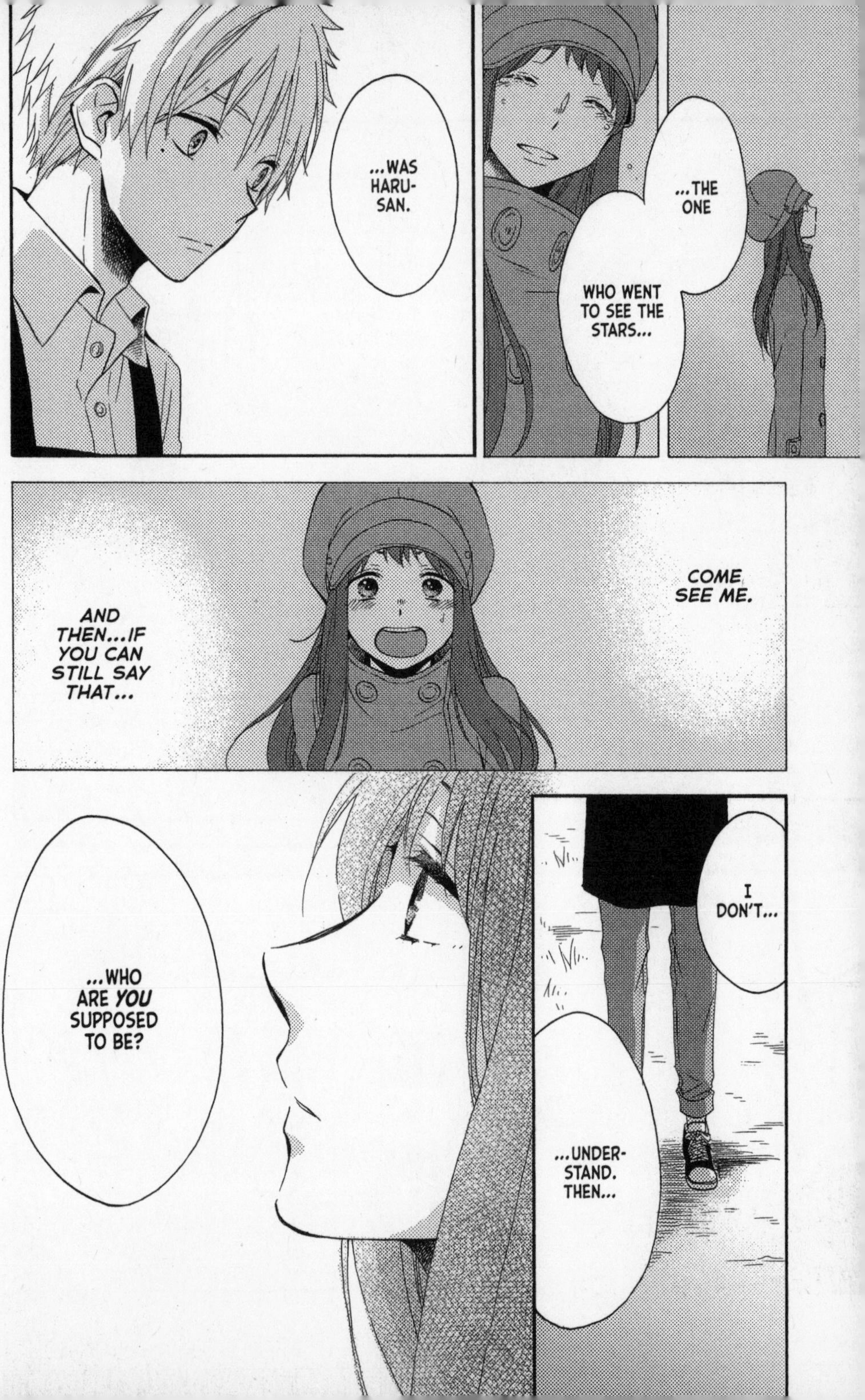
...THE ONE
WHO WENT TO SEE THE STARS...
...WAS HARU-SAN.
COME SEE ME.
AND THEN...IF YOU CAN STILL SAY THAT...
I DON'T...
...UNDER-STAND. THEN...
...WHO ARE *YOU* SUPPOSED TO BE?

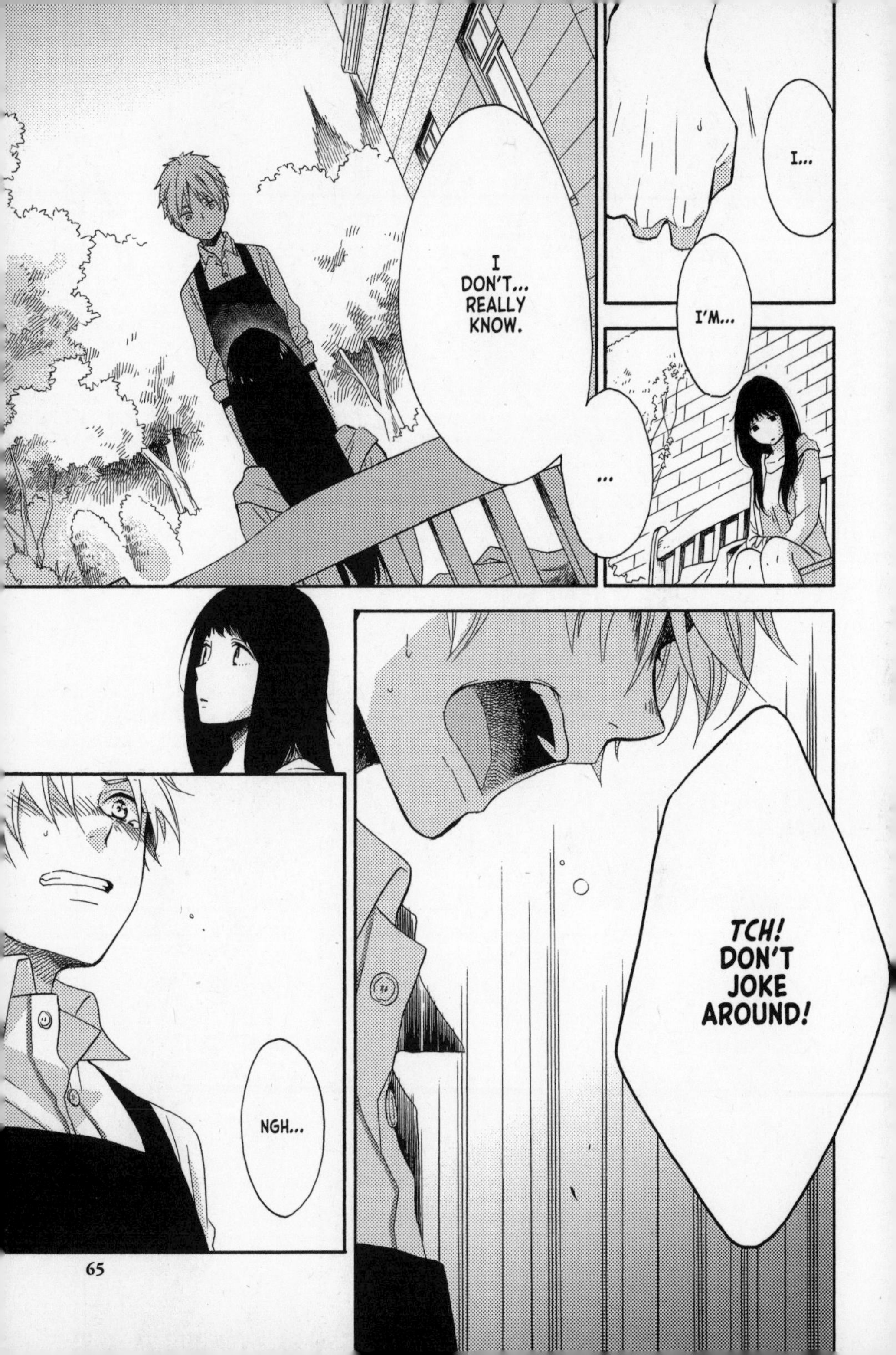
I...
I'M...
I DON'T... REALLY KNOW.
...
TCH! DON'T JOKE AROUND!
NGH...

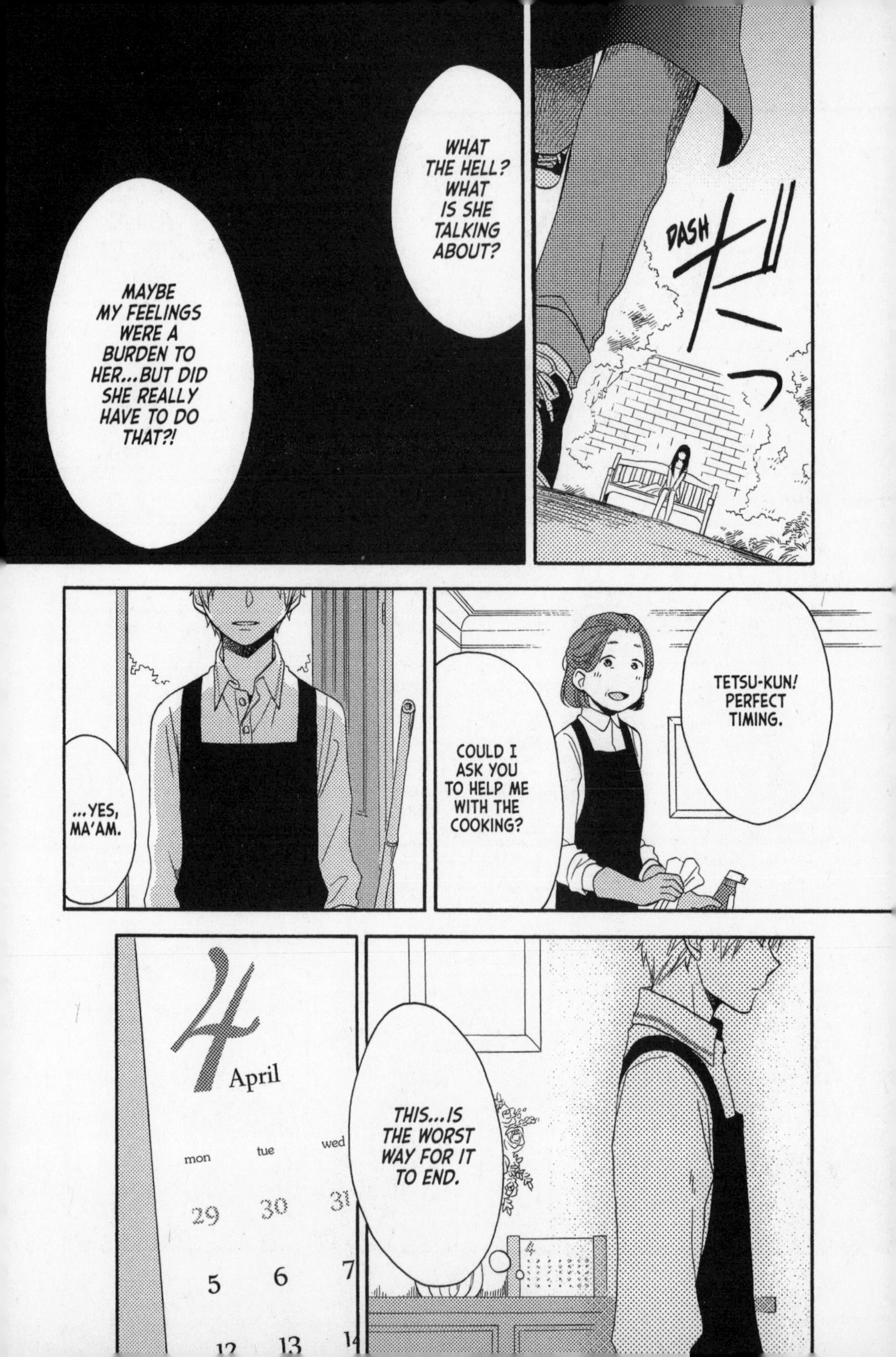
DASH
WHAT THE HELL? WHAT IS SHE TALKING ABOUT?
MAYBE MY FEELINGS WERE A BURDEN TO HER...BUT DID SHE REALLY HAVE TO DO THAT?!
TETSU-KUN! PERFECT TIMING.
COULD I ASK YOU TO HELP ME WITH THE COOKING?
...YES, MA'AM.
THIS...IS THE WORST WAY FOR IT TO END.
4
April
mon tue wed
29 30 31
5 6 7
13 14

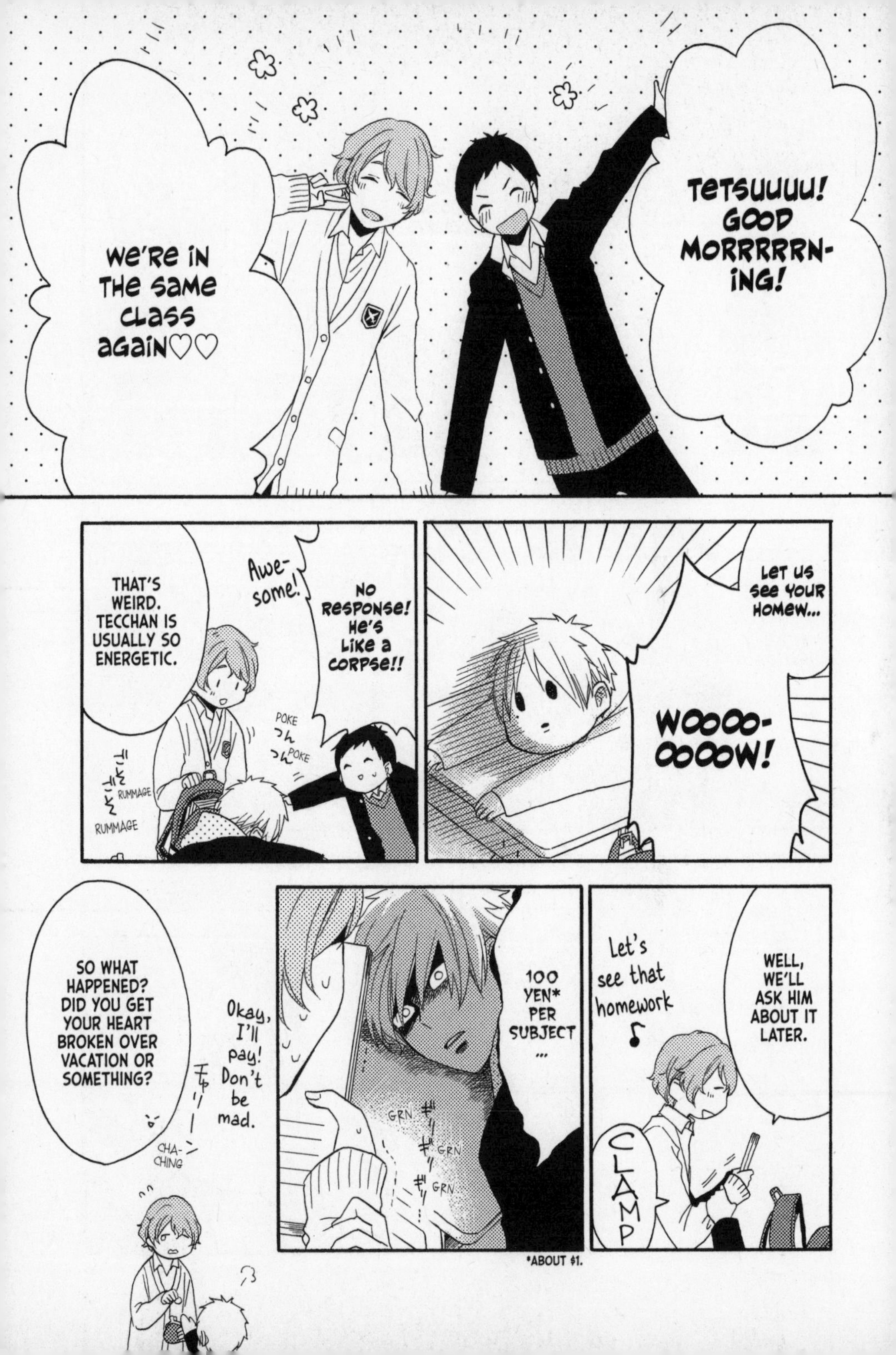
TETSUUUU! GOOD MORRRRN-ING!
WE'RE IN THE SAME CLASS AGAIN♡♡
LET US SEE YOUR HOMEW...
WOOOO-OOOOW!
Awe-some!
NO RESPONSE! HE'S LIKE A CORPSE!!
POKE
POKE
THAT'S WEIRD. TECCHAN IS USUALLY SO ENERGETIC.
RUMMAGE
RUMMAGE
WELL, WE'LL ASK HIM ABOUT IT LATER.
Let's see that homework ♪
CLAMP
100 YEN* PER SUBJECT ...
GRN
GRN
GRN
Okay, I'll pay! Don't be mad.
SO WHAT HAPPENED? DID YOU GET YOUR HEART BROKEN OVER VACATION OR SOMETHING?
CHA-CHING
*ABOUT $1.

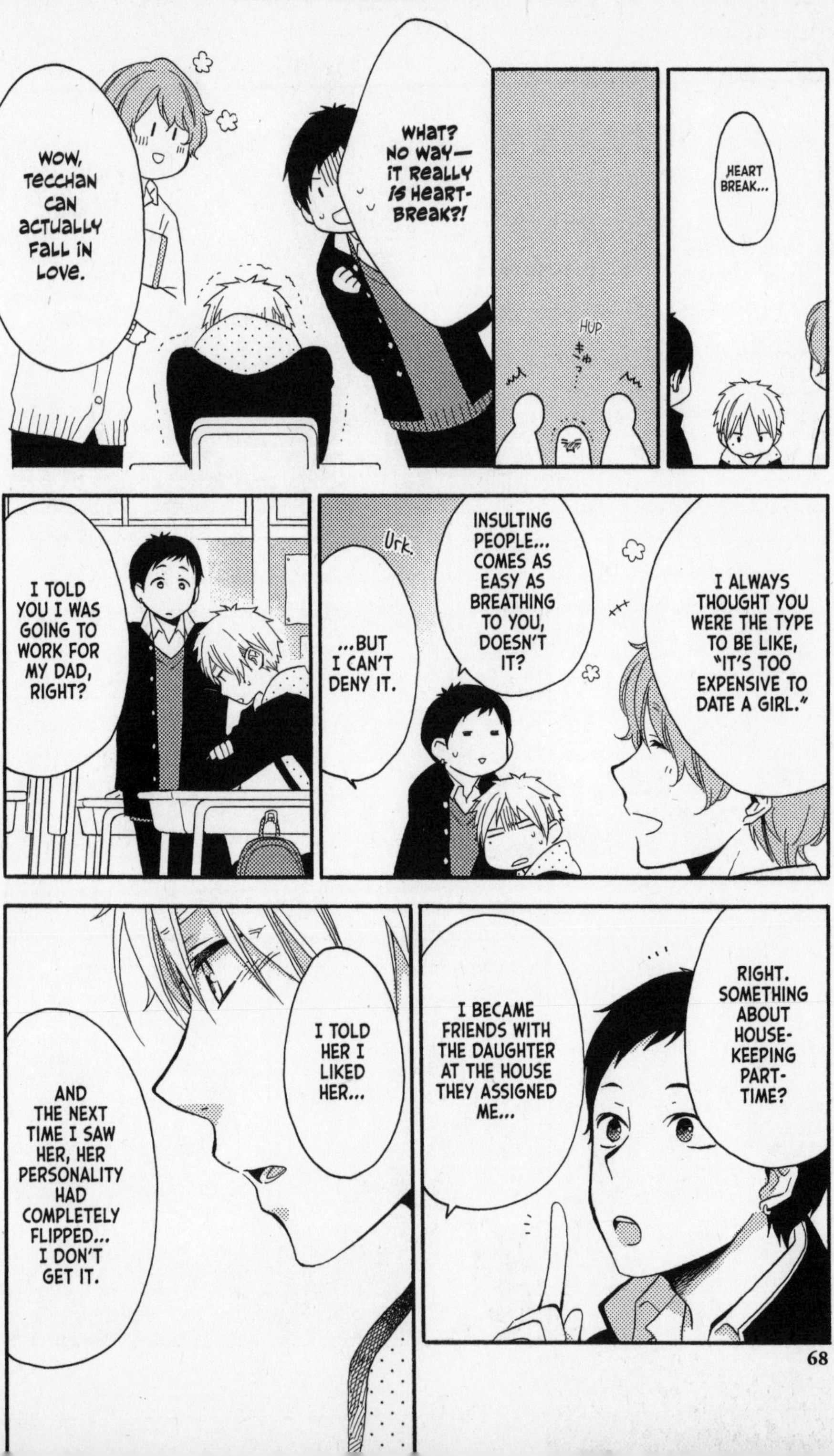

HEART BREAK...
HUP
WHAT? NO WAY— IT REALLY IS HEART-BREAK?!
WOW, TECCHAN CAN ACTUALLY FALL IN LOVE.
I ALWAYS THOUGHT YOU WERE THE TYPE TO BE LIKE, "IT'S TOO EXPENSIVE TO DATE A GIRL."
INSULTING PEOPLE... COMES AS EASY AS BREATHING TO YOU, DOESN'T IT?
Urk.
...BUT I CAN'T DENY IT.
I TOLD YOU I WAS GOING TO WORK FOR MY DAD, RIGHT?
RIGHT. SOMETHING ABOUT HOUSE-KEEPING PART-TIME?
I BECAME FRIENDS WITH THE DAUGHTER AT THE HOUSE THEY ASSIGNED ME...
I TOLD HER I LIKED HER...
AND THE NEXT TIME I SAW HER, HER PERSONALITY HAD COMPLETELY FLIPPED... I DON'T GET IT.

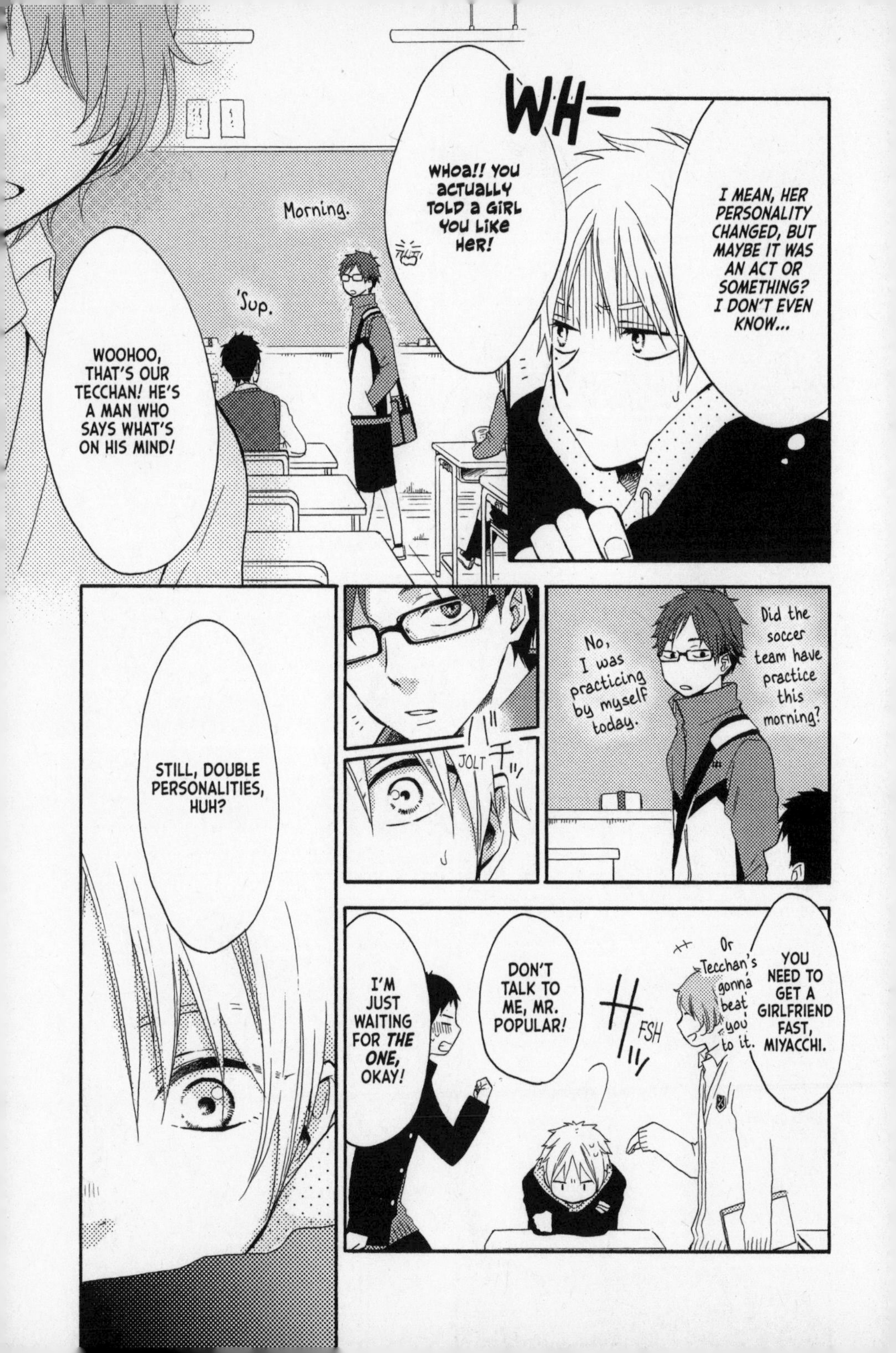
I MEAN, HER PERSONALITY CHANGED, BUT MAYBE IT WAS AN ACT OR SOMETHING? I DON'T EVEN KNOW...
WH-
WHOA!! YOU ACTUALLY TOLD A GIRL YOU LIKE HER!
WOOHOO, THAT'S OUR TECCHAN! HE'S A MAN WHO SAYS WHAT'S ON HIS MIND!
Morning.
'Sup.
Did the soccer team have practice this morning?
No, I was practicing by myself today.
JOLT
YOU NEED TO GET A GIRLFRIEND FAST, MIYACCHI.
Or Tecchan's gonna beat you to it.
DON'T TALK TO ME, MR. POPULAR!
FSH
I'M JUST WAITING FOR *THE ONE*, OKAY!
STILL, DOUBLE PERSONALITIES, HUH?

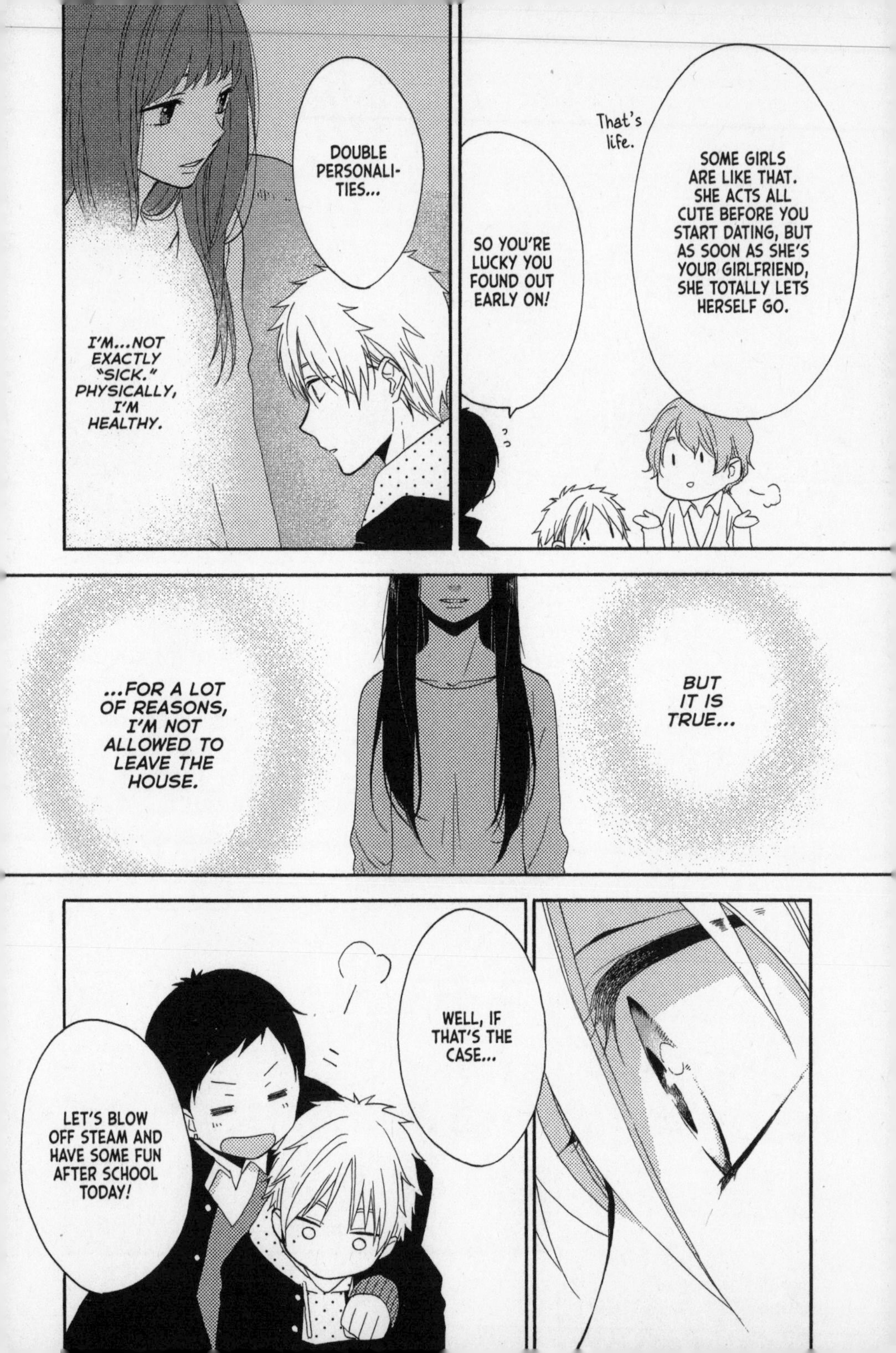
SOME GIRLS ARE LIKE THAT. SHE ACTS ALL CUTE BEFORE YOU START DATING, BUT AS SOON AS SHE'S YOUR GIRLFRIEND, SHE TOTALLY LETS HERSELF GO.
That's life.
SO YOU'RE LUCKY YOU FOUND OUT EARLY ON!
DOUBLE PERSONALITIES...
I'M...NOT EXACTLY "SICK." PHYSICALLY, I'M HEALTHY.
BUT IT IS TRUE...
...FOR A LOT OF REASONS, I'M NOT ALLOWED TO LEAVE THE HOUSE.
WELL, IF THAT'S THE CASE...
LET'S BLOW OFF STEAM AND HAVE SOME FUN AFTER SCHOOL TODAY!

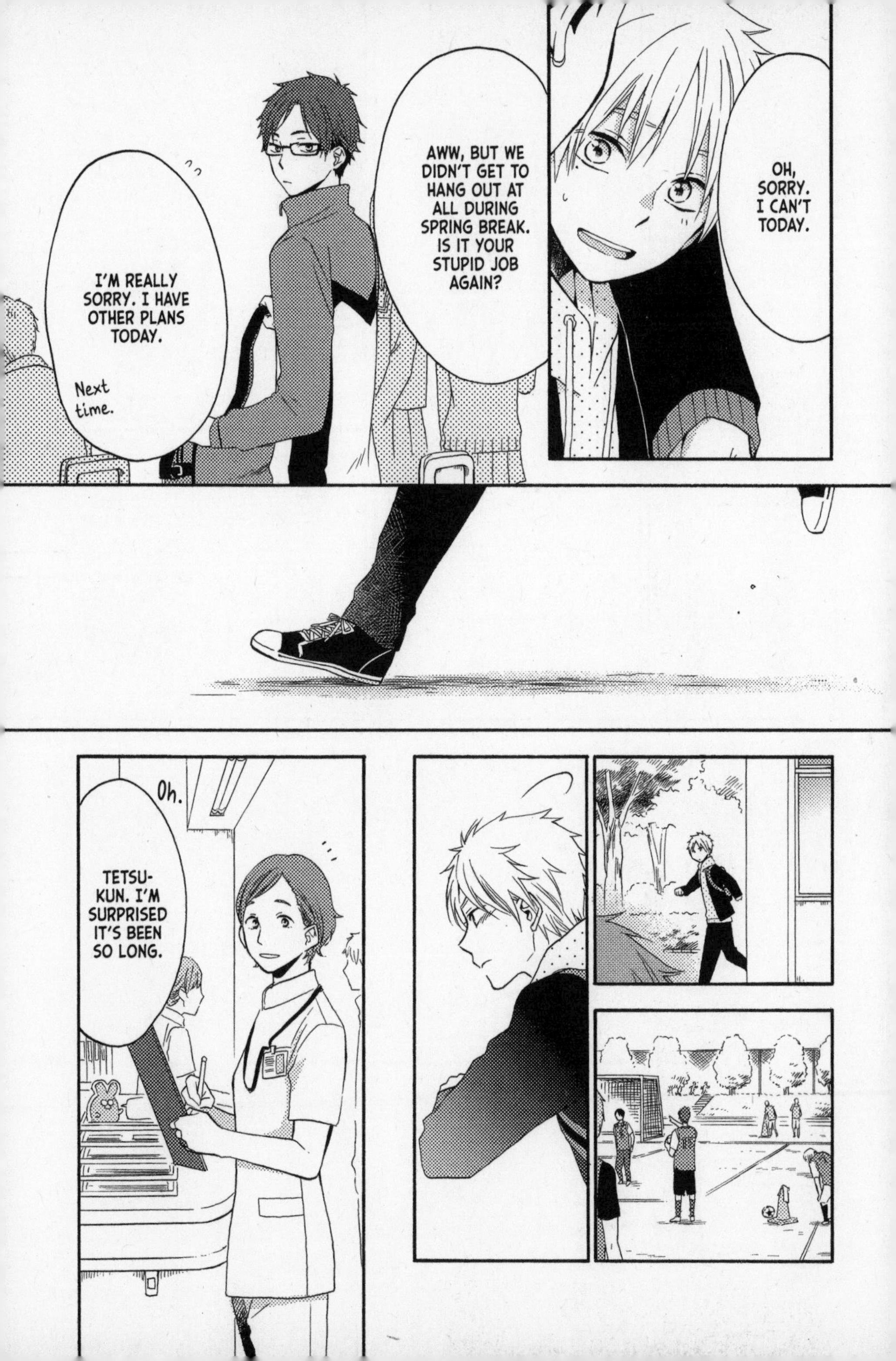
OH, SORRY. I CAN'T TODAY.
AWW, BUT WE DIDN'T GET TO HANG OUT AT ALL DURING SPRING BREAK. IS IT YOUR STUPID JOB AGAIN?
I'M REALLY SORRY. I HAVE OTHER PLANS TODAY.
Next time.
Oh.
TETSU-KUN. I'M SURPRISED IT'S BEEN SO LONG.

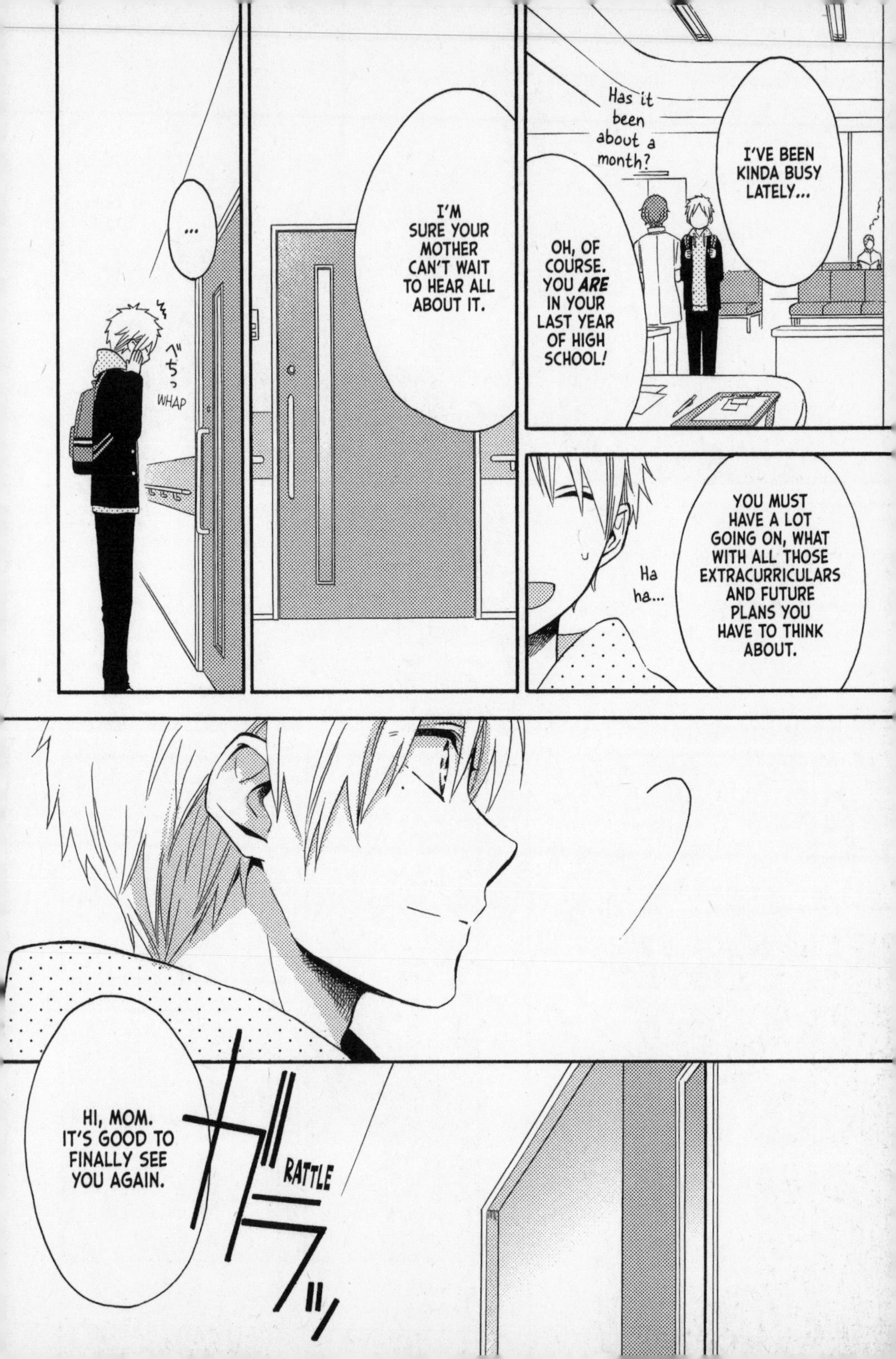
I'VE BEEN KINDA BUSY LATELY...
Has it been about a month?
OH, OF COURSE. YOU *ARE* IN YOUR LAST YEAR OF HIGH SCHOOL!
YOU MUST HAVE A LOT GOING ON, WHAT WITH ALL THOSE EXTRACURRICULARS AND FUTURE PLANS YOU HAVE TO THINK ABOUT.
Ha ha...
I'M SURE YOUR MOTHER CAN'T WAIT TO HEAR ALL ABOUT IT.
...
べちっ
WHAP
ガラッ
RATTLE
HI, MOM. IT'S GOOD TO FINALLY SEE YOU AGAIN.

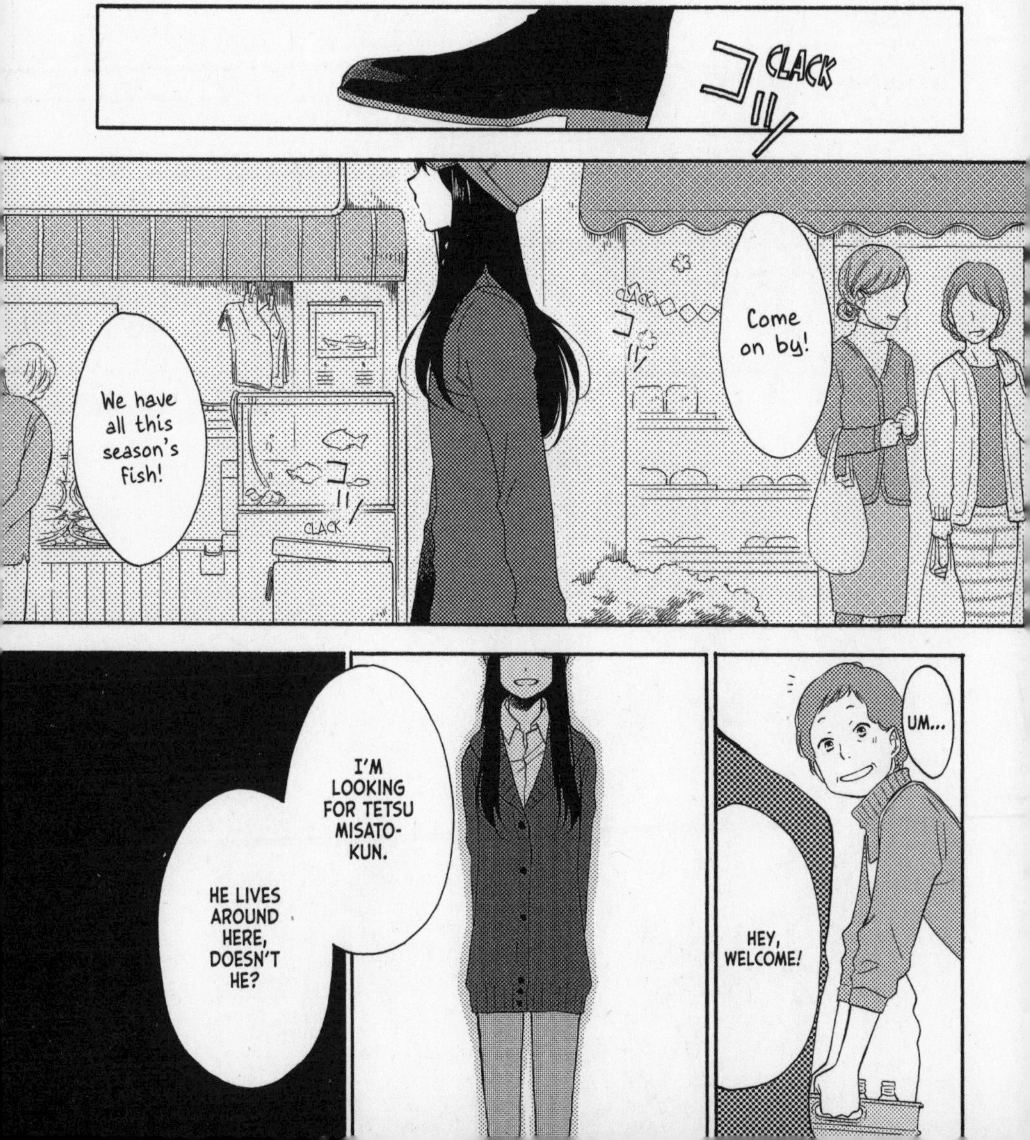
CLACK
Come on by!
CLACK
We have all this season's fish!
CLACK
UM...
HEY, WELCOME!
I'M LOOKING FOR TETSU MISATO-KUN.
HE LIVES AROUND HERE, DOESN'T HE?

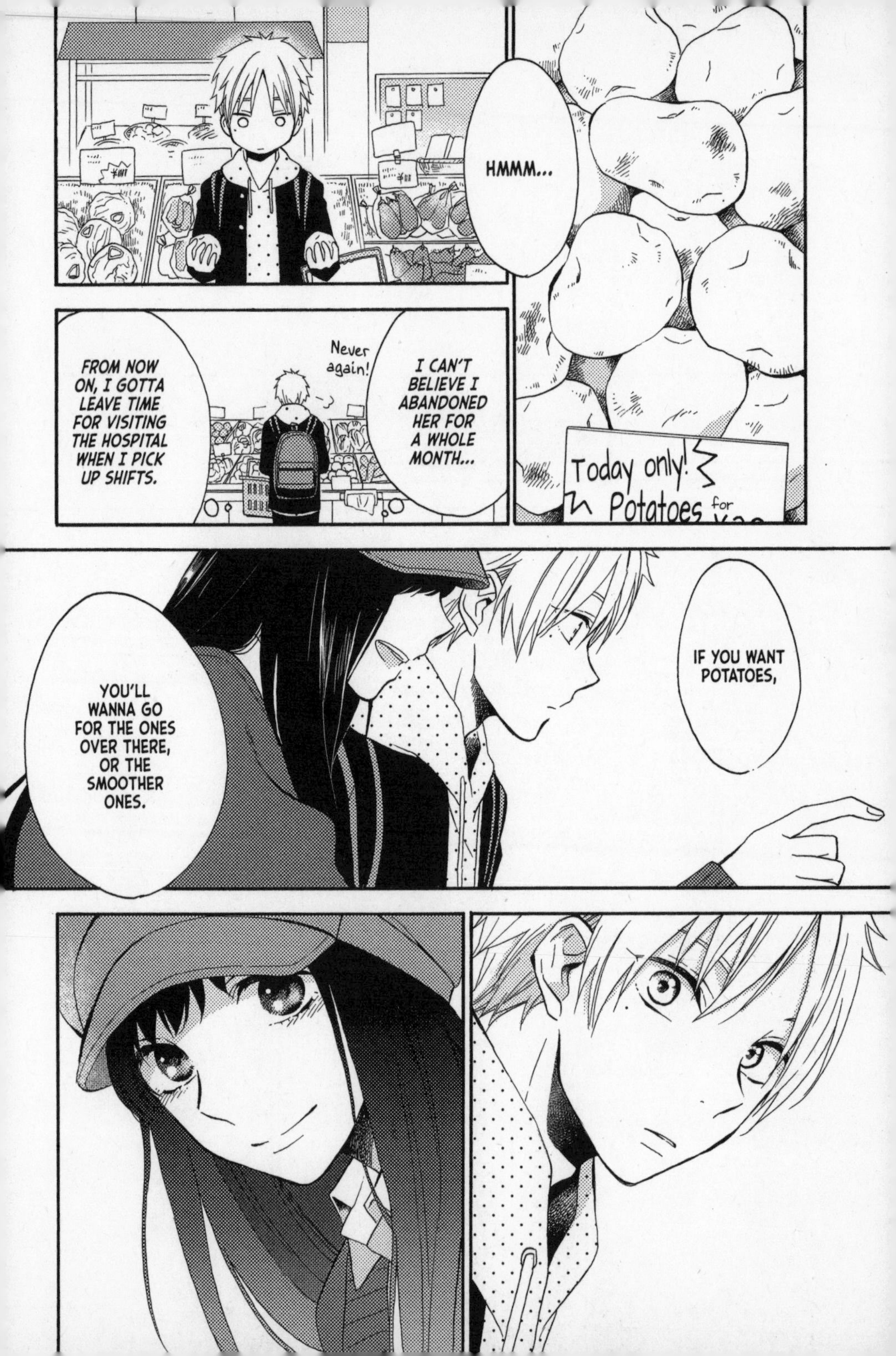
HMMM...
Today only!
Potatoes for
I CAN'T BELIEVE I ABANDONED HER FOR A WHOLE MONTH...
Never again!
FROM NOW ON, I GOTTA LEAVE TIME FOR VISITING THE HOSPITAL WHEN I PICK UP SHIFTS.
IF YOU WANT POTATOES,
YOU'LL WANNA GO FOR THE ONES OVER THERE, OR THE SMOOTHER ONES.

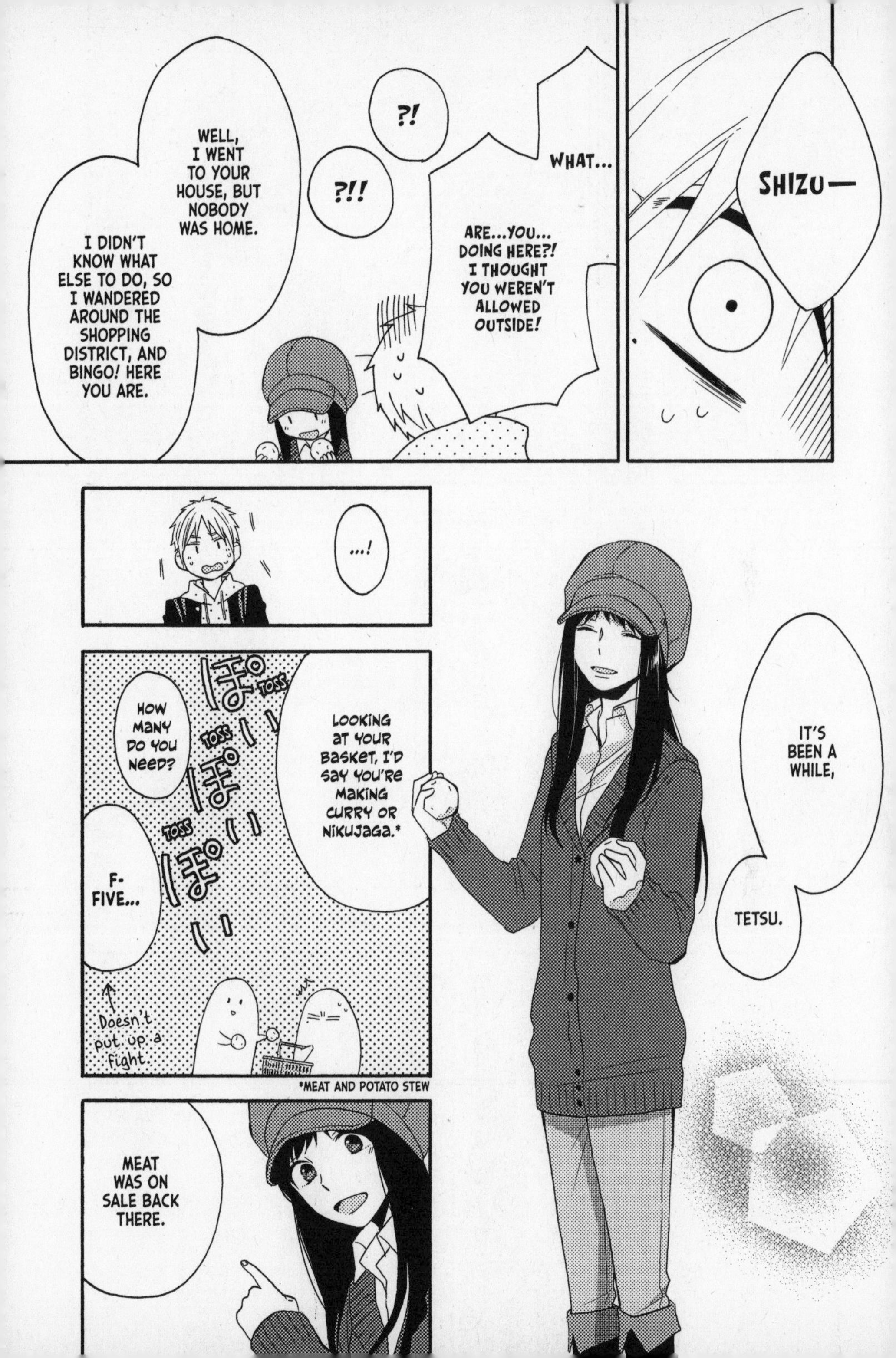
SHIZU—
WHAT...
ARE...YOU... DOING HERE?! I THOUGHT YOU WEREN'T ALLOWED OUTSIDE!
?!
?!!
WELL, I WENT TO YOUR HOUSE, BUT NOBODY WAS HOME.
I DIDN'T KNOW WHAT ELSE TO DO, SO I WANDERED AROUND THE SHOPPING DISTRICT, AND BINGO! HERE YOU ARE.
IT'S BEEN A WHILE,
TETSU.
...!
LOOKING AT YOUR BASKET, I'D SAY YOU'RE MAKING CURRY OR NIKUJAGA.*
HOW MANY DO YOU NEED?
TOSS
TOSS
TOSS
F-FIVE...
Doesn't put up a fight.
*MEAT AND POTATO STEW
MEAT WAS ON SALE BACK THERE.

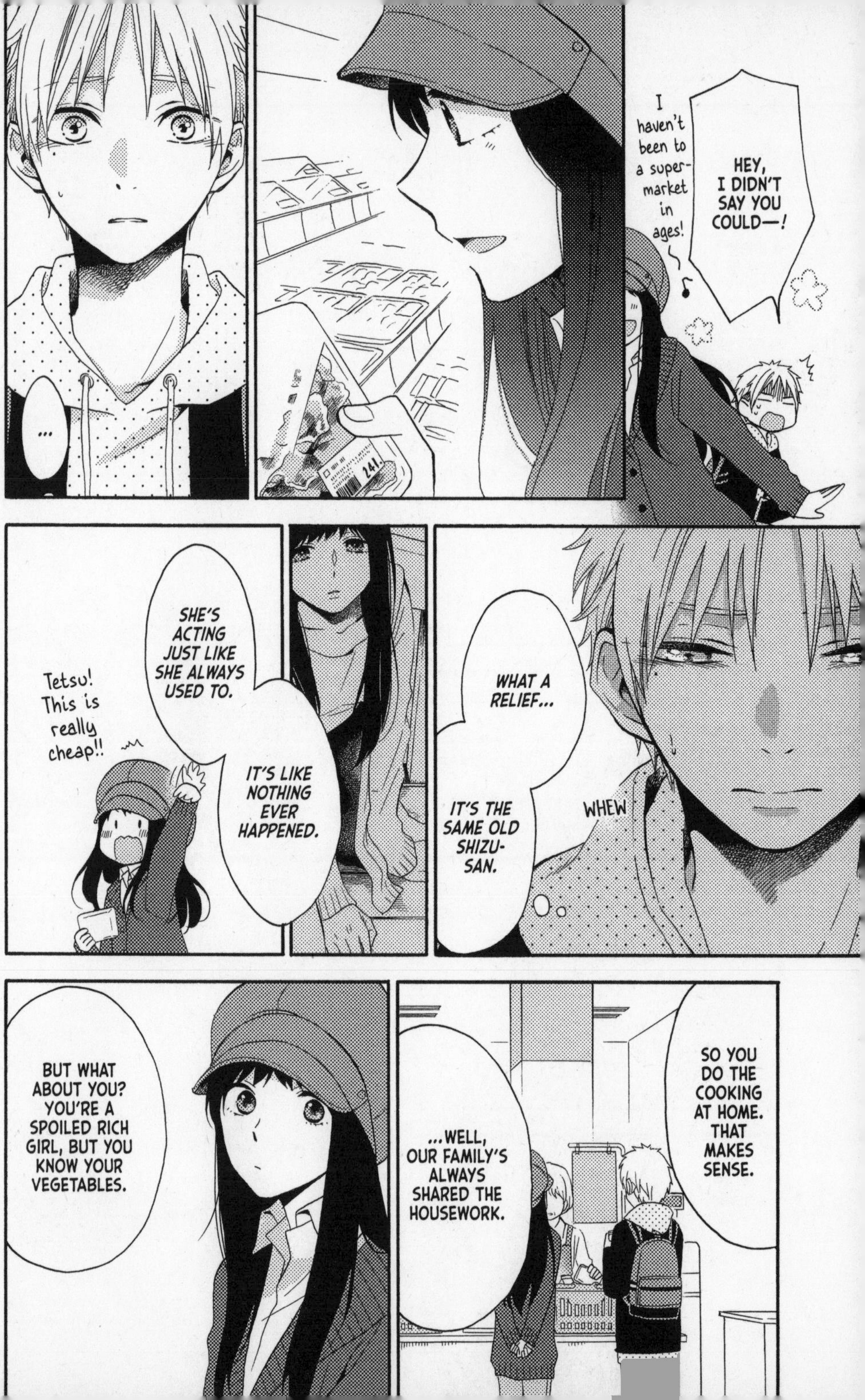
HEY, I DIDN'T SAY YOU COULD—!
I haven't been to a super-market in ages! ~♪
...
WHAT A RELIEF...
WHEW
IT'S THE SAME OLD SHIZU-SAN.
SHE'S ACTING JUST LIKE SHE ALWAYS USED TO.
IT'S LIKE NOTHING EVER HAPPENED.
Tetsu! This is really cheap!!
SO YOU DO THE COOKING AT HOME. THAT MAKES SENSE.
...WELL, OUR FAMILY'S ALWAYS SHARED THE HOUSEWORK.
BUT WHAT ABOUT YOU? YOU'RE A SPOILED RICH GIRL, BUT YOU KNOW YOUR VEGETABLES.

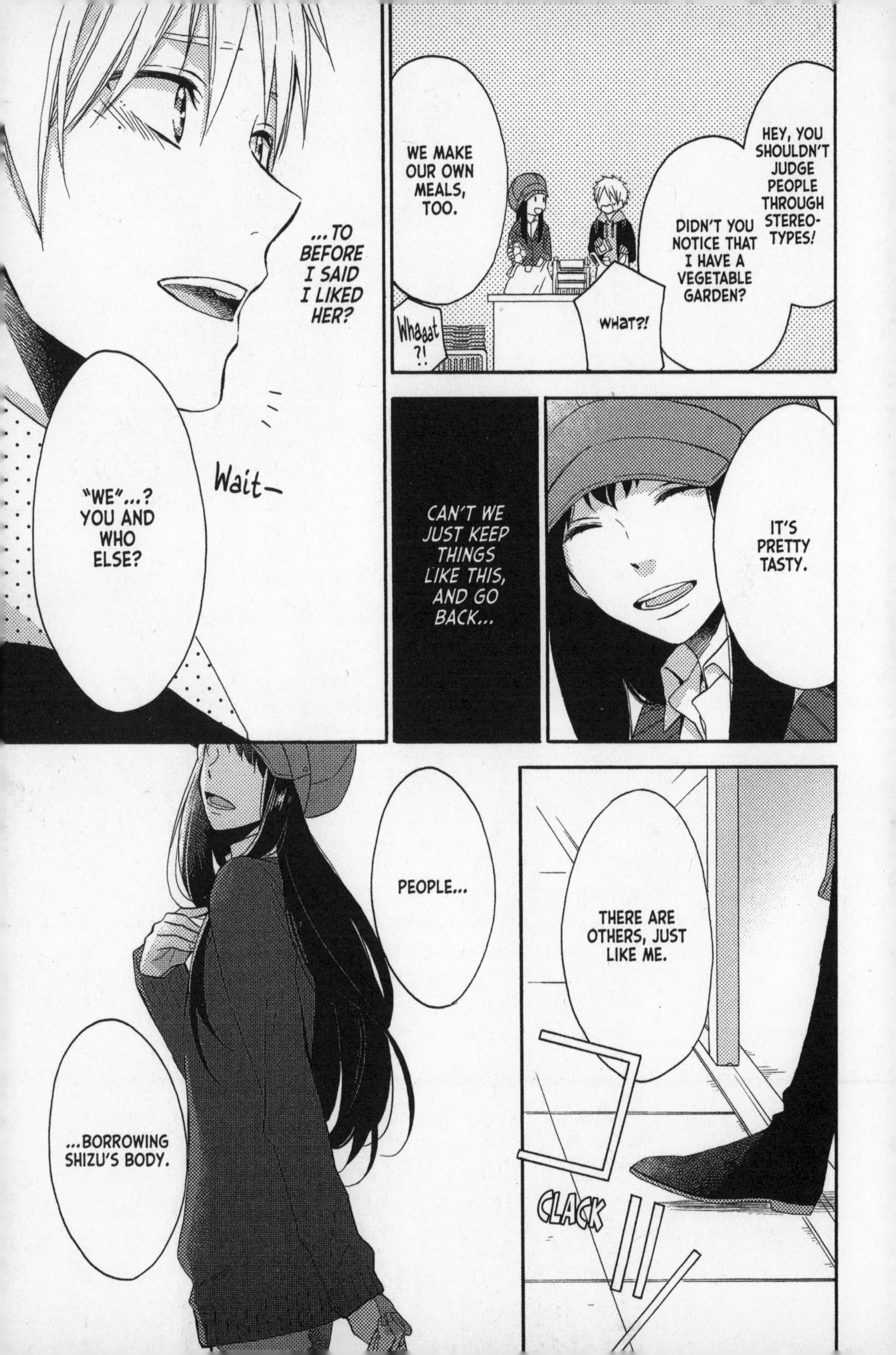

HEY, YOU SHOULDN'T JUDGE PEOPLE THROUGH STEREO-TYPES!
DIDN'T YOU NOTICE THAT I HAVE A VEGETABLE GARDEN?
WHAT?!
WE MAKE OUR OWN MEALS, TOO.
Whaaat?!
IT'S PRETTY TASTY.
CAN'T WE JUST KEEP THINGS LIKE THIS, AND GO BACK...
...TO BEFORE I SAID I LIKED HER?
Wait–
"WE"...? YOU AND WHO ELSE?
THERE ARE OTHERS, JUST LIKE ME.
CLACK
PEOPLE...
...BORROWING SHIZU'S BODY.

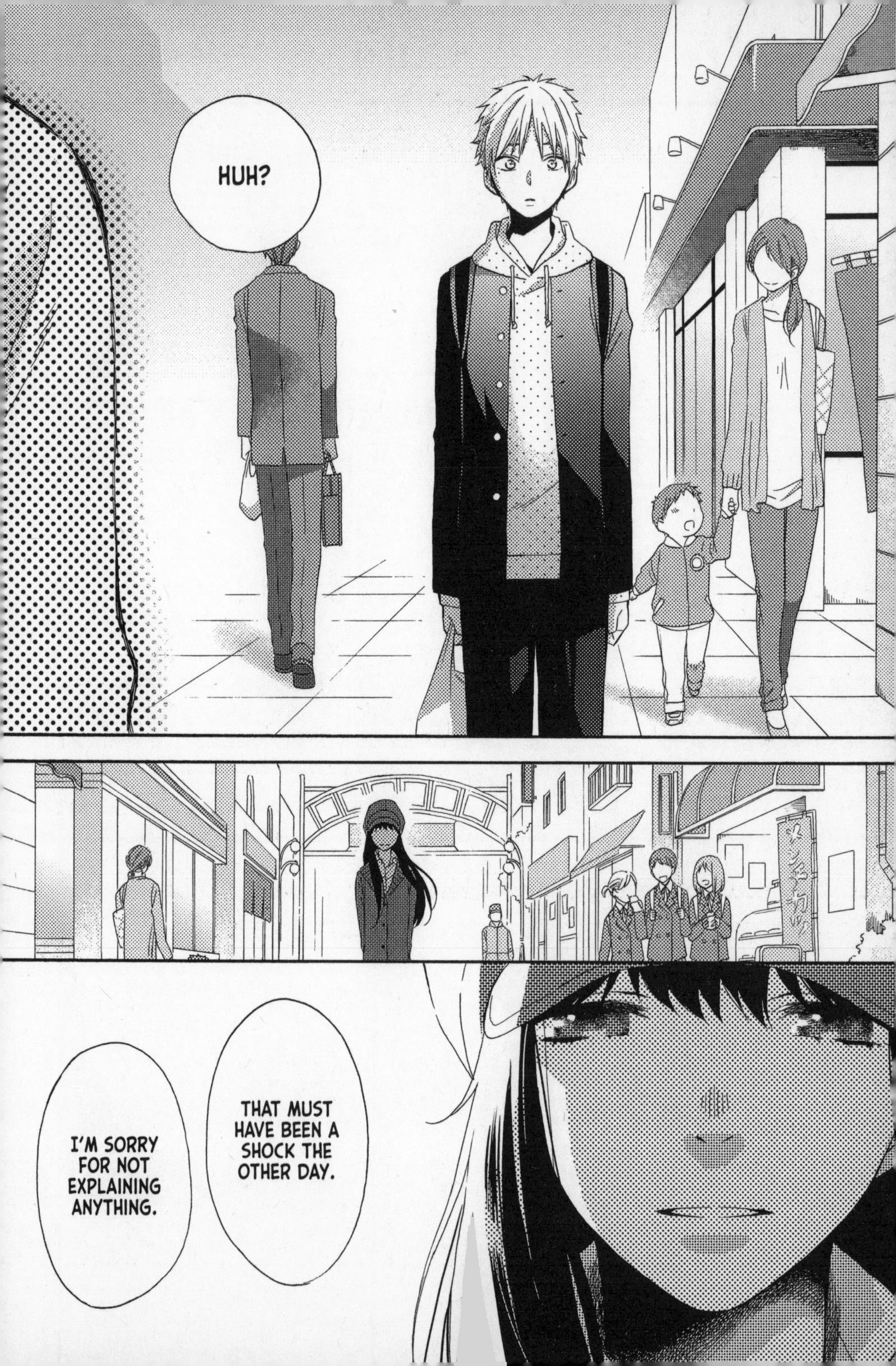
HUH?
THAT MUST HAVE BEEN A SHOCK THE OTHER DAY.
I'M SORRY FOR NOT EXPLAINING ANYTHING.

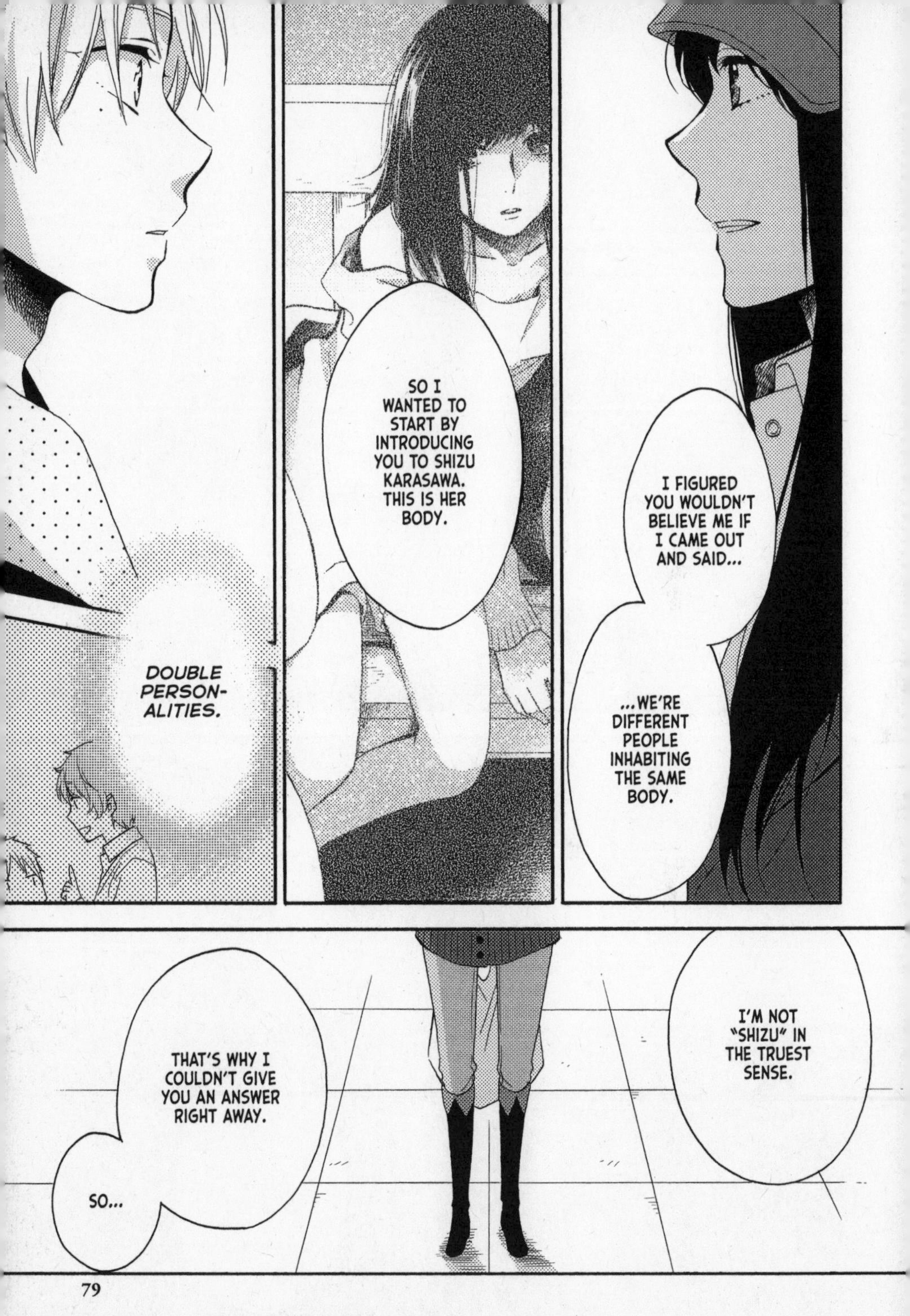
I FIGURED YOU WOULDN'T BELIEVE ME IF I CAME OUT AND SAID...
...WE'RE DIFFERENT PEOPLE INHABITING THE SAME BODY.
SO I WANTED TO START BY INTRODUCING YOU TO SHIZU KARASAWA. THIS IS HER BODY.
DOUBLE PERSON-ALITIES.
I'M NOT "SHIZU" IN THE TRUEST SENSE.
THAT'S WHY I COULDN'T GIVE YOU AN ANSWER RIGHT AWAY.
SO...

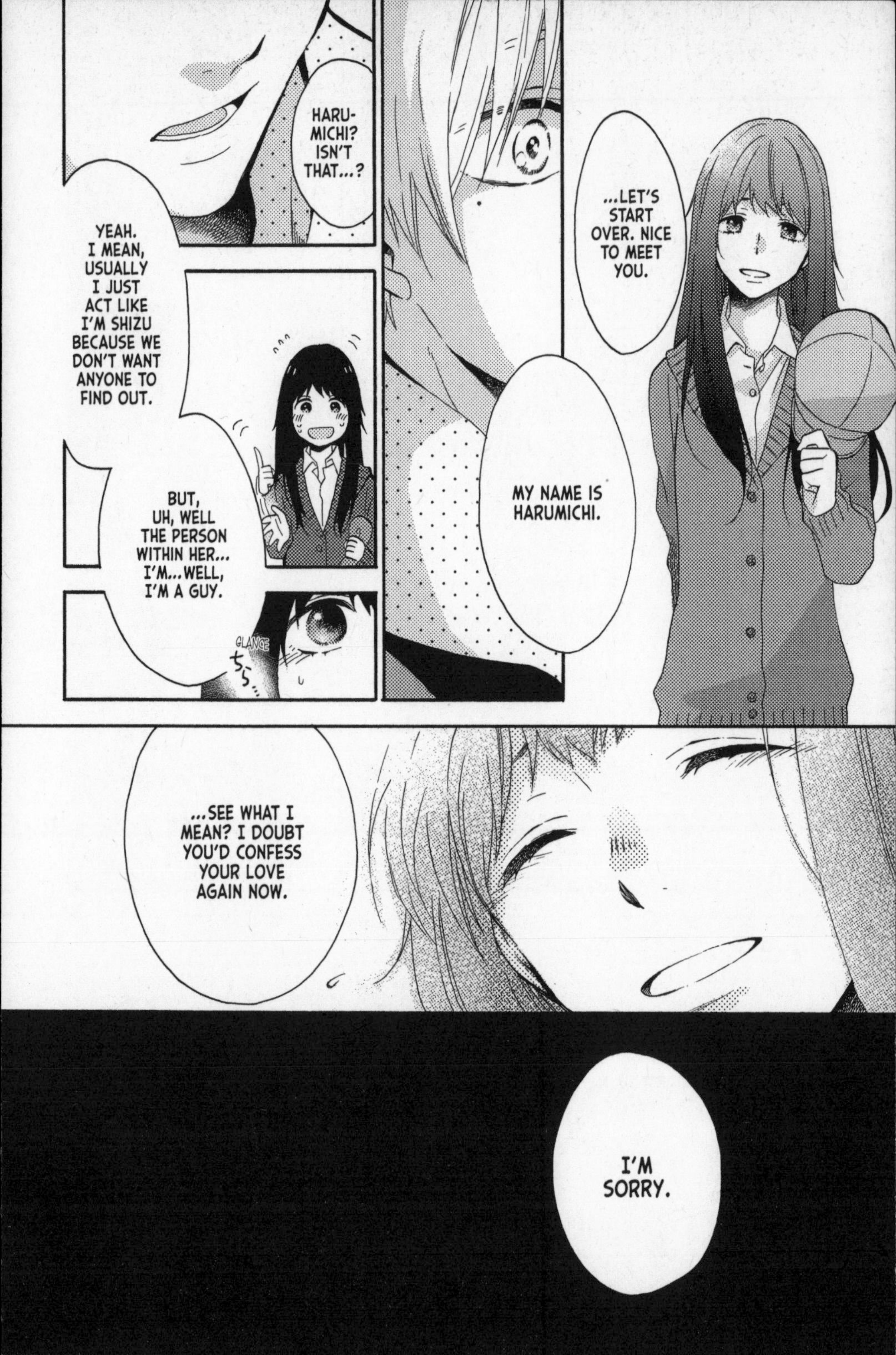
...LET'S START OVER. NICE TO MEET YOU.
MY NAME IS HARUMICHI.
HARU-MICHI? ISN'T THAT...?
YEAH. I MEAN, USUALLY I JUST ACT LIKE I'M SHIZU BECAUSE WE DON'T WANT ANYONE TO FIND OUT.
BUT, UH, WELL THE PERSON WITHIN HER... I'M...WELL, I'M A GUY.
GLANCE
ちら...
...SEE WHAT I MEAN? I DOUBT YOU'D CONFESS YOUR LOVE AGAIN NOW.
I'M SORRY.

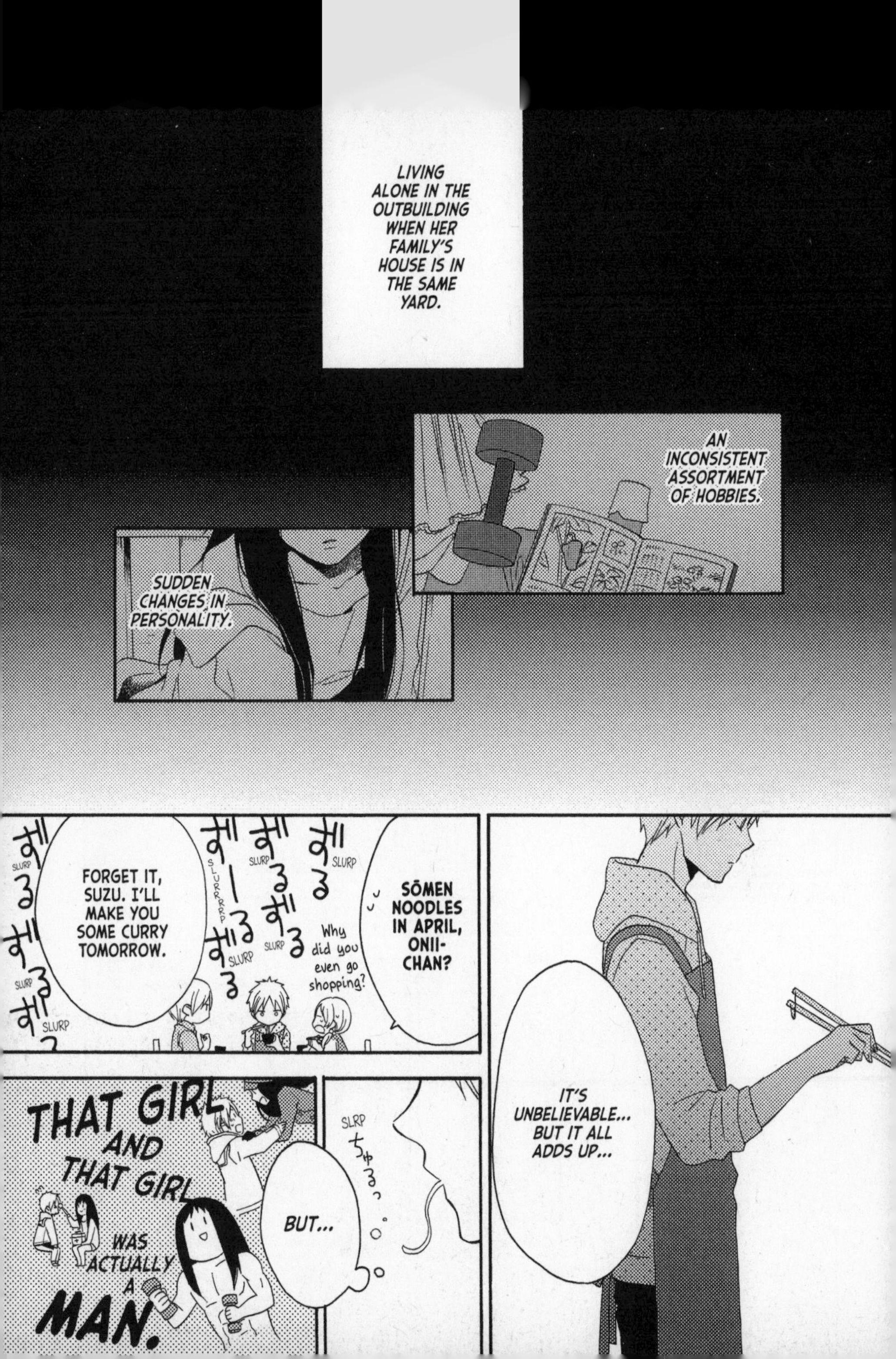
LIVING ALONE IN THE OUTBUILDING WHEN HER FAMILY'S HOUSE IS IN THE SAME YARD.
AN INCONSISTENT ASSORTMENT OF HOBBIES.
SUDDEN CHANGES IN PERSONALITY.
IT'S UNBELIEVABLE... BUT IT ALL ADDS UP...
ずる SLURP
SŌMEN NOODLES IN APRIL, ONII-CHAN?
Why did you even go shopping?
ずるずる SLURP SLURP
ずーる SLURRRRP SLURP
FORGET IT, SUZU. I'LL MAKE YOU SOME CURRY TOMORROW.
ずるずるずる SLURP SLURP SLURP
SLRP ちゅるっ
BUT...
THAT GIRL AND THAT GIRL WAS ACTUALLY A MAN.

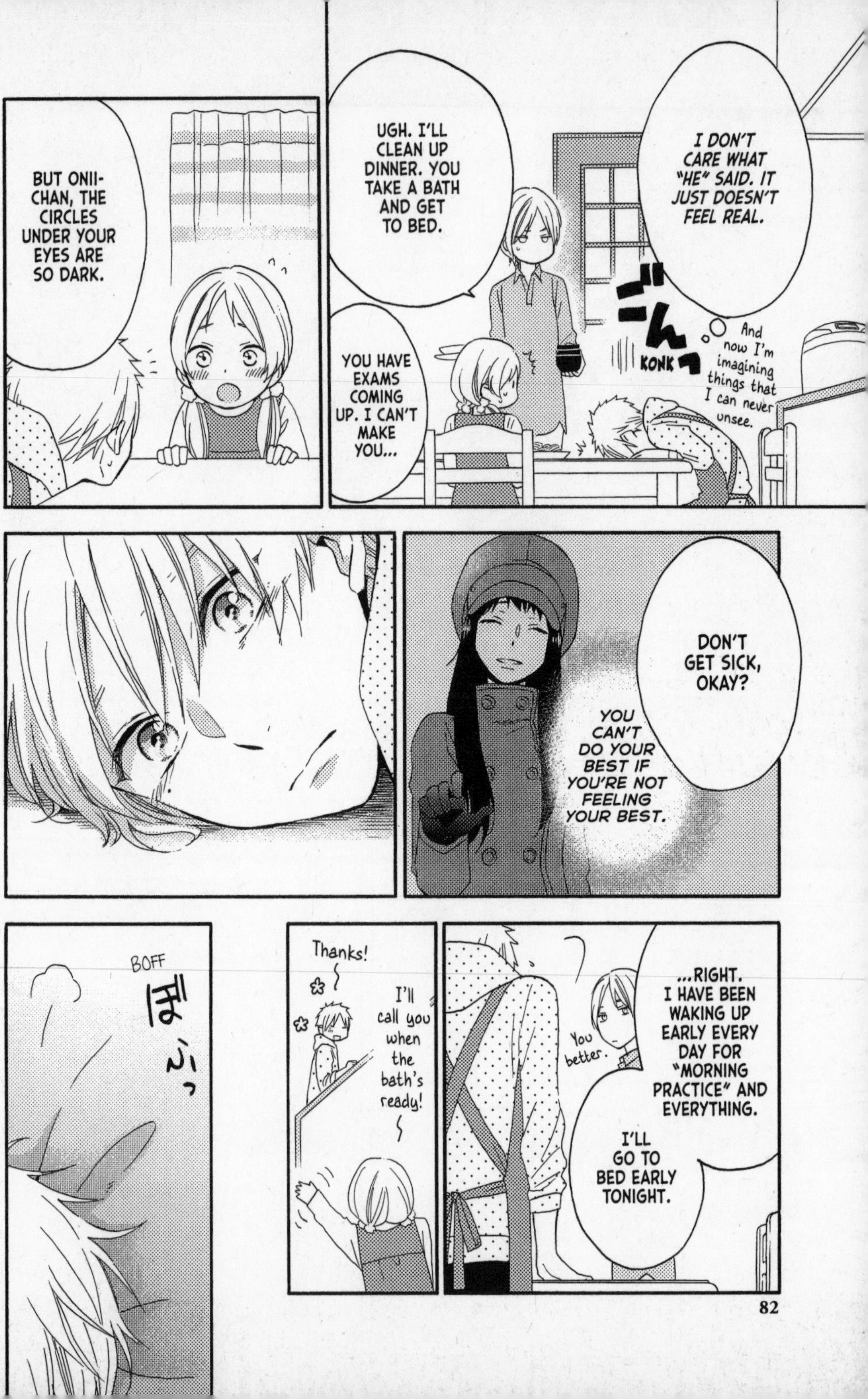
I DON'T CARE WHAT "HE" SAID. IT JUST DOESN'T FEEL REAL.
UGH. I'LL CLEAN UP DINNER. YOU TAKE A BATH AND GET TO BED.
ごんっ
KONK
And now I'm imagining things that I can never unsee.
YOU HAVE EXAMS COMING UP. I CAN'T MAKE YOU...
BUT ONII-CHAN, THE CIRCLES UNDER YOUR EYES ARE SO DARK.
DON'T GET SICK, OKAY?
YOU CAN'T DO YOUR BEST IF YOU'RE NOT FEELING YOUR BEST.
...RIGHT. I HAVE BEEN WAKING UP EARLY EVERY DAY FOR "MORNING PRACTICE" AND EVERYTHING.
I'LL GO TO BED EARLY TONIGHT.
You better.
I'll call you when the bath's ready!
Thanks!
ぼふっ
BOFF

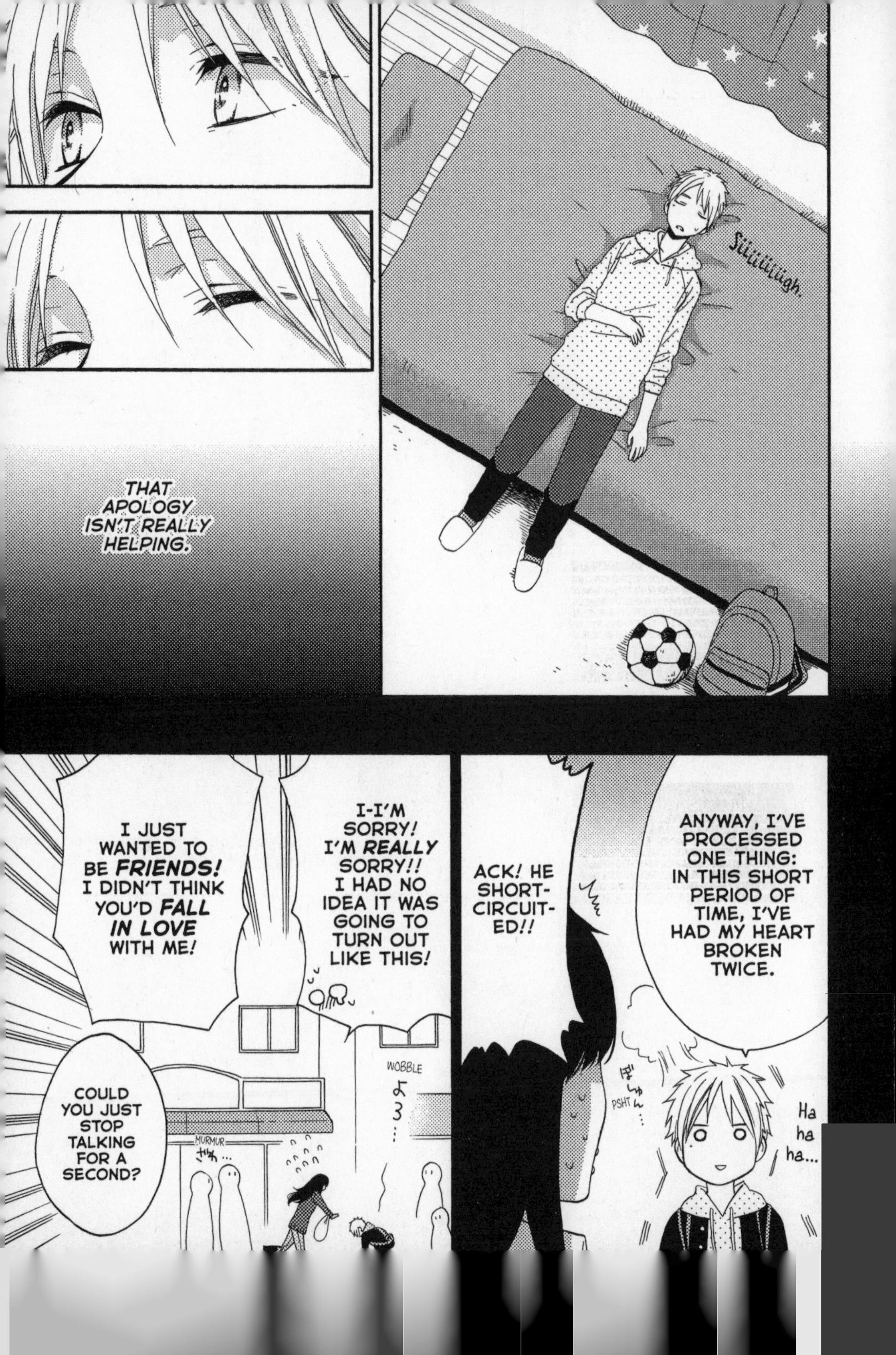
Siiiiiiiigh.
THAT APOLOGY ISN'T REALLY HELPING.
ANYWAY, I'VE PROCESSED ONE THING: IN THIS SHORT PERIOD OF TIME, I'VE HAD MY HEART BROKEN TWICE.
ACK! HE SHORT-CIRCUITED!!
PSHT
Ha ha ha...
I-I'M SORRY! I'M **REALLY** SORRY!! I HAD NO IDEA IT WAS GOING TO TURN OUT LIKE THIS!
I JUST WANTED TO BE **FRIENDS!** I DIDN'T THINK YOU'D **FALL IN LOVE** WITH ME!
WOBBLE
COULD YOU JUST STOP TALKING FOR A SECOND?
MURMUR

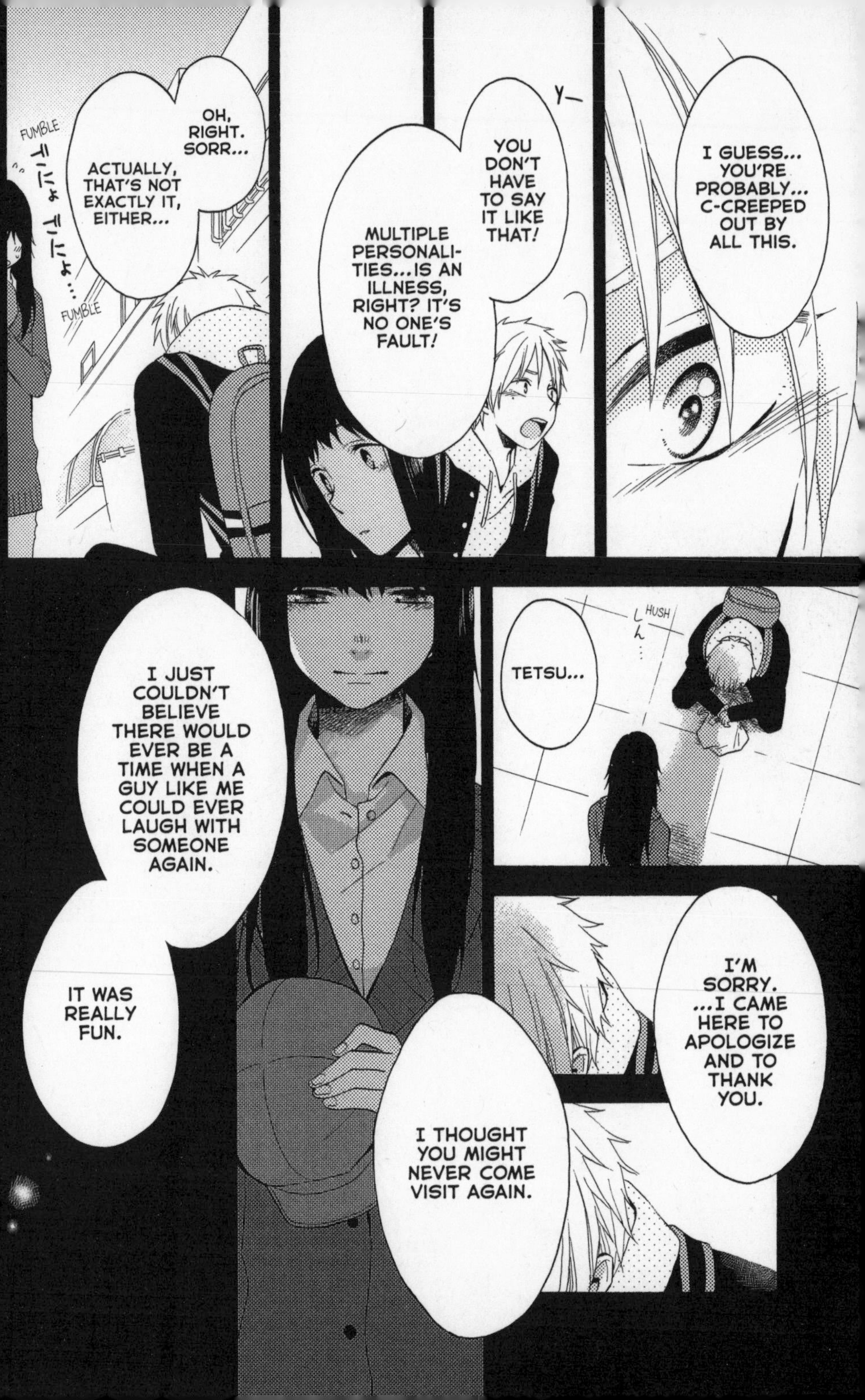
I GUESS... YOU'RE PROBABLY... C-CREEPED OUT BY ALL THIS.
Y—
YOU DON'T HAVE TO SAY IT LIKE THAT!
MULTIPLE PERSONALI-TIES...IS AN ILLNESS, RIGHT? IT'S NO ONE'S FAULT!
OH, RIGHT. SORR...
ACTUALLY, THAT'S NOT EXACTLY IT, EITHER...
FUMBLE
FUMBLE
HUSH
TETSU...
I'M SORRY. ...I CAME HERE TO APOLOGIZE AND TO THANK YOU.
I THOUGHT YOU MIGHT NEVER COME VISIT AGAIN.
I JUST COULDN'T BELIEVE THERE WOULD EVER BE A TIME WHEN A GUY LIKE ME COULD EVER LAUGH WITH SOMEONE AGAIN.
IT WAS REALLY FUN.

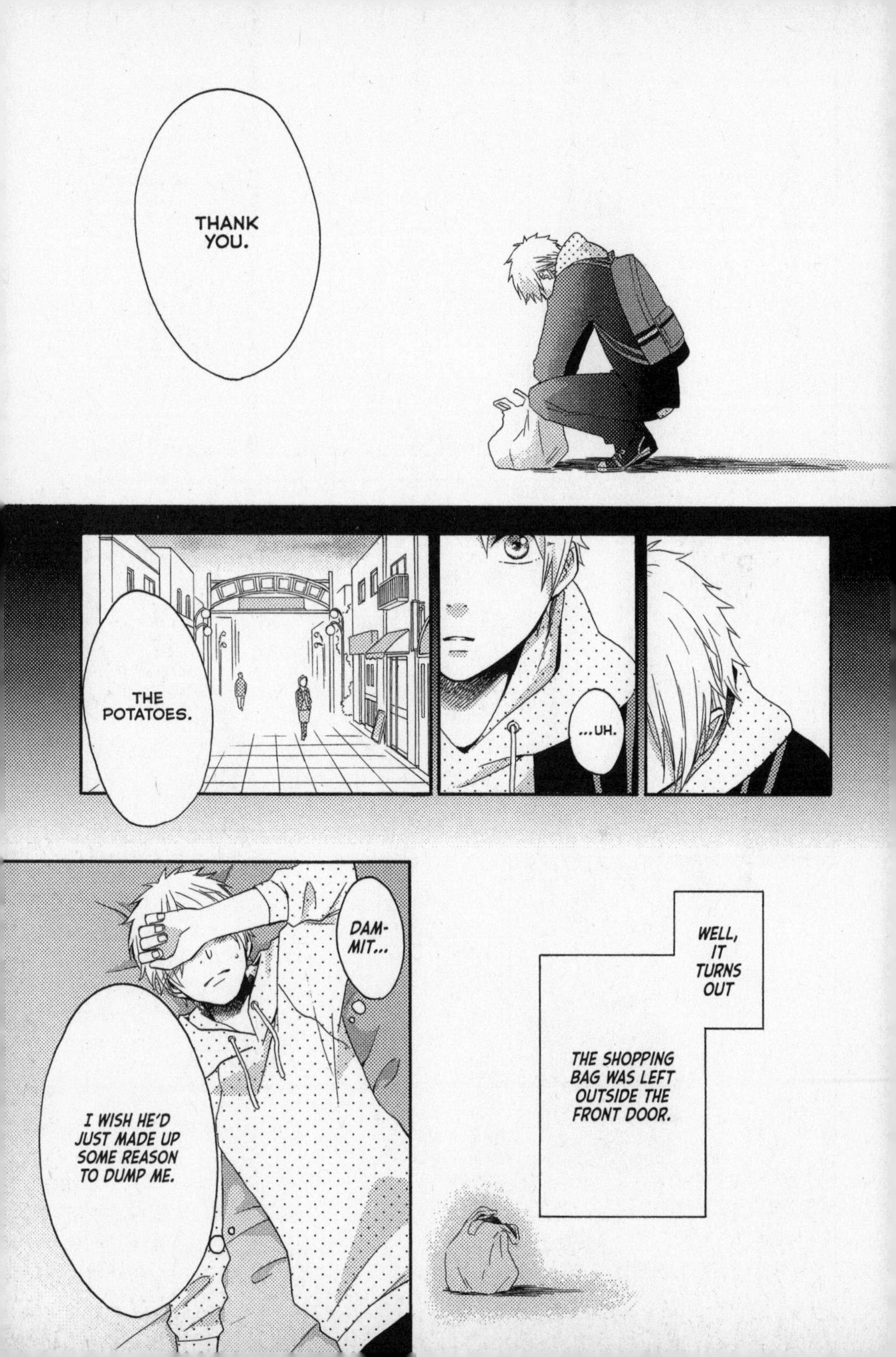
THANK YOU.
...UH.
THE POTATOES.
WELL, IT TURNS OUT
THE SHOPPING BAG WAS LEFT OUTSIDE THE FRONT DOOR.
DAM-MIT...
I WISH HE'D JUST MADE UP SOME REASON TO DUMP ME.

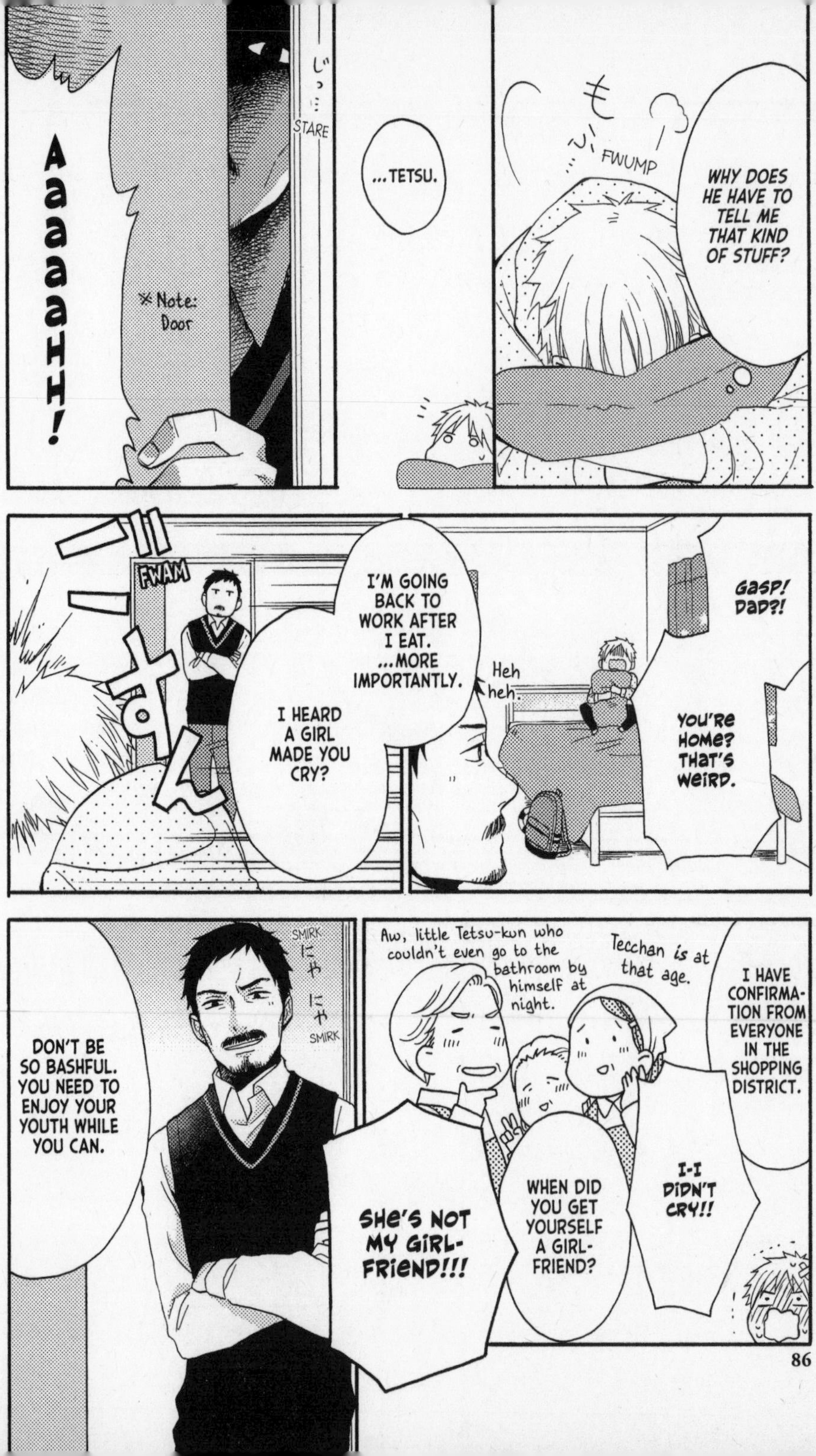
FWUMP
WHY DOES HE HAVE TO TELL ME THAT KIND OF STUFF?
...TETSU.
STARE
Aaaaaahh!
※Note: Door
Gasp! Dad?!
You're home? That's weird.
Heh heh.
FWAM
I'M GOING BACK TO WORK AFTER I EAT. ...MORE IMPORTANTLY.
I HEARD A GIRL MADE YOU CRY?
I HAVE CONFIRMATION FROM EVERYONE IN THE SHOPPING DISTRICT.
Tecchan is at that age.
Aw, little Tetsu-kun who couldn't even go to the bathroom by himself at night.
I-I DIDN'T CRY!!
WHEN DID YOU GET YOURSELF A GIRL-FRIEND?
SHE'S NOT MY GIRL-FRIEND!!!
SMIRK
SMIRK
DON'T BE SO BASHFUL. YOU NEED TO ENJOY YOUR YOUTH WHILE YOU CAN.

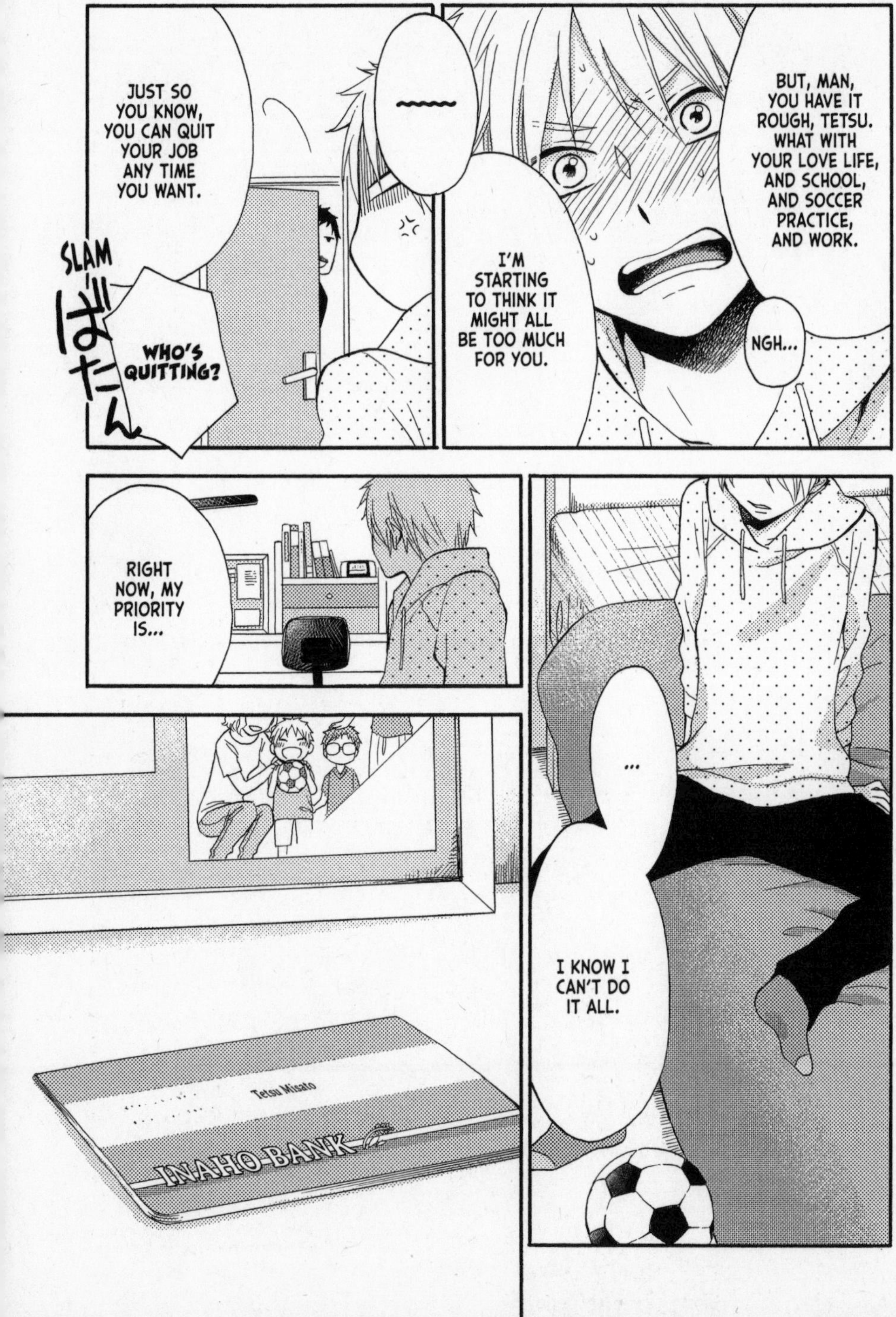
BUT, MAN, YOU HAVE IT ROUGH, TETSU. WHAT WITH YOUR LOVE LIFE, AND SCHOOL, AND SOCCER PRACTICE, AND WORK.
NGH...
I'M STARTING TO THINK IT MIGHT ALL BE TOO MUCH FOR YOU.
~~~~
JUST SO YOU KNOW, YOU CAN QUIT YOUR JOB ANY TIME YOU WANT.
SLAM
ばたん
WHO'S QUITTING?
...
I KNOW I CAN'T DO IT ALL.
RIGHT NOW, MY PRIORITY IS...
Tetsu Misato
INAHO BANK
~~~~

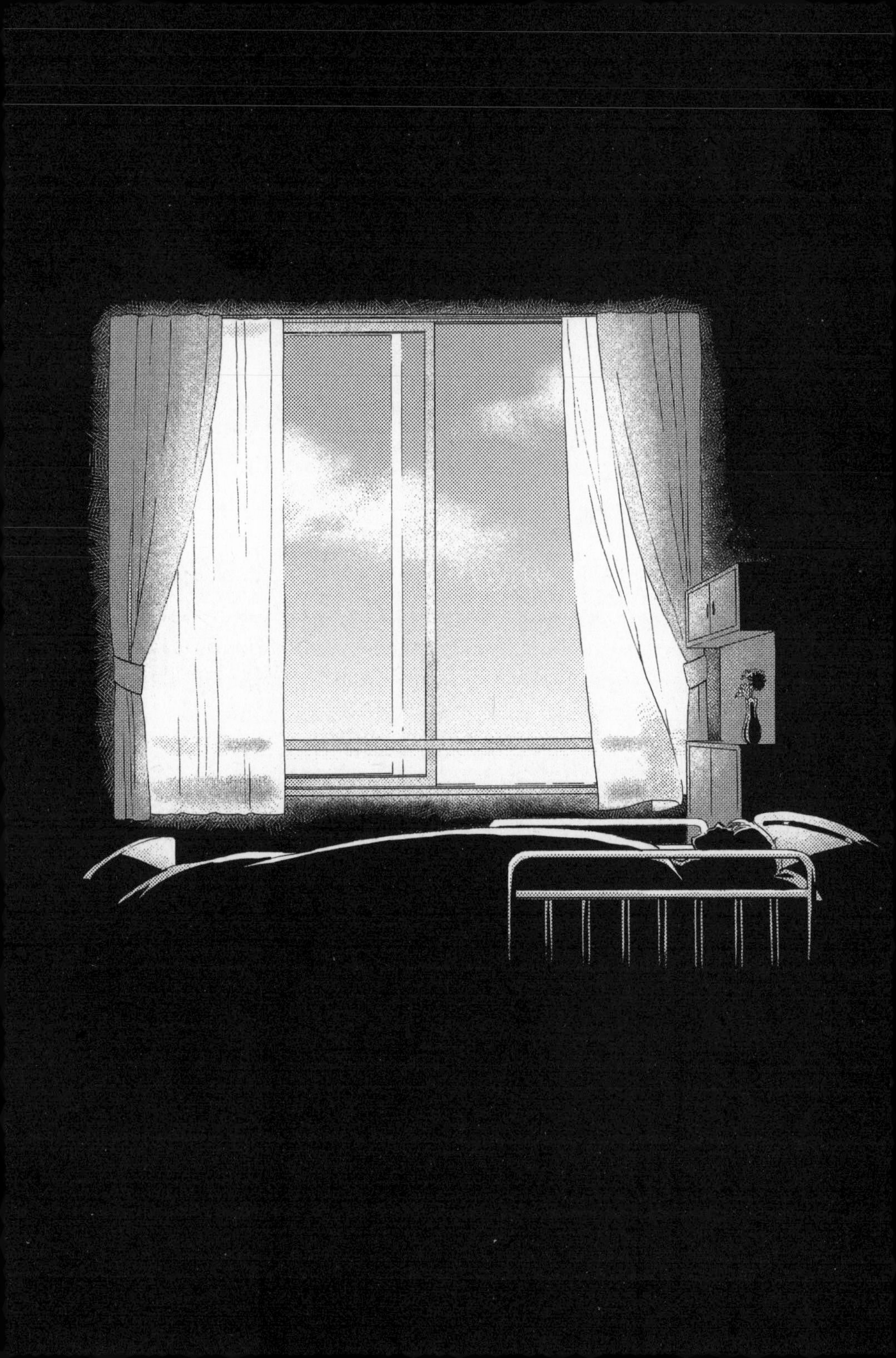

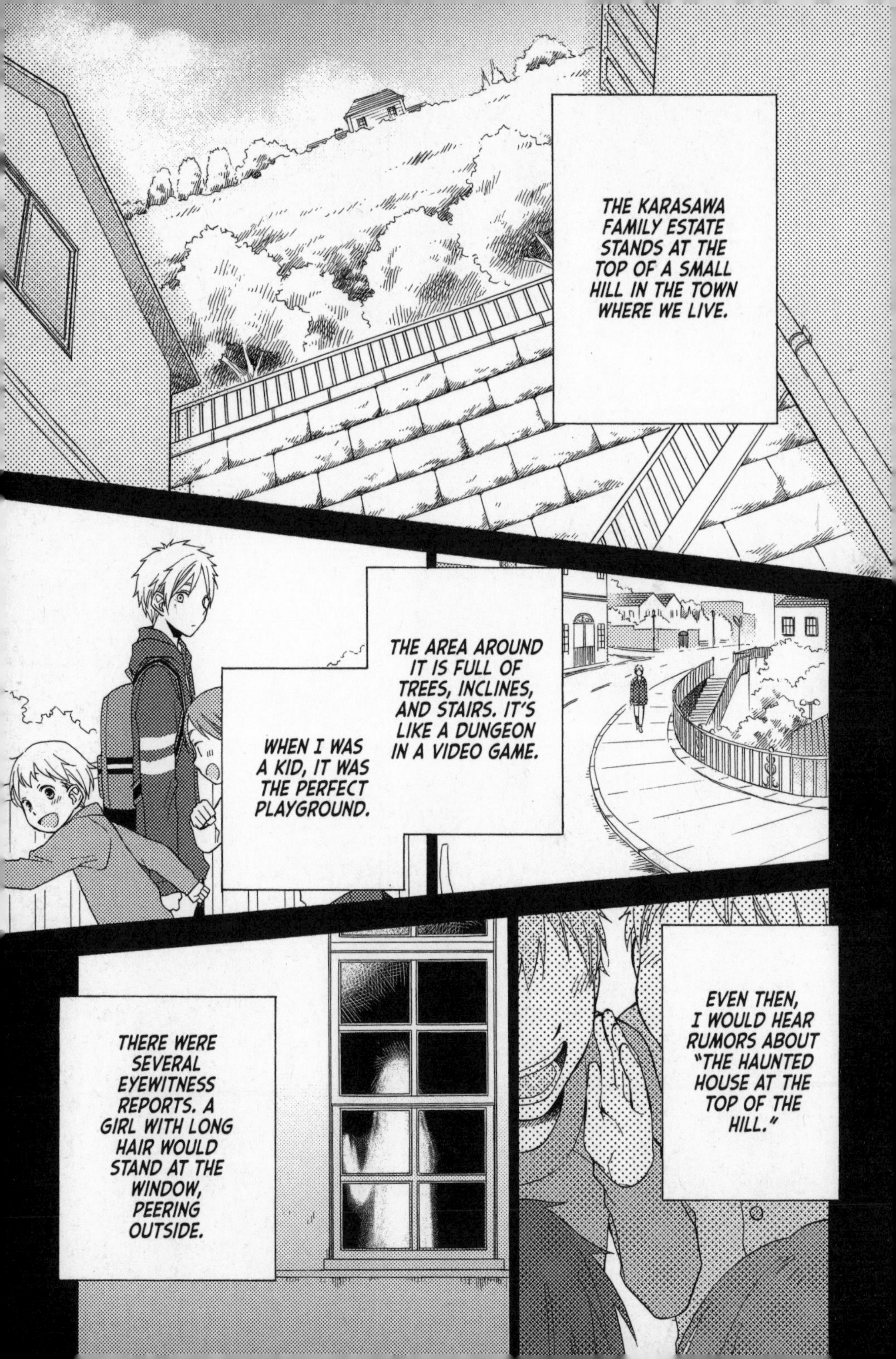
THE KARASAWA FAMILY ESTATE STANDS AT THE TOP OF A SMALL HILL IN THE TOWN WHERE WE LIVE.
THE AREA AROUND IT IS FULL OF TREES, INCLINES, AND STAIRS. IT'S LIKE A DUNGEON IN A VIDEO GAME.
WHEN I WAS A KID, IT WAS THE PERFECT PLAYGROUND.
EVEN THEN, I WOULD HEAR RUMORS ABOUT "THE HAUNTED HOUSE AT THE TOP OF THE HILL."
THERE WERE SEVERAL EYEWITNESS REPORTS. A GIRL WITH LONG HAIR WOULD STAND AT THE WINDOW, PEERING OUTSIDE.

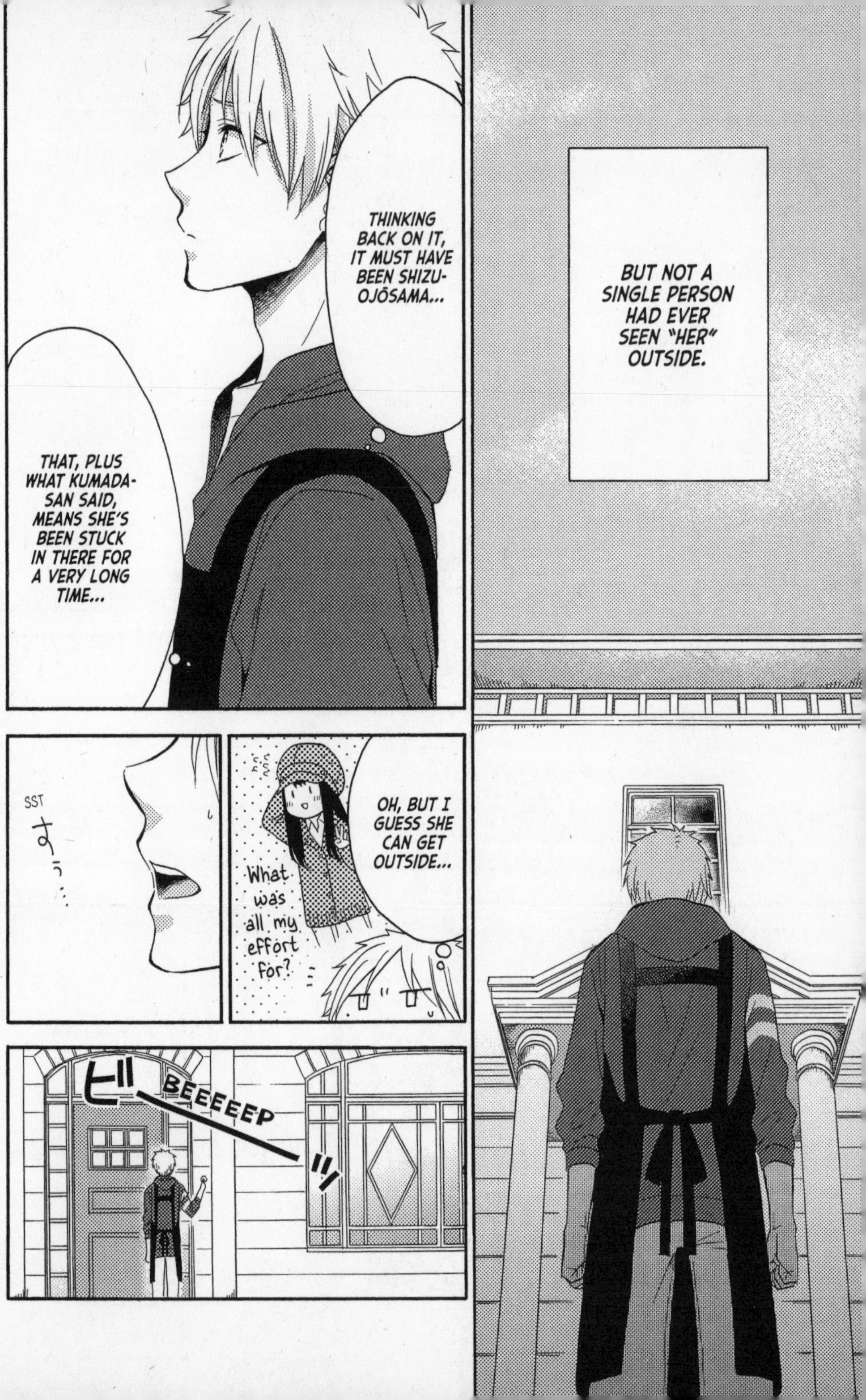
BUT NOT A SINGLE PERSON HAD EVER SEEN "HER" OUTSIDE.
THINKING BACK ON IT, IT MUST HAVE BEEN SHIZU-OJŌSAMA...
THAT, PLUS WHAT KUMADA-SAN SAID, MEANS SHE'S BEEN STUCK IN THERE FOR A VERY LONG TIME...
OH, BUT I GUESS SHE CAN GET OUTSIDE...
What was all my effort for?
SST
すぅ…
ビーッ
BEEEEEP

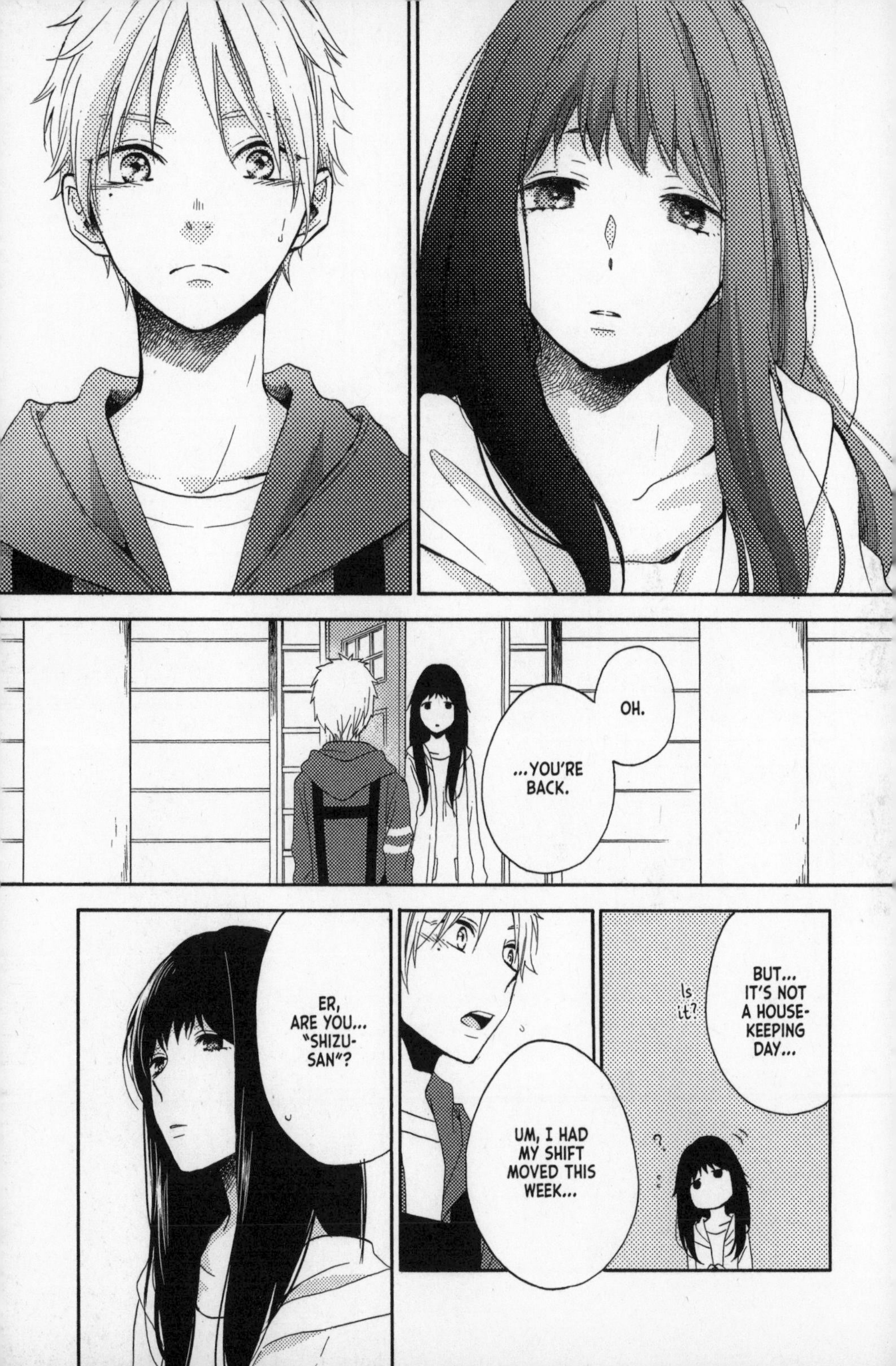
OH.
...YOU'RE BACK.
BUT... IT'S NOT A HOUSE-KEEPING DAY...
Is it?
UM, I HAD MY SHIFT MOVED THIS WEEK...
ER, ARE YOU... "SHIZU-SAN"?

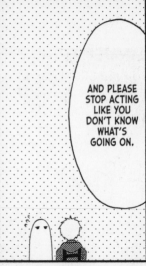

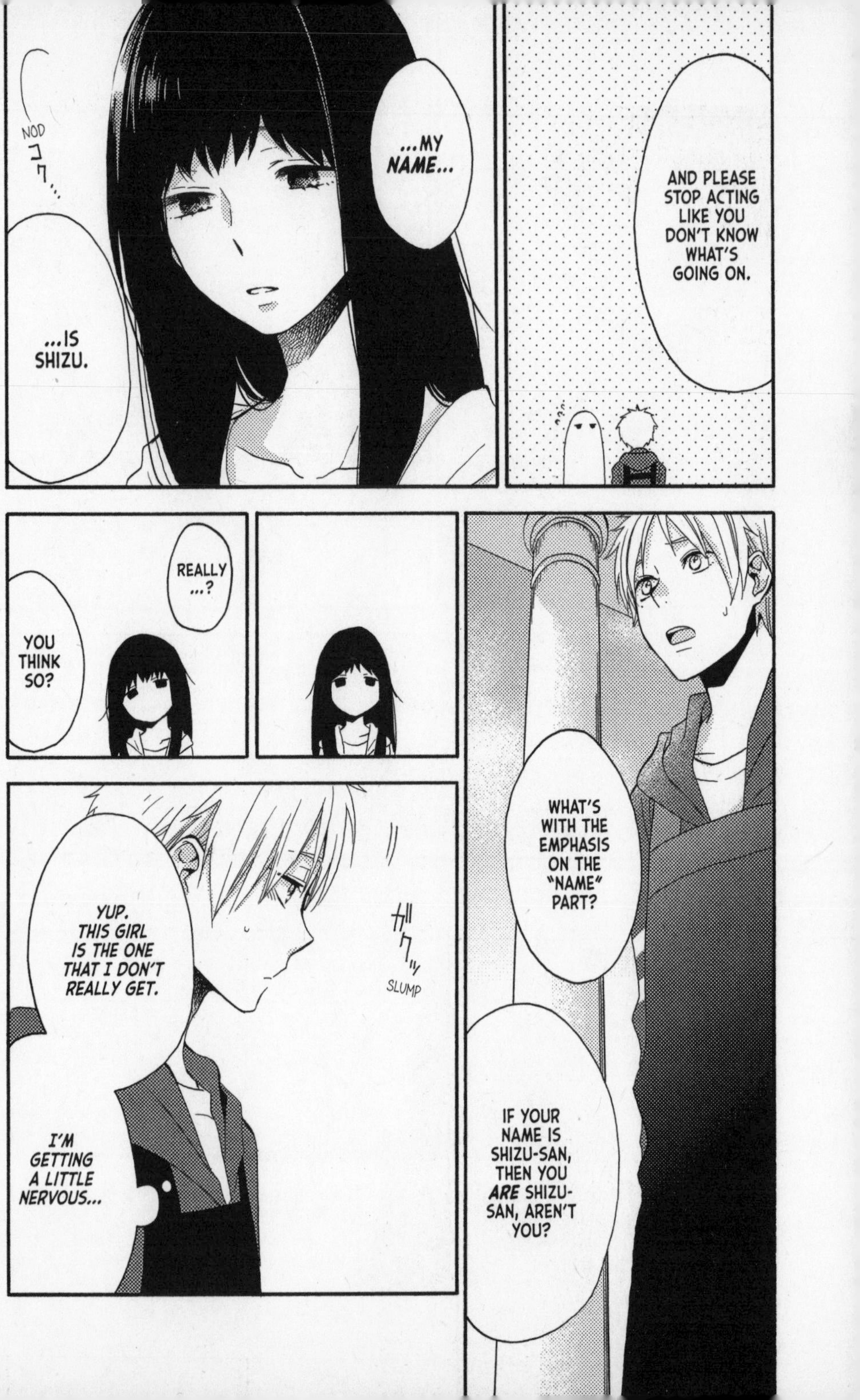
AND PLEASE STOP ACTING LIKE YOU DON'T KNOW WHAT'S GOING ON.
...MY NAME...
NOD
コク...
...IS SHIZU.
WHAT'S WITH THE EMPHASIS ON THE "NAME" PART?
IF YOUR NAME IS SHIZU-SAN, THEN YOU ARE SHIZU-SAN, AREN'T YOU?
REALLY ...?
YOU THINK SO?
ガクッ
SLUMP
YUP. THIS GIRL IS THE ONE THAT I DON'T REALLY GET.
I'M GETTING A LITTLE NERVOUS...

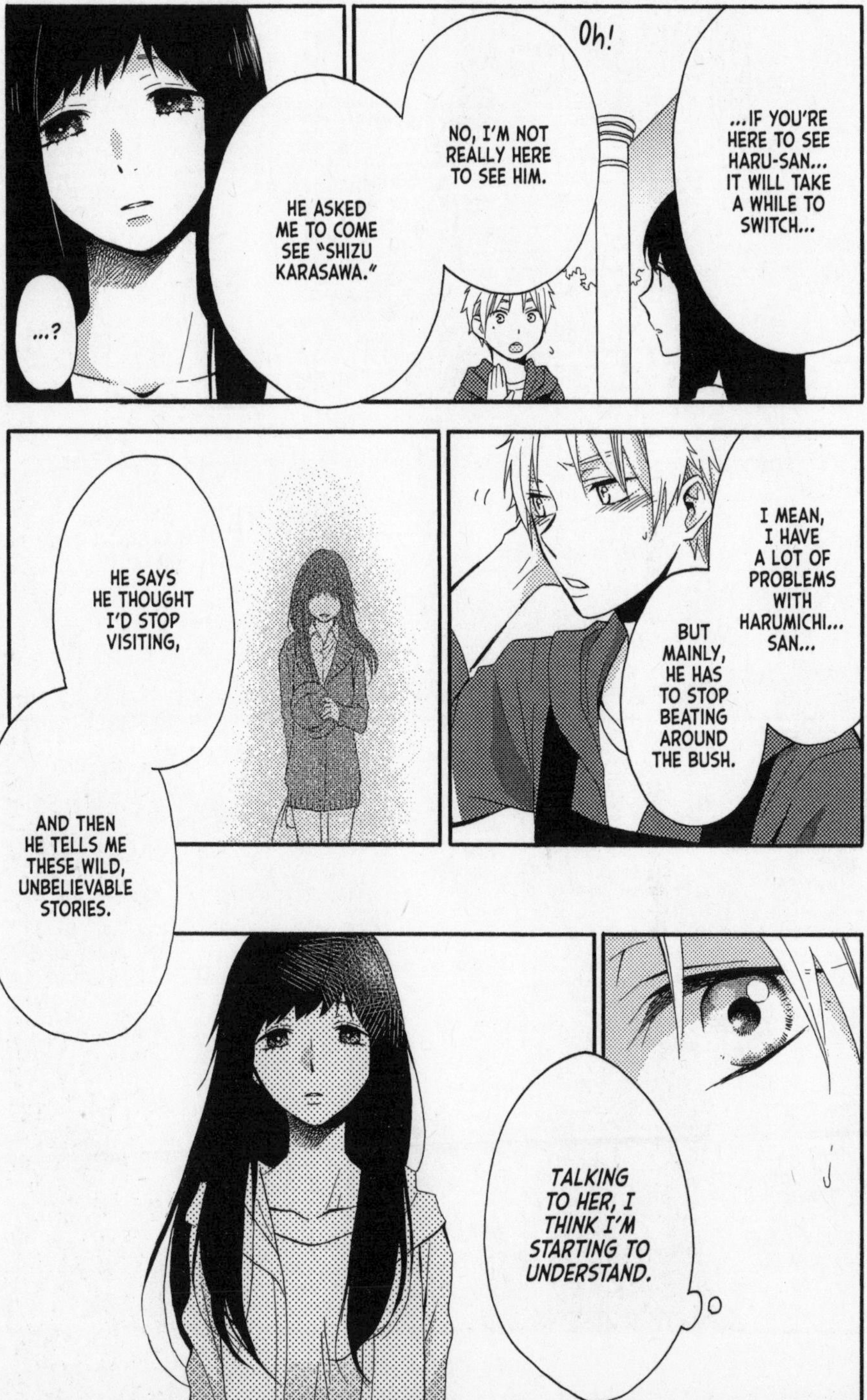
...IF YOU'RE HERE TO SEE HARU-SAN... IT WILL TAKE A WHILE TO SWITCH...
Oh!
NO, I'M NOT REALLY HERE TO SEE HIM.
HE ASKED ME TO COME SEE "SHIZU KARASAWA."
...?
I MEAN, I HAVE A LOT OF PROBLEMS WITH HARUMICHI... SAN...
BUT MAINLY, HE HAS TO STOP BEATING AROUND THE BUSH.
HE SAYS HE THOUGHT I'D STOP VISITING,
AND THEN HE TELLS ME THESE WILD, UNBELIEVABLE STORIES.
TALKING TO HER, I THINK I'M STARTING TO UNDERSTAND.

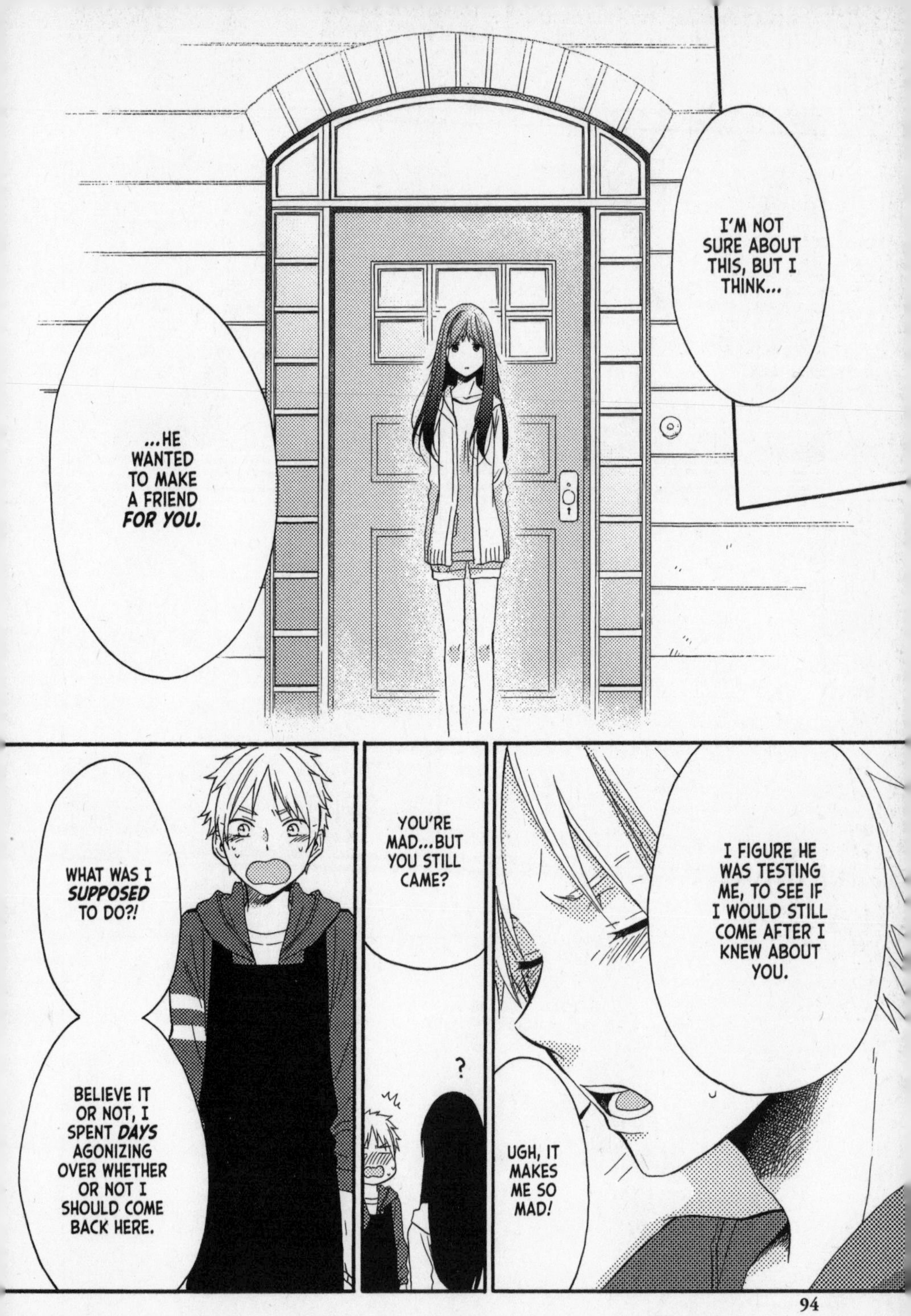
I'M NOT SURE ABOUT THIS, BUT I THINK...
...HE WANTED TO MAKE A FRIEND *FOR YOU.*
I FIGURE HE WAS TESTING ME, TO SEE IF I WOULD STILL COME AFTER I KNEW ABOUT YOU.
UGH, IT MAKES ME SO MAD!
YOU'RE MAD...BUT YOU STILL CAME?
?
WHAT WAS I *SUPPOSED* TO DO?!
BELIEVE IT OR NOT, I SPENT *DAYS* AGONIZING OVER WHETHER OR NOT I SHOULD COME BACK HERE.

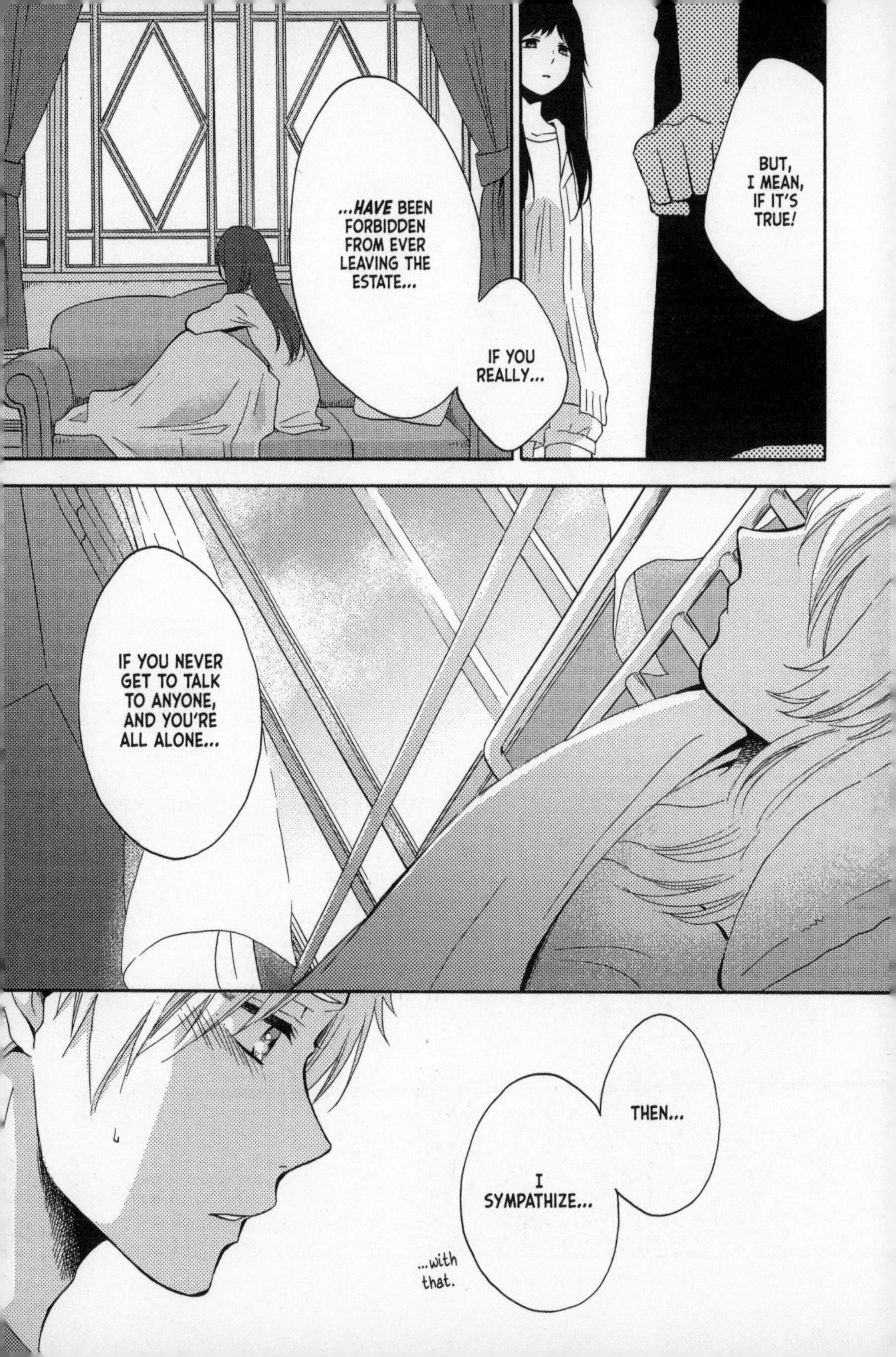
BUT, I MEAN, IF IT'S TRUE!
IF YOU REALLY...
...HAVE BEEN FORBIDDEN FROM EVER LEAVING THE ESTATE...
IF YOU NEVER GET TO TALK TO ANYONE, AND YOU'RE ALL ALONE...
THEN...
I SYMPATHIZE...
...with that.

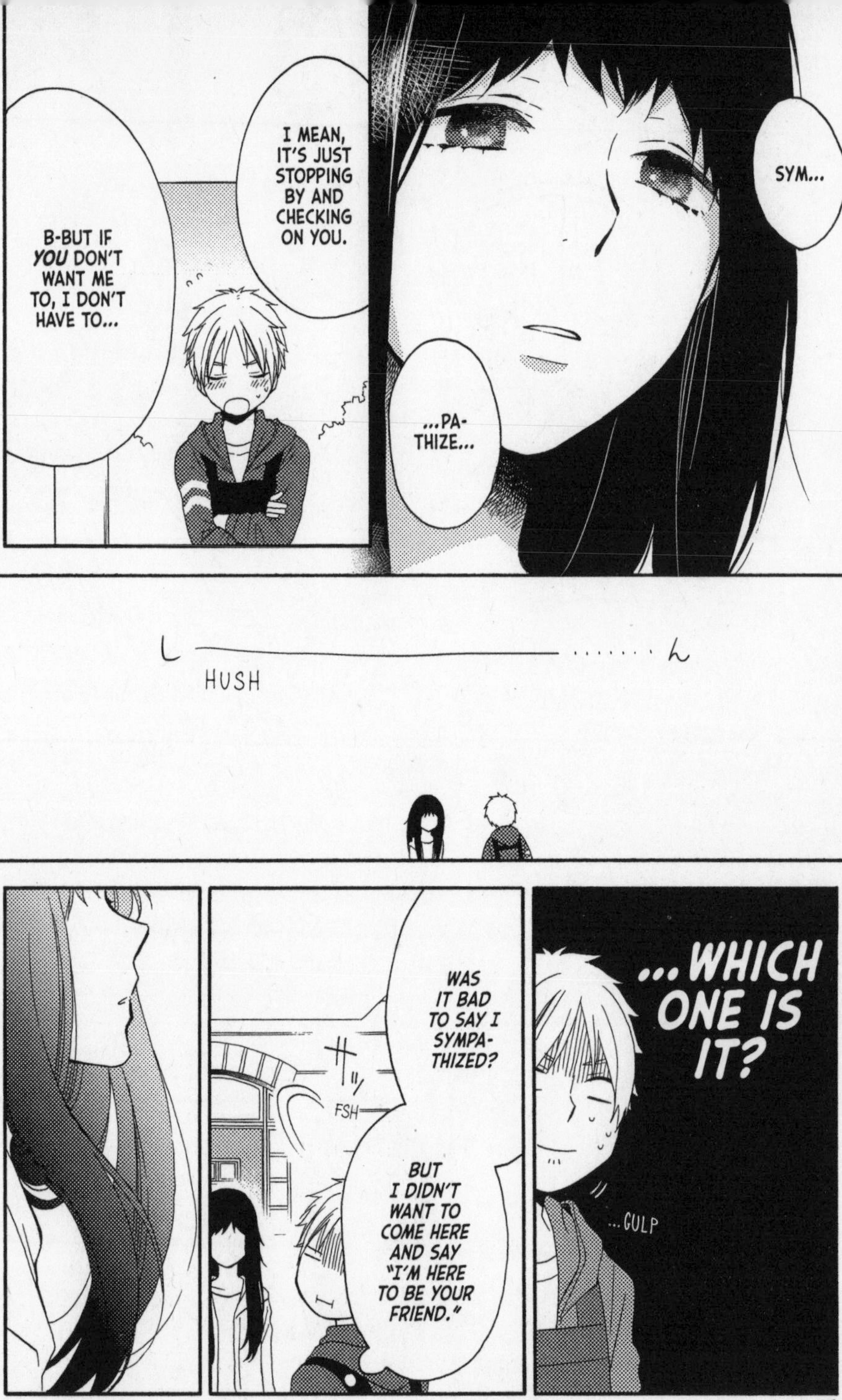
SYM...
...PA-THIZE...
I MEAN, IT'S JUST STOPPING BY AND CHECKING ON YOU.
B-BUT IF *YOU* DON'T WANT ME TO, I DON'T HAVE TO...
HUSH
...WHICH ONE IS IT?
...GULP
WAS IT BAD TO SAY I SYMPA-THIZED?
FSH
BUT I DIDN'T WANT TO COME HERE AND SAY "I'M HERE TO BE YOUR FRIEND."

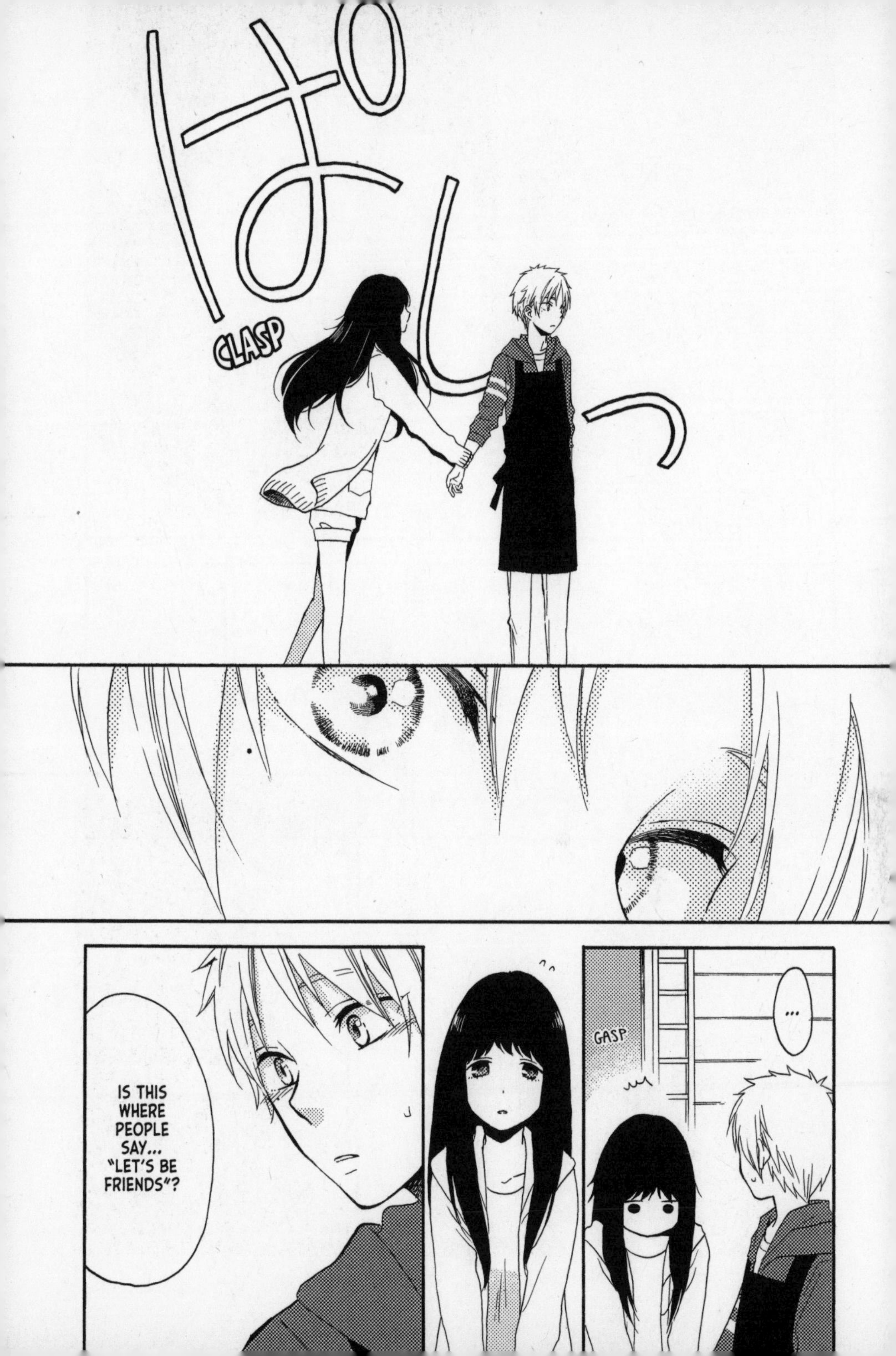
ぱしっ
CLASP
GASP
...
IS THIS WHERE PEOPLE SAY... "LET'S BE FRIENDS"?

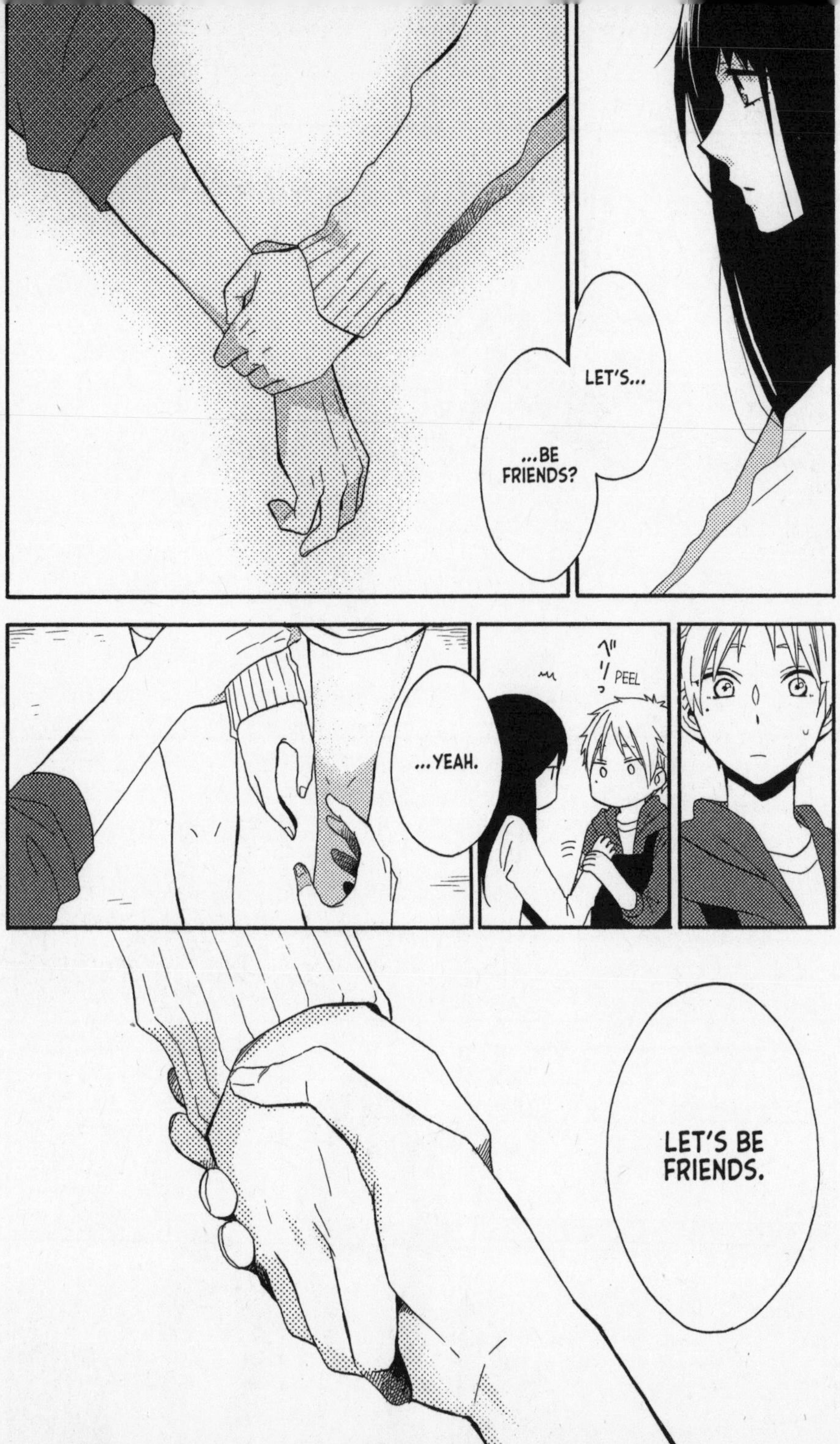
LET'S...
...BE FRIENDS?
PEEL
...YEAH.
LET'S BE FRIENDS.

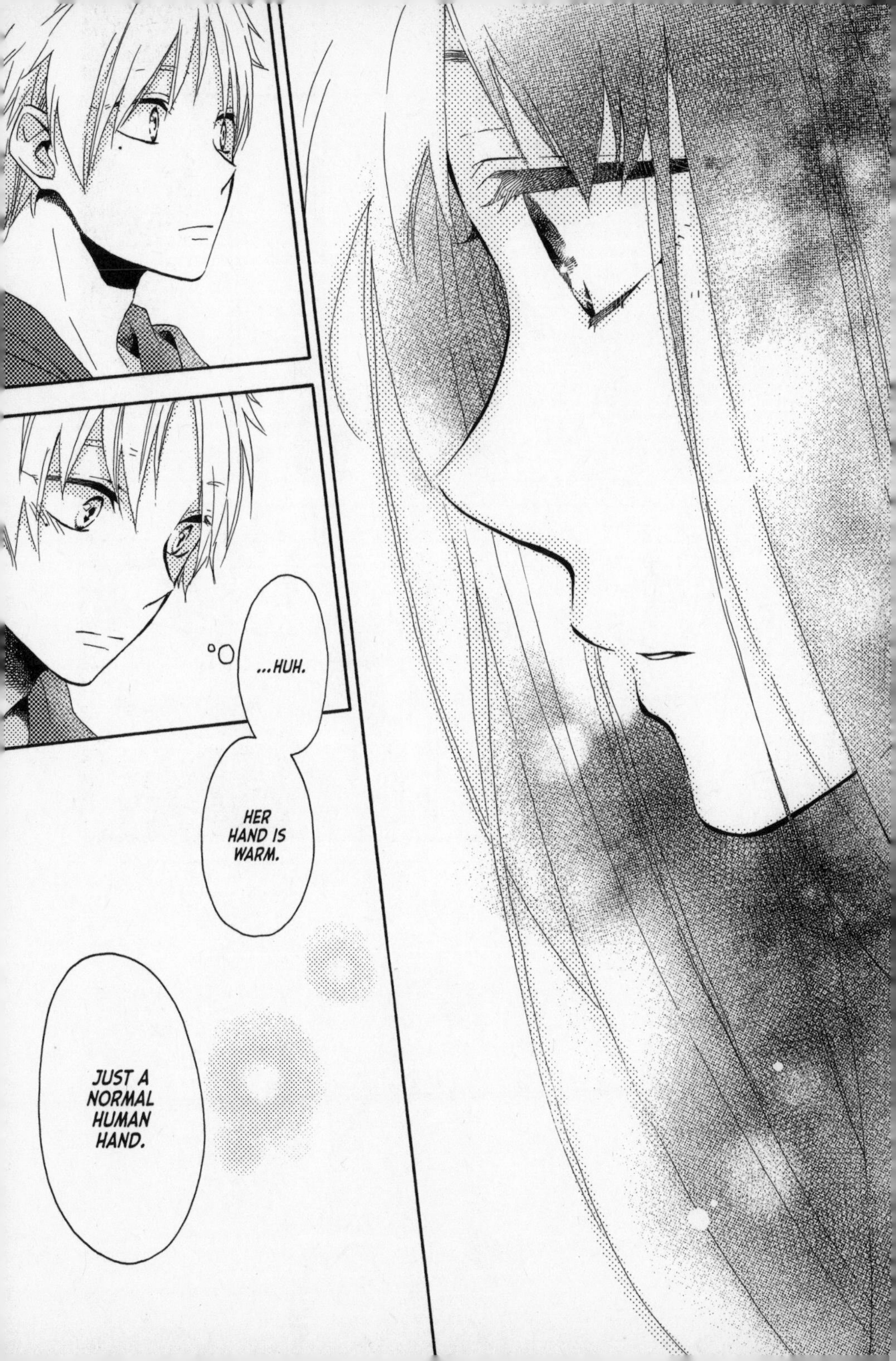
...HUH.
HER HAND IS WARM.
JUST A NORMAL HUMAN HAND.

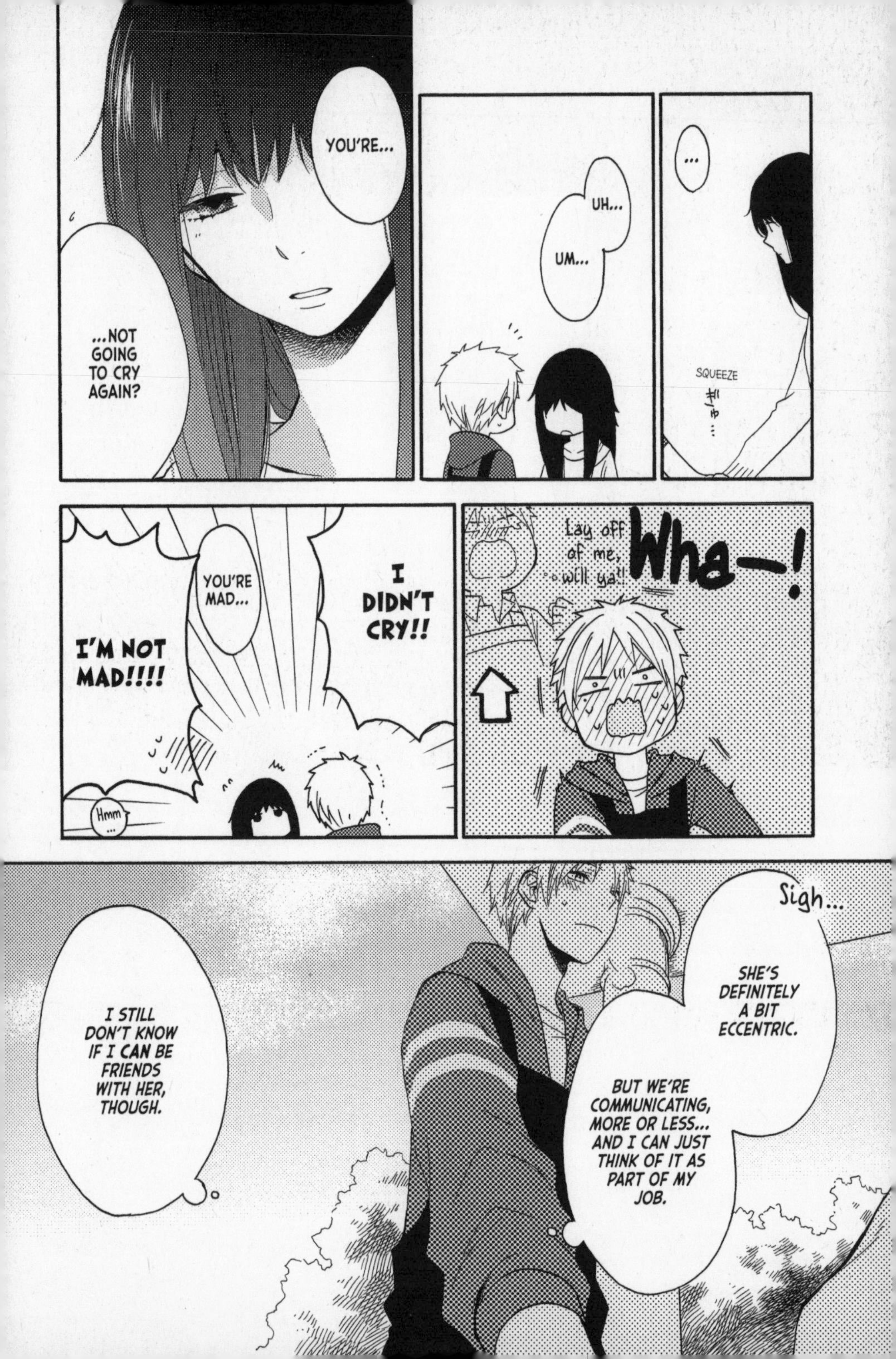
...
SQUEEZE
ギュ…
UH...
UM...
YOU'RE...
...NOT GOING TO CRY AGAIN?
Wha—!
Lay off of me, will ya!!
I DIDN'T CRY!!
YOU'RE MAD...
I'M NOT MAD!!!!
Hmm...
Sigh...
SHE'S DEFINITELY A BIT ECCENTRIC.
BUT WE'RE COMMUNICATING, MORE OR LESS... AND I CAN JUST THINK OF IT AS PART OF MY JOB.
I STILL DON'T KNOW IF I CAN BE FRIENDS WITH HER, THOUGH.

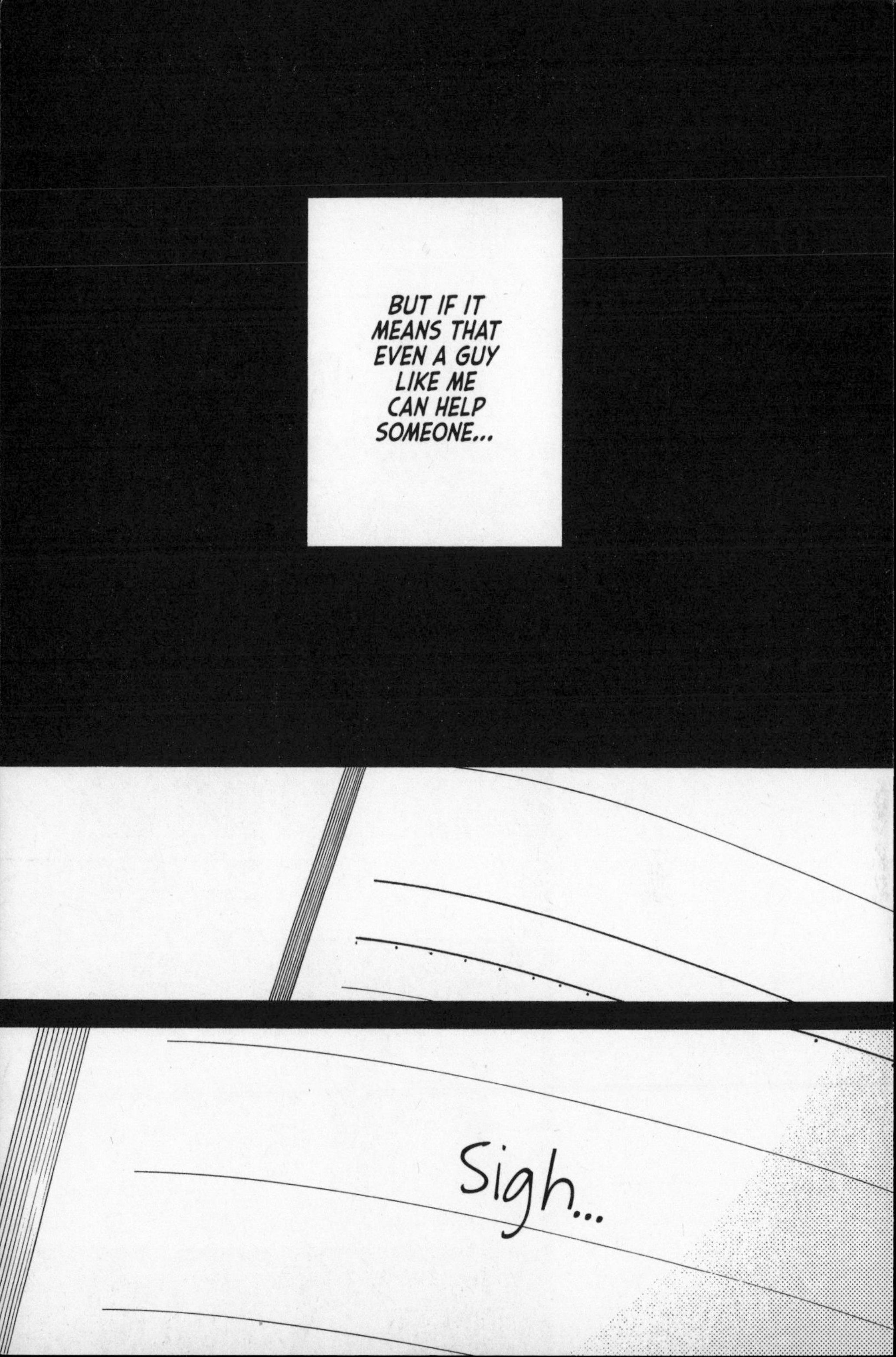
BUT IF IT MEANS THAT EVEN A GUY LIKE ME CAN HELP SOMEONE...
Sigh...

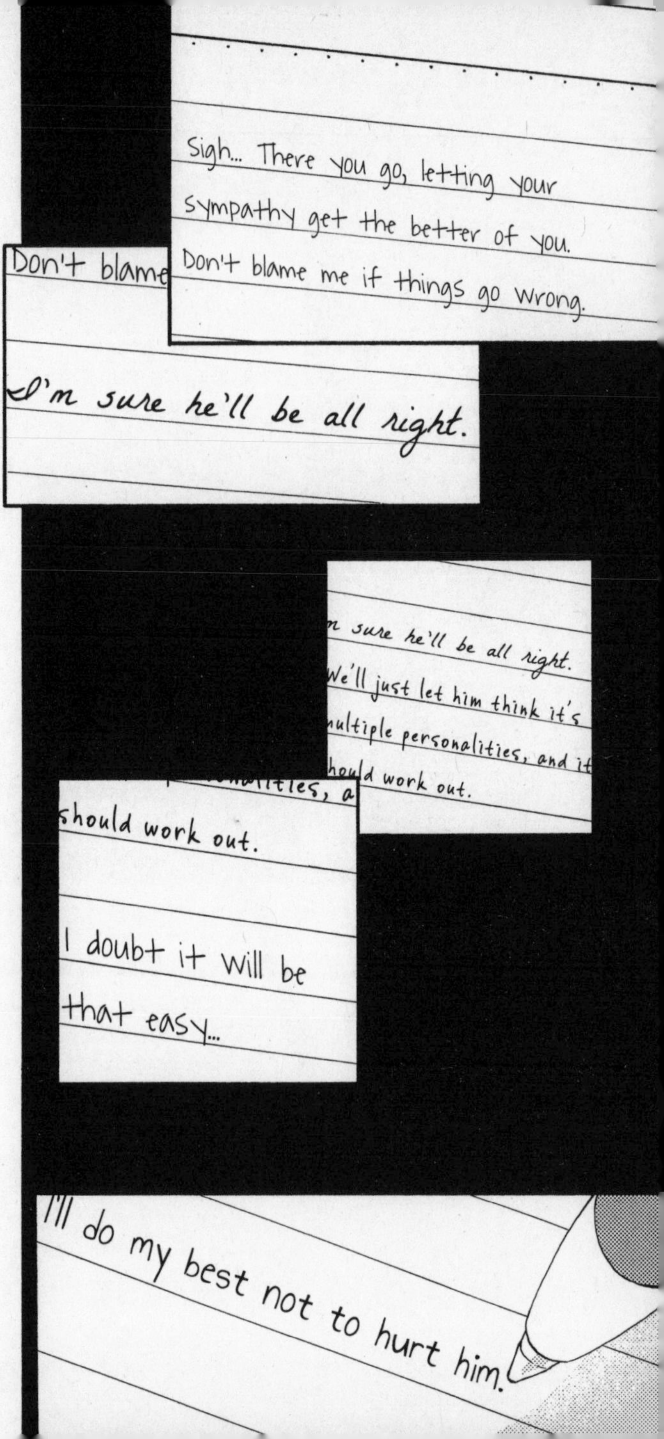
Sigh... There you go, letting your sympathy get the better of you. Don't blame me if things go wrong.
Don't blame
I'm sure he'll be all right.
n sure he'll be all right. We'll just let him think it's multiple personalities, and it should work out.
hould work out.
should work out.
I doubt it will be that easy...
I'll do my best not to hurt him.

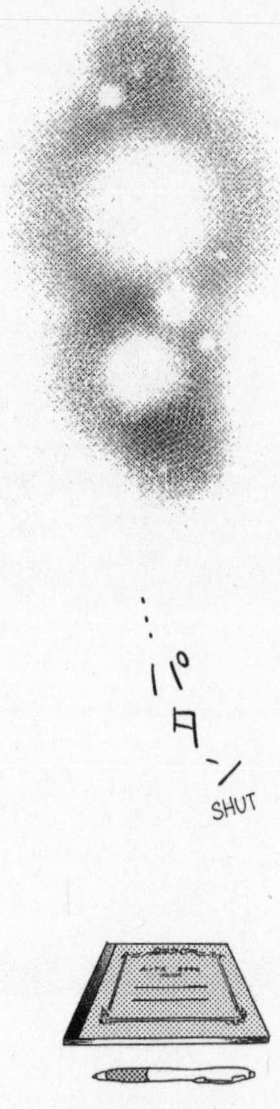
SHUT

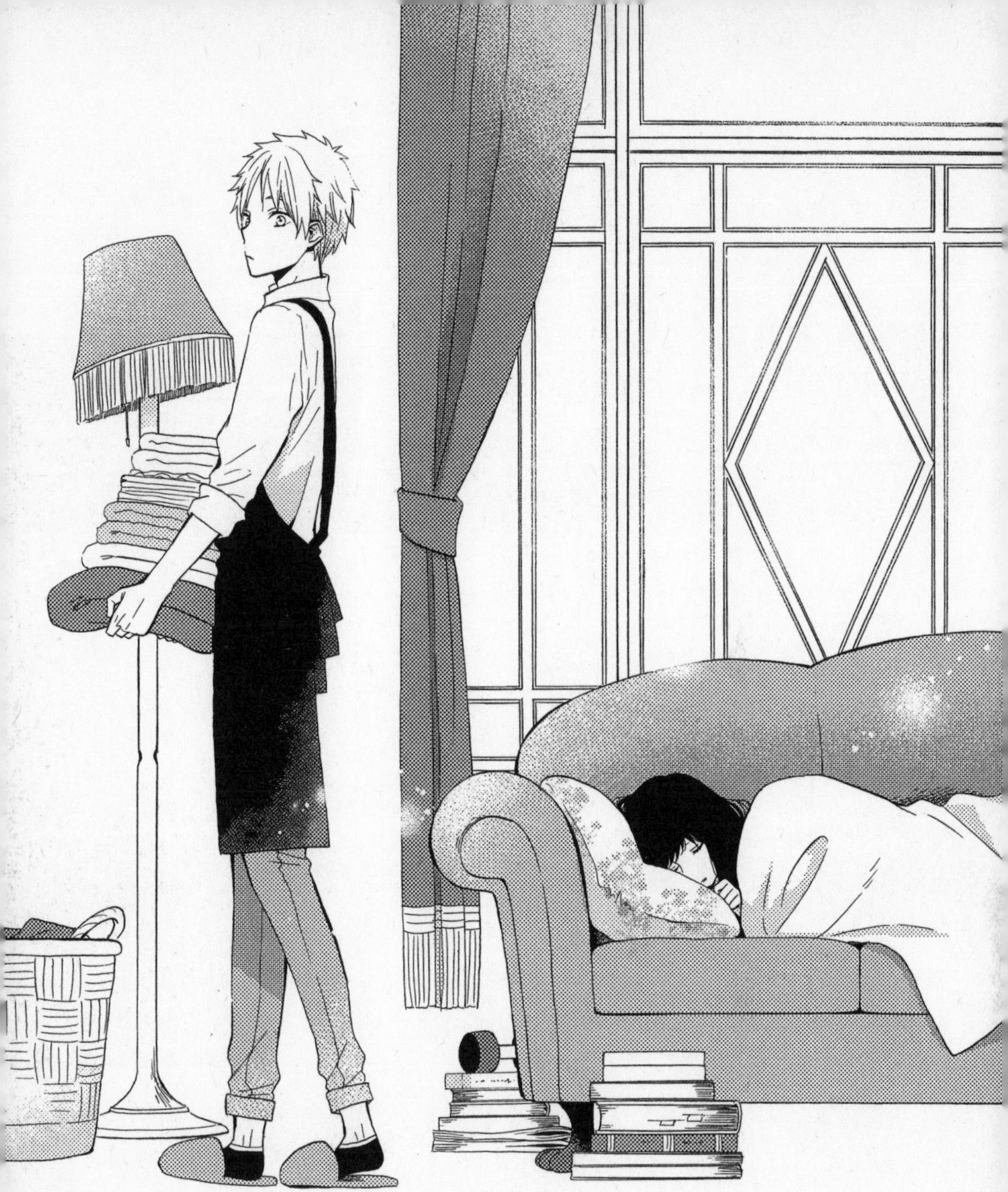

CHAPTER 3

PRELUDE

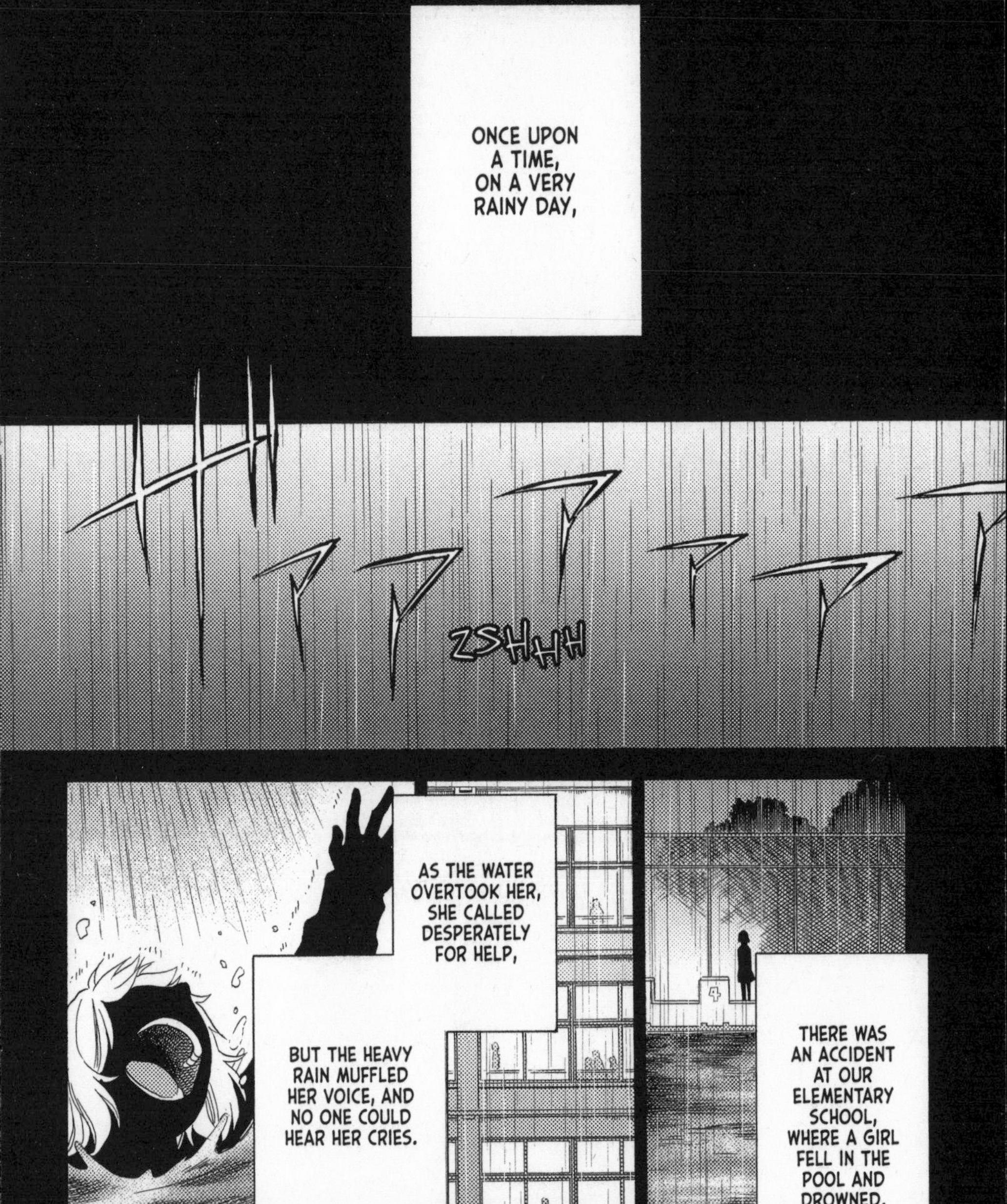
ONCE UPON A TIME, ON A VERY RAINY DAY,
ZSHHH
THERE WAS AN ACCIDENT AT OUR ELEMENTARY SCHOOL, WHERE A GIRL FELL IN THE POOL AND DROWNED.
AS THE WATER OVERTOOK HER, SHE CALLED DESPERATELY FOR HELP,
BUT THE HEAVY RAIN MUFFLED HER VOICE, AND NO ONE COULD HEAR HER CRIES.

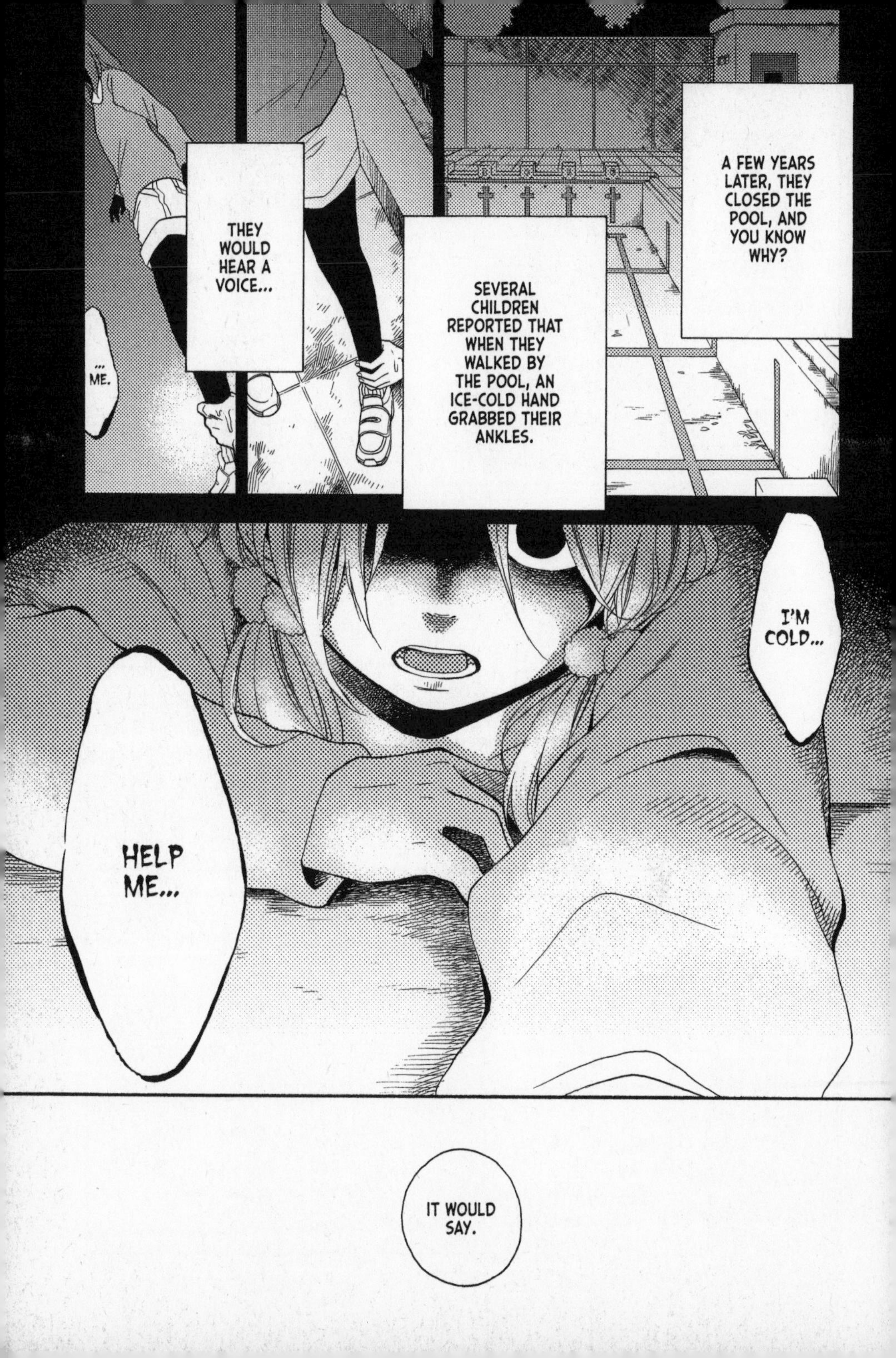
A FEW YEARS LATER, THEY CLOSED THE POOL, AND YOU KNOW WHY?
SEVERAL CHILDREN REPORTED THAT WHEN THEY WALKED BY THE POOL, AN ICE-COLD HAND GRABBED THEIR ANKLES.
THEY WOULD HEAR A VOICE...
... ME.
I'M COLD...
HELP ME...
IT WOULD SAY.

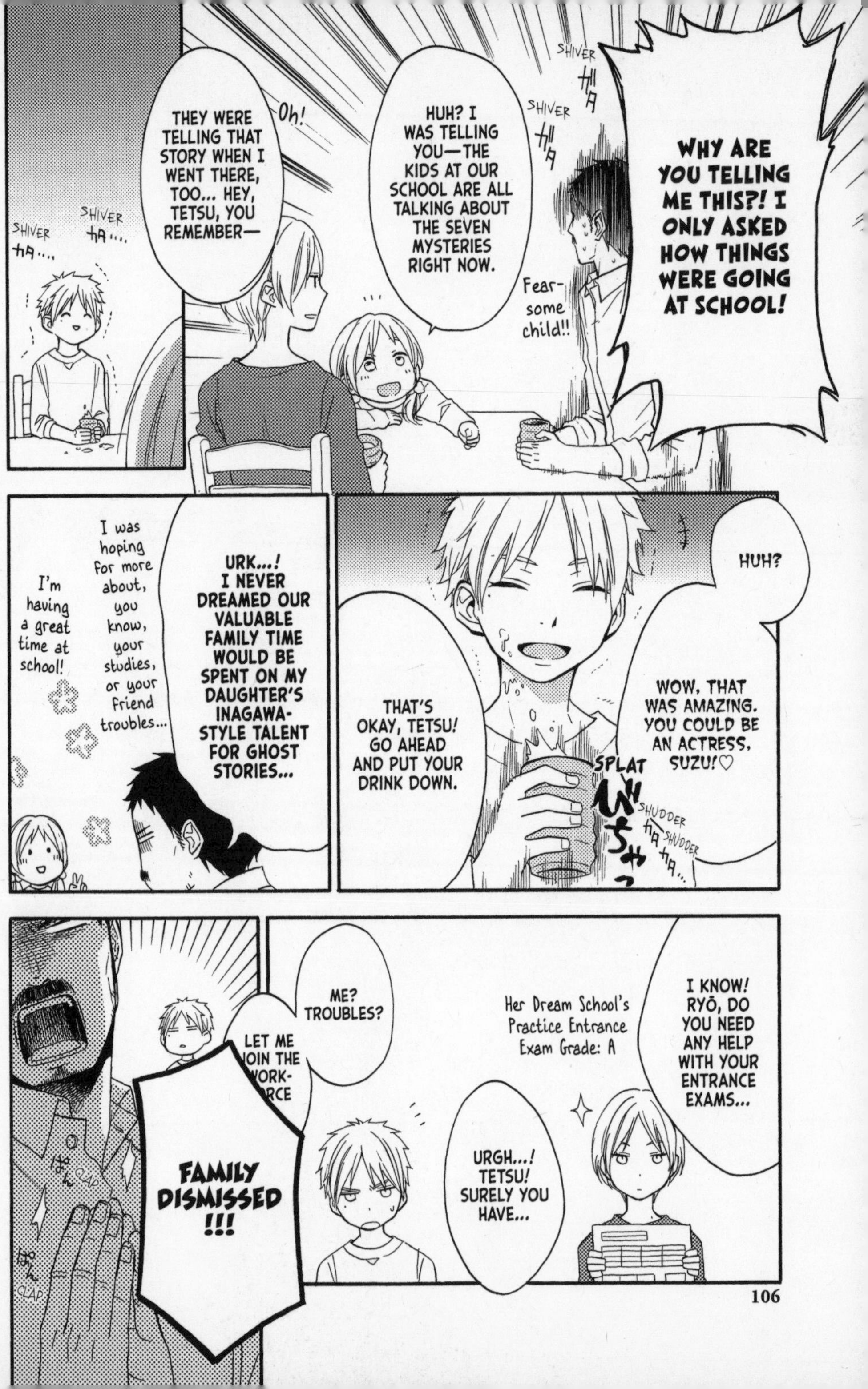
WHY ARE YOU TELLING ME THIS?! I ONLY ASKED HOW THINGS WERE GOING AT SCHOOL!
SHIVER
SHIVER
Fear-some child!!
HUH? I WAS TELLING YOU—THE KIDS AT OUR SCHOOL ARE ALL TALKING ABOUT THE SEVEN MYSTERIES RIGHT NOW.
Oh!
THEY WERE TELLING THAT STORY WHEN I WENT THERE, TOO... HEY, TETSU, YOU REMEMBER—
SHIVER
SHIVER
HUH?
WOW, THAT WAS AMAZING. YOU COULD BE AN ACTRESS, SUZU!♡
SPLAT
SHUDDER
SHUDDER
THAT'S OKAY, TETSU! GO AHEAD AND PUT YOUR DRINK DOWN.
URK...! I NEVER DREAMED OUR VALUABLE FAMILY TIME WOULD BE SPENT ON MY DAUGHTER'S INAGAWA-STYLE TALENT FOR GHOST STORIES...
I was hoping for more about, you know, your studies, or your friend troubles...
I'm having a great time at school!
I KNOW! RYŌ, DO YOU NEED ANY HELP WITH YOUR ENTRANCE EXAMS...
Her Dream School's Practice Entrance Exam Grade: A
URGH...! TETSU! SURELY YOU HAVE...
ME? TROUBLES?
LET ME OIN THE WORK- RCE
FAMILY DISMISSED!!!
CLAP
CLAP

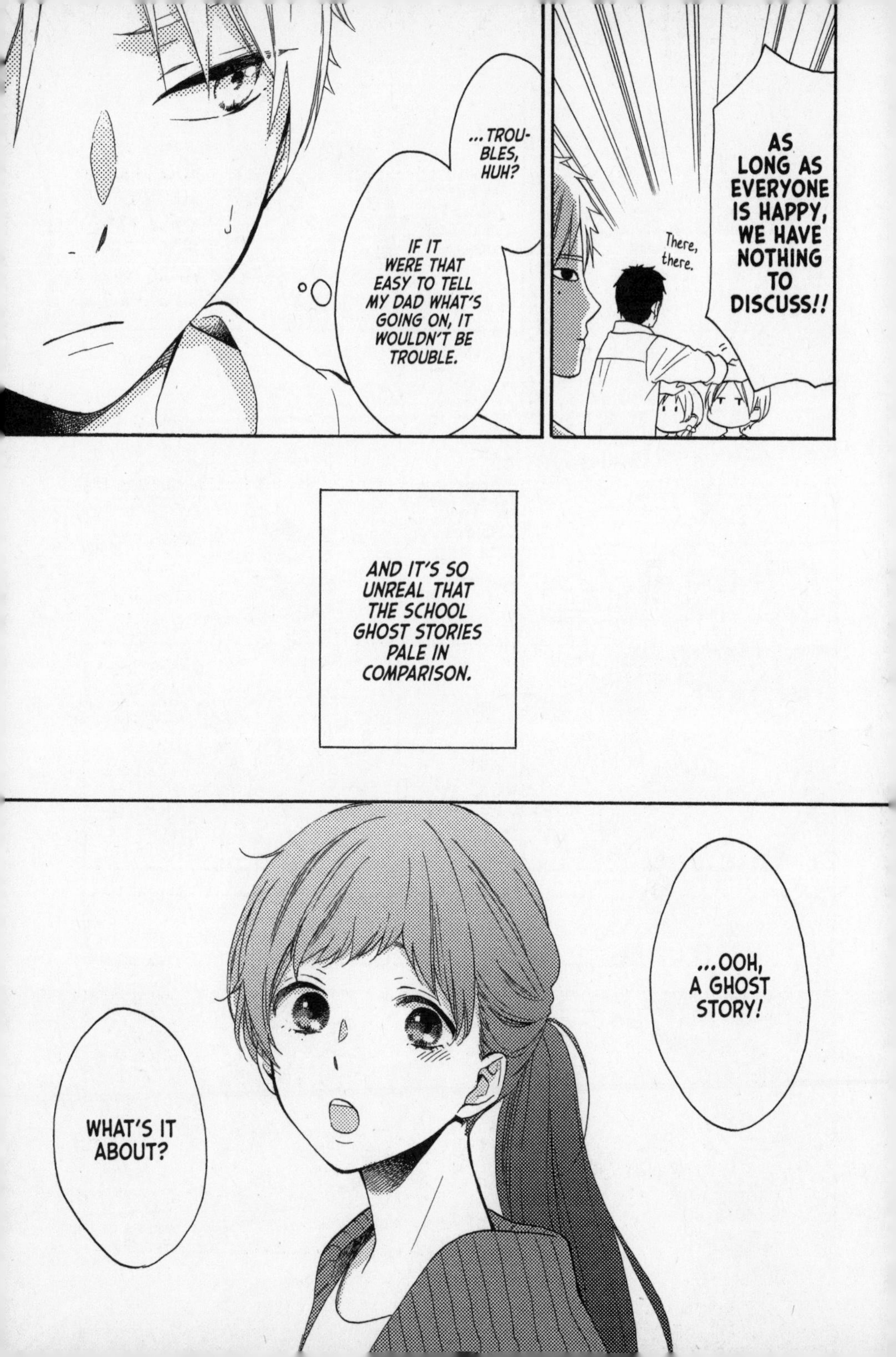
AS LONG AS EVERYONE IS HAPPY, WE HAVE NOTHING TO DISCUSS!!
There, there.
...TROU-BLES, HUH?
IF IT WERE THAT EASY TO TELL MY DAD WHAT'S GOING ON, IT WOULDN'T BE TROUBLE.
AND IT'S SO UNREAL THAT THE SCHOOL GHOST STORIES PALE IN COMPARISON.
...OOH, A GHOST STORY!
WHAT'S IT ABOUT?

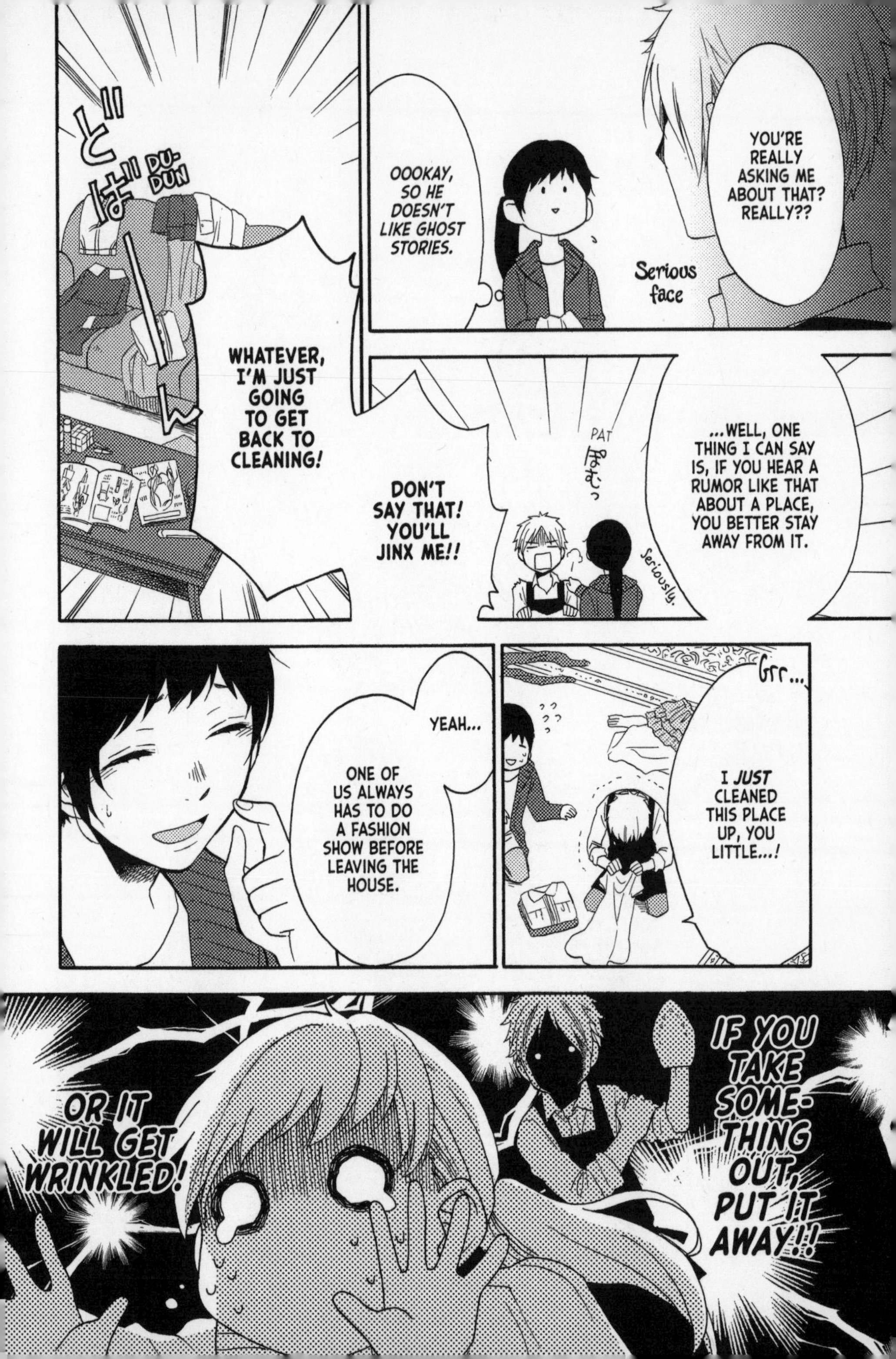
YOU'RE REALLY ASKING ME ABOUT THAT? REALLY??
Serious face
OOOKAY, SO HE DOESN'T LIKE GHOST STORIES.
...WELL, ONE THING I CAN SAY IS, IF YOU HEAR A RUMOR LIKE THAT ABOUT A PLACE, YOU BETTER STAY AWAY FROM IT.
Seriously.
PAT
ぽむっ
DON'T SAY THAT! YOU'LL JINX ME!!
DU-DUN
WHATEVER, I'M JUST GOING TO GET BACK TO CLEANING!
Grrr...
I JUST CLEANED THIS PLACE UP, YOU LITTLE...!
YEAH...
ONE OF US ALWAYS HAS TO DO A FASHION SHOW BEFORE LEAVING THE HOUSE.
IF YOU TAKE SOME-THING OUT, PUT IT AWAY!!
OR IT WILL GET WRINKLED!

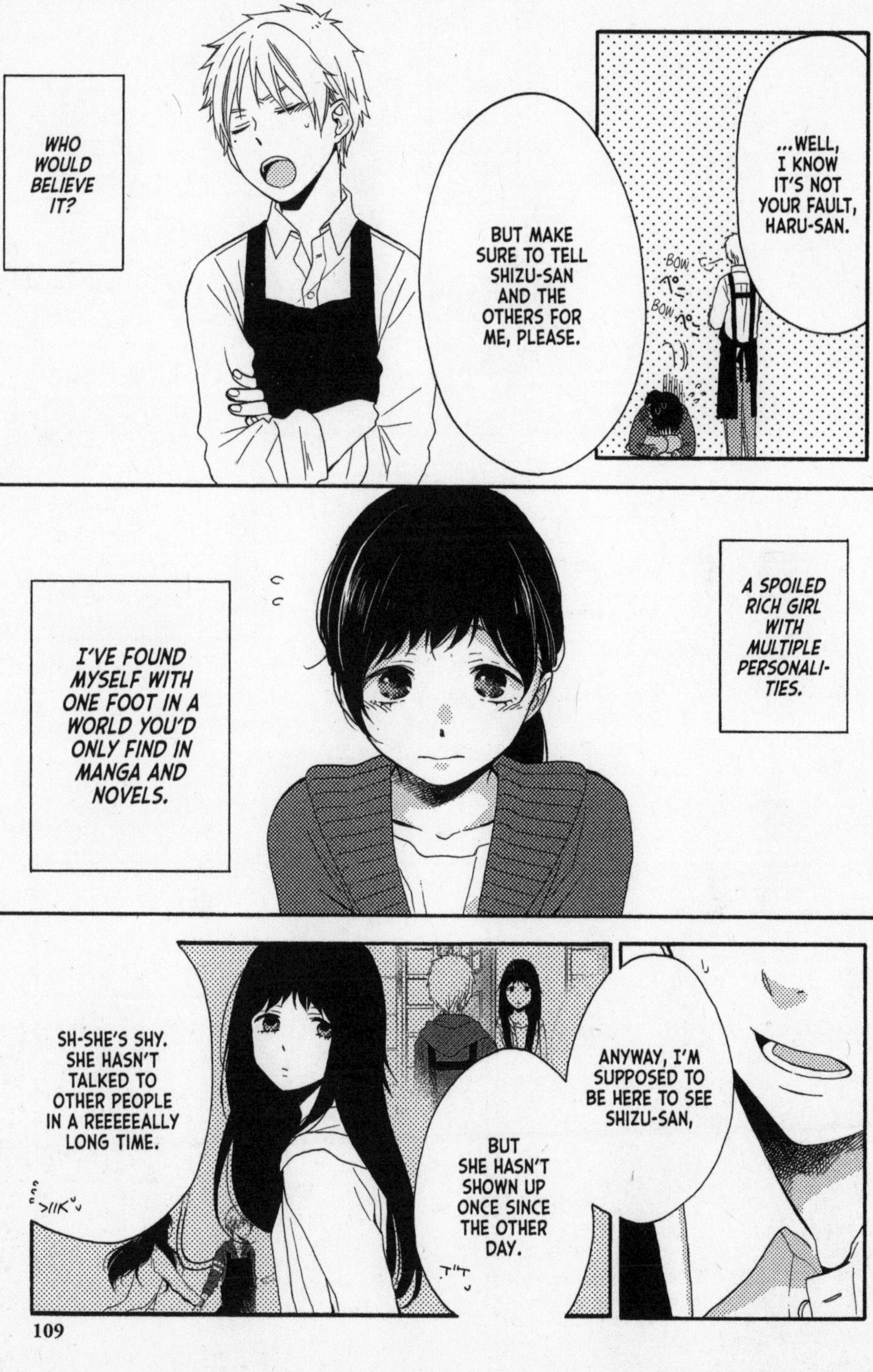
...WELL, I KNOW IT'S NOT YOUR FAULT, HARU-SAN.
BOW
BOW
BUT MAKE SURE TO TELL SHIZU-SAN AND THE OTHERS FOR ME, PLEASE.
WHO WOULD BELIEVE IT?
A SPOILED RICH GIRL WITH MULTIPLE PERSONALITIES.
I'VE FOUND MYSELF WITH ONE FOOT IN A WORLD YOU'D ONLY FIND IN MANGA AND NOVELS.
ANYWAY, I'M SUPPOSED TO BE HERE TO SEE SHIZU-SAN,
BUT SHE HASN'T SHOWN UP ONCE SINCE THE OTHER DAY.
SH-SHE'S SHY. SHE HASN'T TALKED TO OTHER PEOPLE IN A REEEEEALLY LONG TIME.

WE SWITCH OFF ON A DAILY SYSTEM.

?

HMM... WELL, PART OF IT IS BAD TIMING.

WE ALREADY DON'T HAVE THAT MUCH TIME TO SEE EACH OTHER AS IT IS...IF SHE'S GOING TO KEEP HIDING, THEN WHAT'S THE POINT?

YEAH, BUT... I'M SKIPPING OUT ON WORK FOR THIS.

YOU'RE ALWAYS HERE ON TUESDAY AND SATURDAY, SO YOU MISSED HER LAST WEEK.

Mon.	Tue.	Wed.	Thu.	Fri.	Sat.	Sun.
SHIZU	HARU-MICHI	SHIZU	?	SHIZU	HARU-MICHI	SHIZU

Workdays

Last week it was like this

THE DAY AFTER *I* TAKE OVER, SHIZU TAKES OVER, THEN THE NEXT DAY, SOMEONE ELSE GETS TO BE IN CHARGE, THEN SHIZU AGAIN. ...LIKE THAT.

I-I'm sorry!!

SO SHIZU-SAN *CAN* CHANGE THE SCHEDULE IF SHE WANTS...

GULP

UHH, WELL... SHE ASKED *ME* TO COME OUT TODAY...

BUT IN THAT CASE, SHOULDN'T TODAY BE SHIZU-SAN'S DAY?

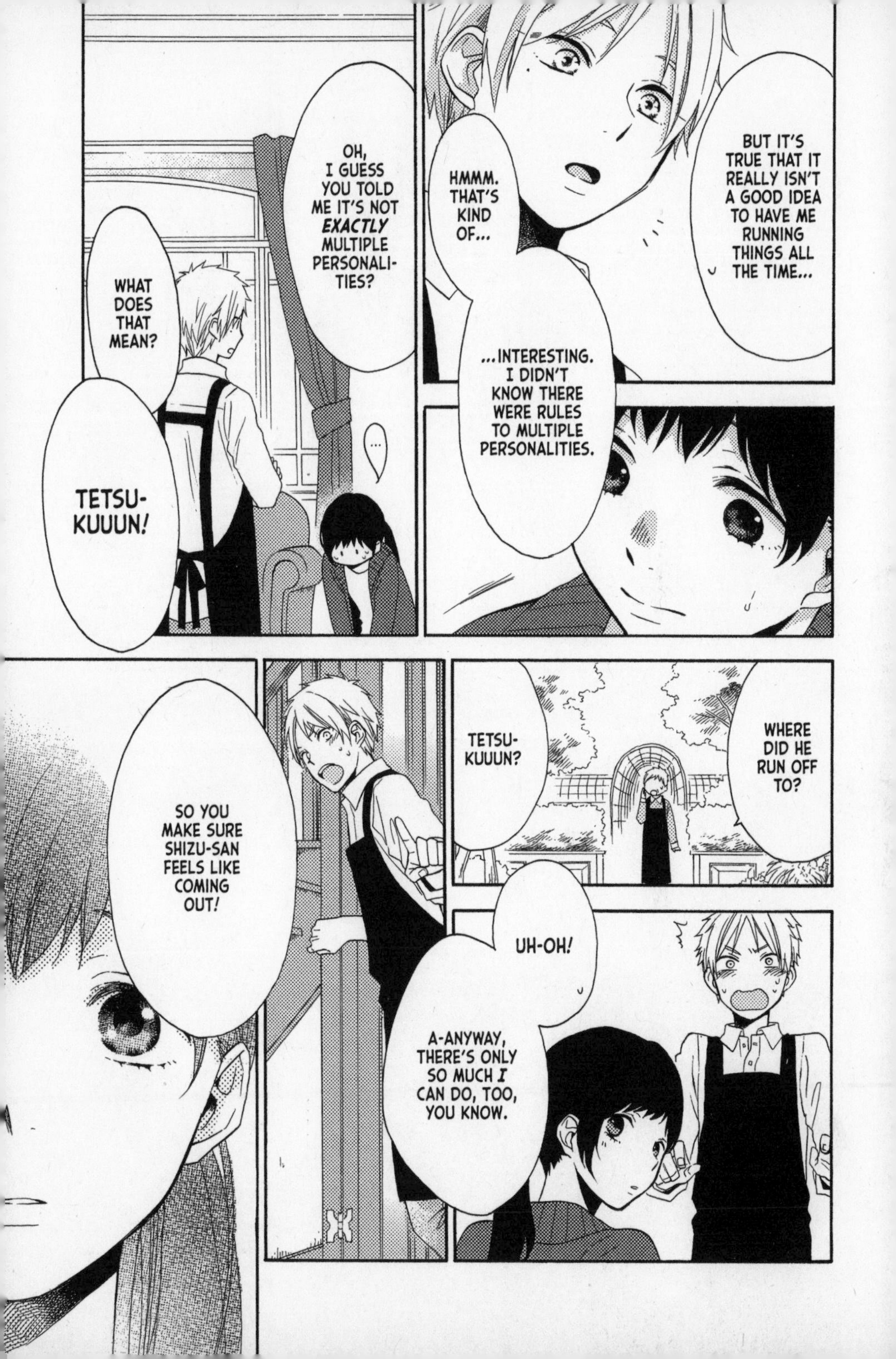
BUT IT'S TRUE THAT IT REALLY ISN'T A GOOD IDEA TO HAVE ME RUNNING THINGS ALL THE TIME...
HMMM. THAT'S KIND OF...
...INTERESTING. I DIDN'T KNOW THERE WERE RULES TO MULTIPLE PERSONALITIES.
OH, I GUESS YOU TOLD ME IT'S NOT *EXACTLY* MULTIPLE PERSONALI-TIES?
WHAT DOES THAT MEAN?
...
TETSU-KUUUN!
WHERE DID HE RUN OFF TO?
TETSU-KUUUN?
UH-OH!
A-ANYWAY, THERE'S ONLY SO MUCH *I* CAN DO, TOO, YOU KNOW.
SO YOU MAKE SURE SHIZU-SAN FEELS LIKE COMING OUT!

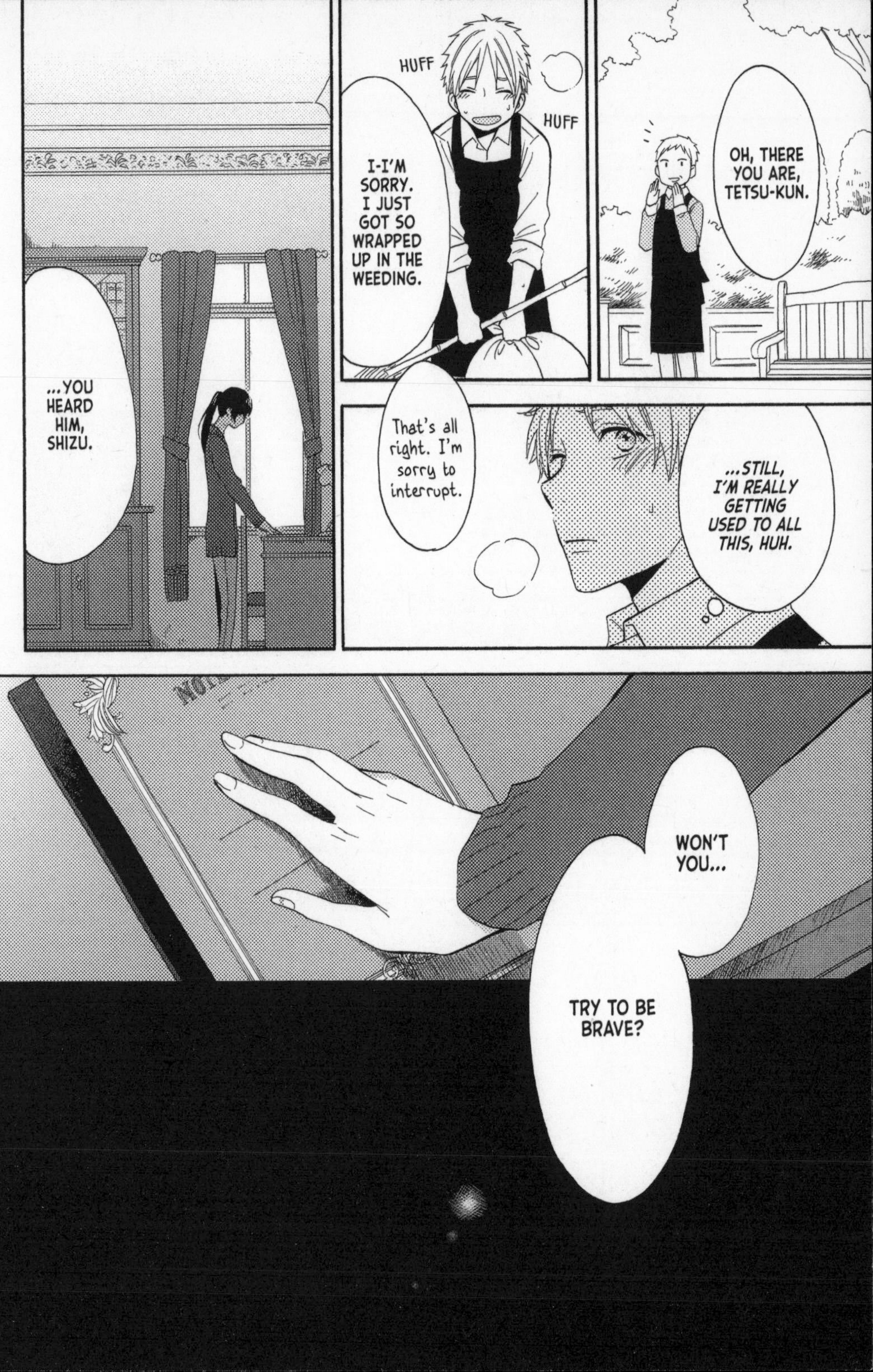
OH, THERE YOU ARE, TETSU-KUN.
HUFF
HUFF
I-I'M SORRY. I JUST GOT SO WRAPPED UP IN THE WEEDING.
That's all right. I'm sorry to interrupt.
...STILL, I'M REALLY GETTING USED TO ALL THIS, HUH.
...YOU HEARD HIM, SHIZU.
WON'T YOU...
TRY TO BE BRAVE?

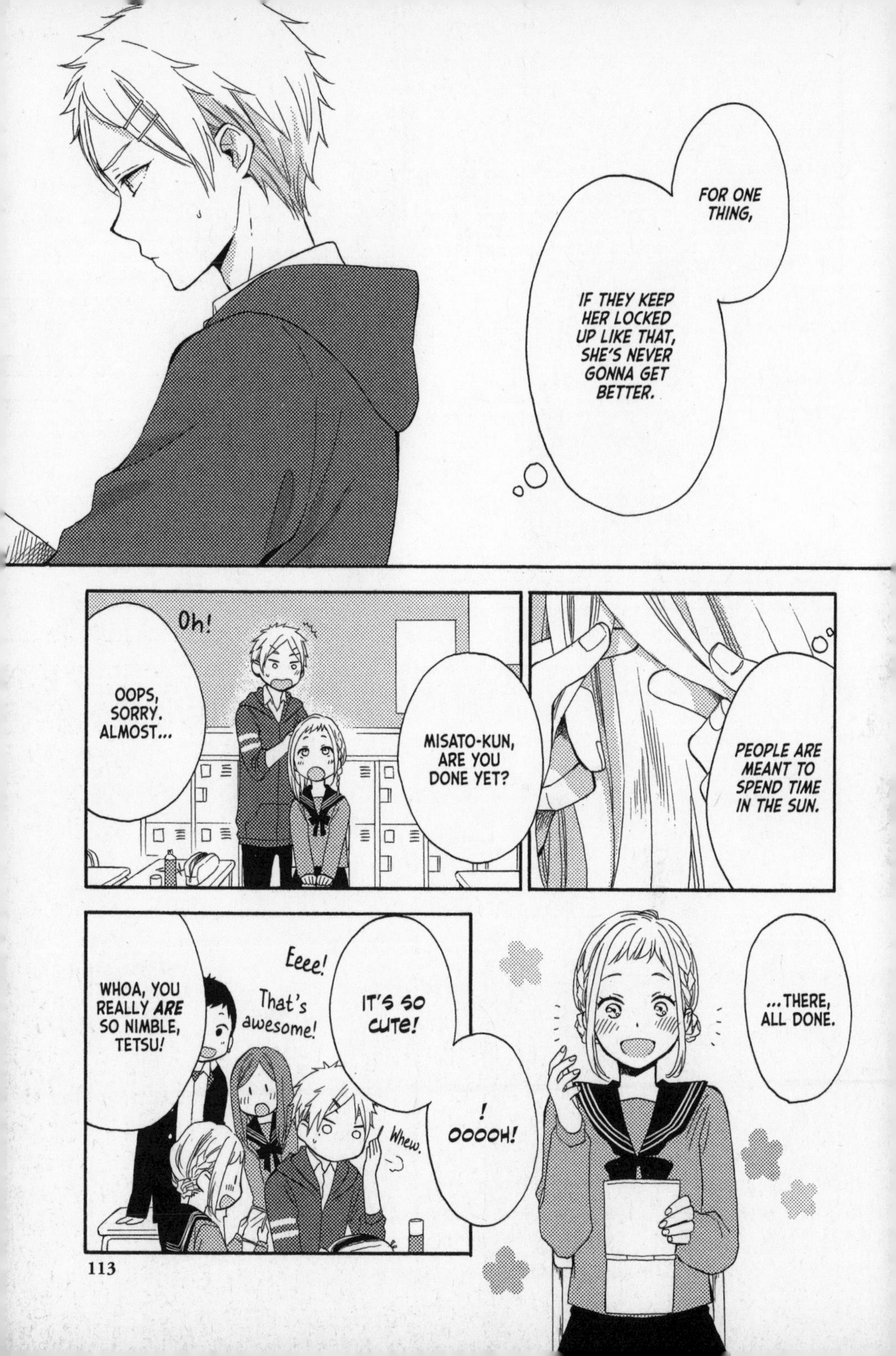
FOR ONE THING,
IF THEY KEEP HER LOCKED UP LIKE THAT, SHE'S NEVER GONNA GET BETTER.
PEOPLE ARE MEANT TO SPEND TIME IN THE SUN.
MISATO-KUN, ARE YOU DONE YET?
Oh!
OOPS, SORRY. ALMOST...
...THERE, ALL DONE.
! OOOOH!
Whew.
IT'S SO CUTE!
Eeee!
That's awesome!
WHOA, YOU REALLY *ARE* SO NIMBLE, TETSU!

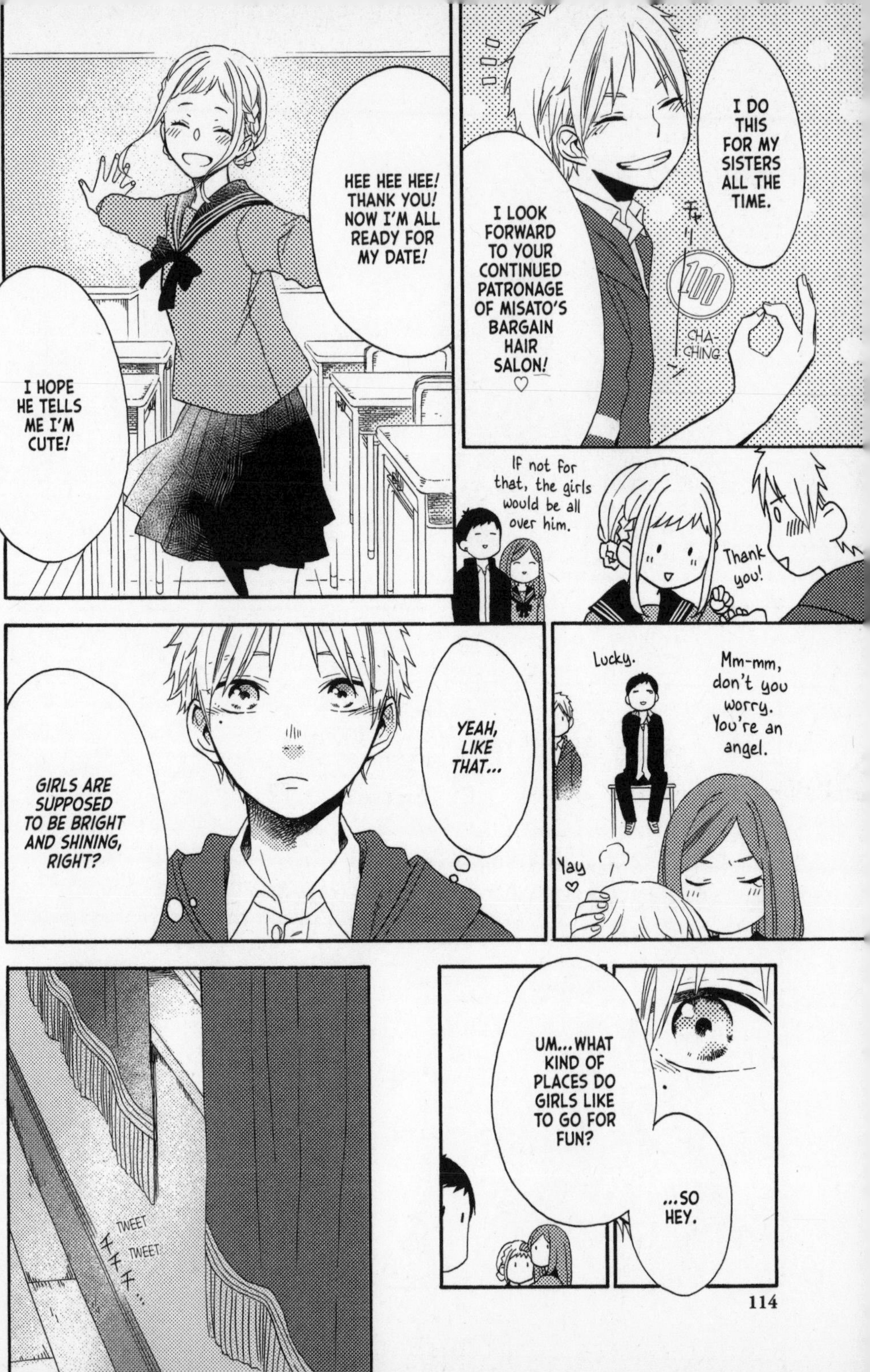
I DO THIS FOR MY SISTERS ALL THE TIME.
CHA-CHING
I LOOK FORWARD TO YOUR CONTINUED PATRONAGE OF MISATO'S BARGAIN HAIR SALON! ♡
Thank you!
If not for that, the girls would be all over him.
HEE HEE HEE! THANK YOU! NOW I'M ALL READY FOR MY DATE!
I HOPE HE TELLS ME I'M CUTE!
Mm-mm, don't you worry. You're an angel.
Lucky.
Yay ♡
YEAH, LIKE THAT...
GIRLS ARE SUPPOSED TO BE BRIGHT AND SHINING, RIGHT?
...SO HEY.
UM...WHAT KIND OF PLACES DO GIRLS LIKE TO GO FOR FUN?
TWEET
TWEET

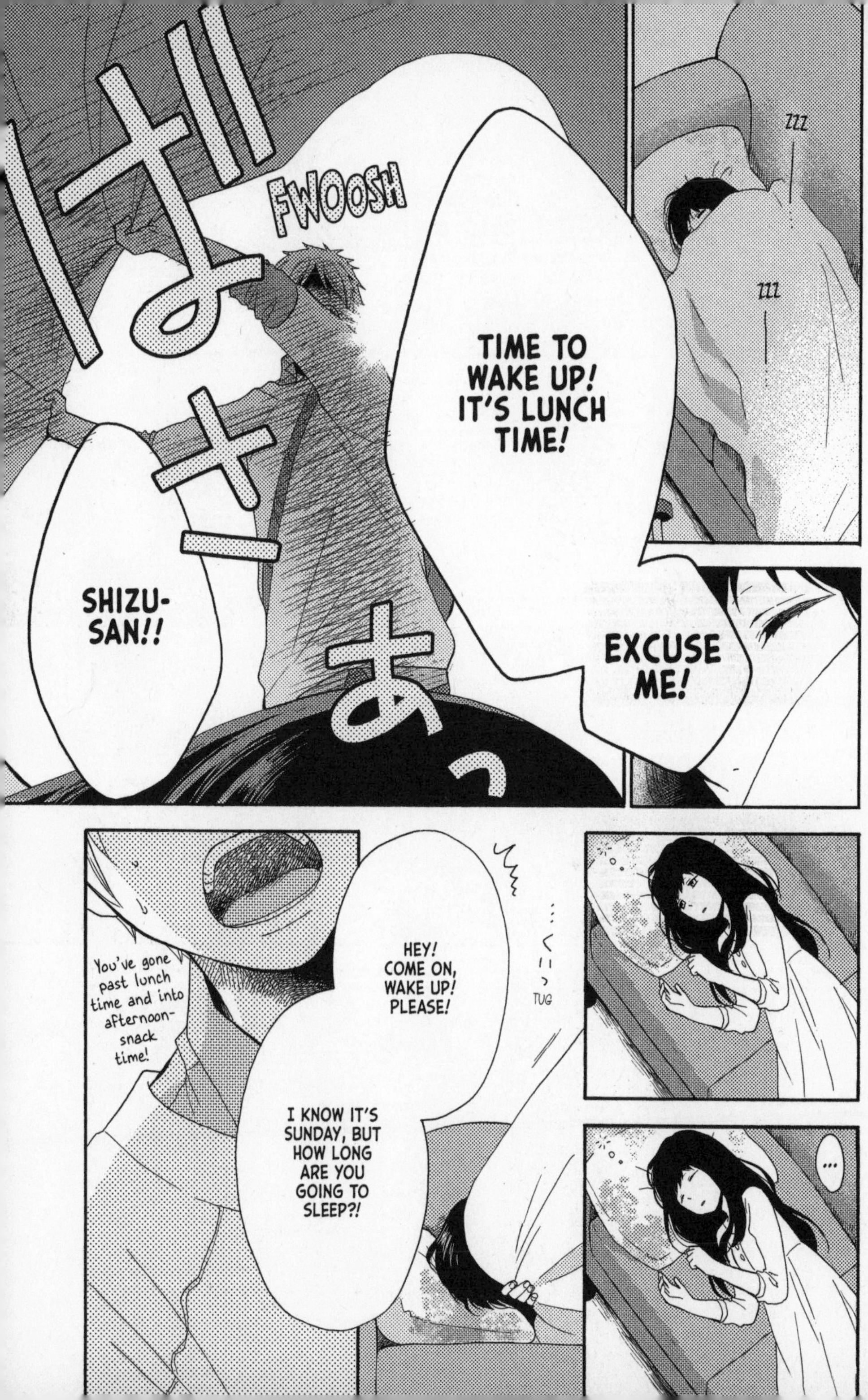
zzz
zzz
EXCUSE ME!
TIME TO WAKE UP! IT'S LUNCH TIME!
FWOOSH
SHIZU-SAN!!
TUG
...
HEY! COME ON, WAKE UP! PLEASE!
I KNOW IT'S SUNDAY, BUT HOW LONG ARE YOU GOING TO SLEEP?!
You've gone past lunch time and into afternoon-snack time!

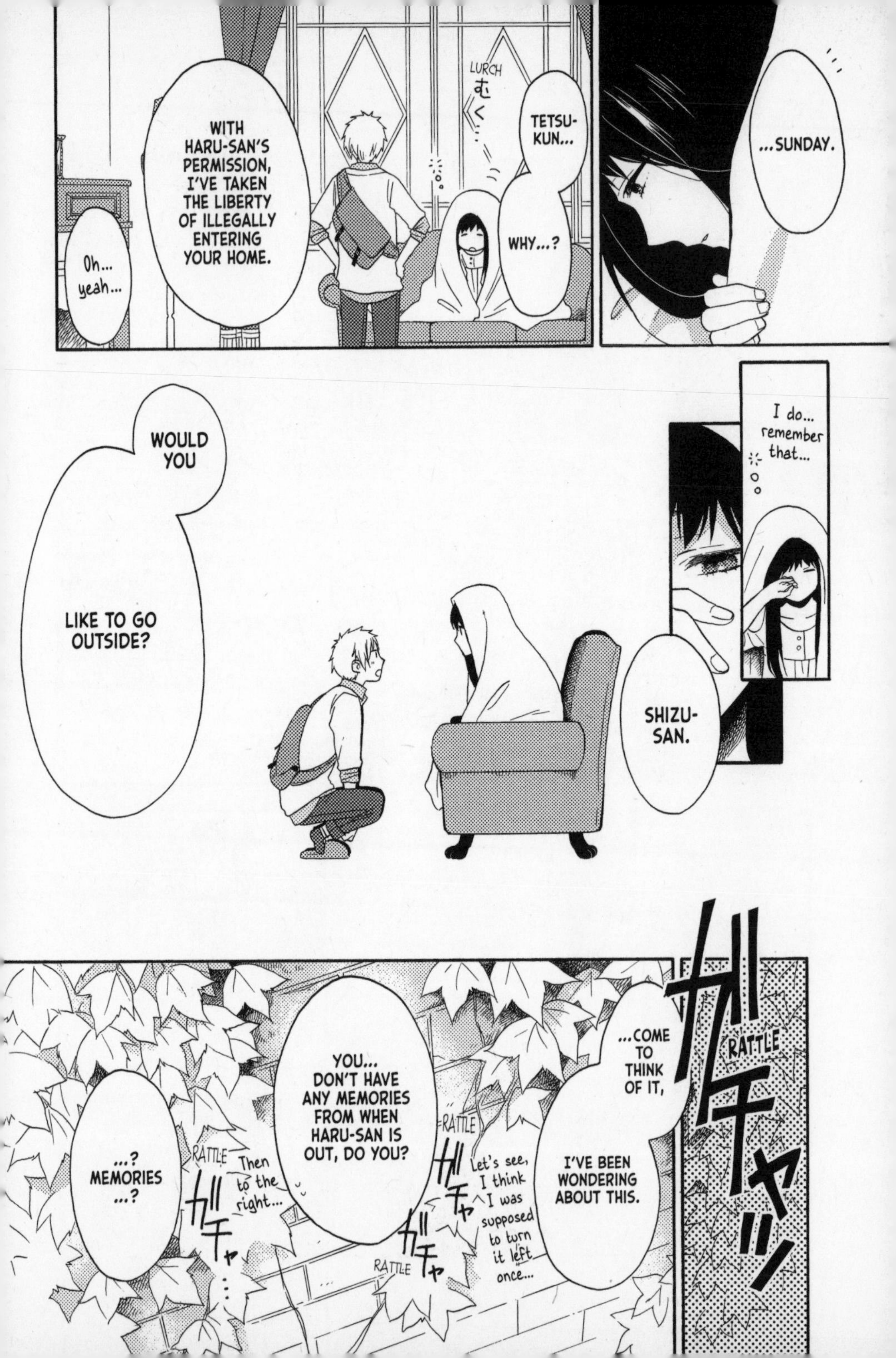
...SUNDAY.
TETSU-KUN...
WHY...?
LURCH
むく
WITH HARU-SAN'S PERMISSION, I'VE TAKEN THE LIBERTY OF ILLEGALLY ENTERING YOUR HOME.
Oh... yeah...
I do... remember that...
SHIZU-SAN.
WOULD YOU
LIKE TO GO OUTSIDE?
RATTLE
ガチャッ
...COME TO THINK OF IT,
I'VE BEEN WONDERING ABOUT THIS.
RATTLE
ガチャ
Let's see, I think I was supposed to turn it left once...
RATTLE
ガチャ
YOU... DON'T HAVE ANY MEMORIES FROM WHEN HARU-SAN IS OUT, DO YOU?
Then to the right...
RATTLE
ガチャ...
...? MEMORIES ...?

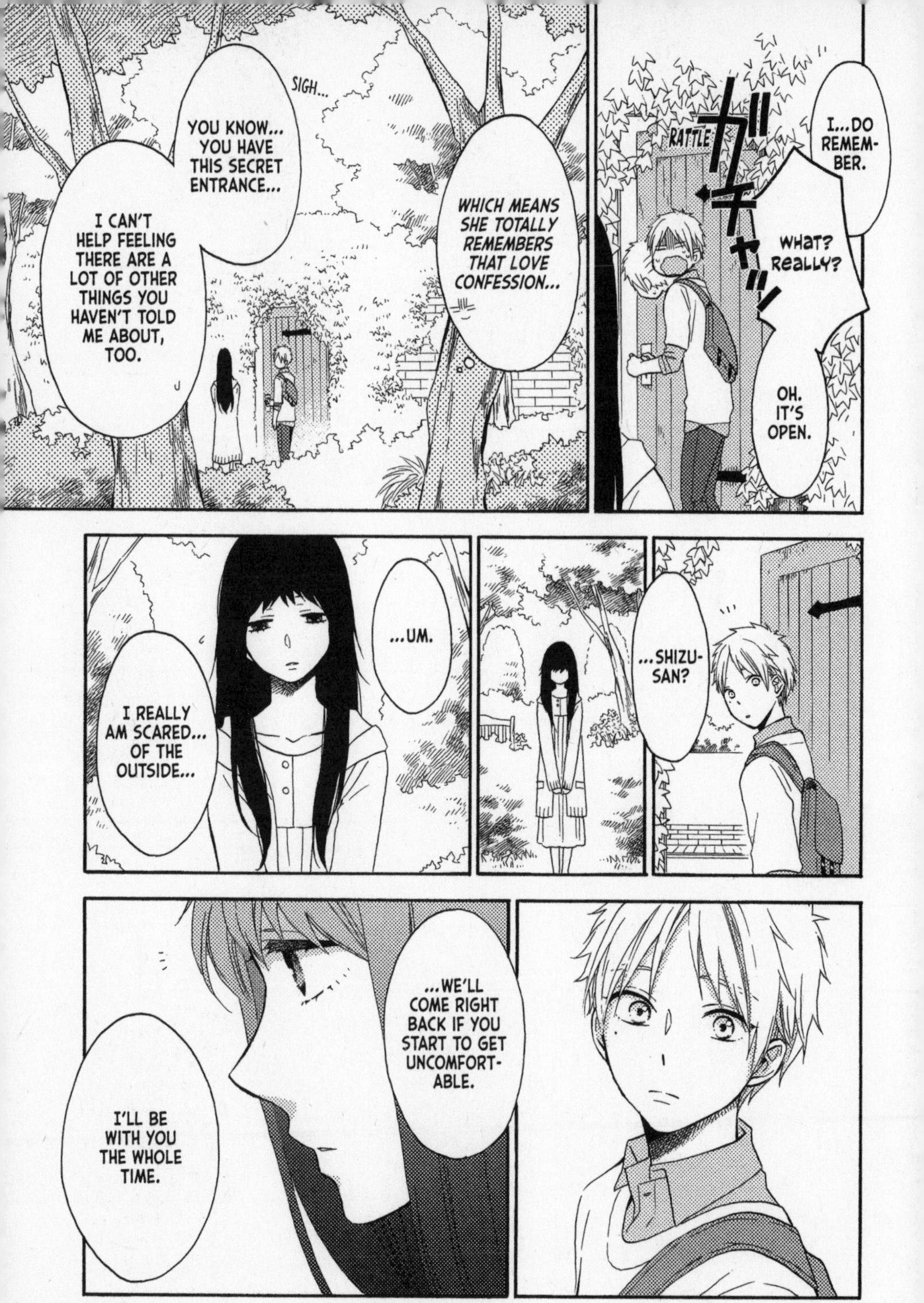
I...DO REMEMBER.
WHAT? REALLY?
RATTLE
OH. IT'S OPEN.
WHICH MEANS SHE TOTALLY REMEMBERS THAT LOVE CONFESSION...
SIGH...
YOU KNOW... YOU HAVE THIS SECRET ENTRANCE...
I CAN'T HELP FEELING THERE ARE A LOT OF OTHER THINGS YOU HAVEN'T TOLD ME ABOUT, TOO.
...SHIZU-SAN?
...UM.
I REALLY AM SCARED... OF THE OUTSIDE...
...WE'LL COME RIGHT BACK IF YOU START TO GET UNCOMFORTABLE.
I'LL BE WITH YOU THE WHOLE TIME.

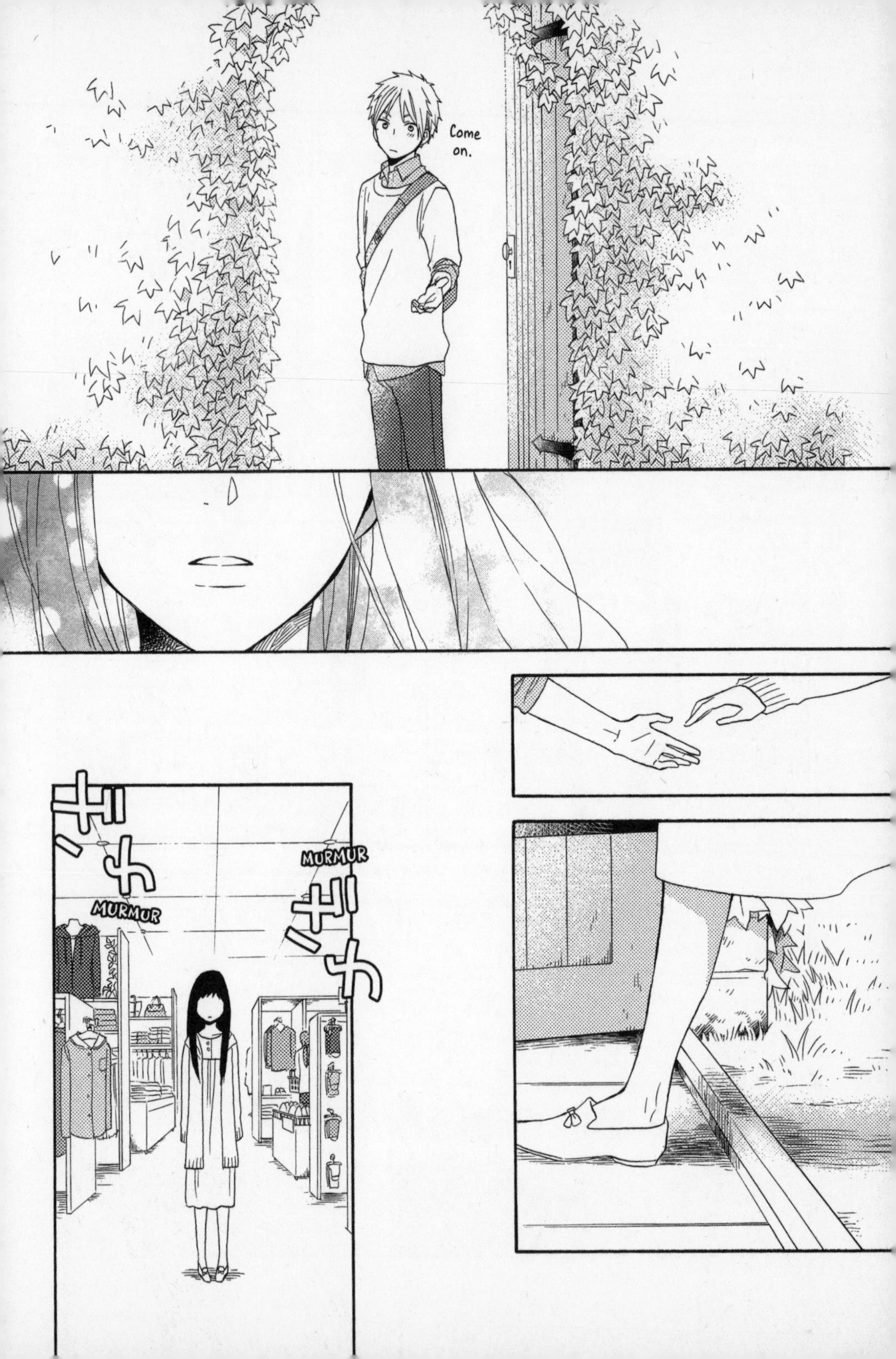
Come on.
MURMUR
ざわ
ざわ
MURMUR

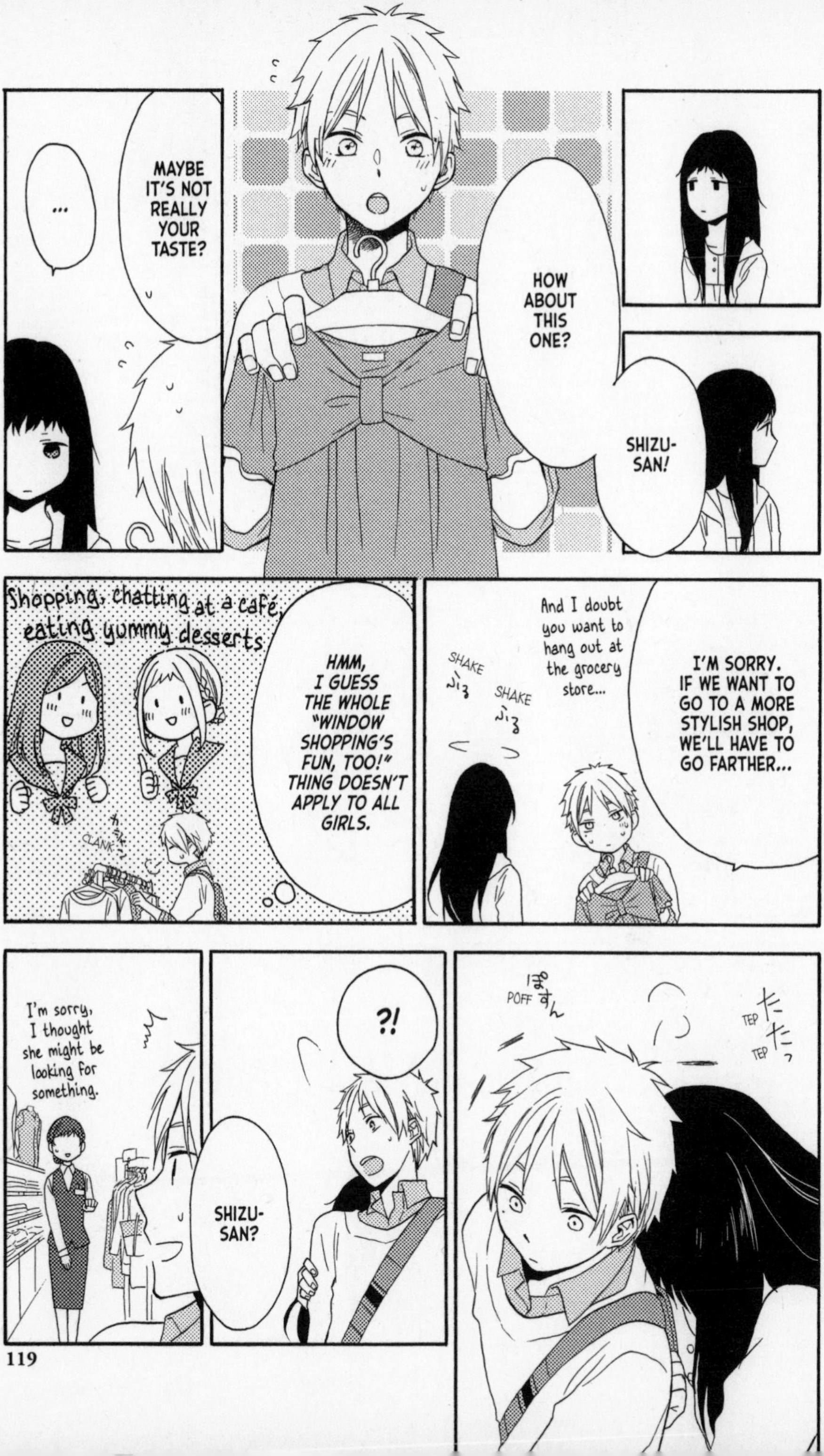
SHIZU-SAN!
HOW ABOUT THIS ONE?
MAYBE IT'S NOT REALLY YOUR TASTE?
...
I'M SORRY. IF WE WANT TO GO TO A MORE STYLISH SHOP, WE'LL HAVE TO GO FARTHER...
And I doubt you want to hang out at the grocery store...
SHAKE
SHAKE
HMM, I GUESS THE WHOLE "WINDOW SHOPPING'S FUN, TOO!" THING DOESN'T APPLY TO ALL GIRLS.
Shopping, chatting at a café, eating yummy desserts
CLANK
TEP
TEP
POFF
?!
SHIZU-SAN?
I'm sorry, I thought she might be looking for something.

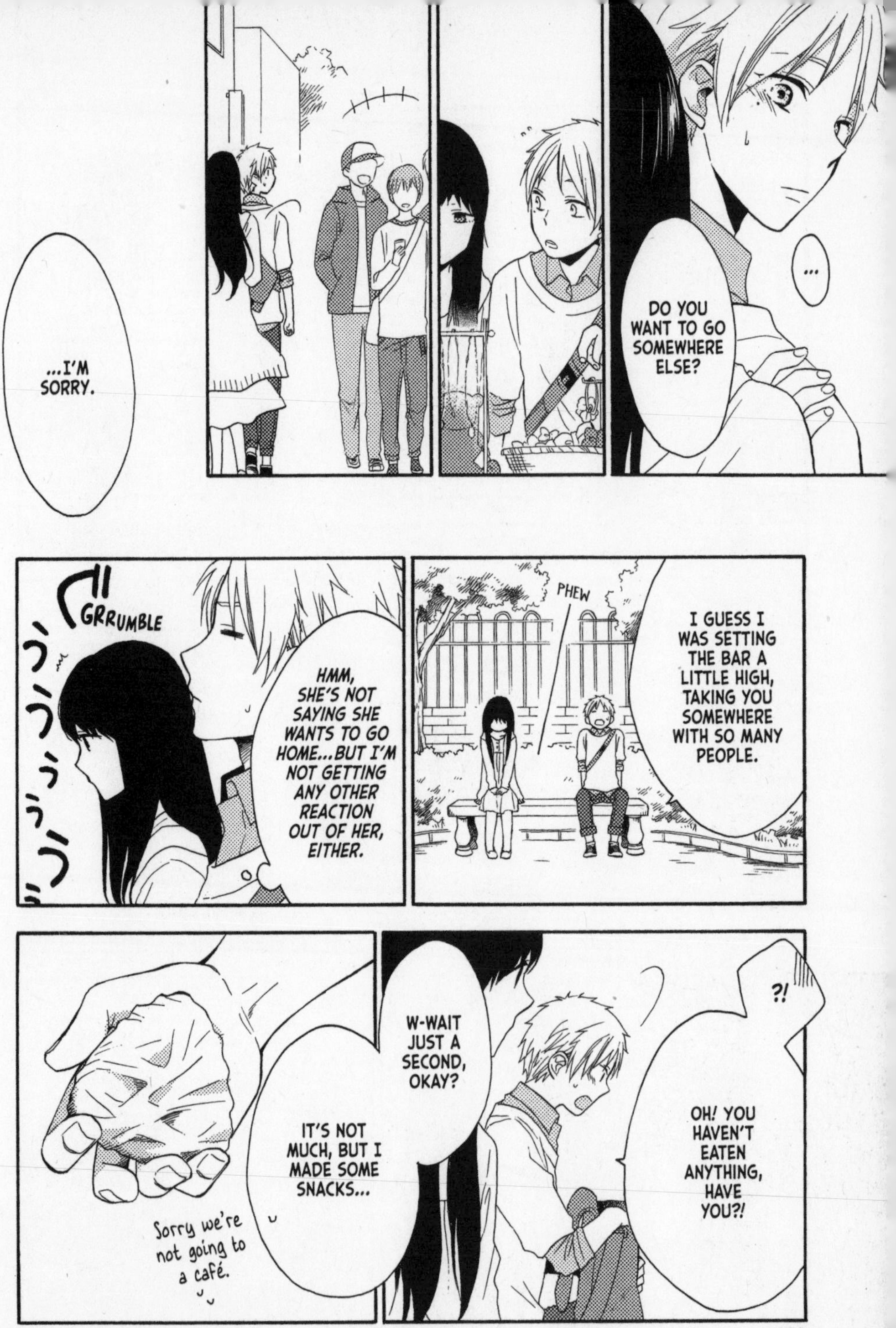
...
DO YOU WANT TO GO SOMEWHERE ELSE?
...I'M SORRY.
PHEW
I GUESS I WAS SETTING THE BAR A LITTLE HIGH, TAKING YOU SOMEWHERE WITH SO MANY PEOPLE.
HMM, SHE'S NOT SAYING SHE WANTS TO GO HOME...BUT I'M NOT GETTING ANY OTHER REACTION OUT OF HER, EITHER.
GRRUMBLE
?!
OH! YOU HAVEN'T EATEN ANYTHING, HAVE YOU?!
W-WAIT JUST A SECOND, OKAY?
IT'S NOT MUCH, BUT I MADE SOME SNACKS...
Sorry we're not going to a café.

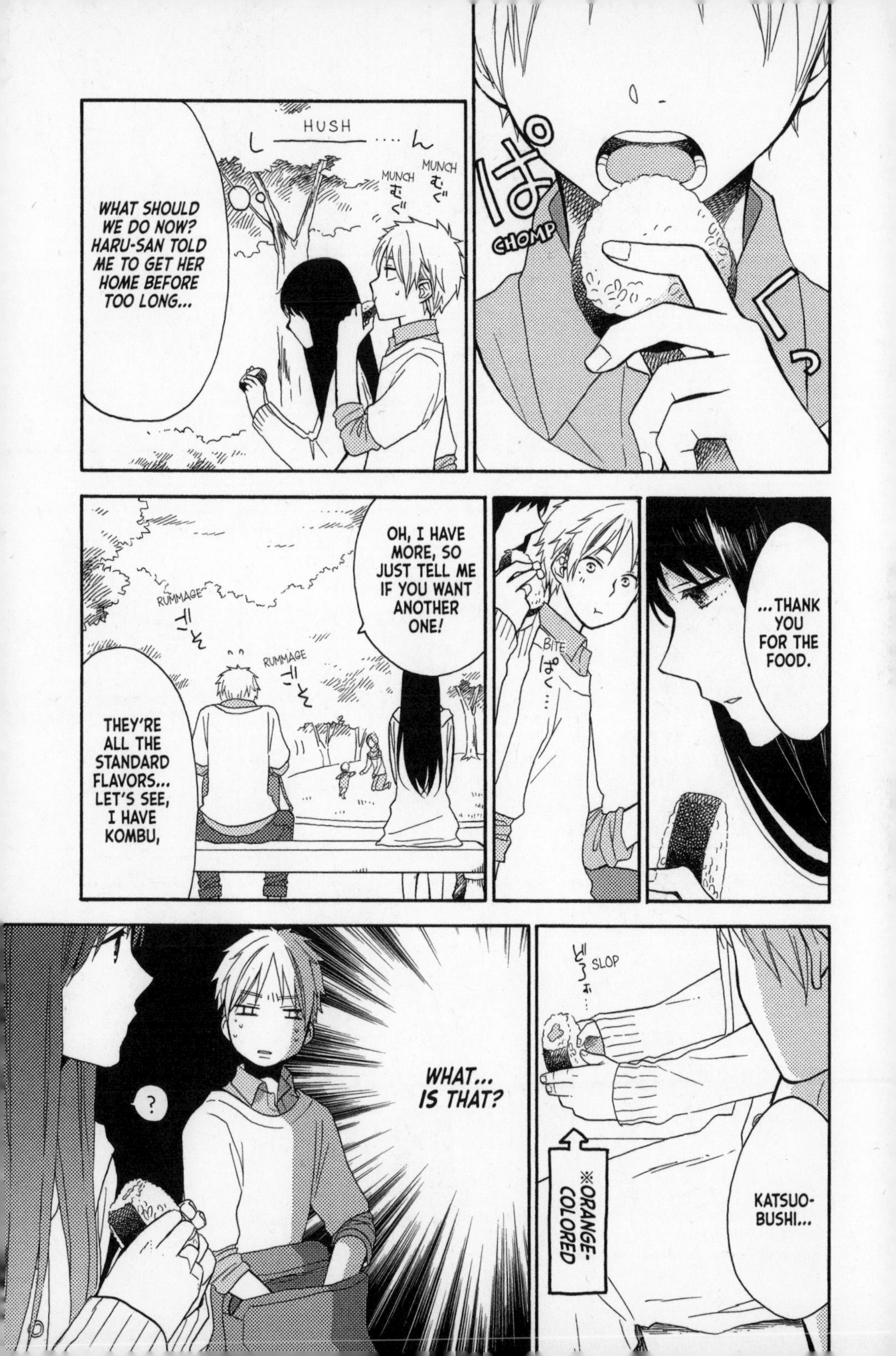
ぱ
CHOMP
HUSH
し——……ん
MUNCH むぐ
MUNCH むぐ
WHAT SHOULD WE DO NOW? HARU-SAN TOLD ME TO GET HER HOME BEFORE TOO LONG...
...THANK YOU FOR THE FOOD.
BITE
OH, I HAVE MORE, SO JUST TELL ME IF YOU WANT ANOTHER ONE!
RUMMAGE
RUMMAGE
THEY'RE ALL THE STANDARD FLAVORS... LET'S SEE, I HAVE KOMBU,
SLOP
※ORANGE-COLORED
KATSUO-BUSHI...
WHAT... IS THAT?
?

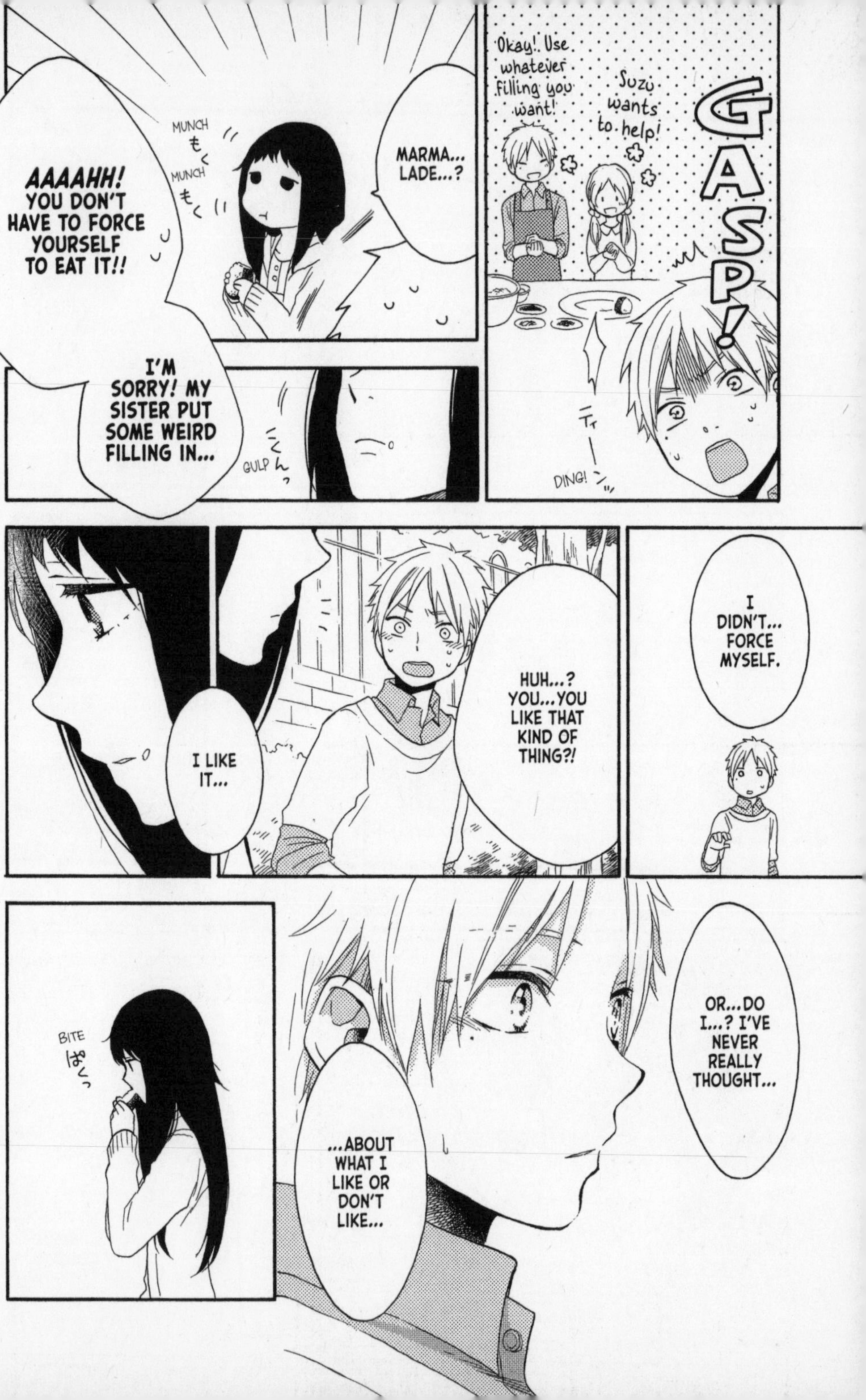
Okay! Use whatever filling you want!
Suzu wants to help!
GASP!
DING!
MARMA... LADE...?
MUNCH もく
MUNCH もく
AAAAHH! YOU DON'T HAVE TO FORCE YOURSELF TO EAT IT!!
I'M SORRY! MY SISTER PUT SOME WEIRD FILLING IN...
GULP ごくん
I DIDN'T... FORCE MYSELF.
HUH...? YOU...YOU LIKE THAT KIND OF THING?!
I LIKE IT...
OR...DO I...? I'VE NEVER REALLY THOUGHT...
...ABOUT WHAT I LIKE OR DON'T LIKE...
BITE ぱくっ

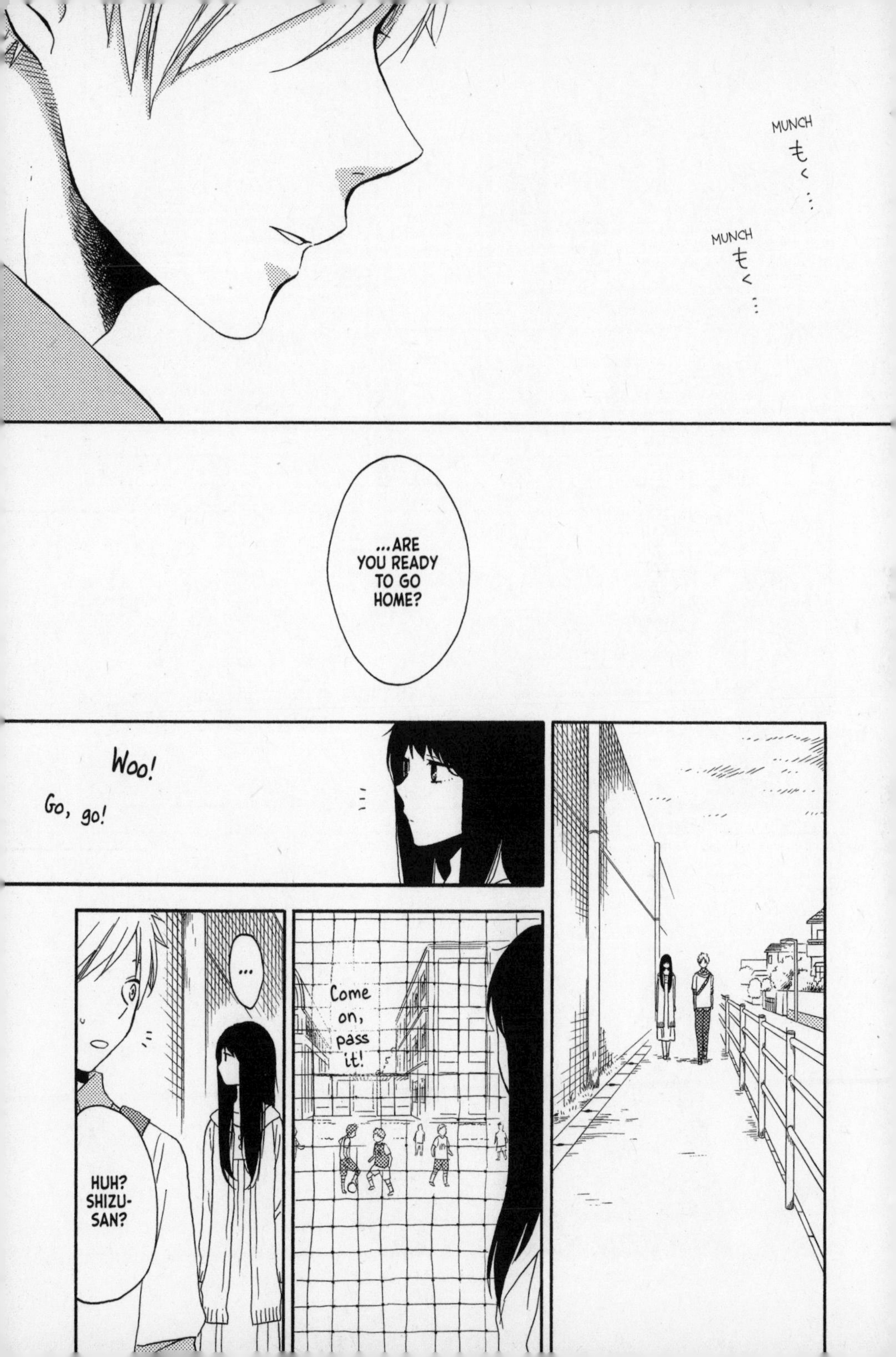
MUNCH
もく…
MUNCH
もく…
...ARE YOU READY TO GO HOME?
Woo!
Go, go!
Come on, pass it!
...
HUH? SHIZU-SAN?

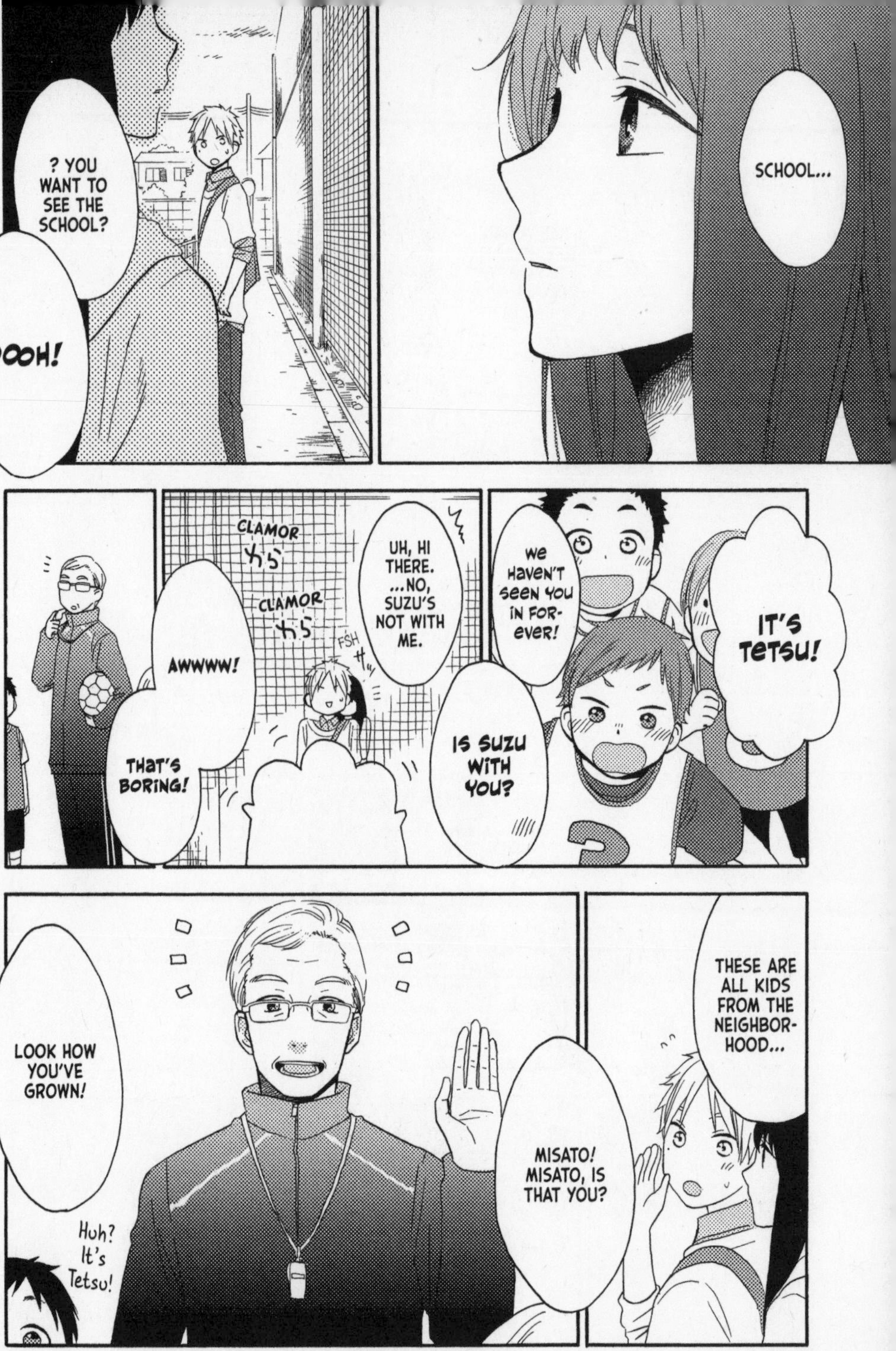
SCHOOL...
? YOU WANT TO SEE THE SCHOOL?
OOOH!
IT'S TETSU!
WE HAVEN'T SEEN YOU IN FOR-EVER!
IS SUZU WITH YOU?
CLAMOR
CLAMOR
UH, HI THERE. ...NO, SUZU'S NOT WITH ME.
FSH
AWWWW!
THAT'S BORING!
THESE ARE ALL KIDS FROM THE NEIGHBOR-HOOD...
MISATO! MISATO, IS THAT YOU?
LOOK HOW YOU'VE GROWN!
Huh? It's Tetsu!

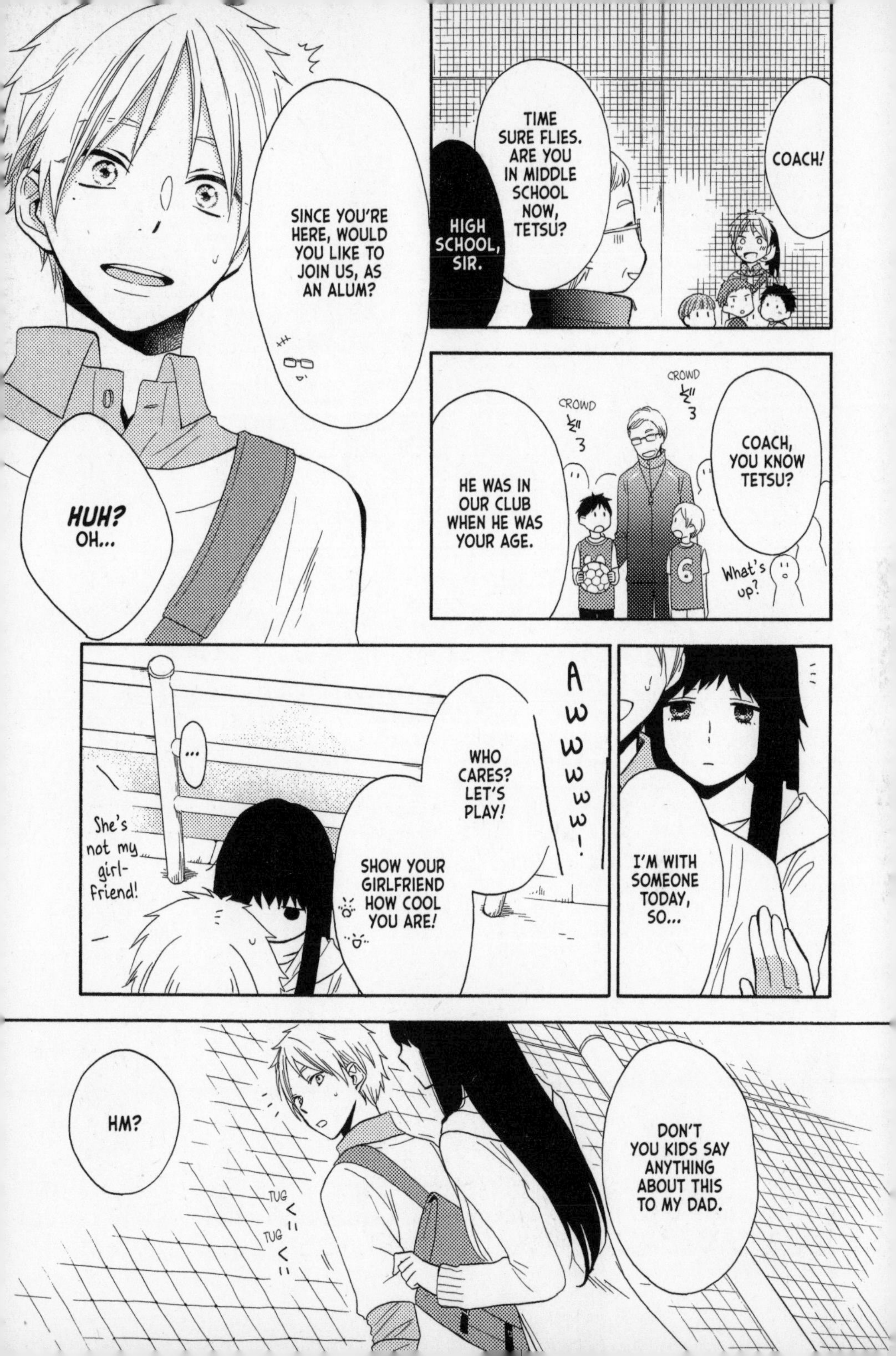
COACH!
TIME SURE FLIES. ARE YOU IN MIDDLE SCHOOL NOW, TETSU?
HIGH SCHOOL, SIR.
COACH, YOU KNOW TETSU?
CROWD
CROWD
HE WAS IN OUR CLUB WHEN HE WAS YOUR AGE.
What's up?
SINCE YOU'RE HERE, WOULD YOU LIKE TO JOIN US, AS AN ALUM?
HUH? OH...
I'M WITH SOMEONE TODAY, SO...
AWWWWW!
WHO CARES? LET'S PLAY!
SHOW YOUR GIRLFRIEND HOW COOL YOU ARE!
...
She's not my girl-friend!
DON'T YOU KIDS SAY ANYTHING ABOUT THIS TO MY DAD.
TUG
TUG
HM?

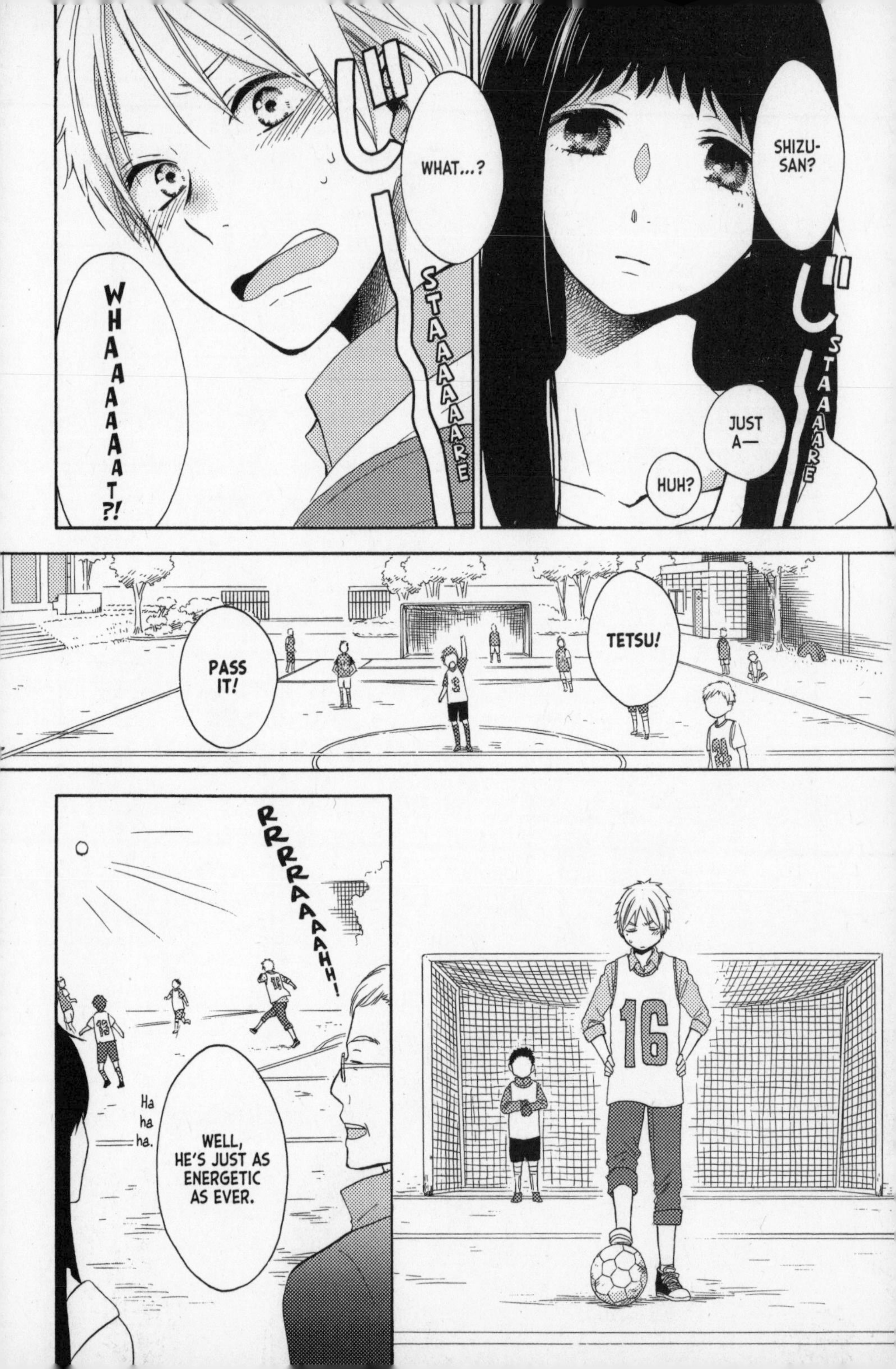
SHIZU-SAN?
じー
STAAAARE
JUST A—
HUH?
WHAT...?
じー
STAAAAARE
WHAAAAAAT?!
TETSU!
PASS IT!
RRRRAAAAHH!
WELL, HE'S JUST AS ENERGETIC AS EVER.
Ha ha ha.

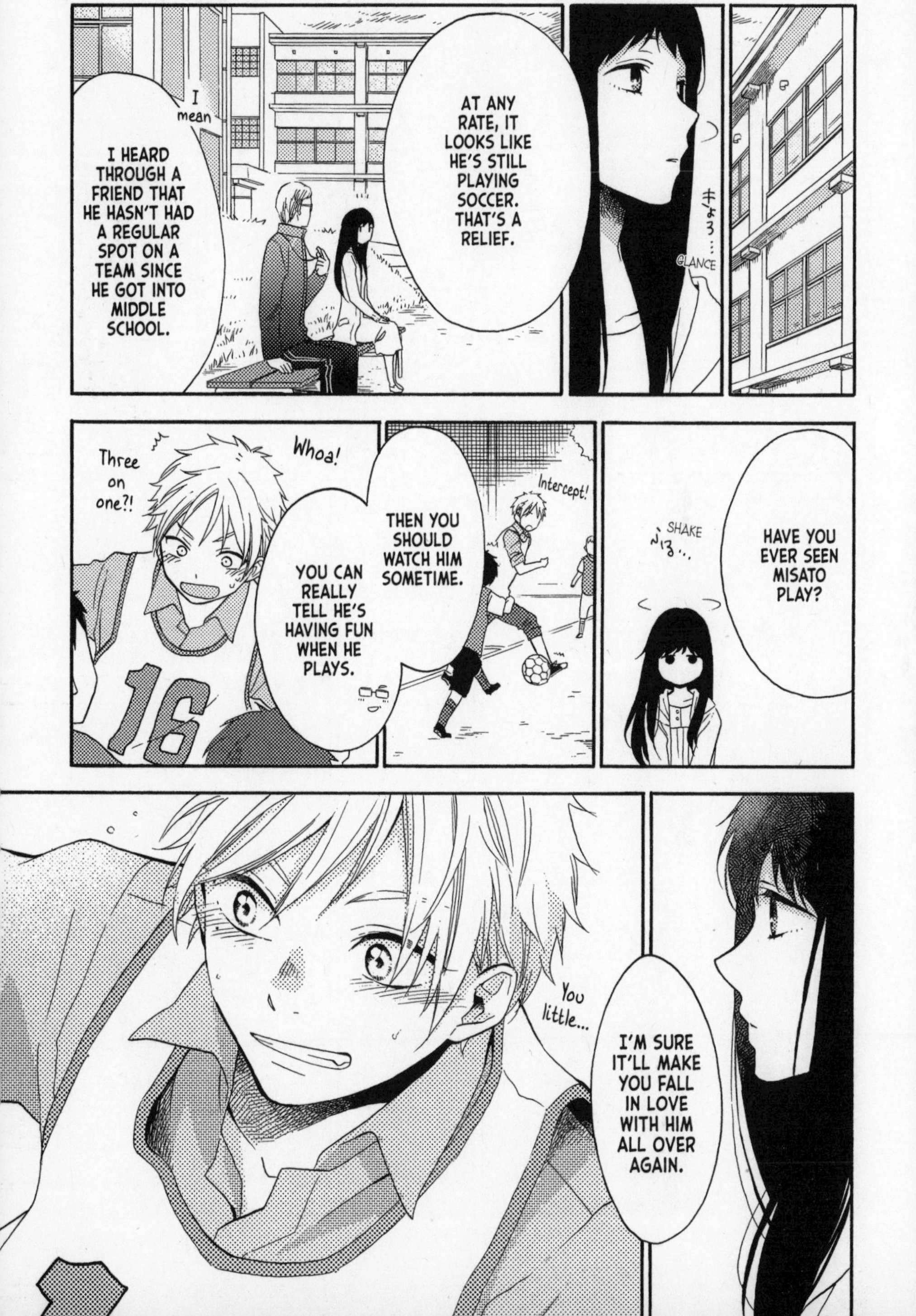
キョロ…
GLANCE
AT ANY RATE, IT LOOKS LIKE HE'S STILL PLAYING SOCCER. THAT'S A RELIEF.
I mean
I HEARD THROUGH A FRIEND THAT HE HASN'T HAD A REGULAR SPOT ON A TEAM SINCE HE GOT INTO MIDDLE SCHOOL.
HAVE YOU EVER SEEN MISATO PLAY?
SHAKE
Intercept!
THEN YOU SHOULD WATCH HIM SOMETIME.
YOU CAN REALLY TELL HE'S HAVING FUN WHEN HE PLAYS.
Whoa!
Three on one?!
I'M SURE IT'LL MAKE YOU FALL IN LOVE WITH HIM ALL OVER AGAIN.
You little...

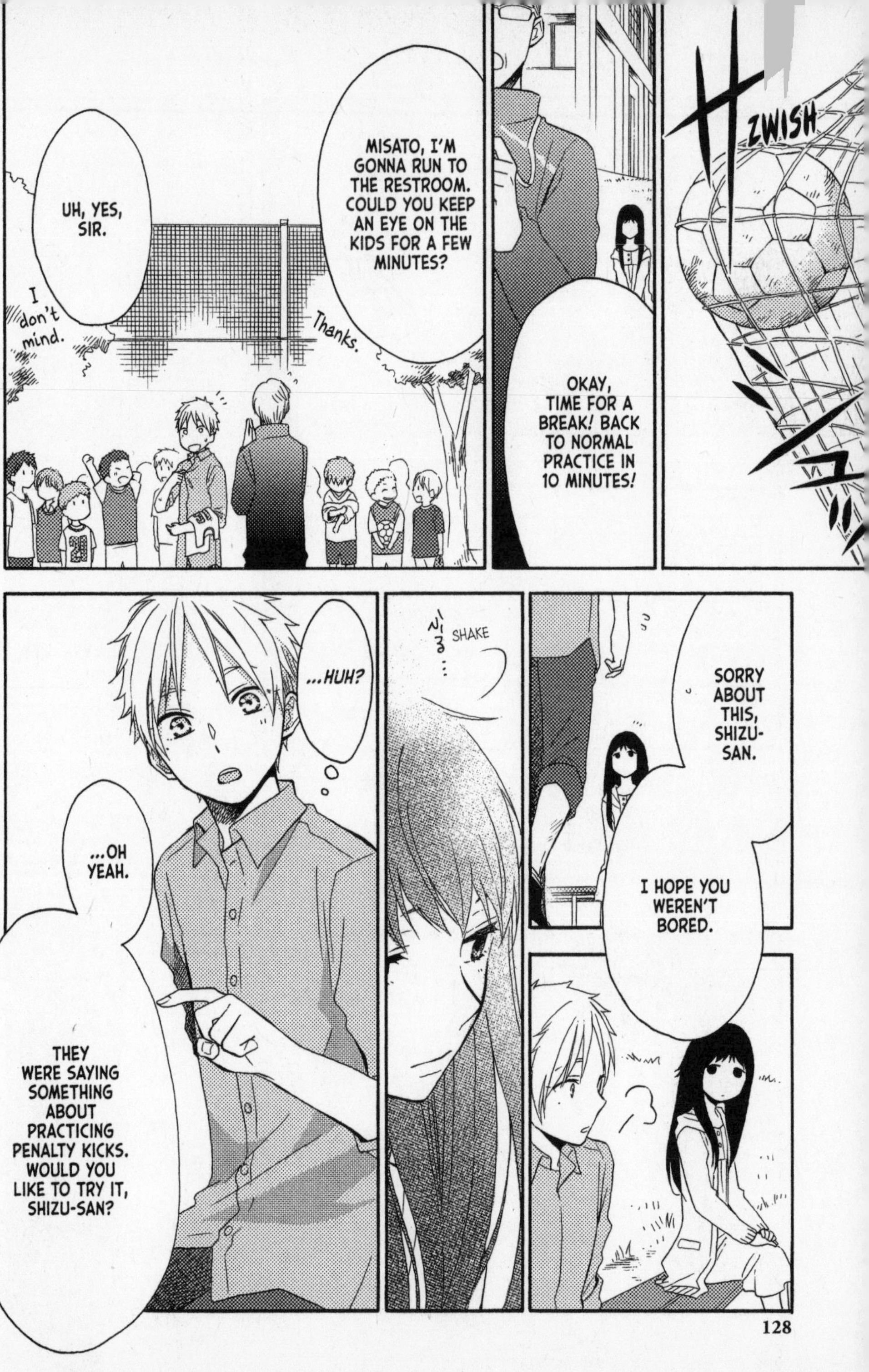
ZWISH
OKAY, TIME FOR A BREAK! BACK TO NORMAL PRACTICE IN 10 MINUTES!
MISATO, I'M GONNA RUN TO THE RESTROOM. COULD YOU KEEP AN EYE ON THE KIDS FOR A FEW MINUTES?
Thanks.
UH, YES, SIR.
I don't mind.
SORRY ABOUT THIS, SHIZU-SAN.
I HOPE YOU WEREN'T BORED.
SHAKE
...HUH?
...OH YEAH.
THEY WERE SAYING SOMETHING ABOUT PRACTICING PENALTY KICKS. WOULD YOU LIKE TO TRY IT, SHIZU-SAN?

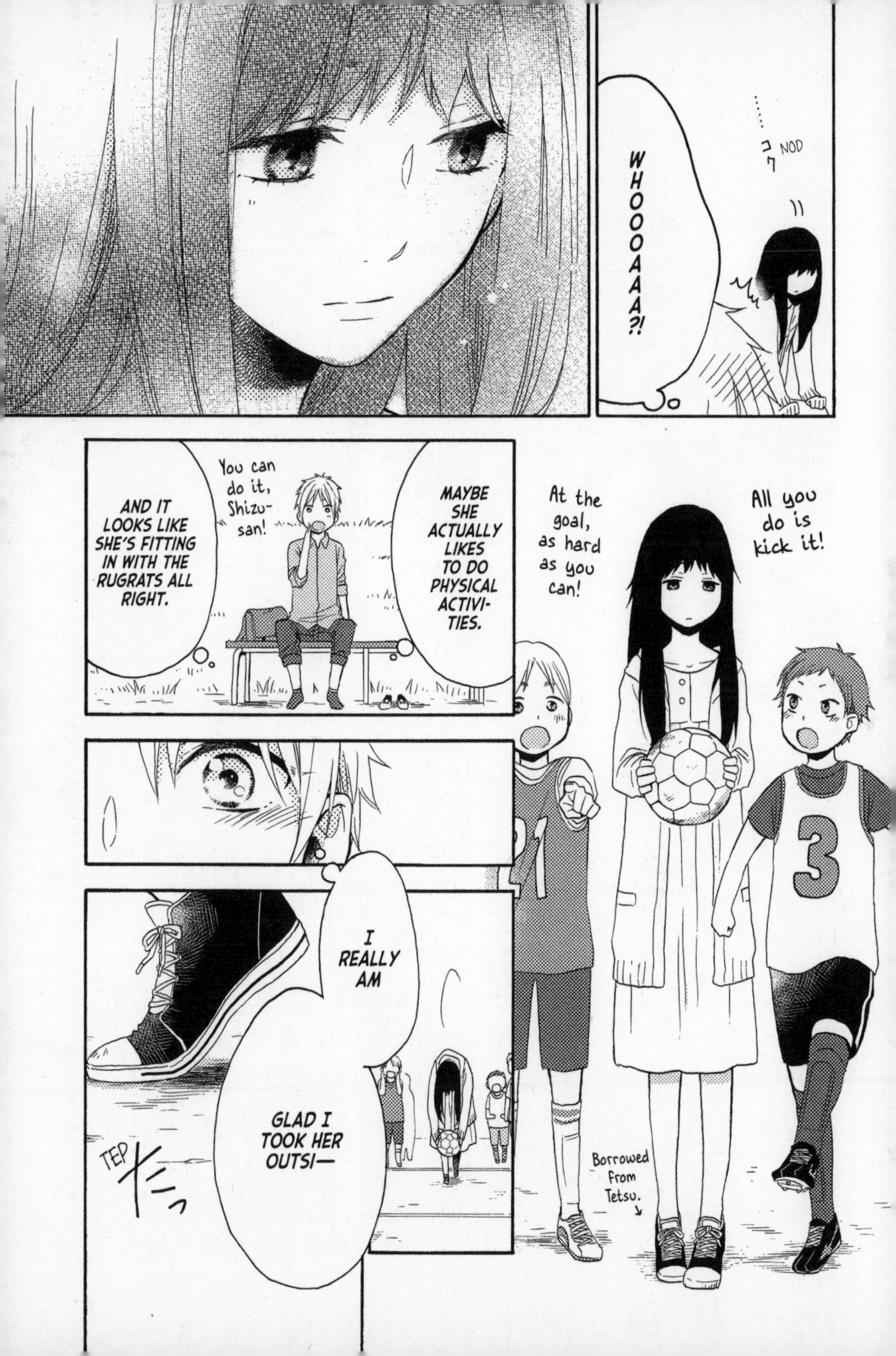

……
NOD
WHOOOAAA?!
All you do is kick it!
At the goal, as hard as you can!
Borrowed from Tetsu.
MAYBE SHE ACTUALLY LIKES TO DO PHYSICAL ACTIVITIES.
You can do it, Shizu-san!
AND IT LOOKS LIKE SHE'S FITTING IN WITH THE RUGRATS ALL RIGHT.
I REALLY AM
GLAD I TOOK HER OUTSI—
TEP

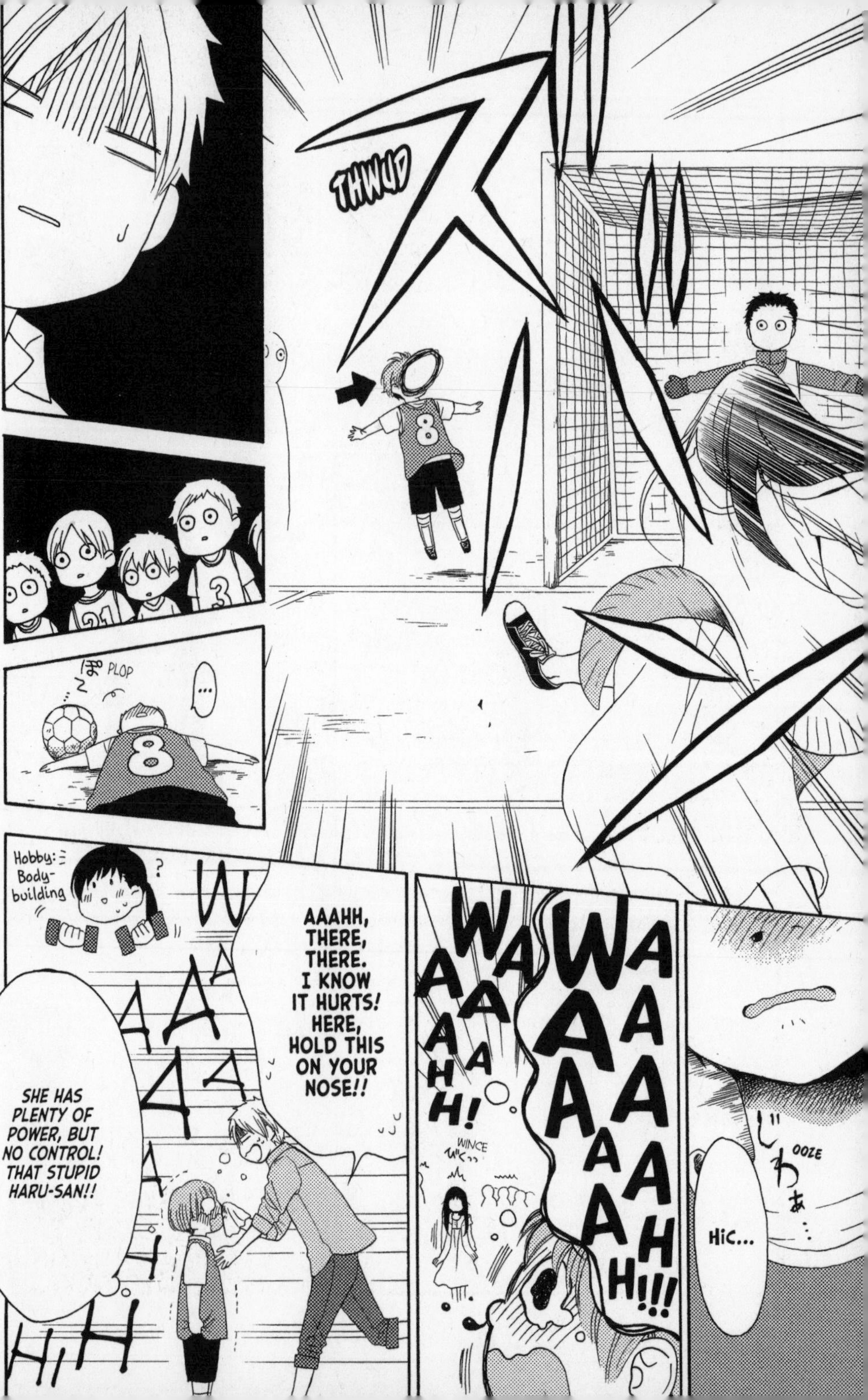
THWUD
ぽ PLOP
...
HIC...
じわぁ... OOZE
WAAAAAAAAAAH!!!
WAAAAAAAH!
びくっ WINCE
AAAHH, THERE, THERE. I KNOW IT HURTS! HERE, HOLD THIS ON YOUR NOSE!!
WAAAAAHH
SHE HAS PLENTY OF POWER, BUT NO CONTROL! THAT STUPID HARU-SAN!!
Hobby: Body-building
?

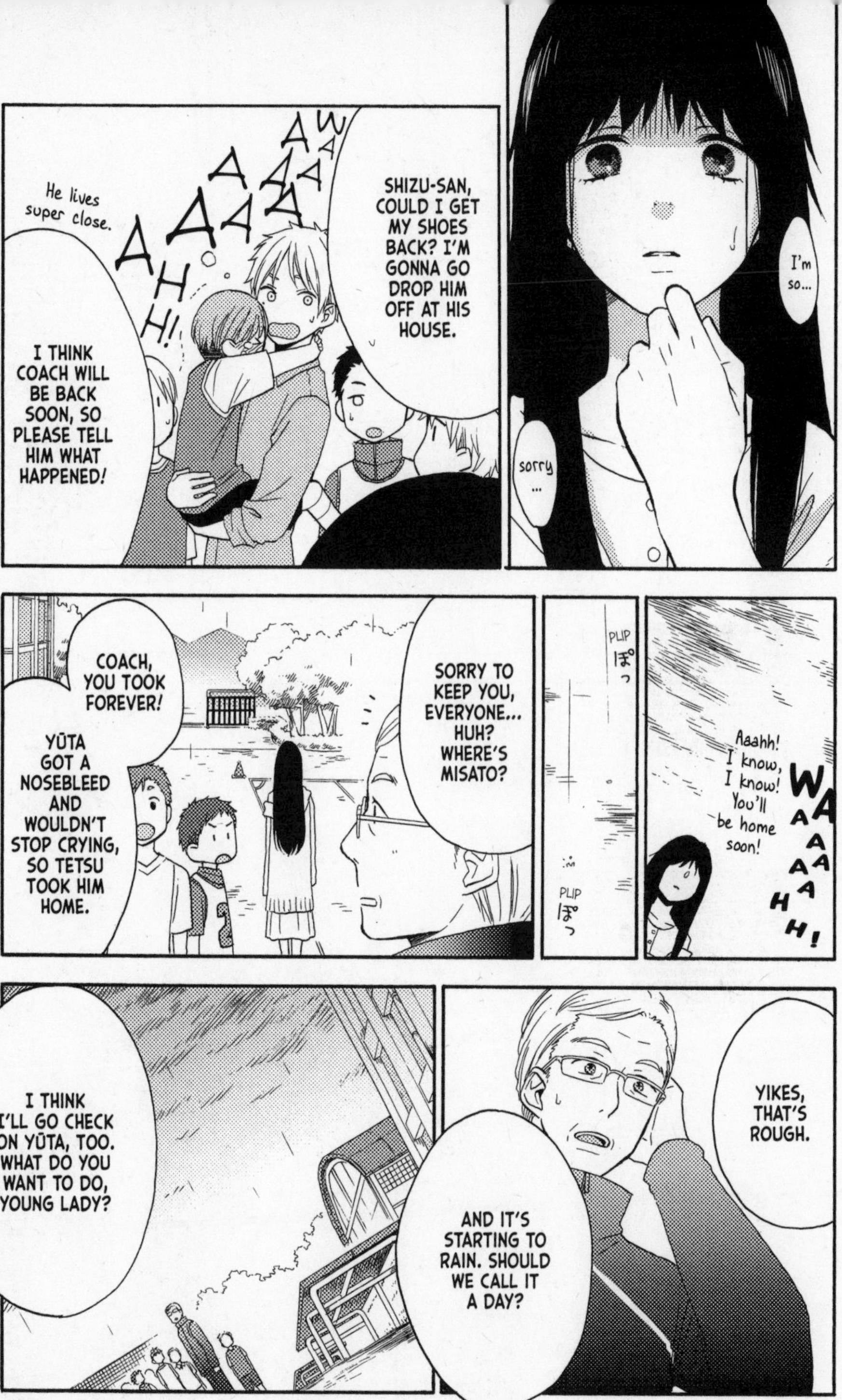
I'm so...
sorry...
SHIZU-SAN, COULD I GET MY SHOES BACK? I'M GONNA GO DROP HIM OFF AT HIS HOUSE.
WAAAAAAAAHH!
He lives super close.
I THINK COACH WILL BE BACK SOON, SO PLEASE TELL HIM WHAT HAPPENED!
Aaahh! I know, I know! You'll be home soon!
WAAAAAAHH!
PLIP ぽっ
PLIP ぽっ
SORRY TO KEEP YOU, EVERYONE... HUH? WHERE'S MISATO?
COACH, YOU TOOK FOREVER!
YŪTA GOT A NOSEBLEED AND WOULDN'T STOP CRYING, SO TETSU TOOK HIM HOME.
YIKES, THAT'S ROUGH.
AND IT'S STARTING TO RAIN. SHOULD WE CALL IT A DAY?
I THINK I'LL GO CHECK ON YŪTA, TOO. WHAT DO YOU WANT TO DO, YOUNG LADY?

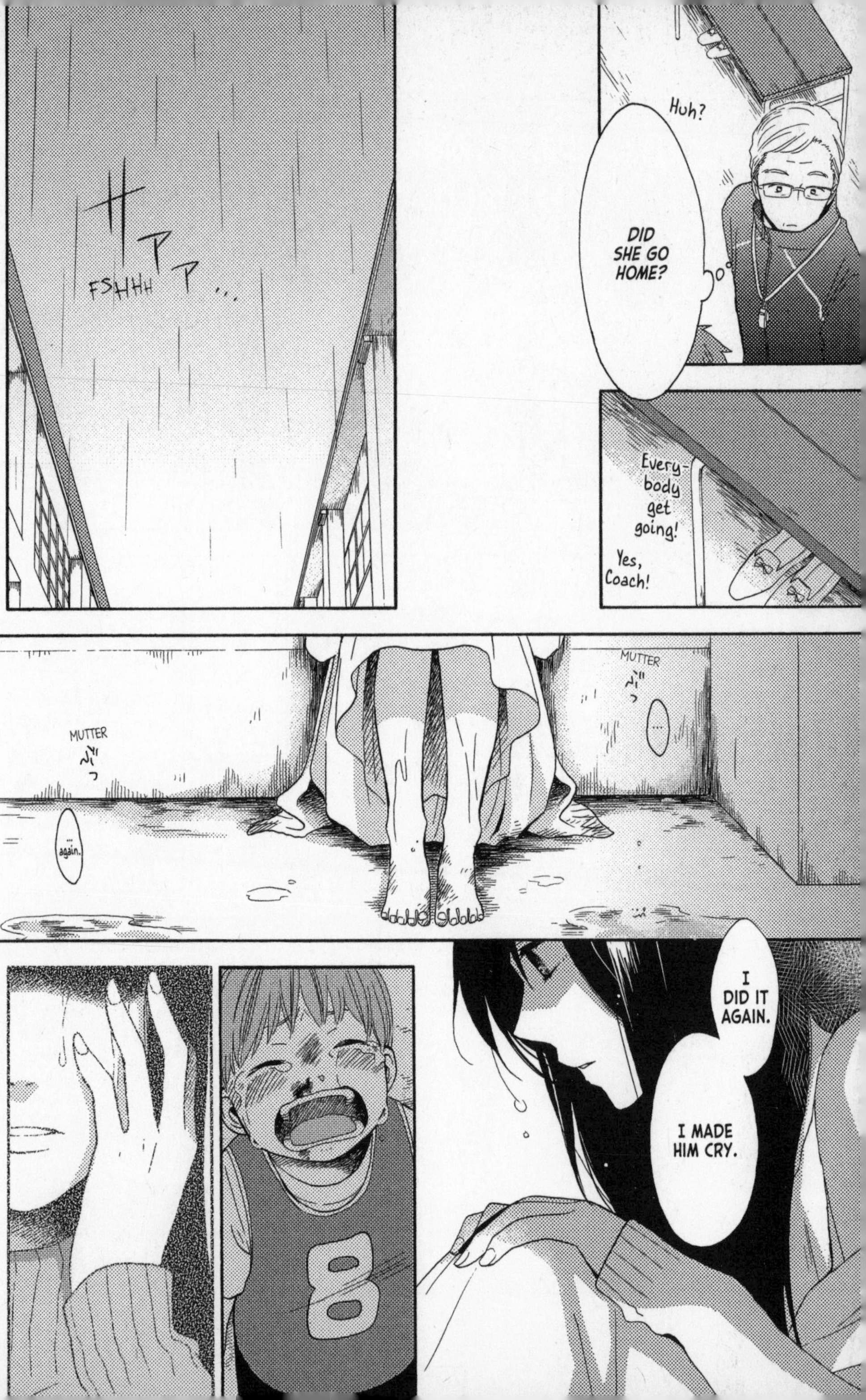
Huh?
DID SHE GO HOME?
Every-body get going!
Yes, Coach!
FSHHH...
MUTTER
...
MUTTER
... again.
I DID IT AGAIN.
I MADE HIM CRY.

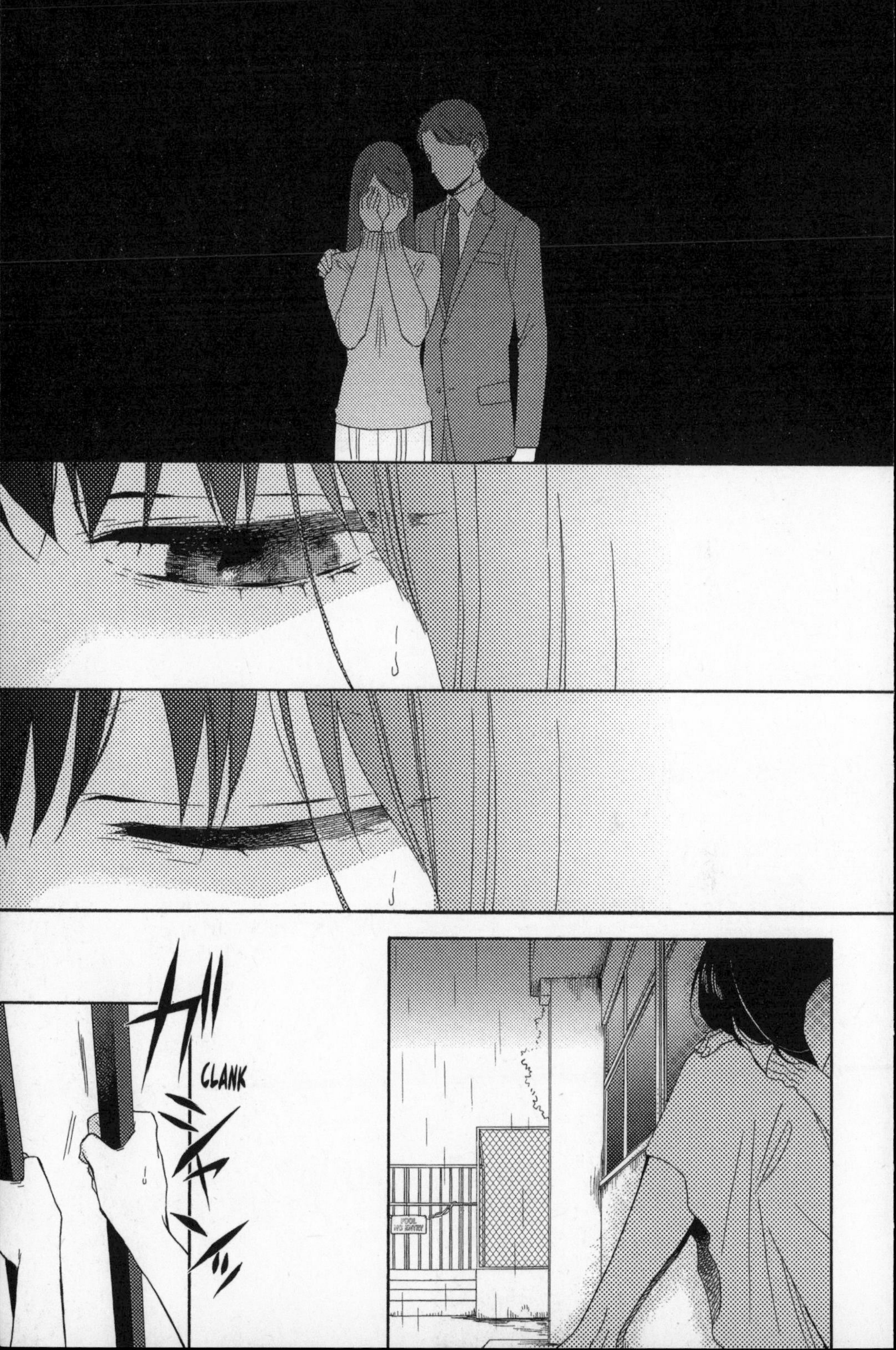
POOL
NO ENTRY
CLANK

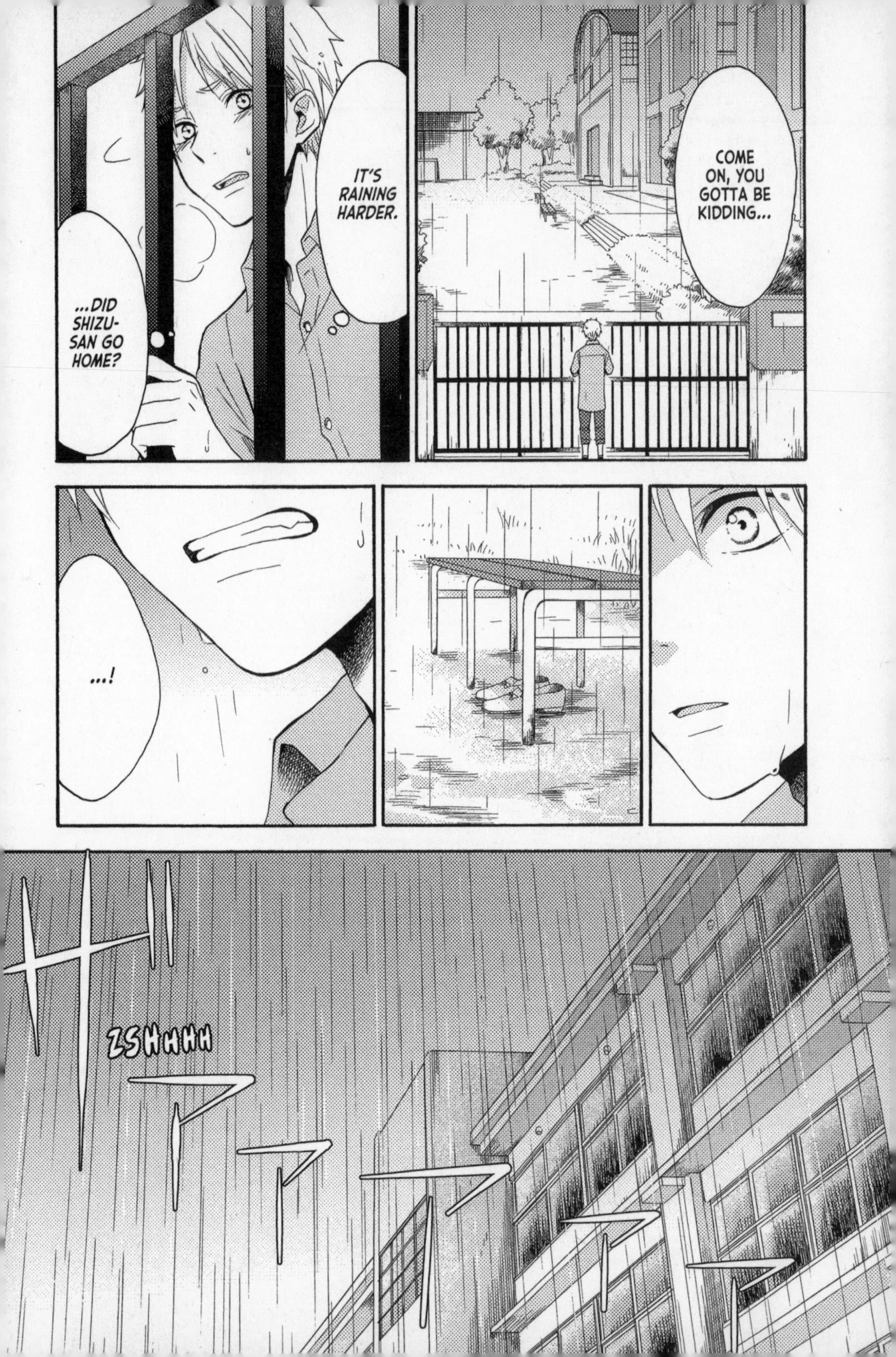
COME ON, YOU GOTTA BE KIDDING...
IT'S RAINING HARDER.
...DID SHIZU-SAN GO HOME?
...!
ZSHHHH

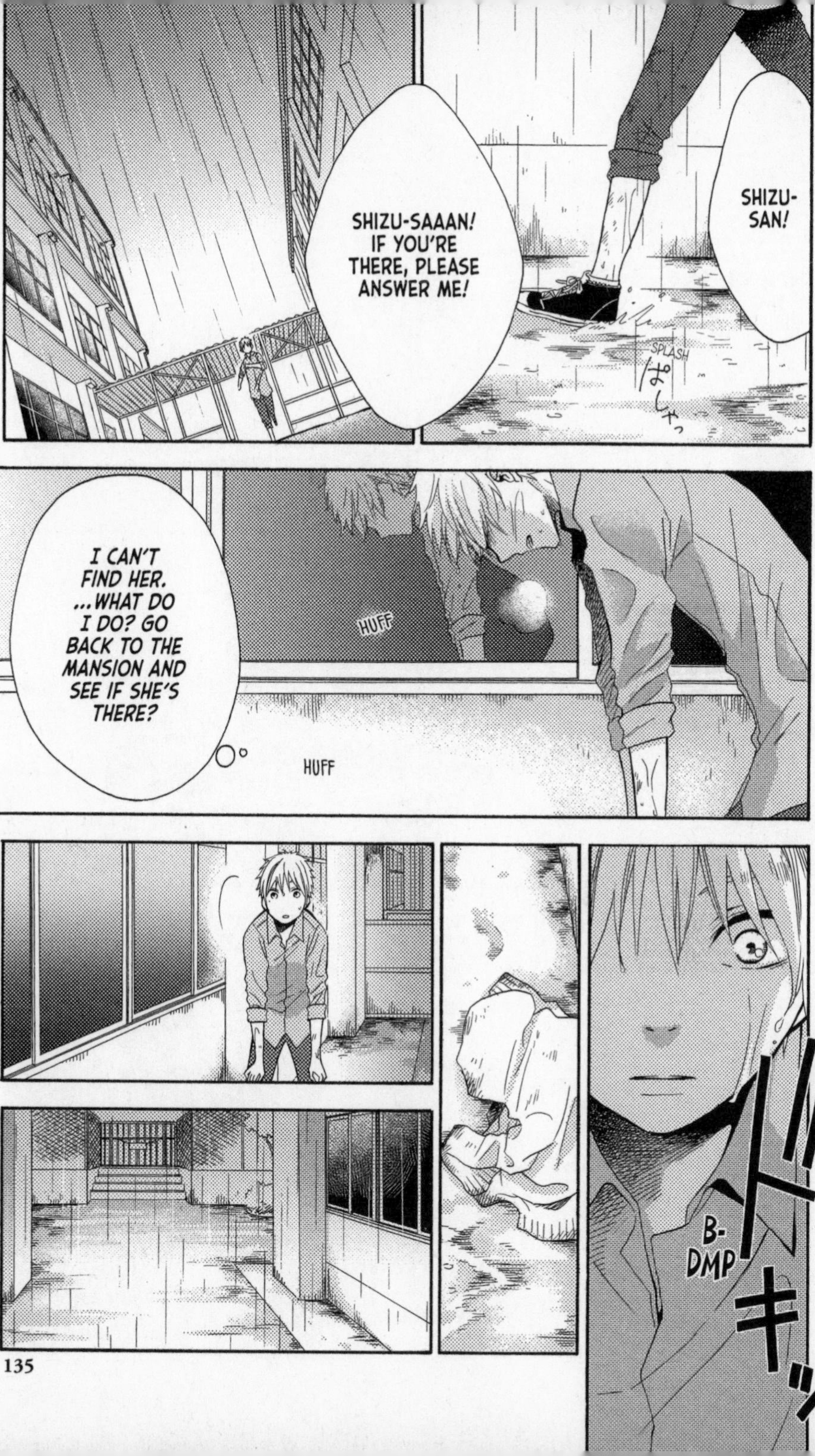
SHIZU-SAN!
SPLASH
ぱしゃっ
SHIZU-SAAAN! IF YOU'RE THERE, PLEASE ANSWER ME!
I CAN'T FIND HER. ...WHAT DO I DO? GO BACK TO THE MANSION AND SEE IF SHE'S THERE?
HUFF
HUFF
B-DMP
ドキッ

SHIZU-SAN, ARE YOU ALL RIGHT?!

CLANK

SHIZU-SAN!!

CLANK

GASP!

POOL
O ENTRY

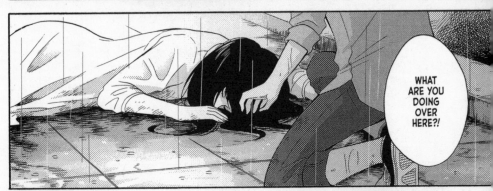

WHAT ARE YOU DOING OVER HERE?!

URGH... ANYWAY... I HAVE TO GET HER OUT OF THE RAIN!

SHIZU-SAN!

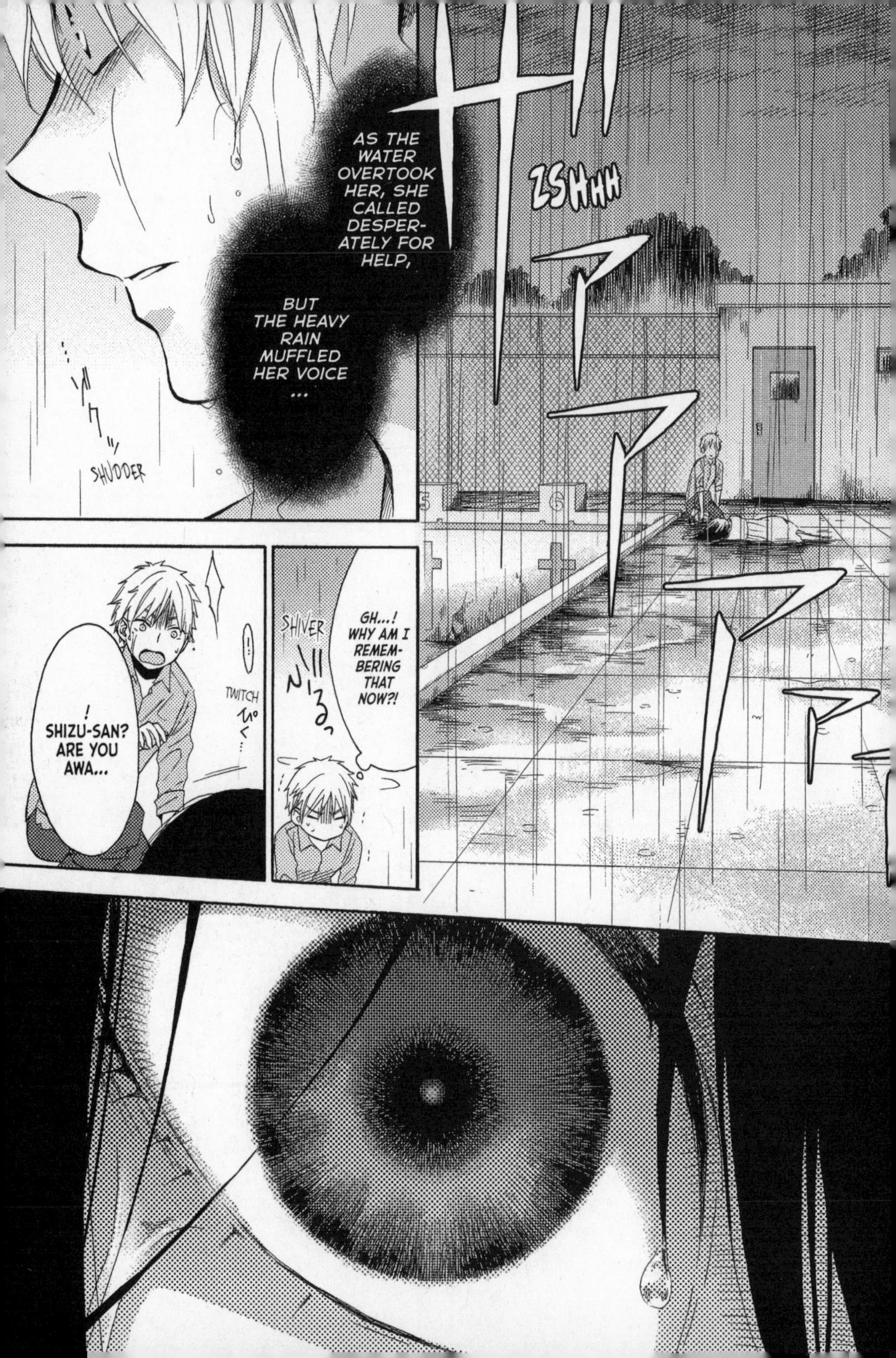
ZSHHH
AS THE WATER OVERTOOK HER, SHE CALLED DESPERATELY FOR HELP,
BUT THE HEAVY RAIN MUFFLED HER VOICE ...
SHUDDER
SHIVER
GH...! WHY AM I REMEMBERING THAT NOW?!
TWITCH
!
! SHIZU-SAN? ARE YOU AWA...

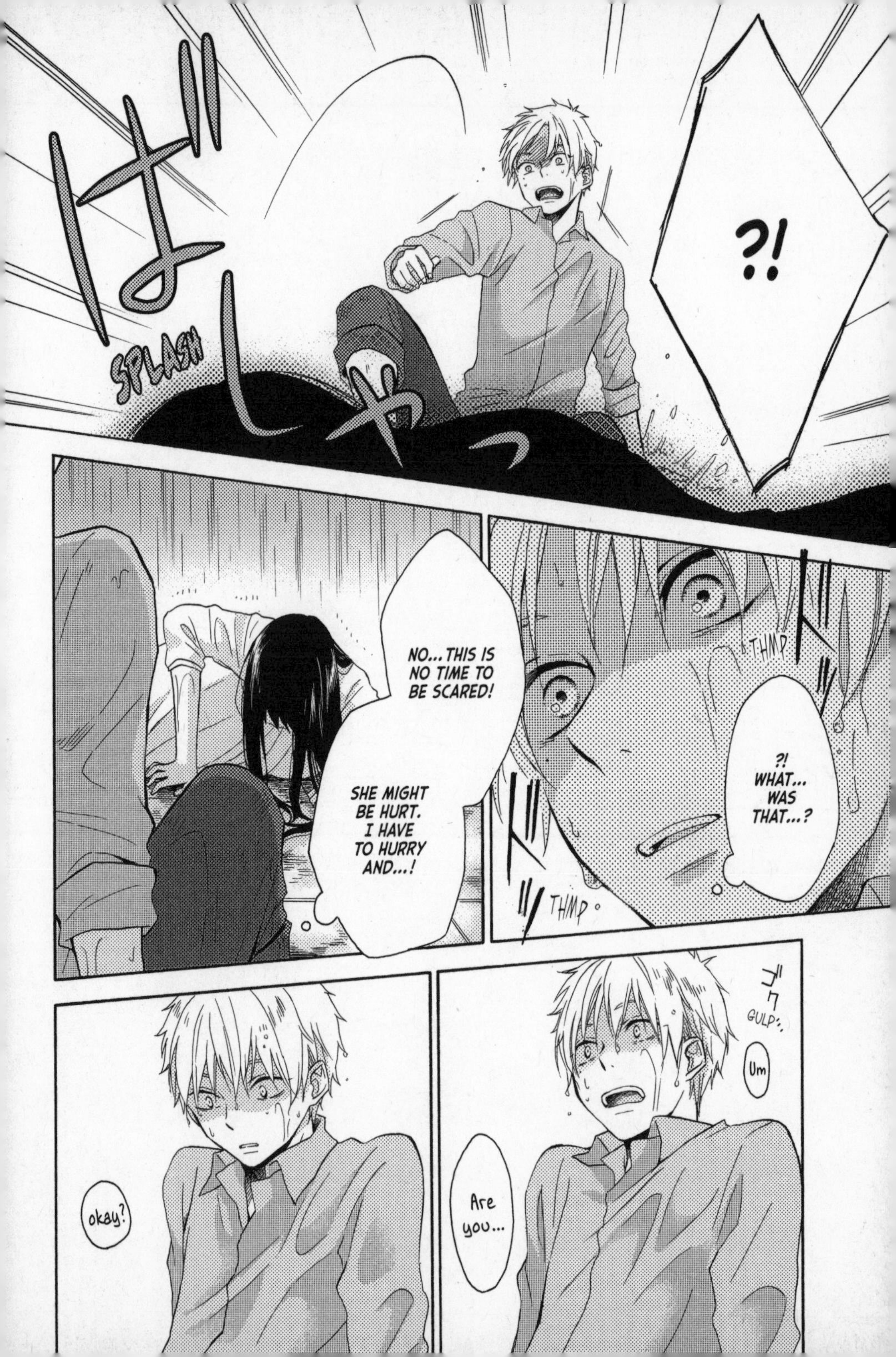
?!
ばしゃっ
SPLASH
THMP
?! WHAT... WAS THAT...?
THMP
NO...THIS IS NO TIME TO BE SCARED!
SHE MIGHT BE HURT. I HAVE TO HURRY AND...!
ゴク
GULP
Um
Are you...
okay?

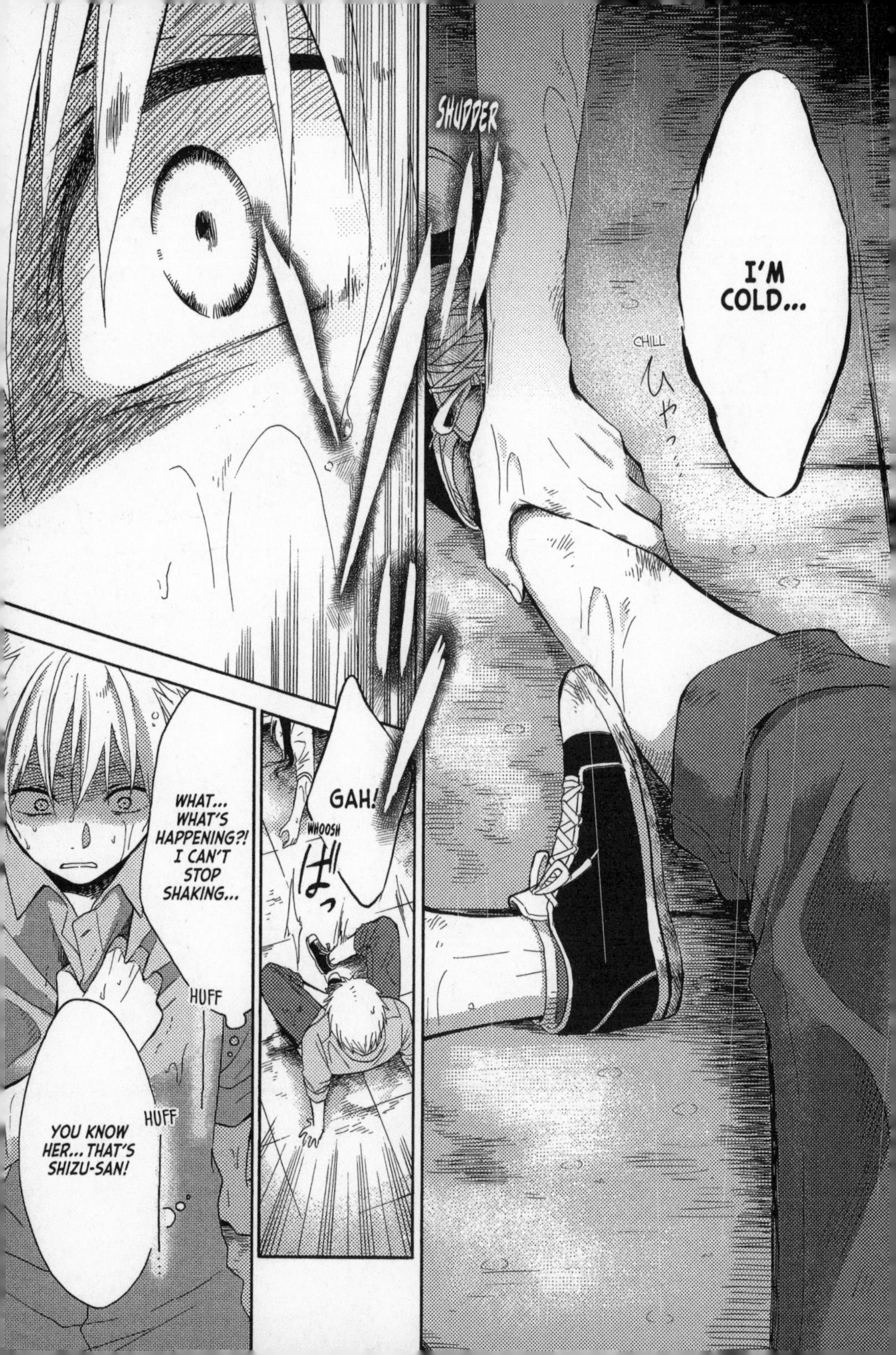
I'M COLD...
CHILL
ひやっ…
SHUDDER
GAH!
WHOOSH
ぱっ
WHAT... WHAT'S HAPPENING?! I CAN'T STOP SHAKING...
HUFF
HUFF
YOU KNOW HER... THAT'S SHIZU-SAN!

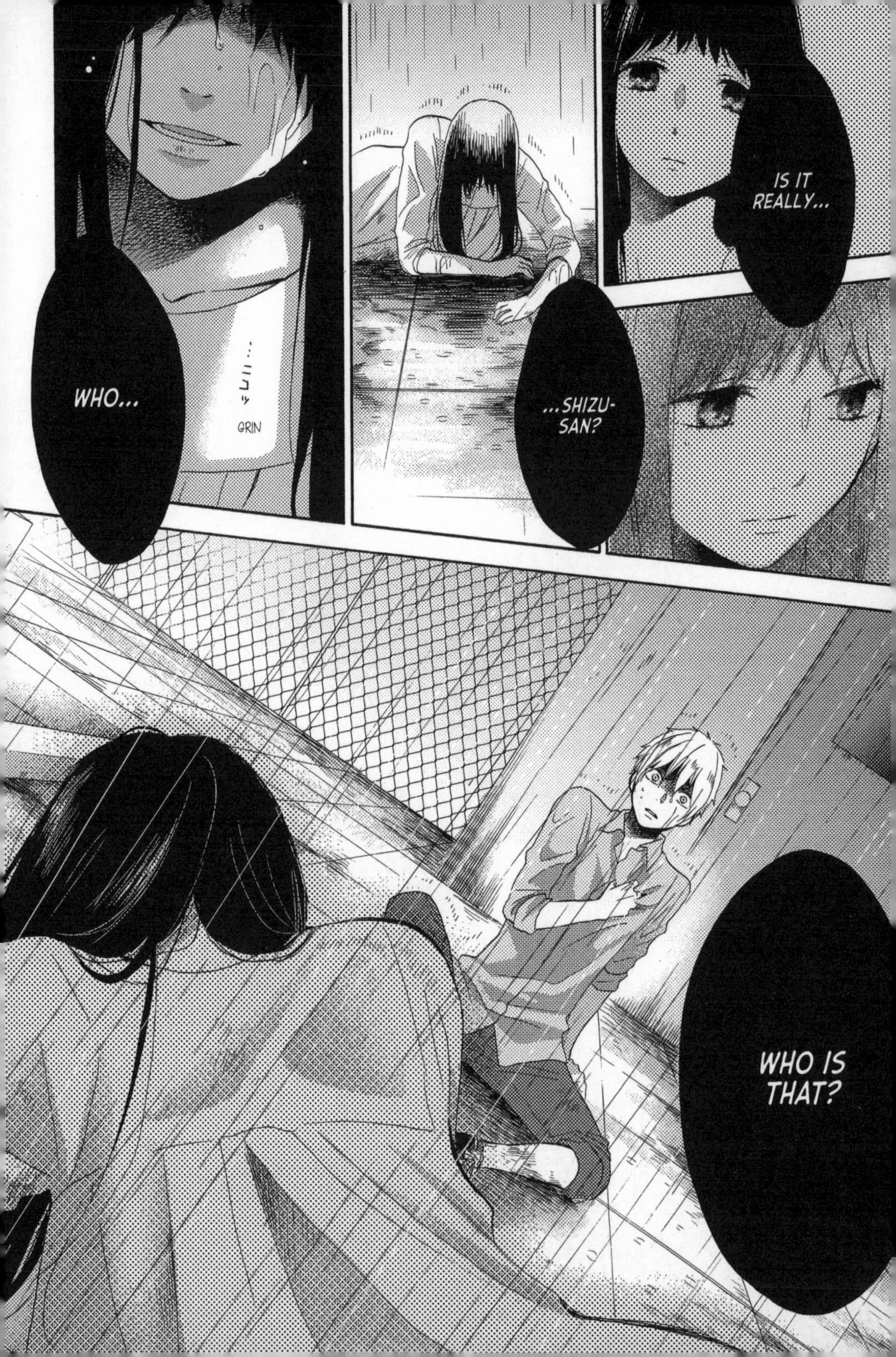
IS IT REALLY...
...SHIZU-SAN?
WHO...
GRIN
WHO IS THAT?

CHAPTER 4

SCALES

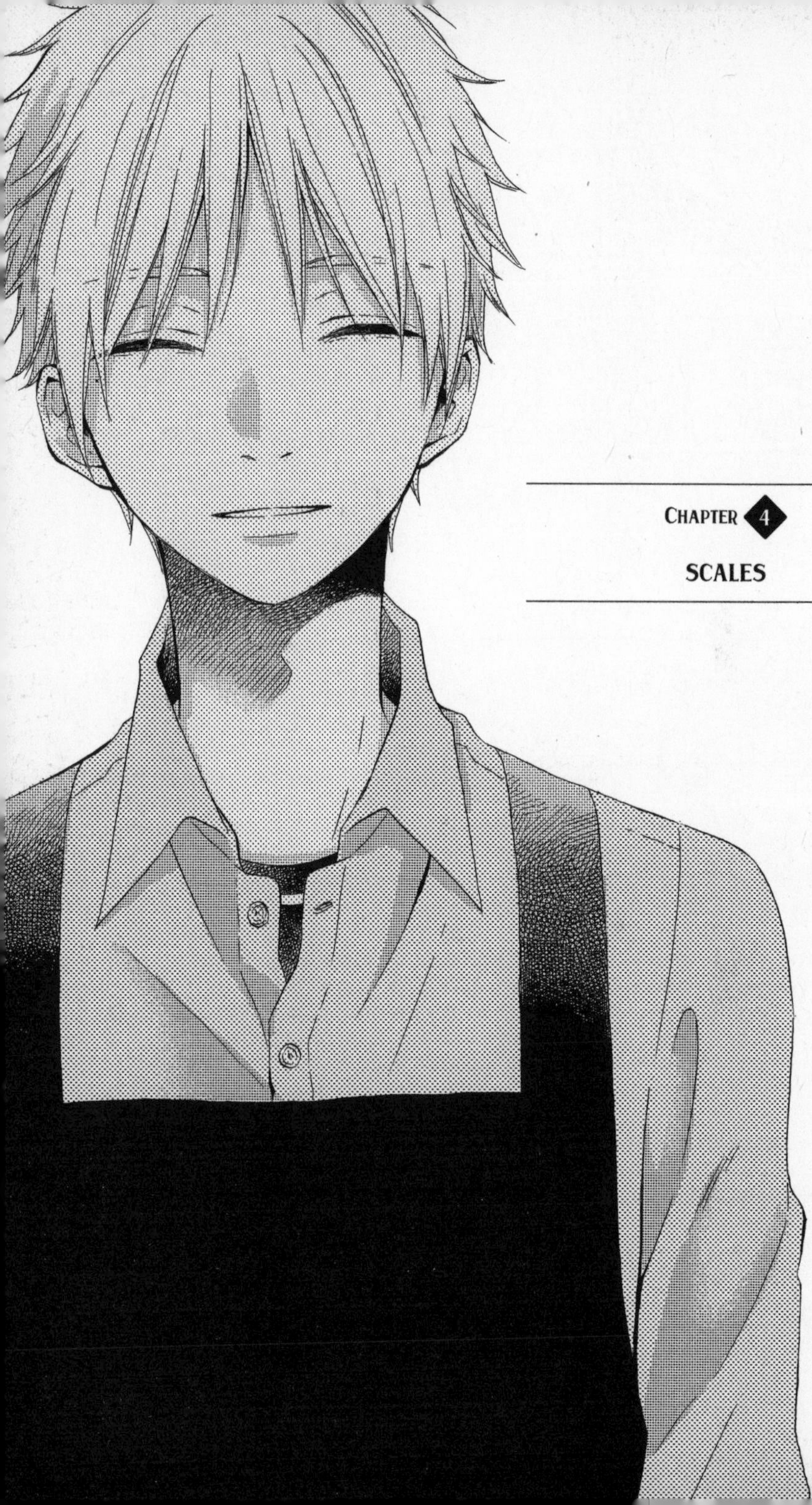

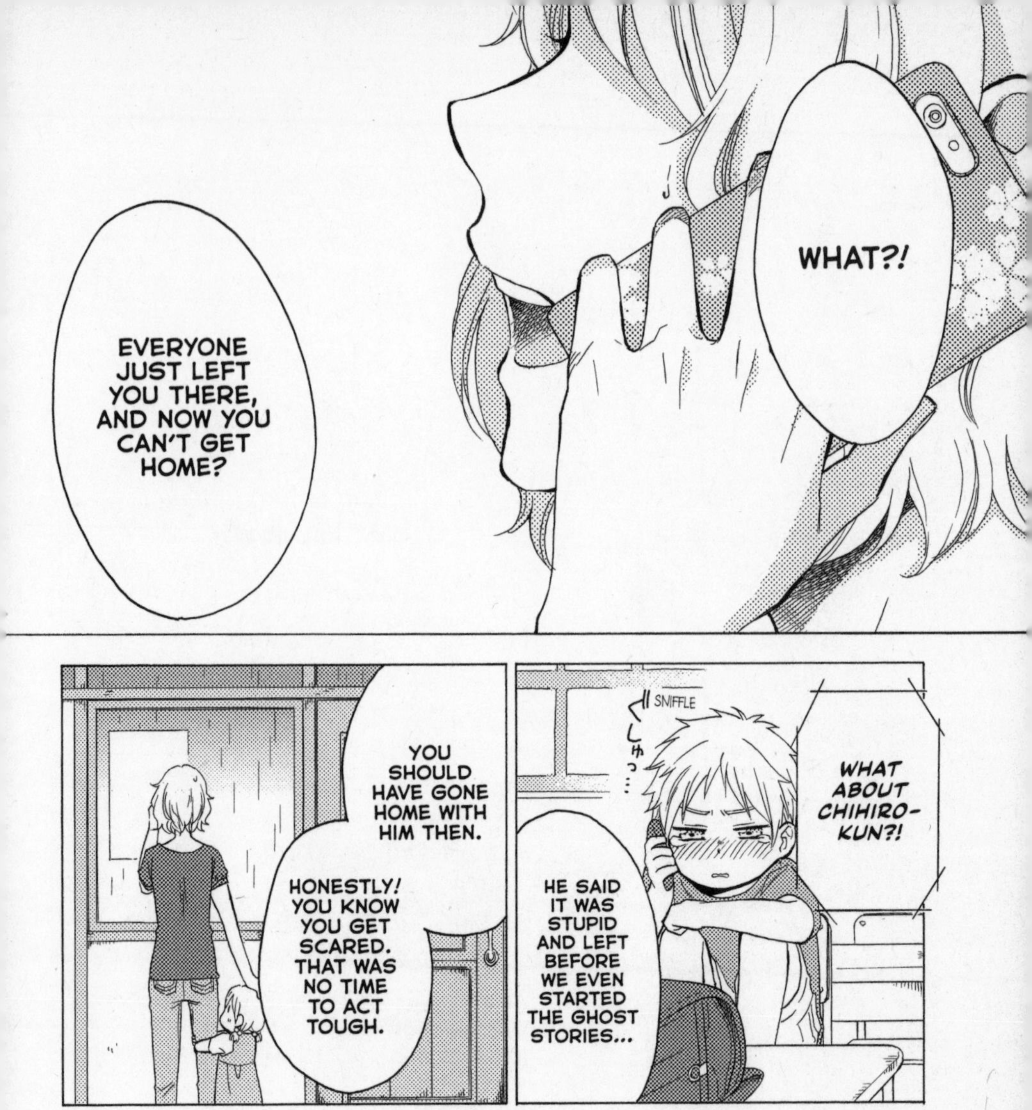
WHAT?!
EVERYONE JUST LEFT YOU THERE, AND NOW YOU CAN'T GET HOME?
WHAT ABOUT CHIHIRO-KUN?!
SNIFFLE
くしゅっ…
HE SAID IT WAS STUPID AND LEFT BEFORE WE EVEN STARTED THE GHOST STORIES...
YOU SHOULD HAVE GONE HOME WITH HIM THEN.
HONESTLY! YOU KNOW YOU GET SCARED. THAT WAS NO TIME TO ACT TOUGH.

Wake Up, Sleeping Beauty

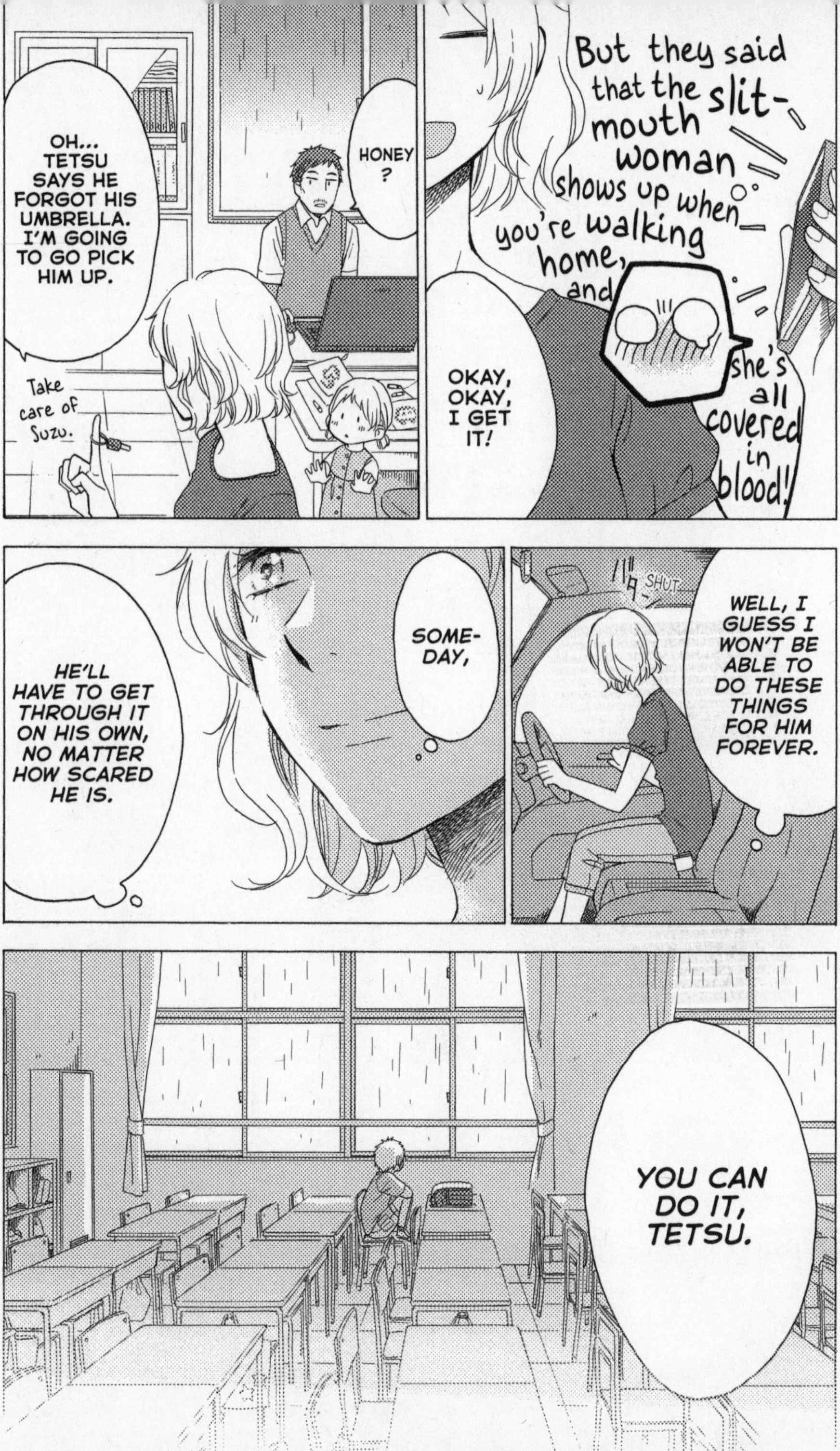
But they said that the slit-mouth woman shows up when you're walking home, and she's all covered in blood!
OKAY, OKAY, I GET IT!
HONEY?
OH... TETSU SAYS HE FORGOT HIS UMBRELLA. I'M GOING TO GO PICK HIM UP.
Take care of Suzu.
SHUT
WELL, I GUESS I WON'T BE ABLE TO DO THESE THINGS FOR HIM FOREVER.
SOME-DAY,
HE'LL HAVE TO GET THROUGH IT ON HIS OWN, NO MATTER HOW SCARED HE IS.
YOU CAN DO IT, TETSU.

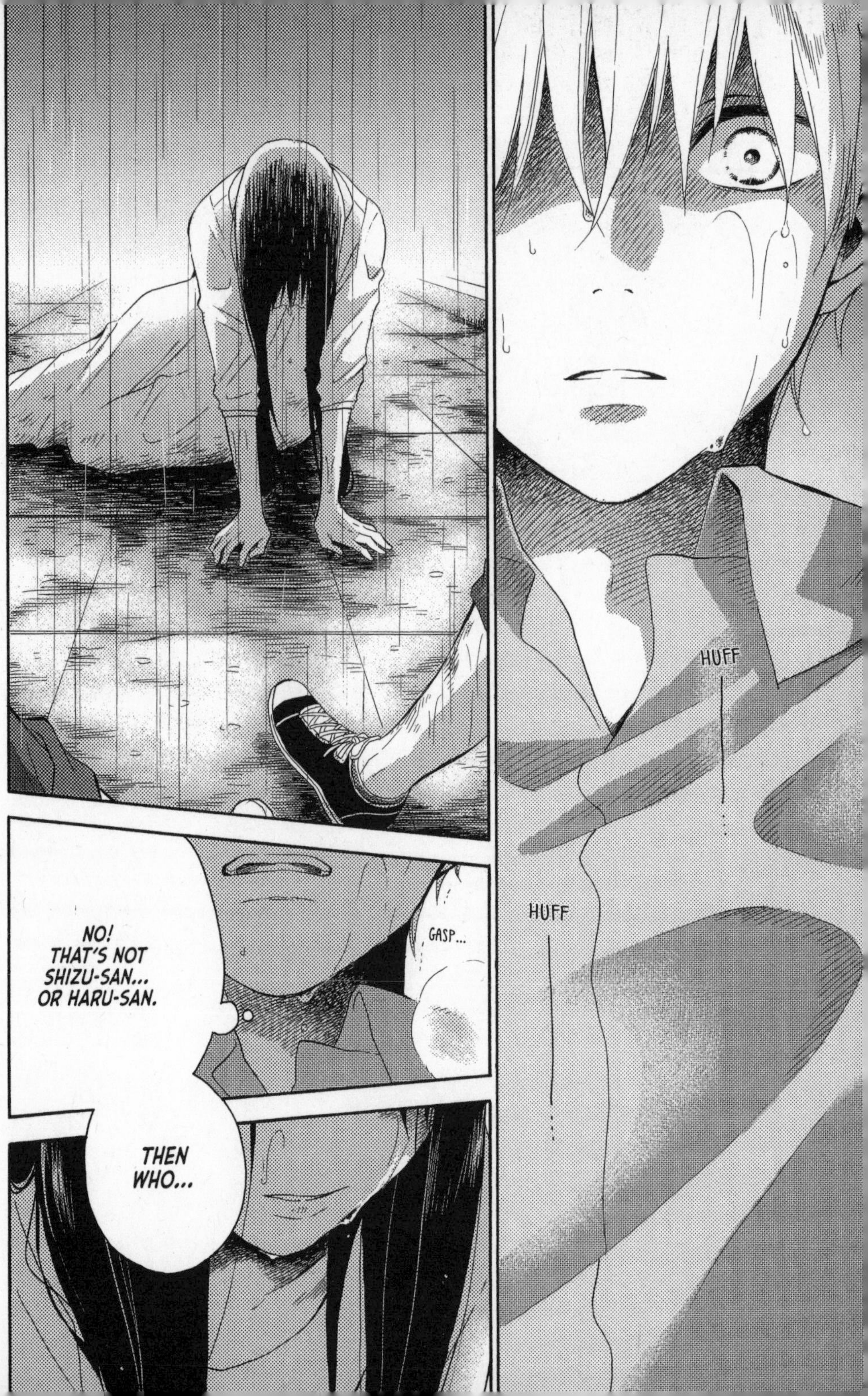
HUFF
HUFF
GASP...
NO! THAT'S NOT SHIZU-SAN... OR HARU-SAN.
THEN WHO...

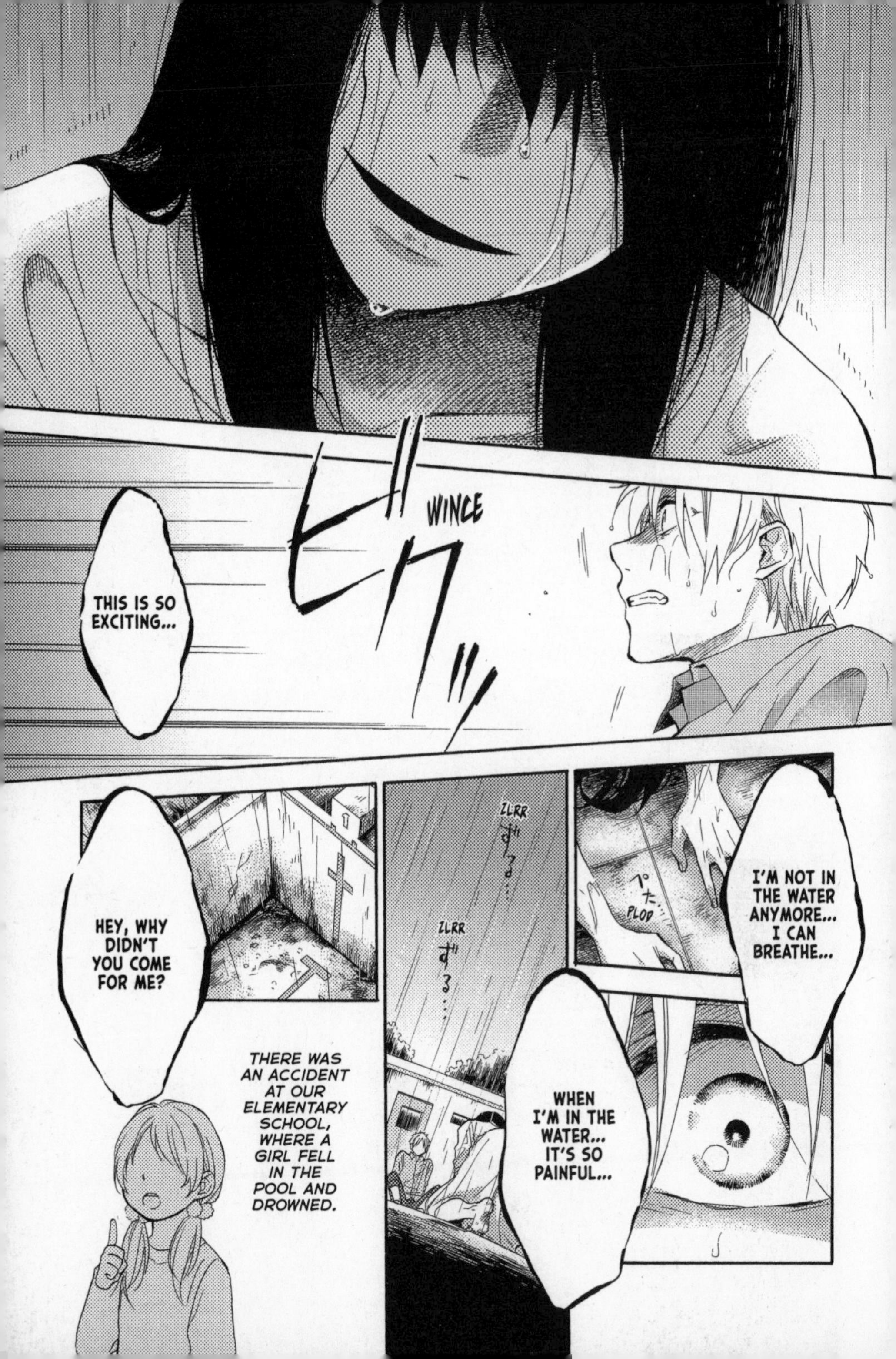
WINCE
THIS IS SO EXCITING...
I'M NOT IN THE WATER ANYMORE... I CAN BREATHE...
PLOD
WHEN I'M IN THE WATER... IT'S SO PAINFUL...
ZLRR
ZLRR
HEY, WHY DIDN'T YOU COME FOR ME?
THERE WAS AN ACCIDENT AT OUR ELEMENTARY SCHOOL, WHERE A GIRL FELL IN THE POOL AND DROWNED.

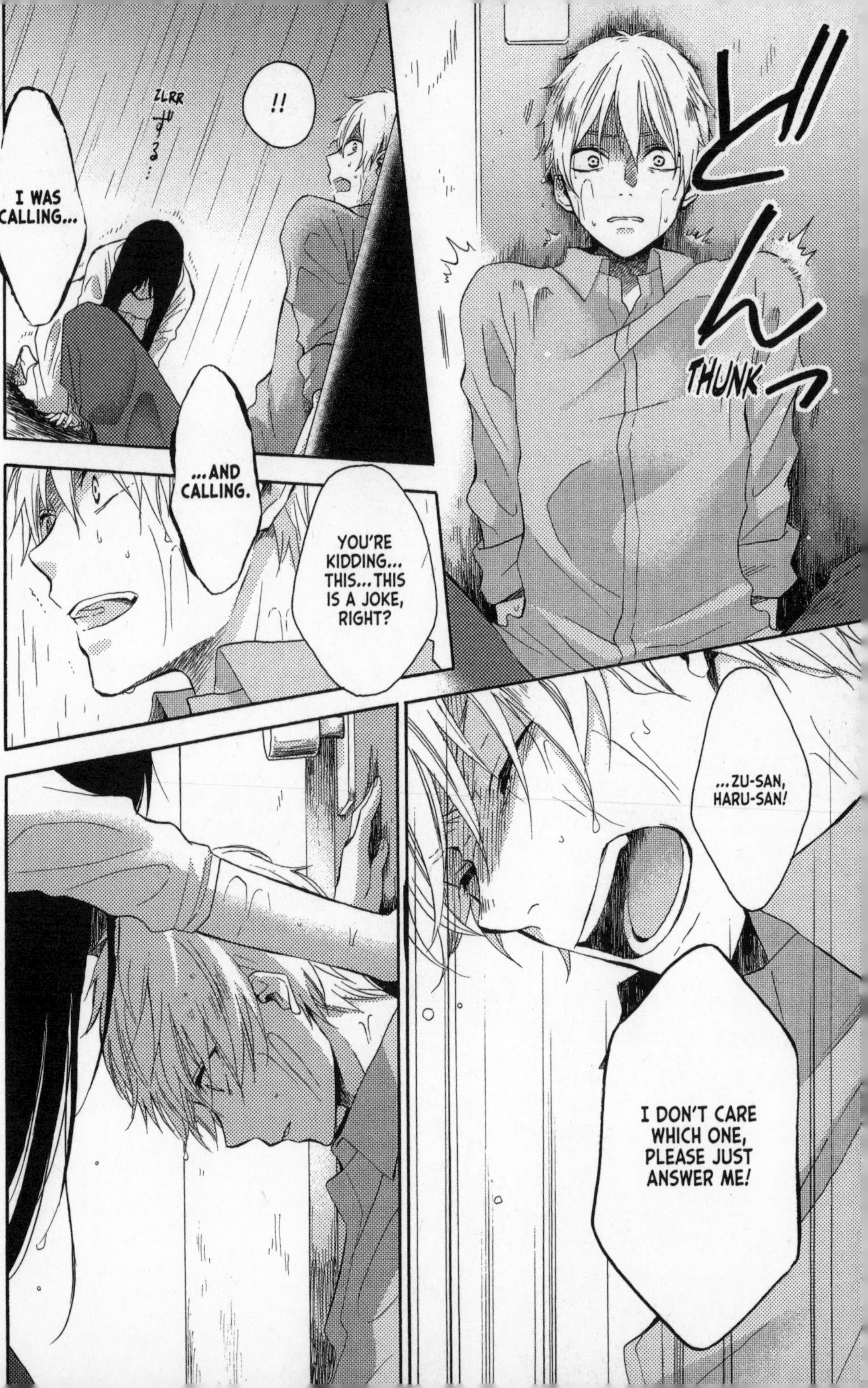
どんっ
THUNK
!!
ZLRR
ずる…
I WAS CALLING...
...AND CALLING.
YOU'RE KIDDING... THIS...THIS IS A JOKE, RIGHT?
...ZU-SAN, HARU-SAN!
I DON'T CARE WHICH ONE, PLEASE JUST ANSWER ME!

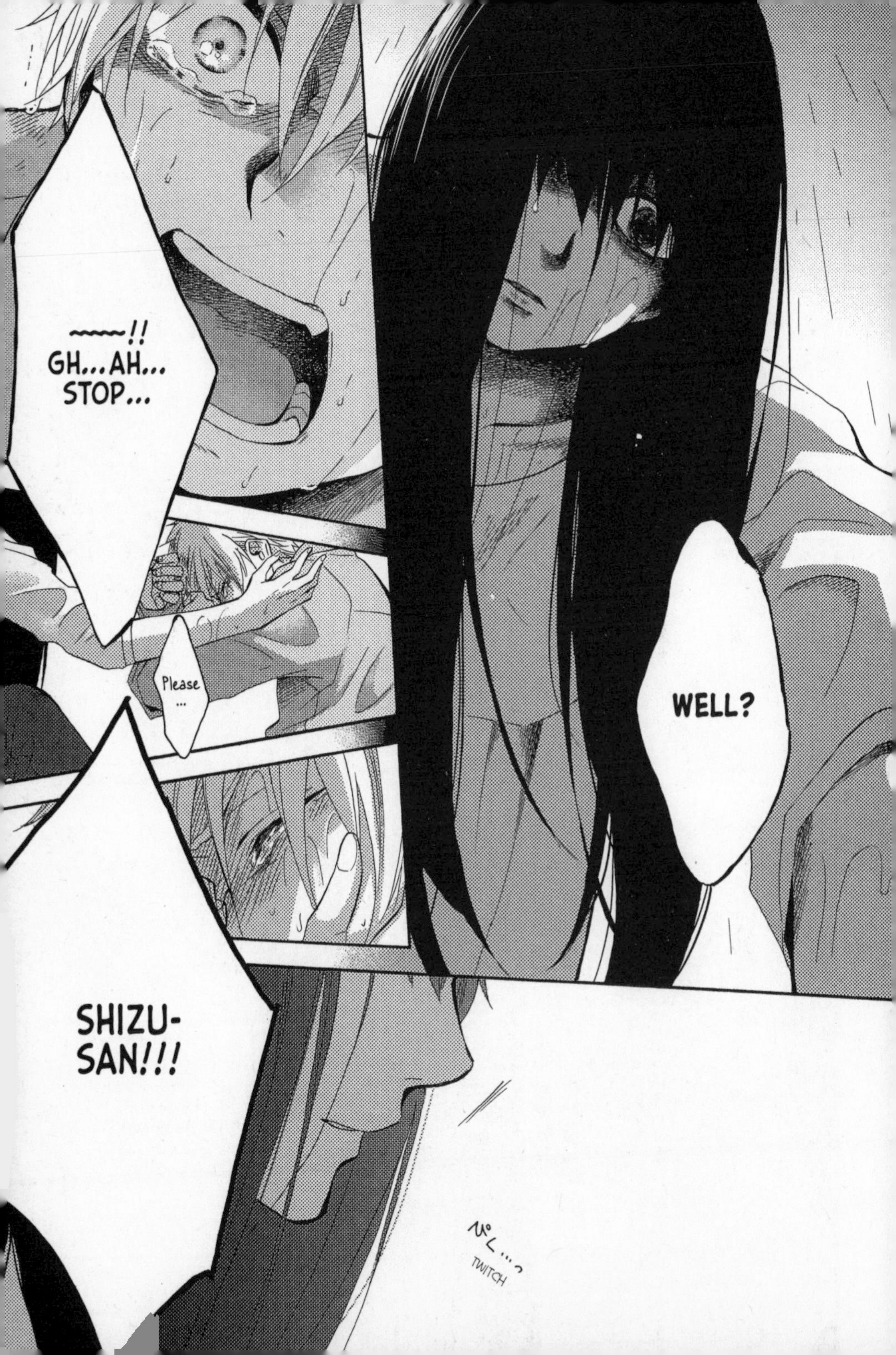
WELL?
~~~!! GH...AH... STOP...
Please ...
SHIZU-SAN!!!
ぴく…っ
TWITCH
~~~

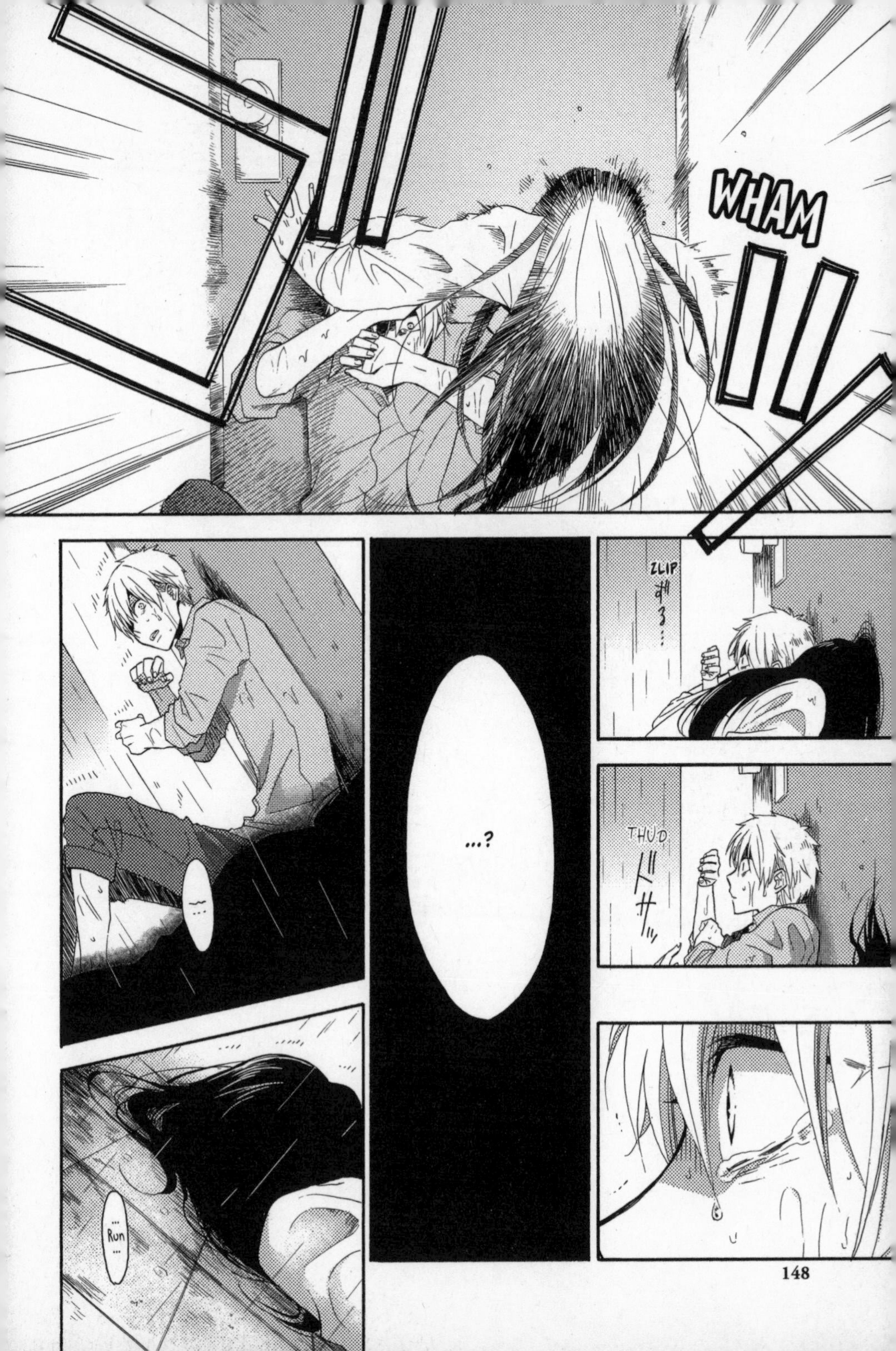
WHAM
ZLIP
ずる…
THUD
ドサッ
...?
... Run ...

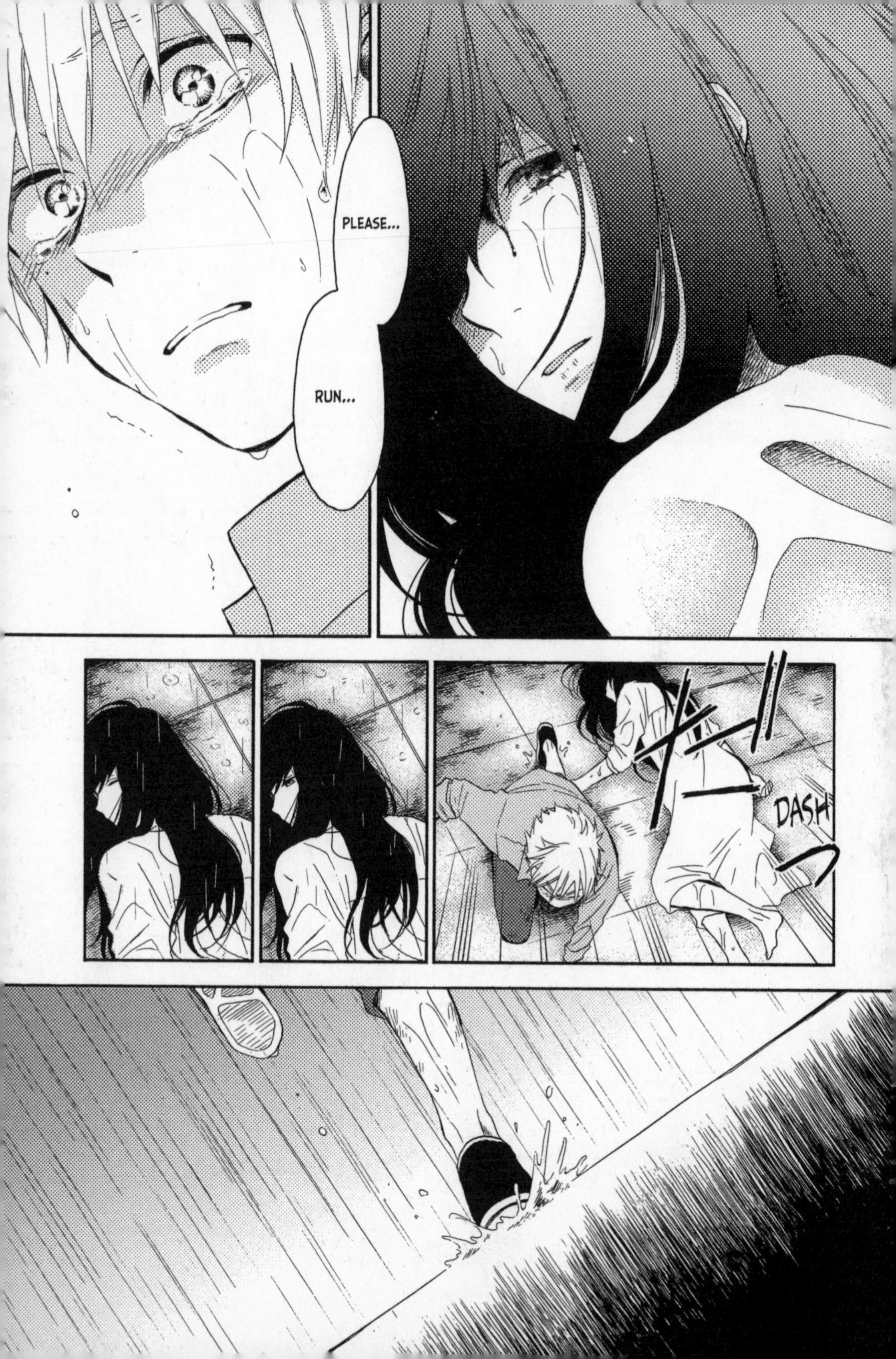
PLEASE...
RUN...
DASH

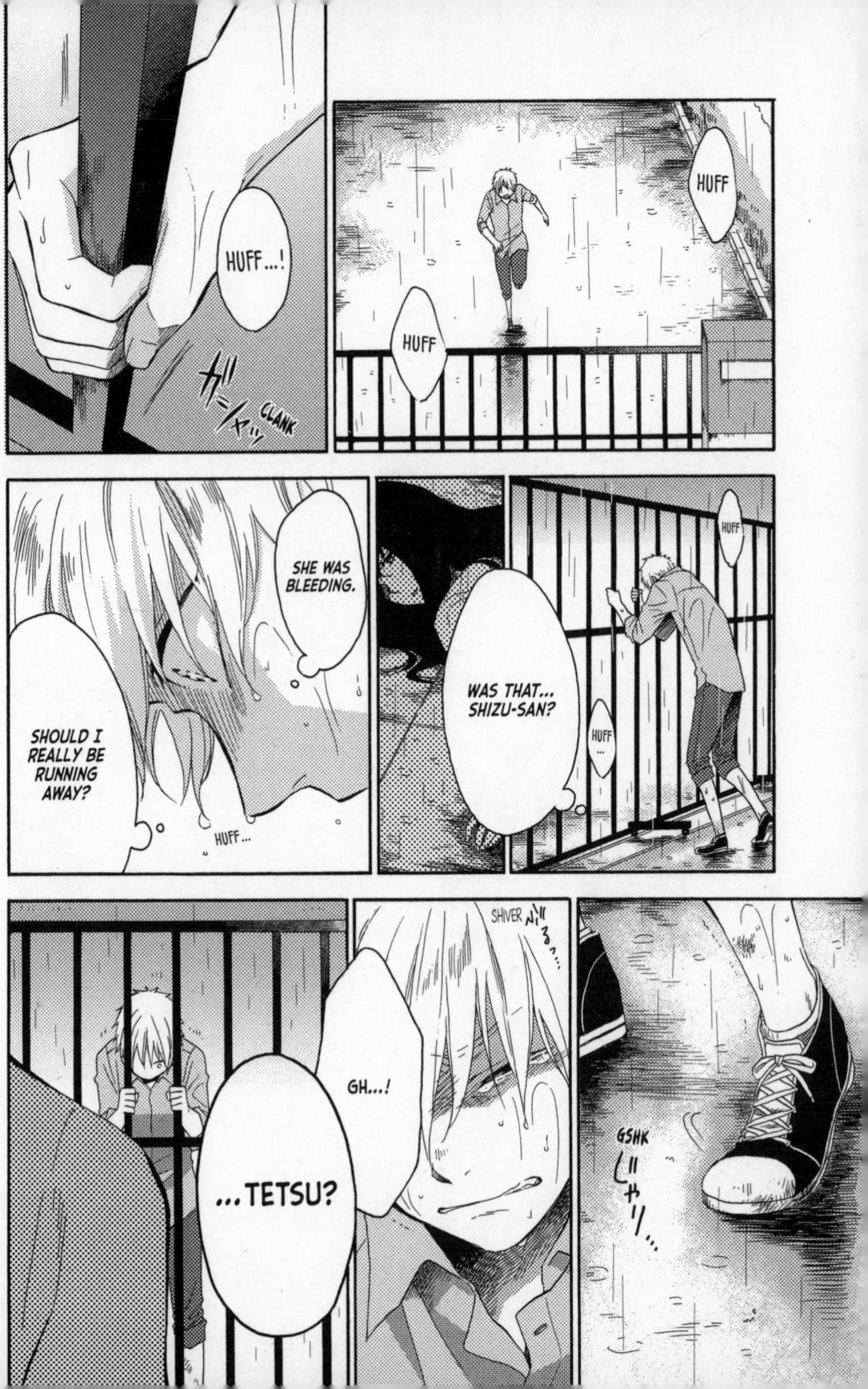
HUFF
HUFF
HUFF...!
CLANK
HUFF
HUFF...
WAS THAT... SHIZU-SAN?
SHE WAS BLEEDING.
SHOULD I REALLY BE RUNNING AWAY?
HUFF...
GSHK
SHIVER
GH...!
...TETSU?

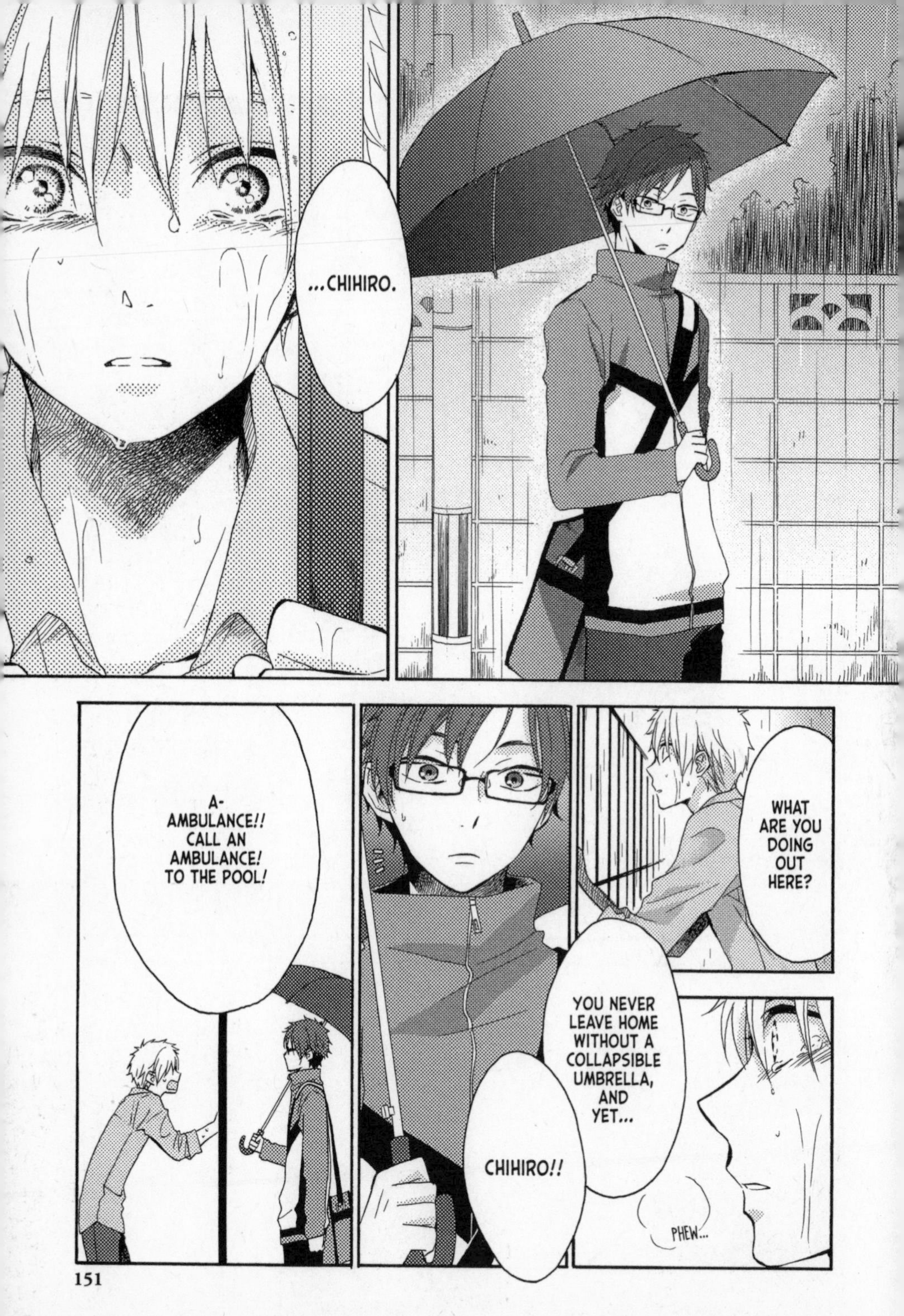
...CHIHIRO.
WHAT ARE YOU DOING OUT HERE?
YOU NEVER LEAVE HOME WITHOUT A COLLAPSIBLE UMBRELLA, AND YET...
PHEW...
CHIHIRO!!
A- AMBULANCE!! CALL AN AMBULANCE! TO THE POOL!

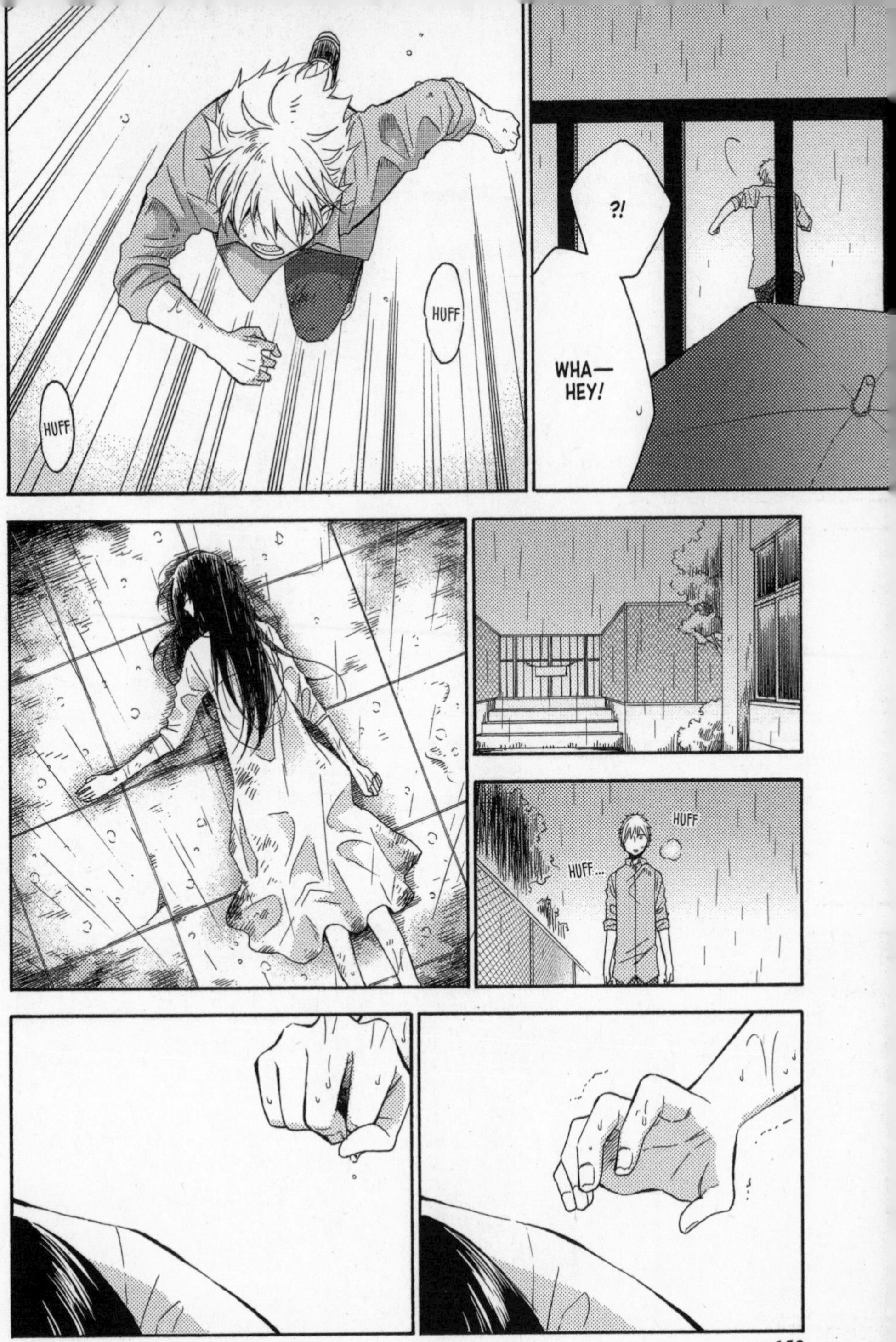
?!
WHA— HEY!
HUFF
HUFF
HUFF
HUFF...

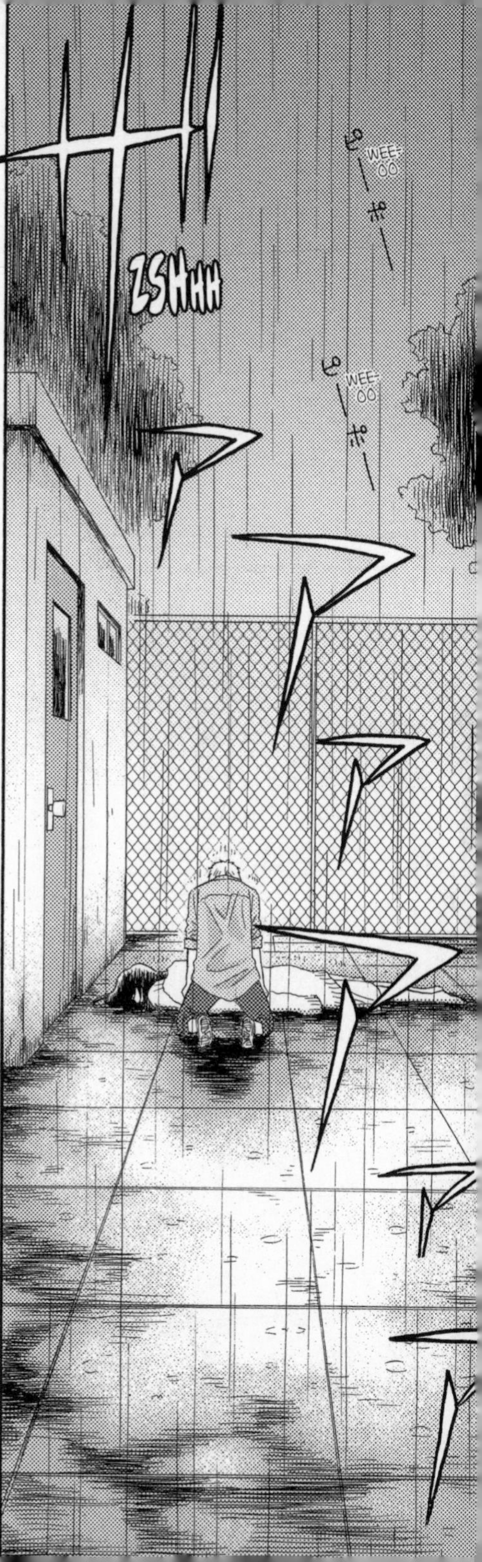
ピーポー
WEE-OO
ZSHHH
ピーポー
WEE-OO

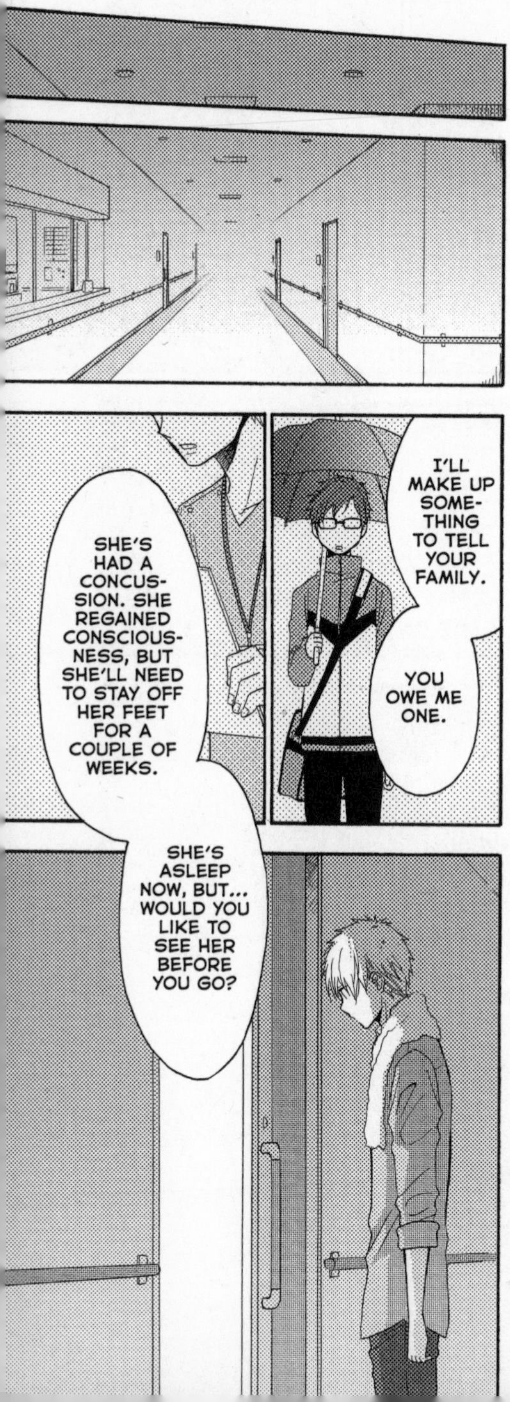
I'LL MAKE UP SOMETHING TO TELL YOUR FAMILY.
YOU OWE ME ONE.
SHE'S HAD A CONCUSSION. SHE REGAINED CONSCIOUSNESS, BUT SHE'LL NEED TO STAY OFF HER FEET FOR A COUPLE OF WEEKS.
SHE'S ASLEEP NOW, BUT... WOULD YOU LIKE TO SEE HER BEFORE YOU GO?

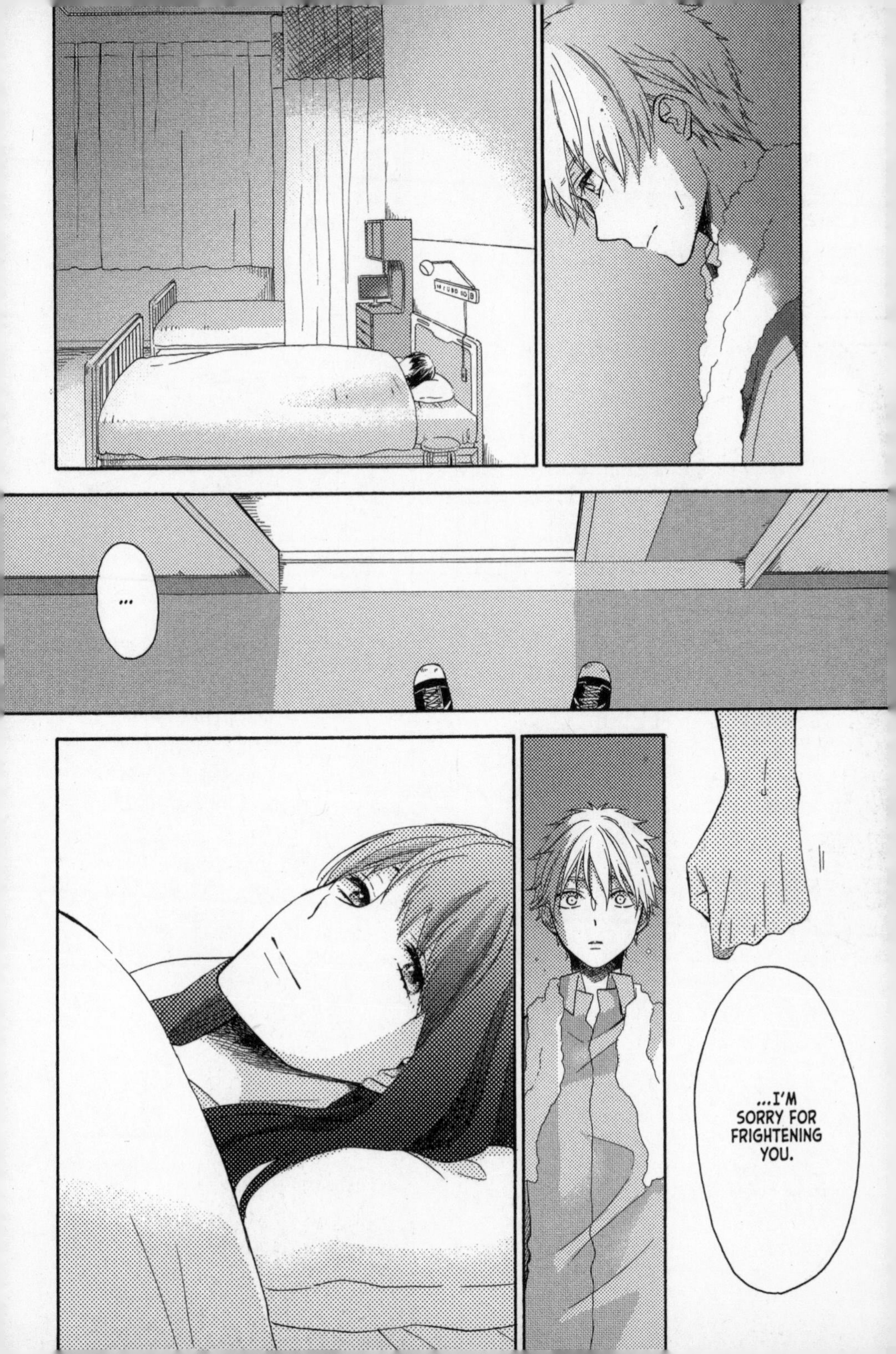
...
...I'M SORRY FOR FRIGHTENING YOU.

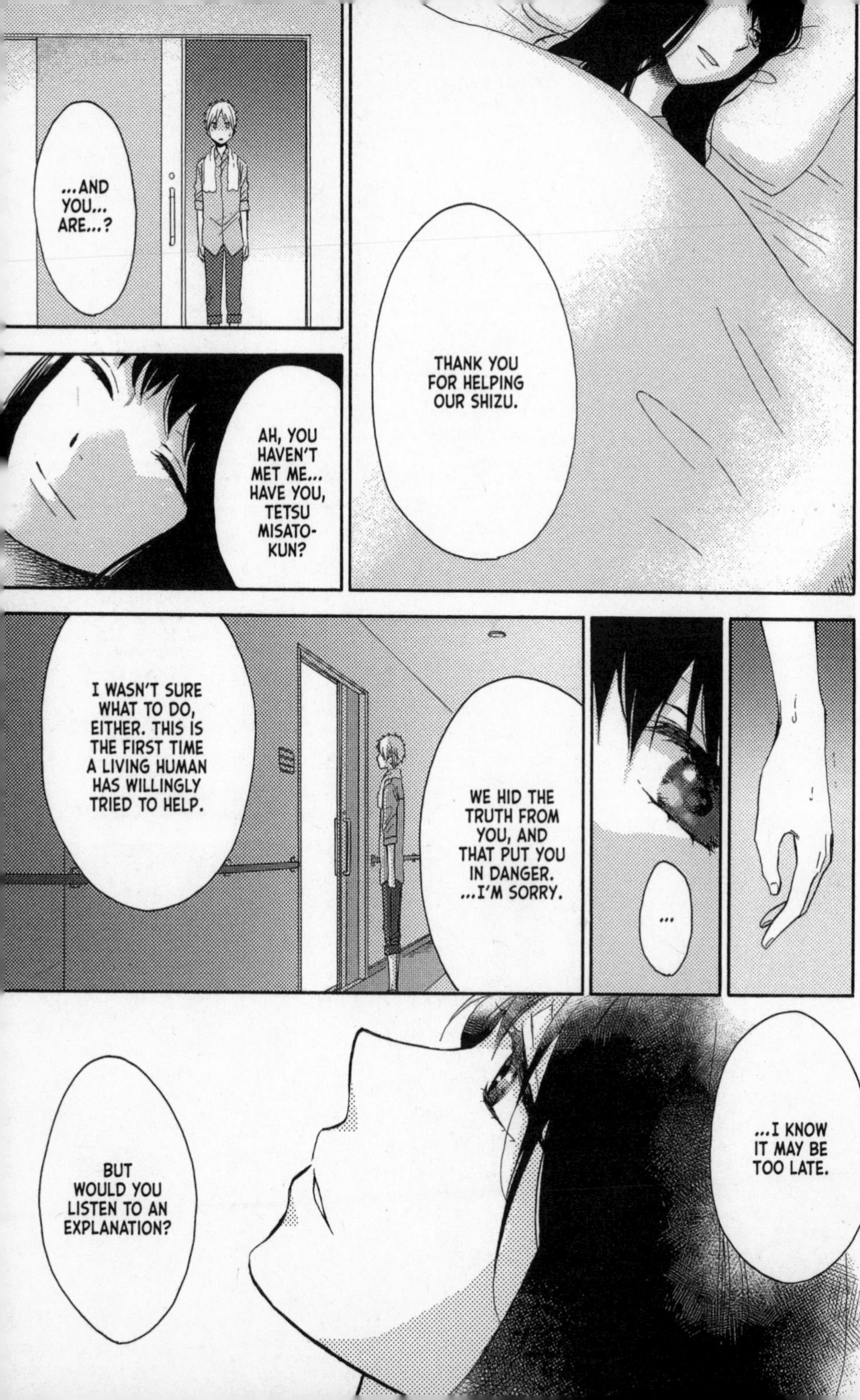
THANK YOU FOR HELPING OUR SHIZU.
...AND YOU... ARE...?
AH, YOU HAVEN'T MET ME... HAVE YOU, TETSU MISATO-KUN?
...
WE HID THE TRUTH FROM YOU, AND THAT PUT YOU IN DANGER. ...I'M SORRY.
I WASN'T SURE WHAT TO DO, EITHER. THIS IS THE FIRST TIME A LIVING HUMAN HAS WILLINGLY TRIED TO HELP.
...I KNOW IT MAY BE TOO LATE.
BUT WOULD YOU LISTEN TO AN EXPLANATION?

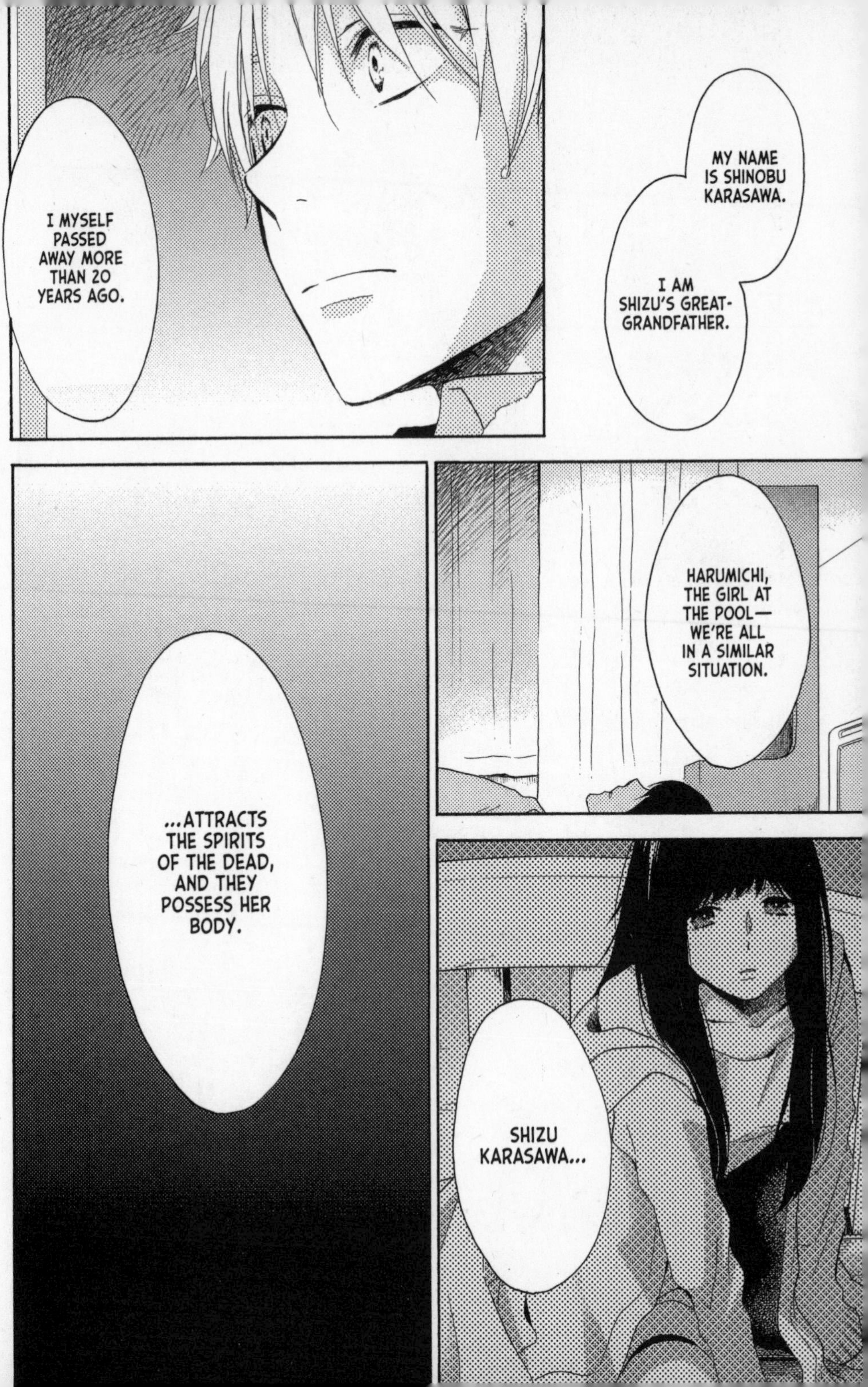
MY NAME IS SHINOBU KARASAWA.
I AM SHIZU'S GREAT-GRANDFATHER.
I MYSELF PASSED AWAY MORE THAN 20 YEARS AGO.
HARUMICHI, THE GIRL AT THE POOL— WE'RE ALL IN A SIMILAR SITUATION.
SHIZU KARASAWA...
...ATTRACTS THE SPIRITS OF THE DEAD, AND THEY POSSESS HER BODY.

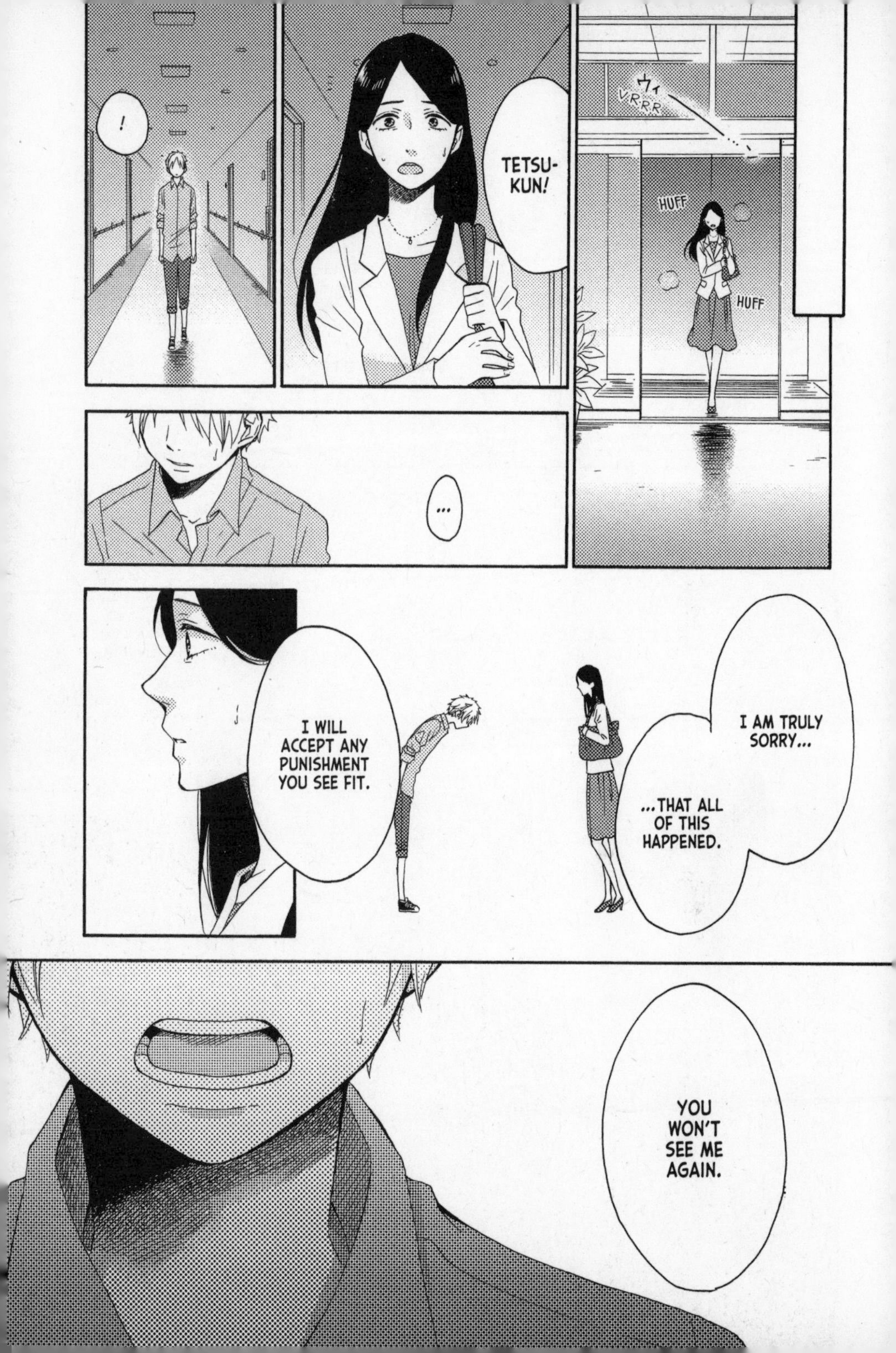
ウィ
VRRR
HUFF
HUFF
TETSU-KUN!
!
...
I AM TRULY SORRY...
...THAT ALL OF THIS HAPPENED.
I WILL ACCEPT ANY PUNISHMENT YOU SEE FIT.
YOU WON'T SEE ME AGAIN.

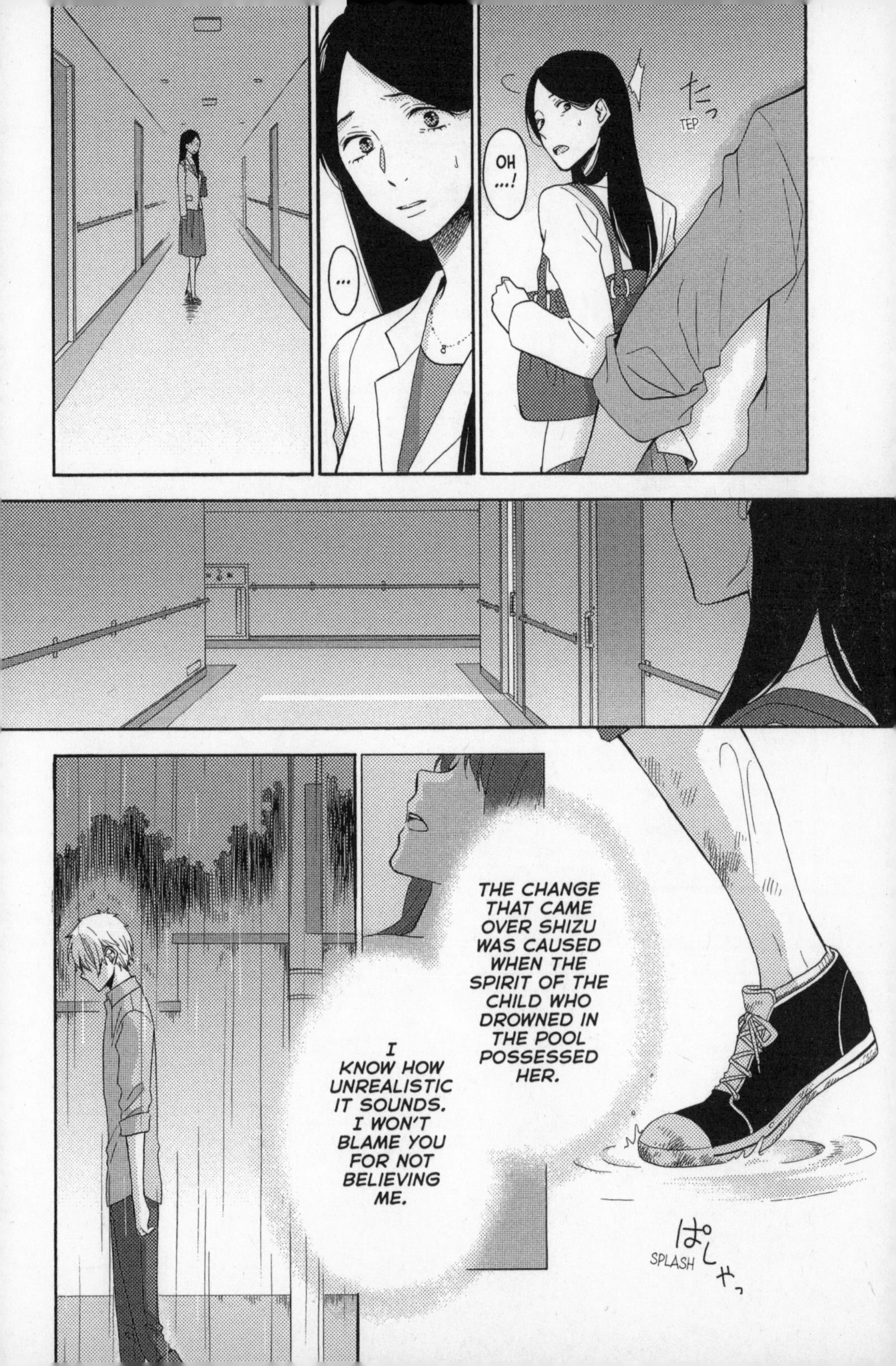
たっ
TEP
OH ...!
...
THE CHANGE THAT CAME OVER SHIZU WAS CAUSED WHEN THE SPIRIT OF THE CHILD WHO DROWNED IN THE POOL POSSESSED HER.
I KNOW HOW UNREALISTIC IT SOUNDS. I WON'T BLAME YOU FOR NOT BELIEVING ME.
ぱしゃっ
SPLASH

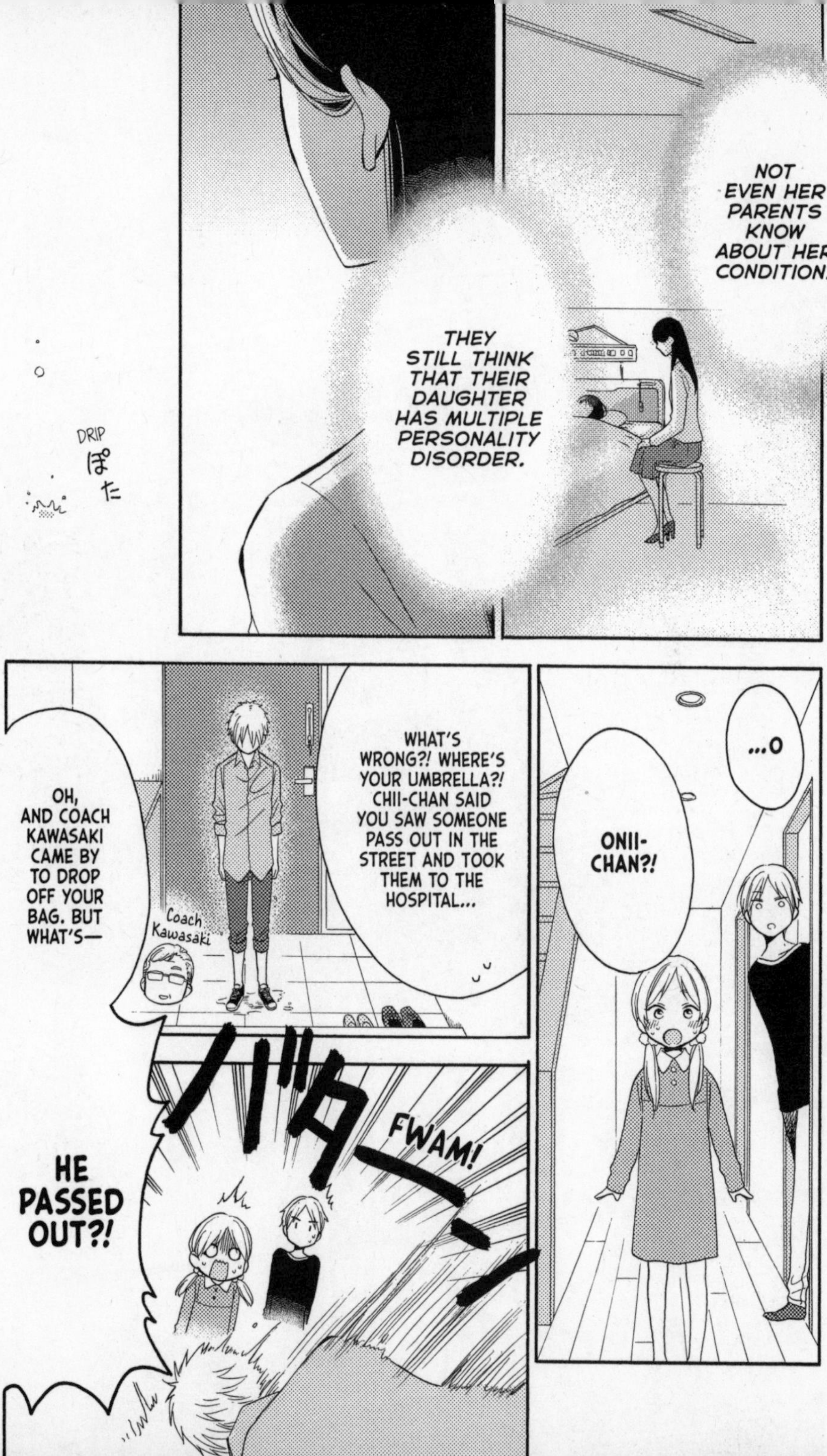
NOT EVEN HER PARENTS KNOW ABOUT HER CONDITION.
THEY STILL THINK THAT THEIR DAUGHTER HAS MULTIPLE PERSONALITY DISORDER.
DRIP
ぽた
...O
ONII-CHAN?!
WHAT'S WRONG?! WHERE'S YOUR UMBRELLA?! CHII-CHAN SAID YOU SAW SOMEONE PASS OUT IN THE STREET AND TOOK THEM TO THE HOSPITAL...
OH, AND COACH KAWASAKI CAME BY TO DROP OFF YOUR BAG. BUT WHAT'S—
Coach Kawasaki
バタ
FWAM!
HE PASSED OUT?!

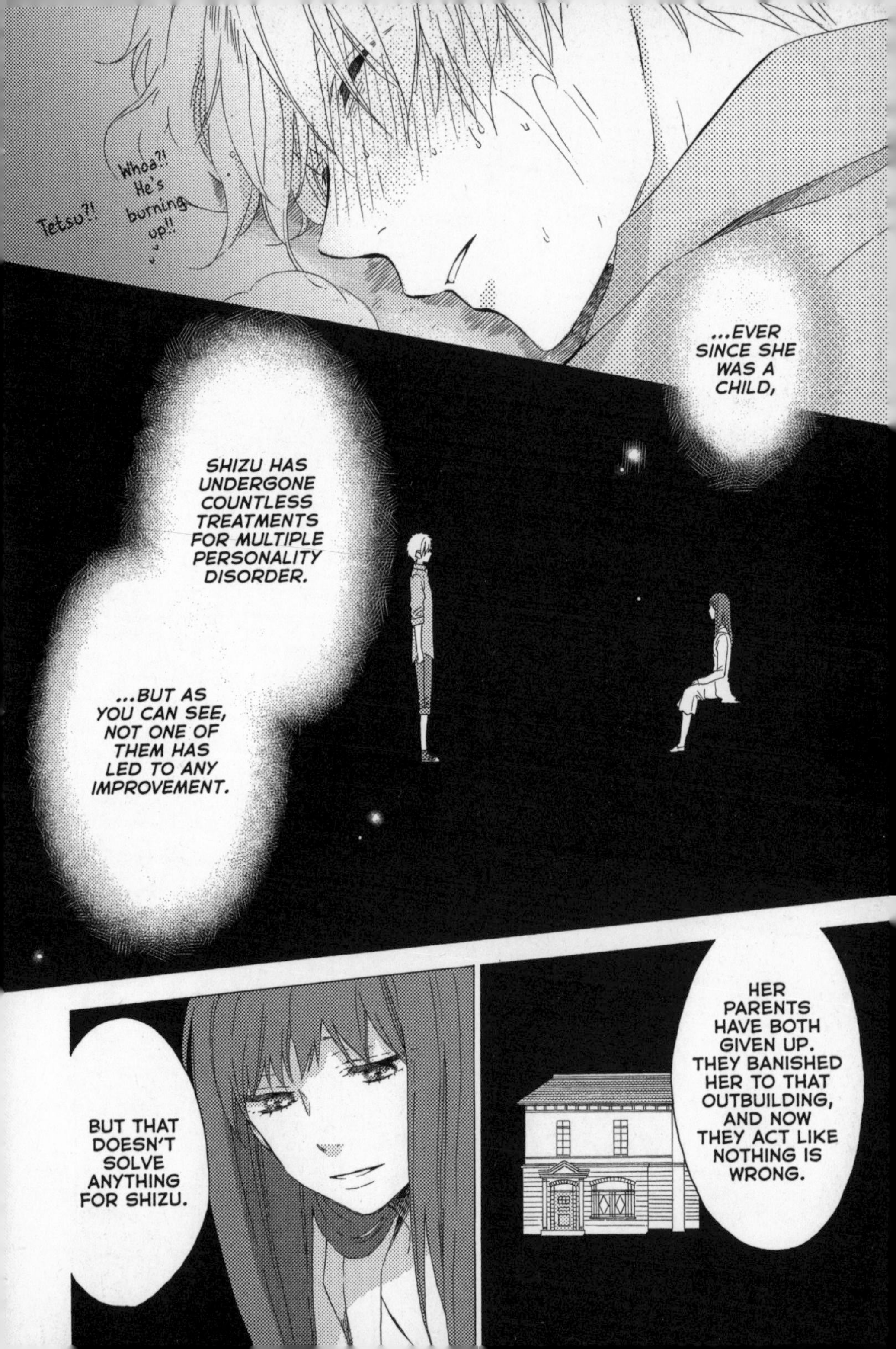
Whoa?! He's burning up!!
Tetsu?!
...EVER SINCE SHE WAS A CHILD,
SHIZU HAS UNDERGONE COUNTLESS TREATMENTS FOR MULTIPLE PERSONALITY DISORDER.
...BUT AS YOU CAN SEE, NOT ONE OF THEM HAS LED TO ANY IMPROVEMENT.
HER PARENTS HAVE BOTH GIVEN UP. THEY BANISHED HER TO THAT OUTBUILDING, AND NOW THEY ACT LIKE NOTHING IS WRONG.
BUT THAT DOESN'T SOLVE ANYTHING FOR SHIZU.

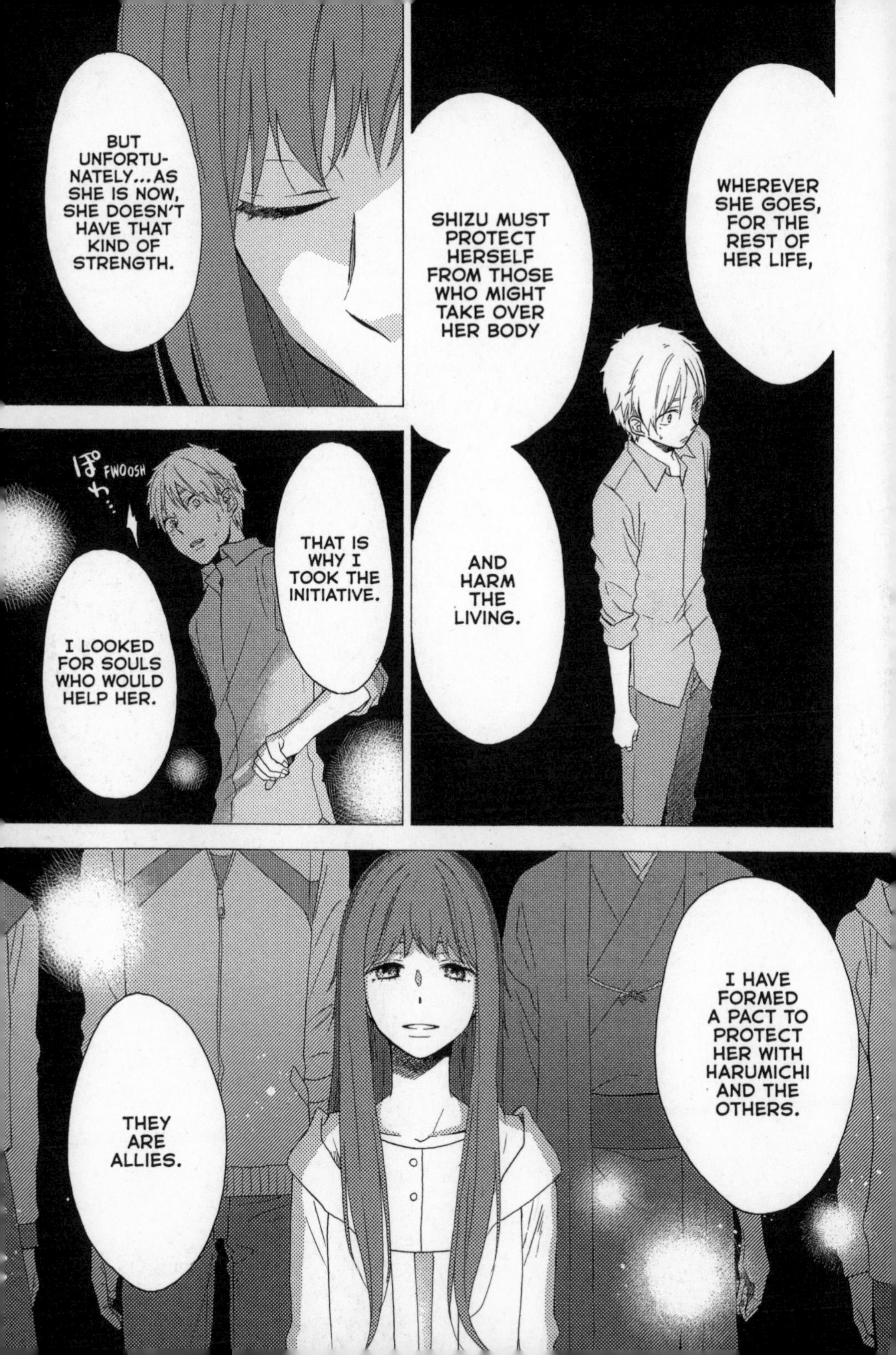
WHEREVER SHE GOES, FOR THE REST OF HER LIFE,
SHIZU MUST PROTECT HERSELF FROM THOSE WHO MIGHT TAKE OVER HER BODY
AND HARM THE LIVING.
BUT UNFORTUNATELY...AS SHE IS NOW, SHE DOESN'T HAVE THAT KIND OF STRENGTH.
THAT IS WHY I TOOK THE INITIATIVE.
ぽわ… FWOOSH
I LOOKED FOR SOULS WHO WOULD HELP HER.
I HAVE FORMED A PACT TO PROTECT HER WITH HARUMICHI AND THE OTHERS.
THEY ARE ALLIES.

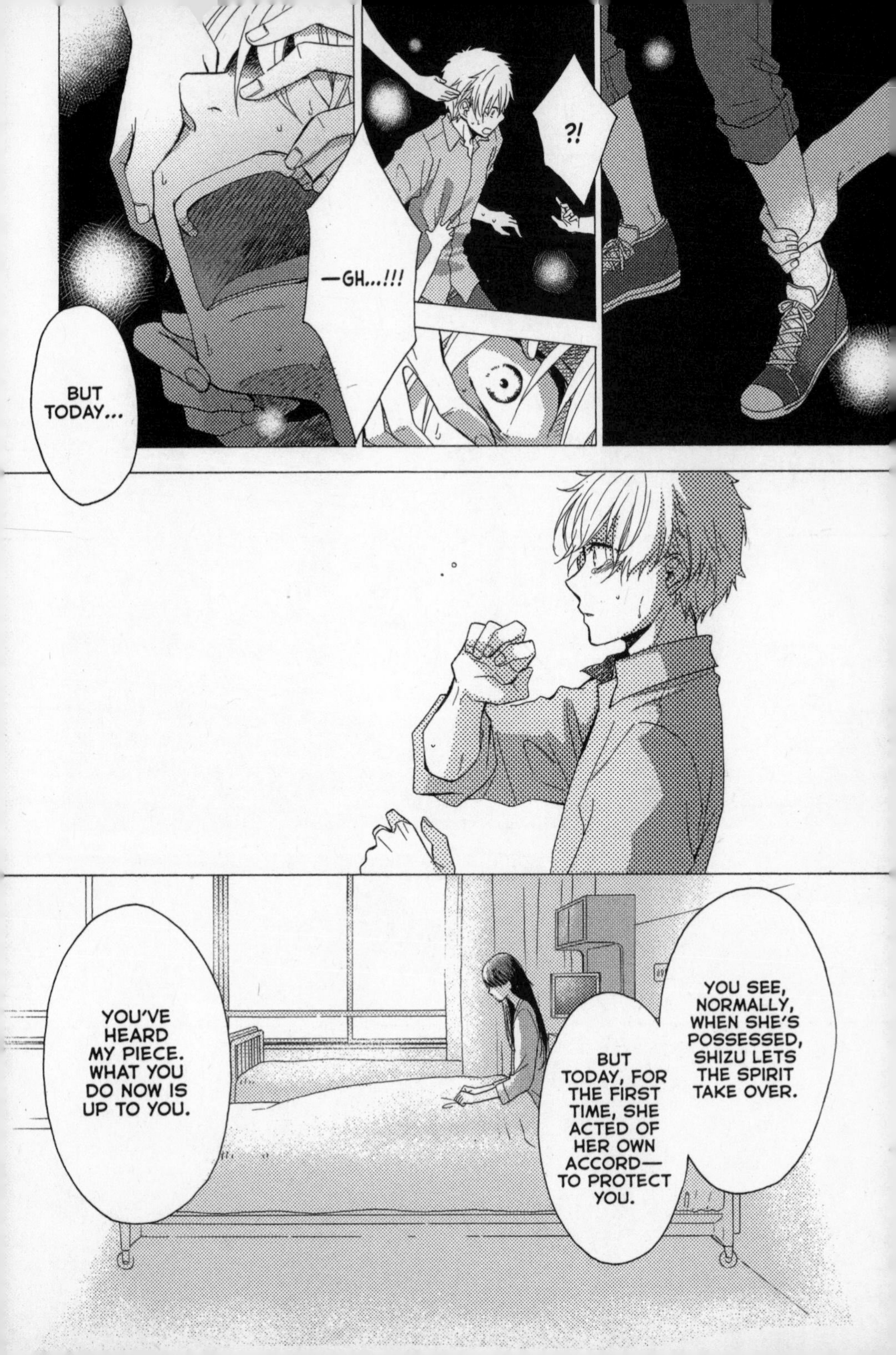
?!
—GH...!!!
BUT TODAY...
YOU SEE, NORMALLY, WHEN SHE'S POSSESSED, SHIZU LETS THE SPIRIT TAKE OVER.
BUT TODAY, FOR THE FIRST TIME, SHE ACTED OF HER OWN ACCORD—TO PROTECT YOU.
YOU'VE HEARD MY PIECE. WHAT YOU DO NOW IS UP TO YOU.

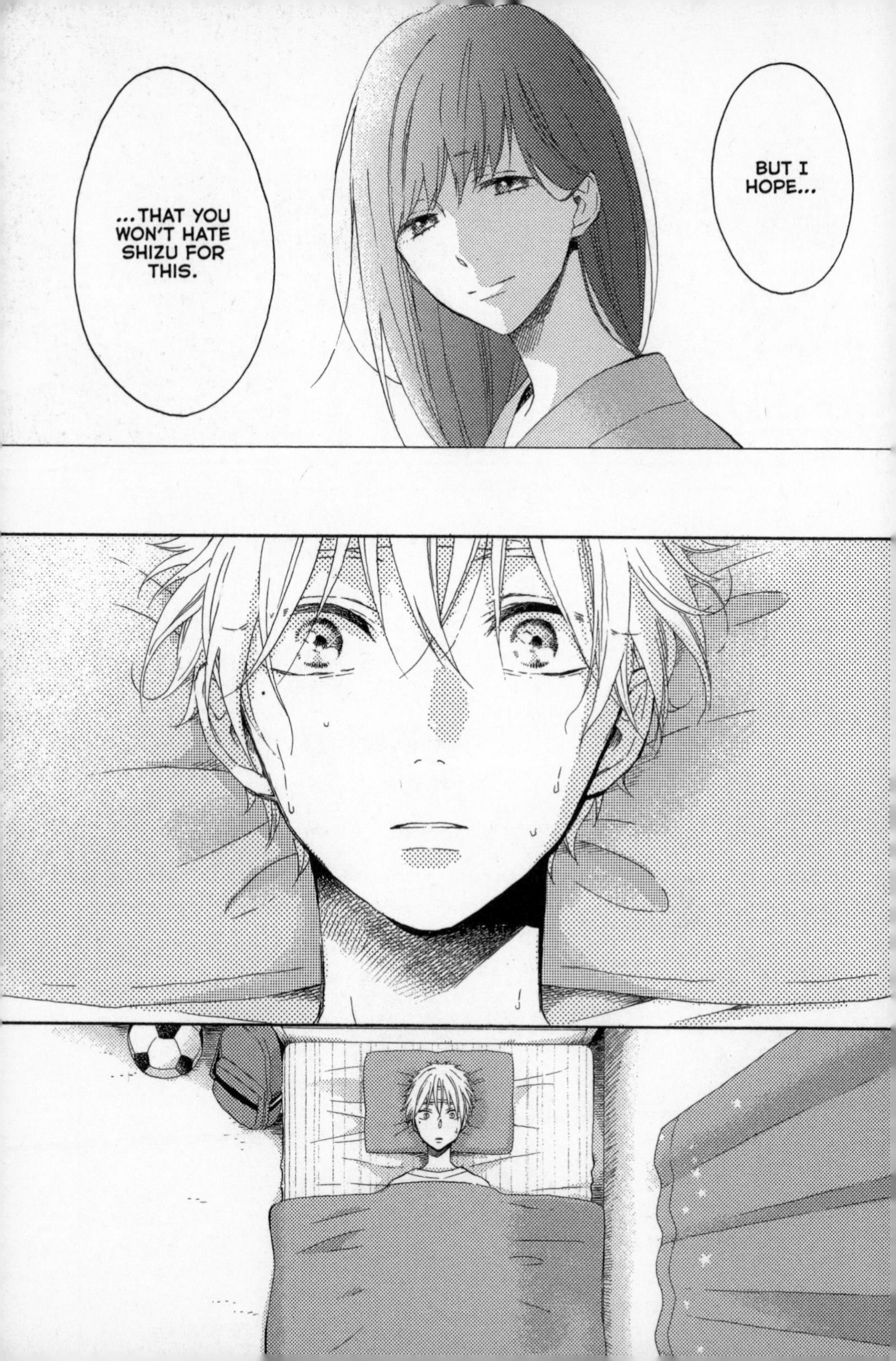
BUT I HOPE...
...THAT YOU WON'T HATE SHIZU FOR THIS.

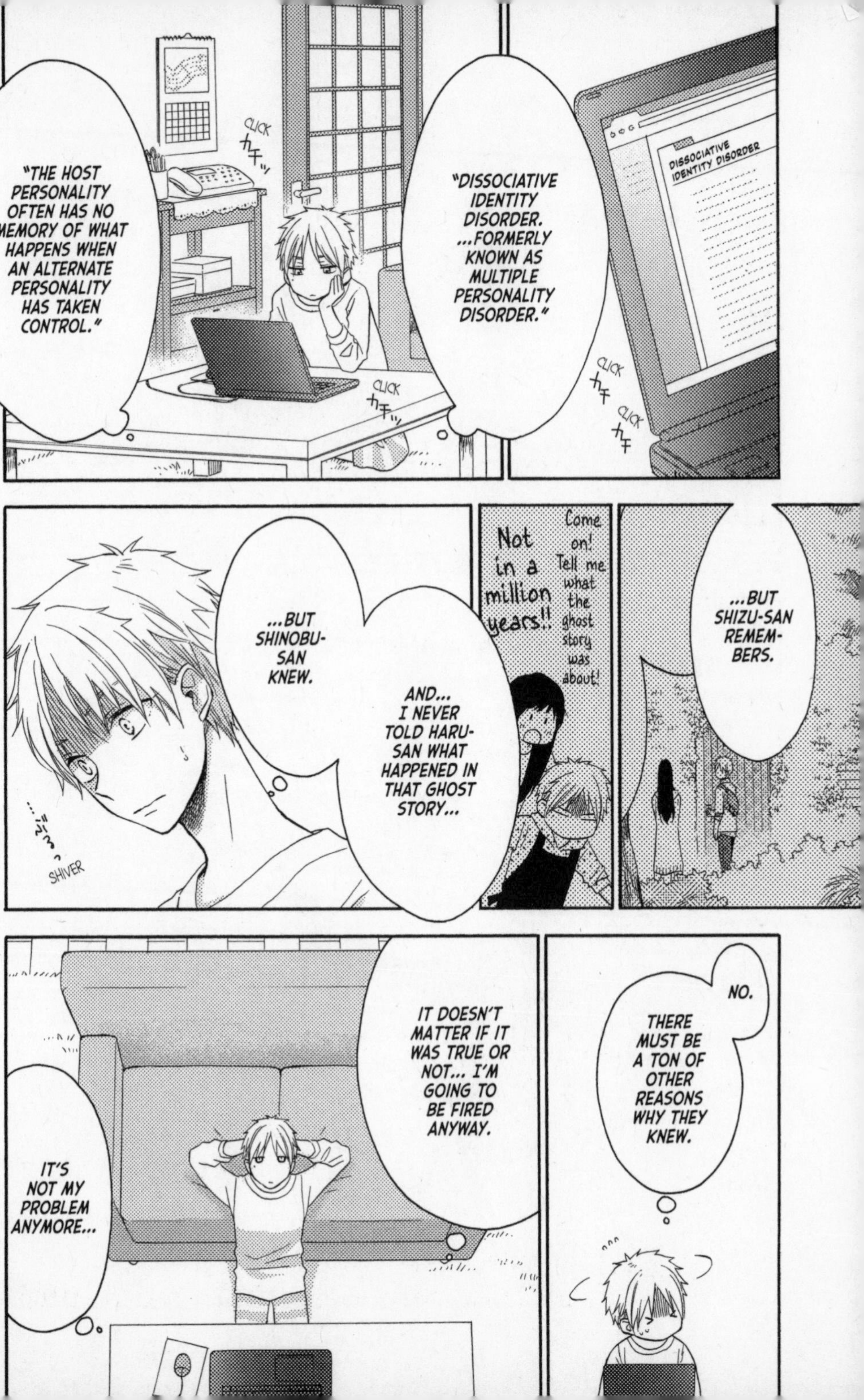
DISSOCIATIVE IDENTITY DISORDER
CLICK
CLICK
"DISSOCIATIVE IDENTITY DISORDER. ...FORMERLY KNOWN AS MULTIPLE PERSONALITY DISORDER."
CLICK
CLICK
"THE HOST PERSONALITY OFTEN HAS NO MEMORY OF WHAT HAPPENS WHEN AN ALTERNATE PERSONALITY HAS TAKEN CONTROL."
...BUT SHIZU-SAN REMEMBERS.
Come on! Tell me what the ghost story was about!
Not in a million years!!
...BUT SHINOBU-SAN KNEW.
AND... I NEVER TOLD HARU-SAN WHAT HAPPENED IN THAT GHOST STORY...
SHIVER
NO.
THERE MUST BE A TON OF OTHER REASONS WHY THEY KNEW.
IT DOESN'T MATTER IF IT WAS TRUE OR NOT... I'M GOING TO BE FIRED ANYWAY.
IT'S NOT MY PROBLEM ANYMORE...

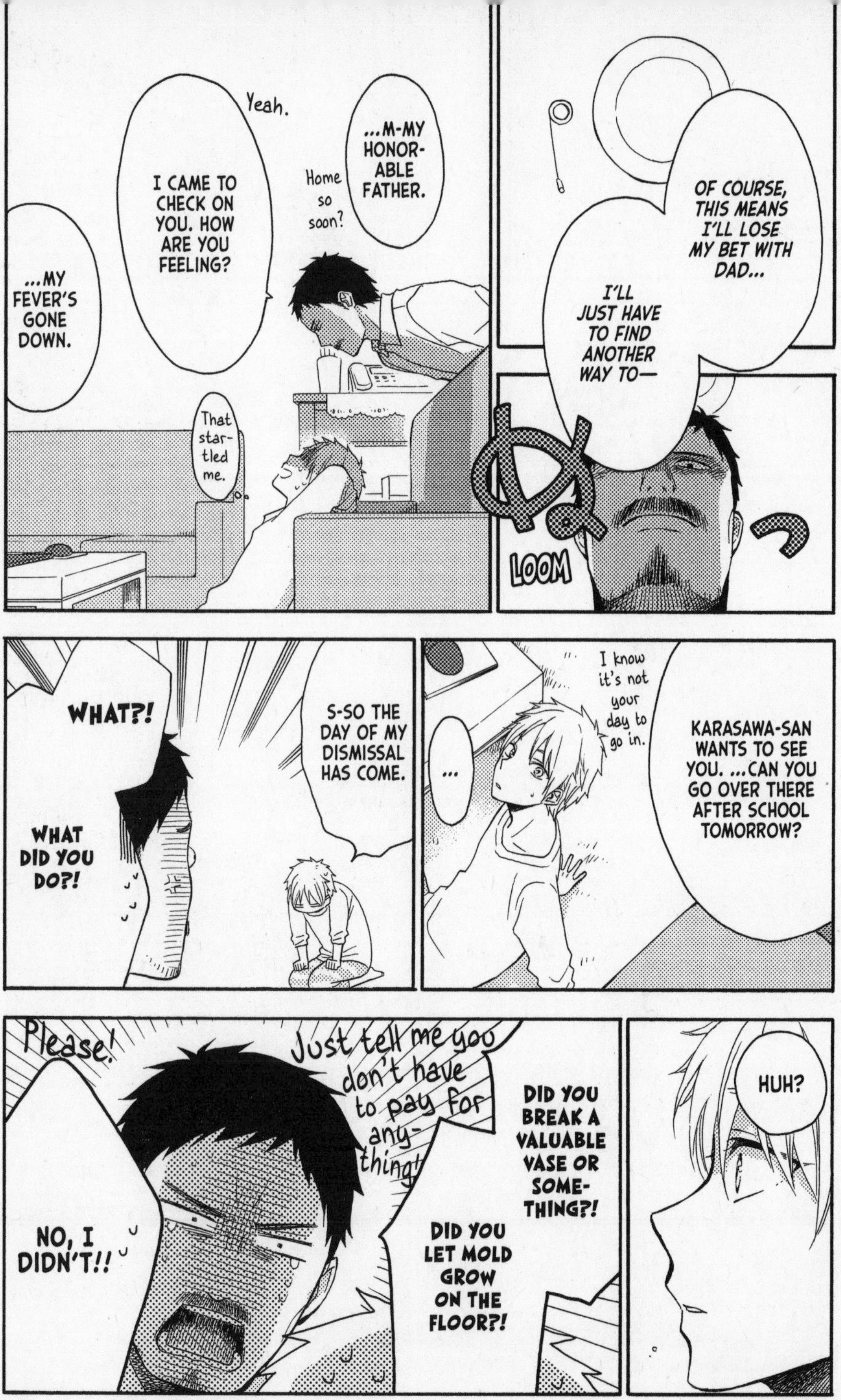
OF COURSE, THIS MEANS I'LL LOSE MY BET WITH DAD...
I'LL JUST HAVE TO FIND ANOTHER WAY TO—
LOOM
...M-MY HONORABLE FATHER.
Home so soon?
Yeah.
I CAME TO CHECK ON YOU. HOW ARE YOU FEELING?
...MY FEVER'S GONE DOWN.
That startled me.
KARASAWA-SAN WANTS TO SEE YOU. ...CAN YOU GO OVER THERE AFTER SCHOOL TOMORROW?
I know it's not your day to go in.
...
S-SO THE DAY OF MY DISMISSAL HAS COME.
WHAT?!
WHAT DID YOU DO?!
HUH?
DID YOU BREAK A VALUABLE VASE OR SOME-THING?!
DID YOU LET MOLD GROW ON THE FLOOR?!
Just tell me you don't have to pay for any-thing!
Please!
NO, I DIDN'T!!

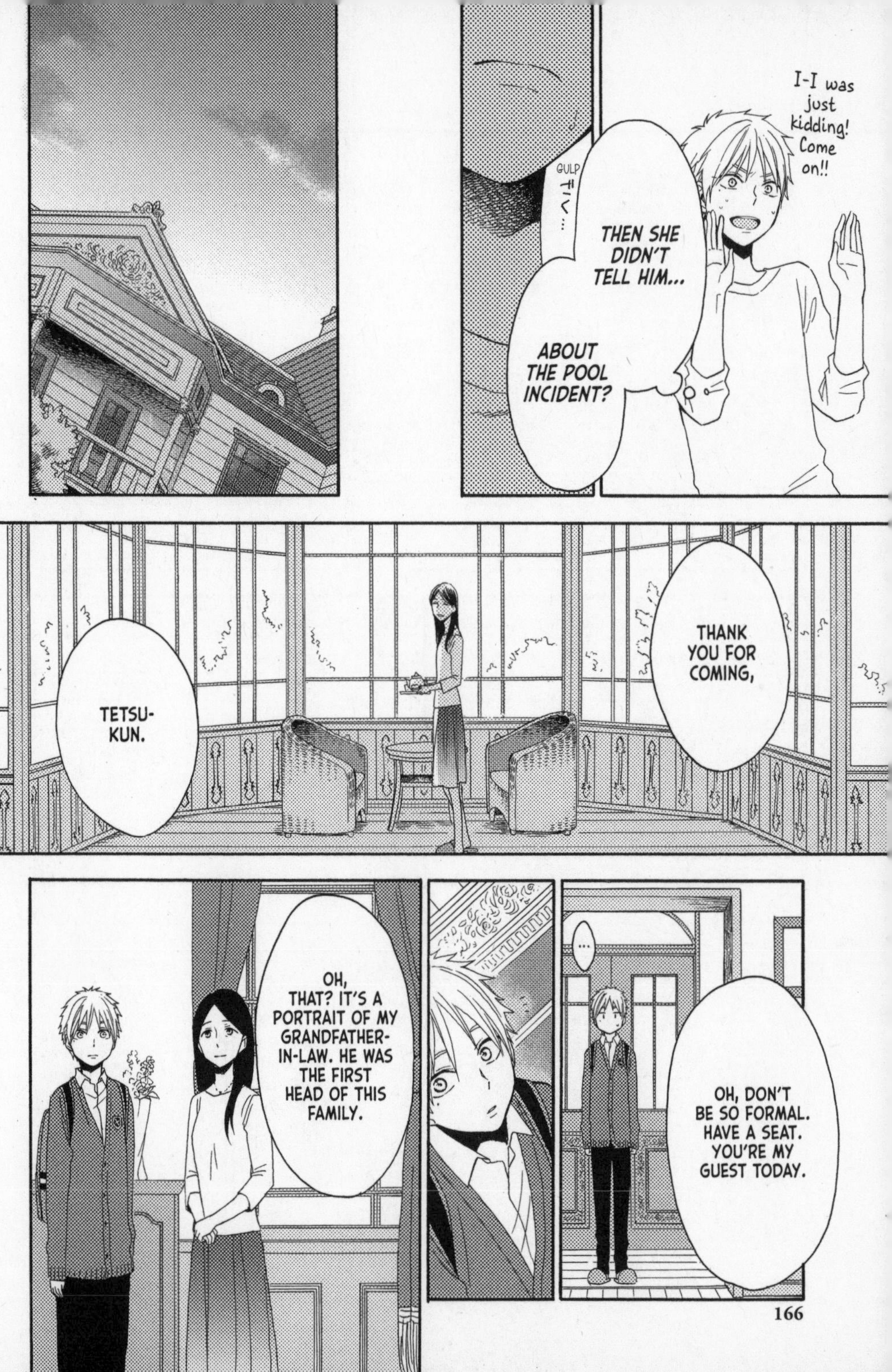
I-I was just kidding! Come on!!
GULP
THEN SHE DIDN'T TELL HIM...
ABOUT THE POOL INCIDENT?
THANK YOU FOR COMING,
TETSU-KUN.
...
OH, DON'T BE SO FORMAL. HAVE A SEAT. YOU'RE MY GUEST TODAY.
OH, THAT? IT'S A PORTRAIT OF MY GRANDFATHER-IN-LAW. HE WAS THE FIRST HEAD OF THIS FAMILY.

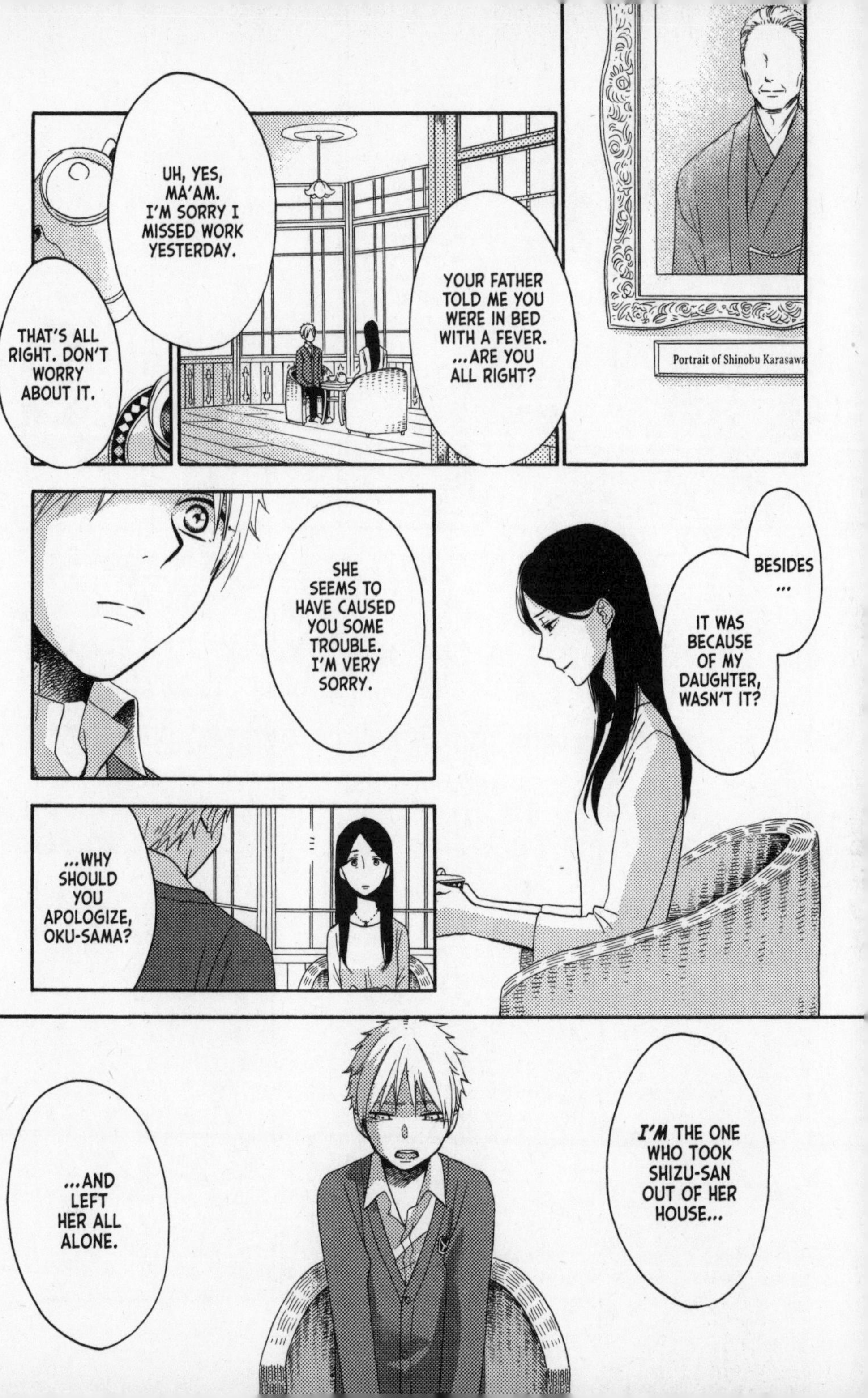
Portrait of Shinobu Karasawa
YOUR FATHER TOLD ME YOU WERE IN BED WITH A FEVER. ...ARE YOU ALL RIGHT?
UH, YES, MA'AM. I'M SORRY I MISSED WORK YESTERDAY.
THAT'S ALL RIGHT. DON'T WORRY ABOUT IT.
BESIDES ...
IT WAS BECAUSE OF MY DAUGHTER, WASN'T IT?
SHE SEEMS TO HAVE CAUSED YOU SOME TROUBLE. I'M VERY SORRY.
...WHY SHOULD YOU APOLOGIZE, OKU-SAMA?
I'M THE ONE WHO TOOK SHIZU-SAN OUT OF HER HOUSE...
...AND LEFT HER ALL ALONE.

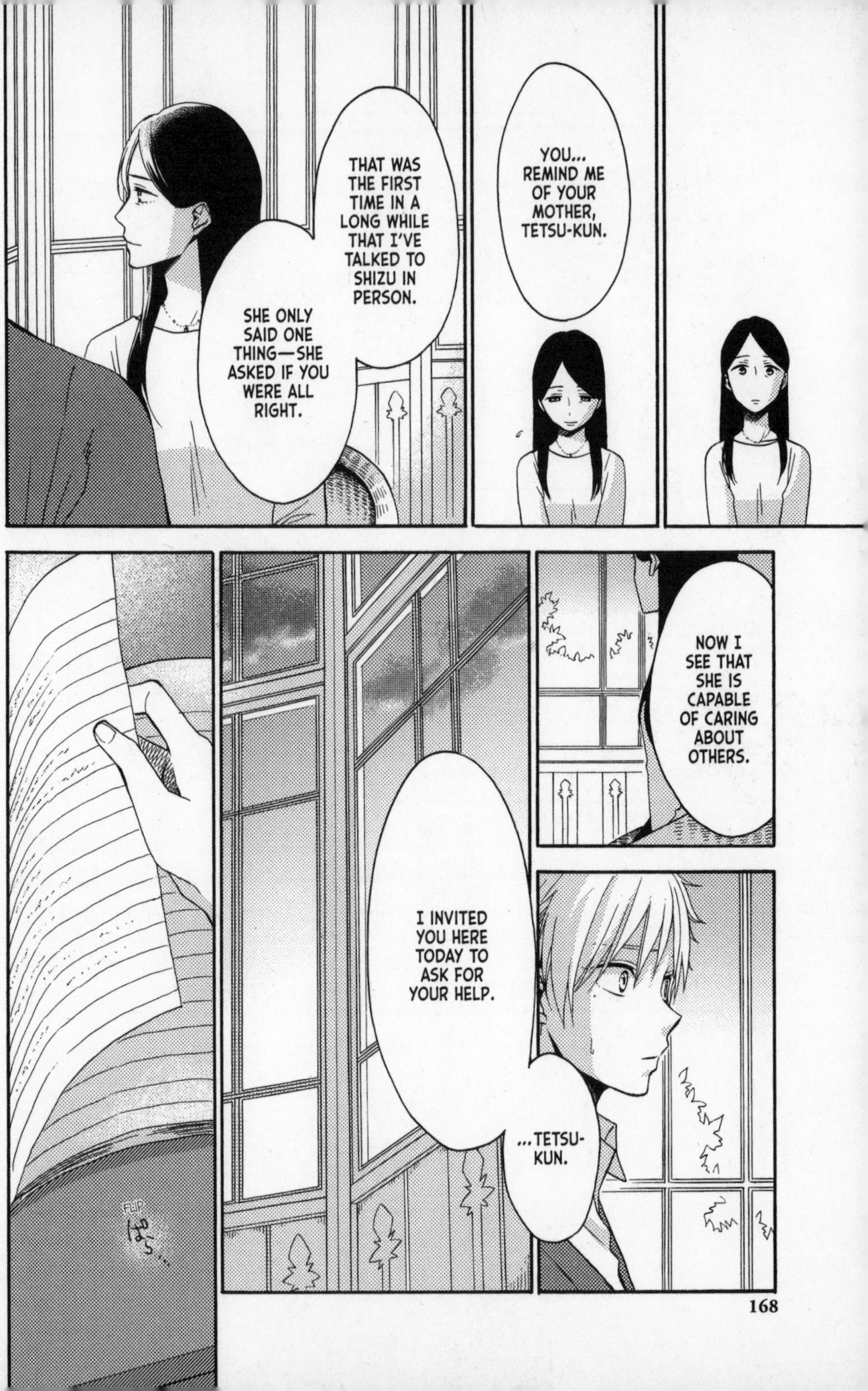
YOU... REMIND ME OF YOUR MOTHER, TETSU-KUN.
THAT WAS THE FIRST TIME IN A LONG WHILE THAT I'VE TALKED TO SHIZU IN PERSON.
SHE ONLY SAID ONE THING—SHE ASKED IF YOU WERE ALL RIGHT.
NOW I SEE THAT SHE IS CAPABLE OF CARING ABOUT OTHERS.
I INVITED YOU HERE TODAY TO ASK FOR YOUR HELP.
...TETSU-KUN.
FLIP
ぱら…

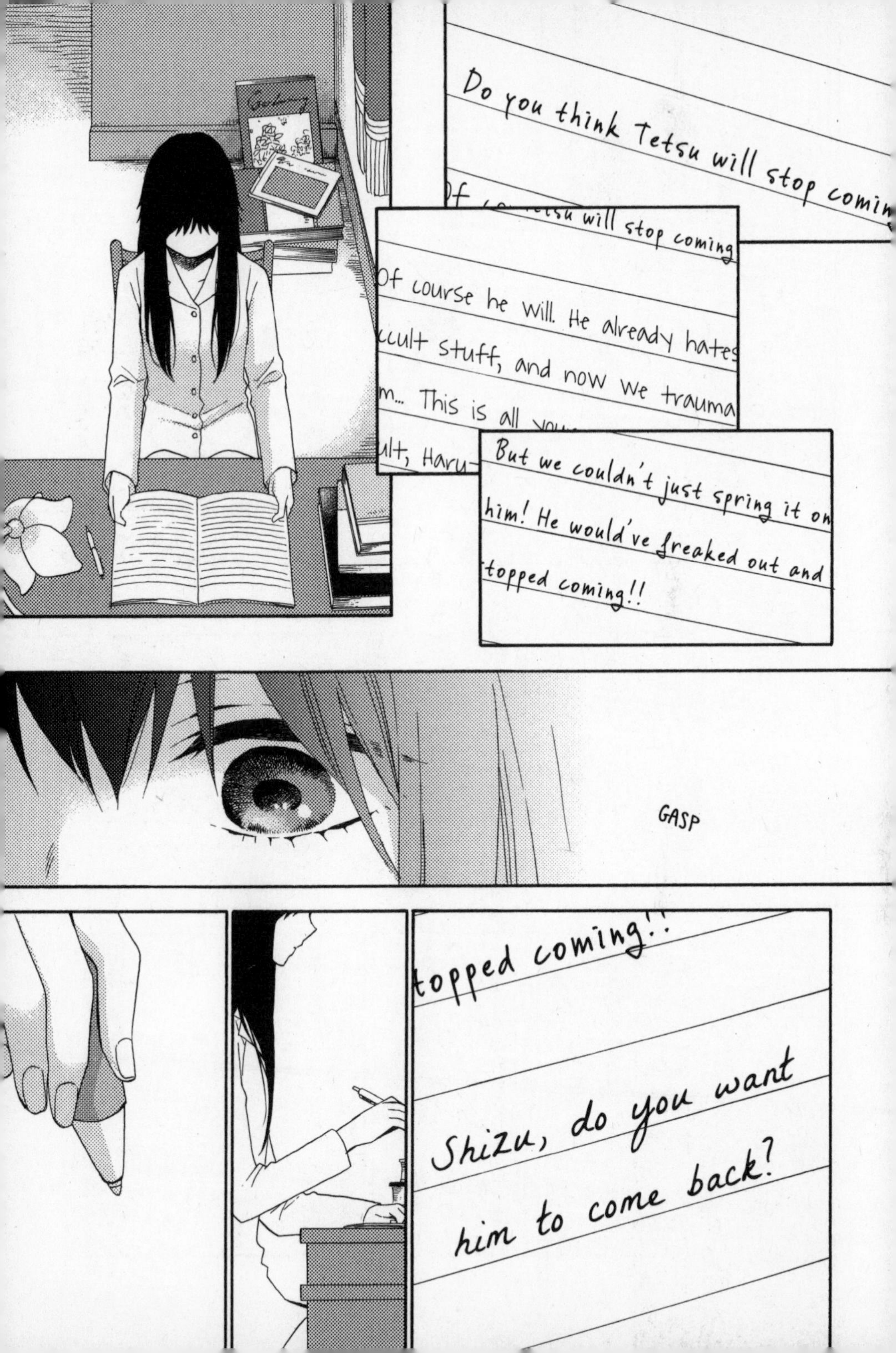

Do you think Tetsu will stop comin
etsu will stop coming
Of course he will. He already hates
ccult stuff, and now we trauma
m... This is all you
lt, Haru-
But we couldn't just spring it on
him! He would've freaked out and
topped coming!!
GASP
topped coming!!
Shizu, do you want
him to come back?

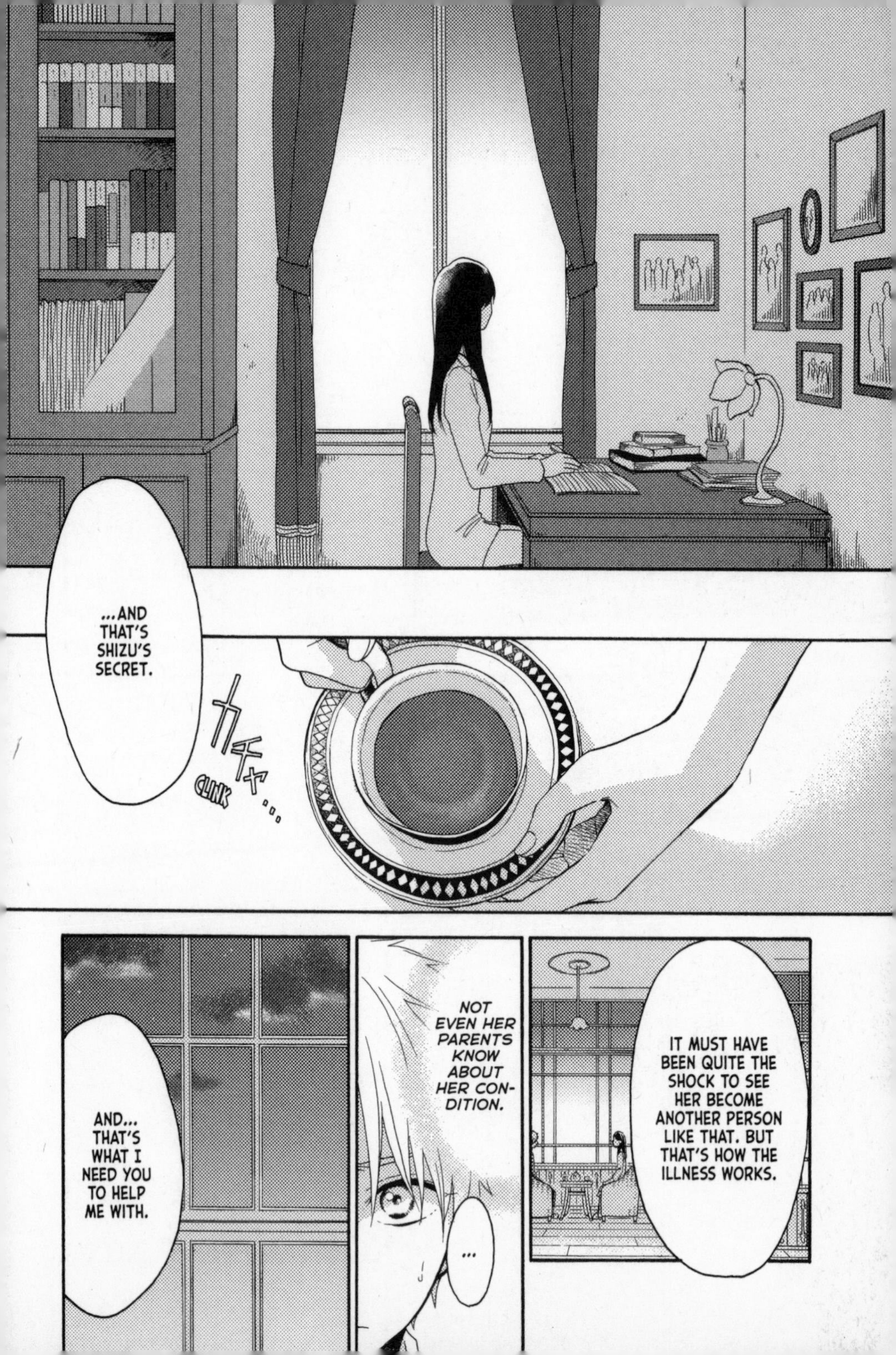
...AND THAT'S SHIZU'S SECRET.
カチャ...
CLINK
IT MUST HAVE BEEN QUITE THE SHOCK TO SEE HER BECOME ANOTHER PERSON LIKE THAT. BUT THAT'S HOW THE ILLNESS WORKS.
NOT EVEN HER PARENTS KNOW ABOUT HER CON-DITION.
...
AND... THAT'S WHAT I NEED YOU TO HELP ME WITH.

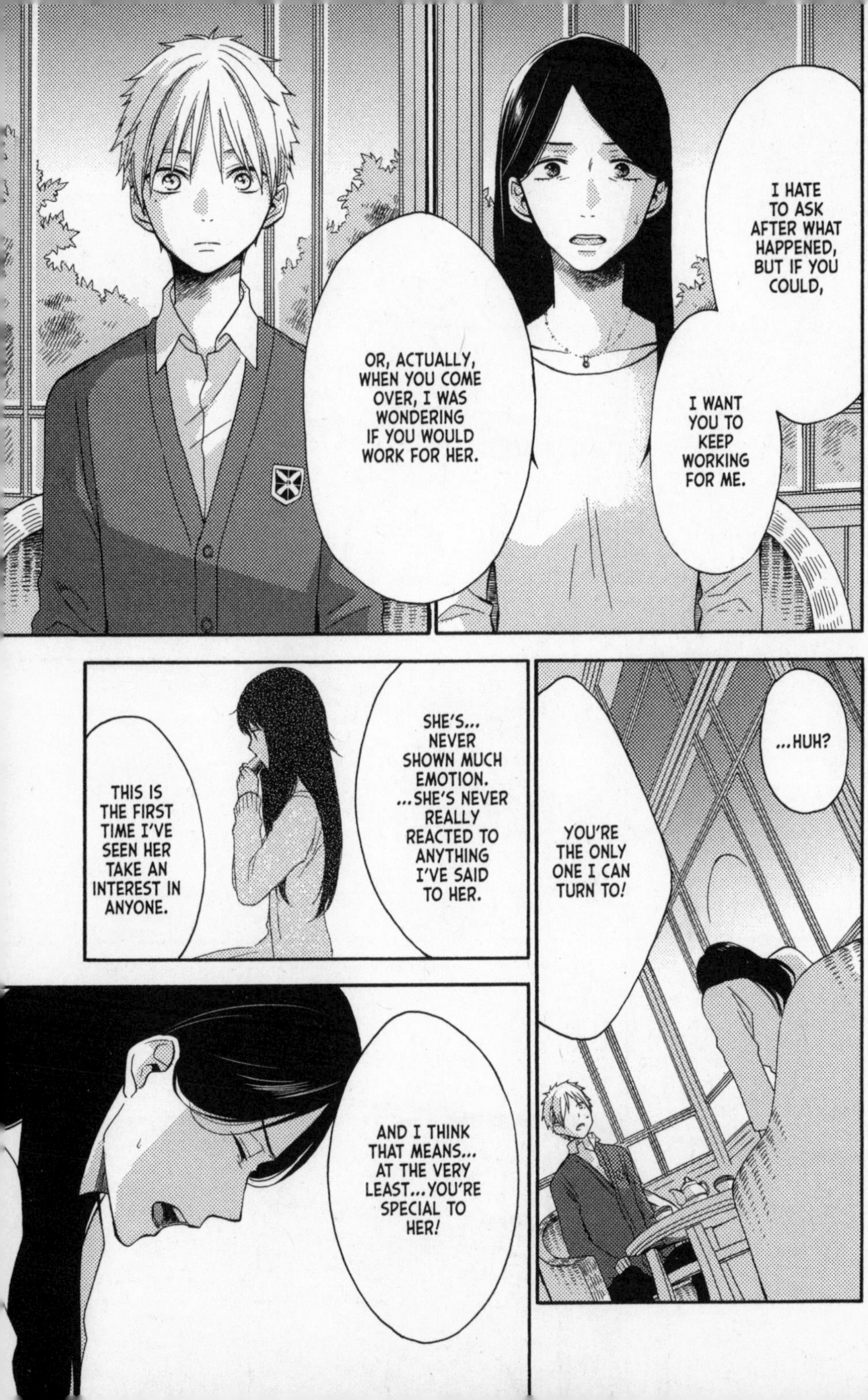
I HATE TO ASK AFTER WHAT HAPPENED, BUT IF YOU COULD,
I WANT YOU TO KEEP WORKING FOR ME.
OR, ACTUALLY, WHEN YOU COME OVER, I WAS WONDERING IF YOU WOULD WORK FOR HER.
...HUH?
YOU'RE THE ONLY ONE I CAN TURN TO!
SHE'S... NEVER SHOWN MUCH EMOTION. ...SHE'S NEVER REALLY REACTED TO ANYTHING I'VE SAID TO HER.
THIS IS THE FIRST TIME I'VE SEEN HER TAKE AN INTEREST IN ANYONE.
AND I THINK THAT MEANS... AT THE VERY LEAST...YOU'RE SPECIAL TO HER!

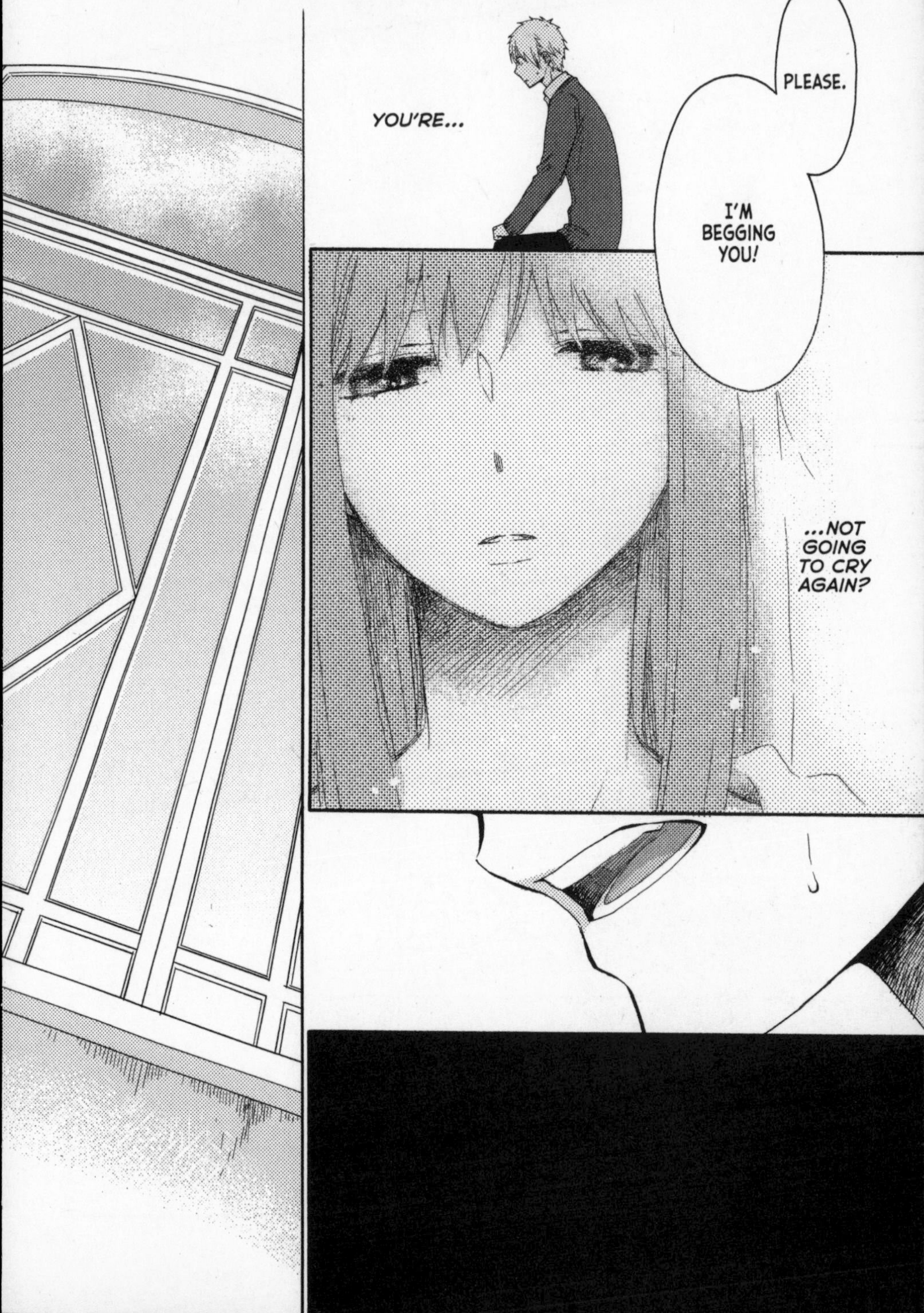
PLEASE.
I'M BEGGING YOU!
YOU'RE...
...NOT GOING TO CRY AGAIN?

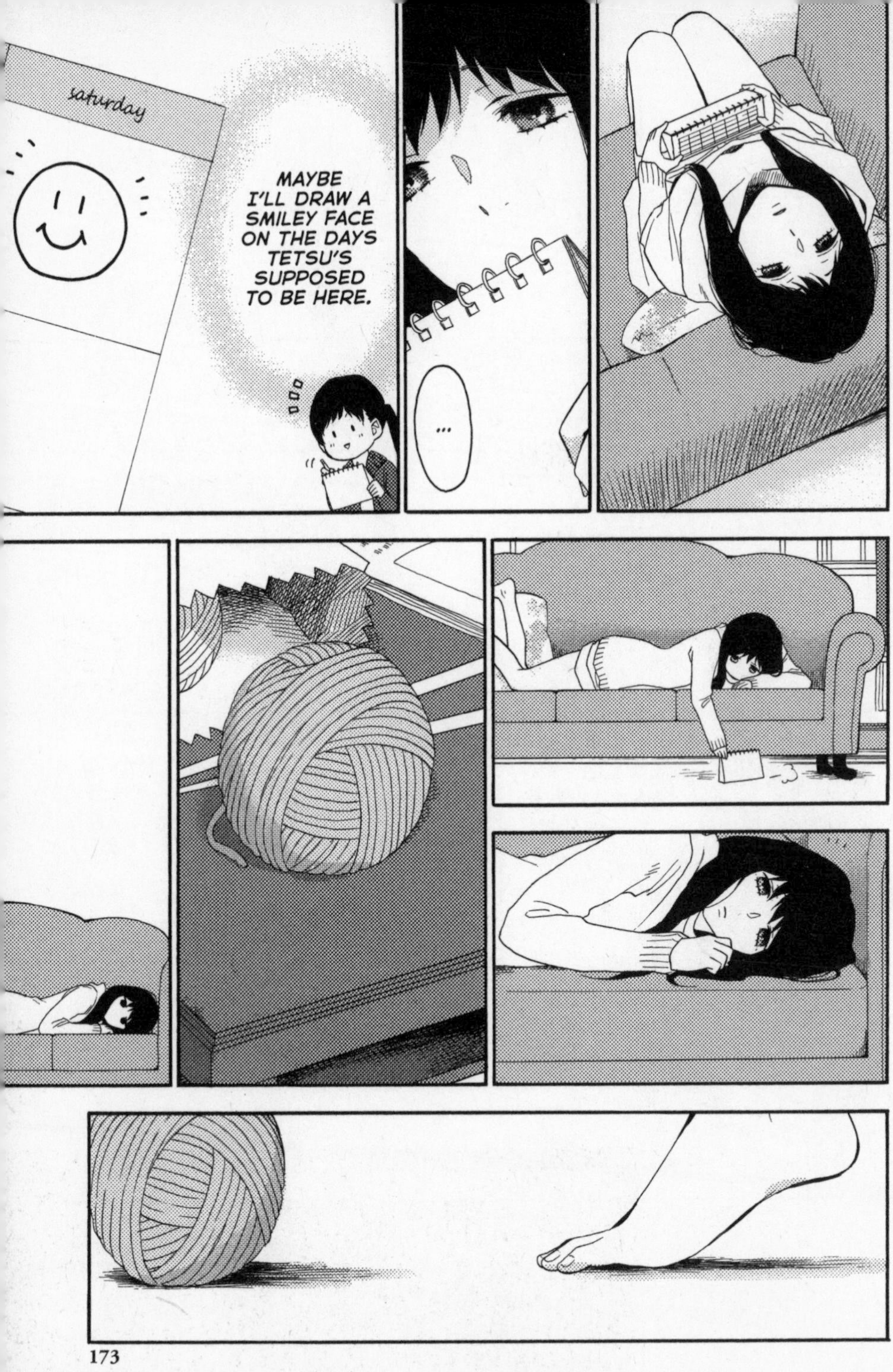
...
saturday
MAYBE I'LL DRAW A SMILEY FACE ON THE DAYS TETSU'S SUPPOSED TO BE HERE.

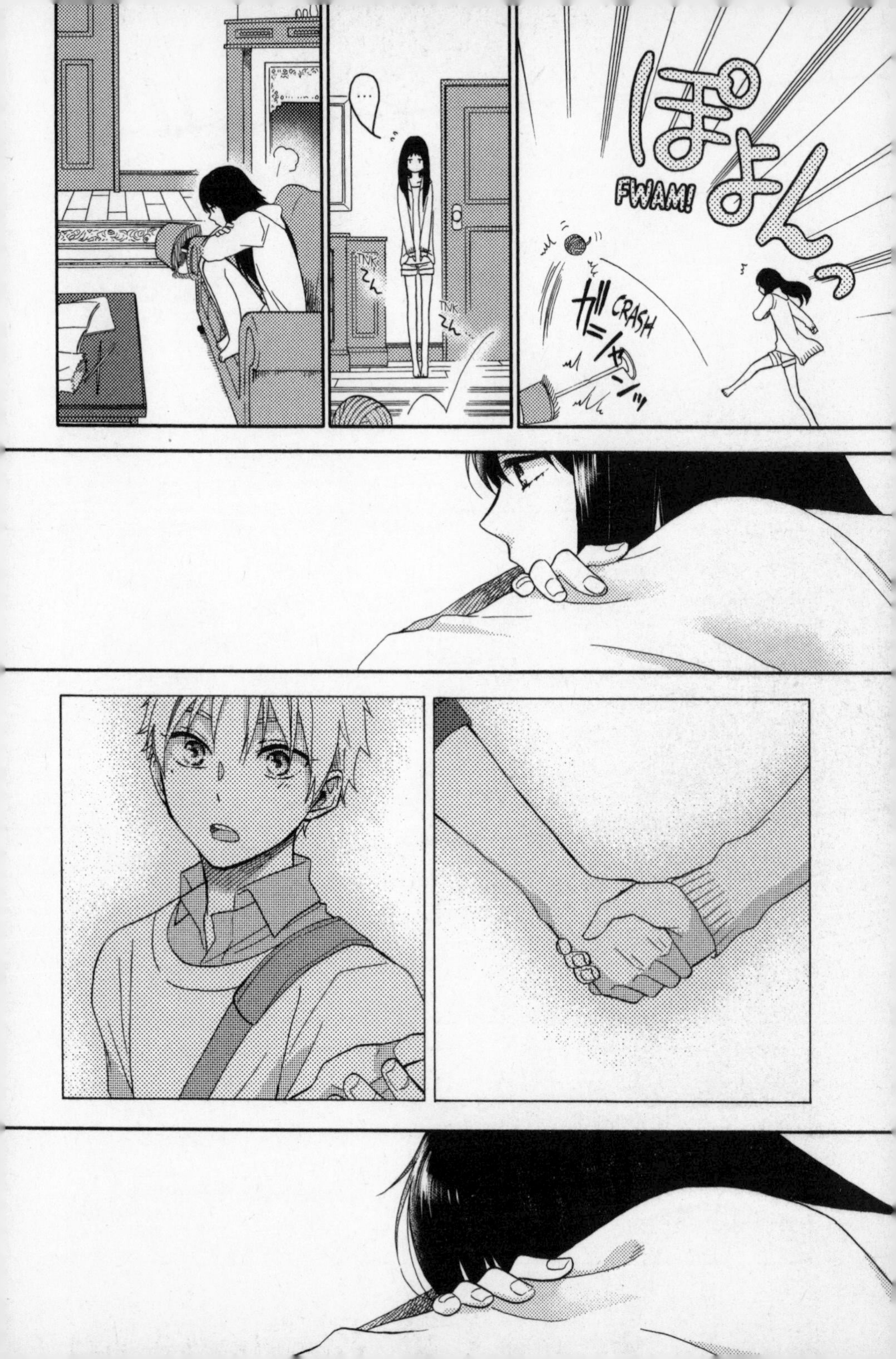
ぽよんっ
FWAM!
ガシャンッ
CRASH
…
TNK
こん
TNK
こん

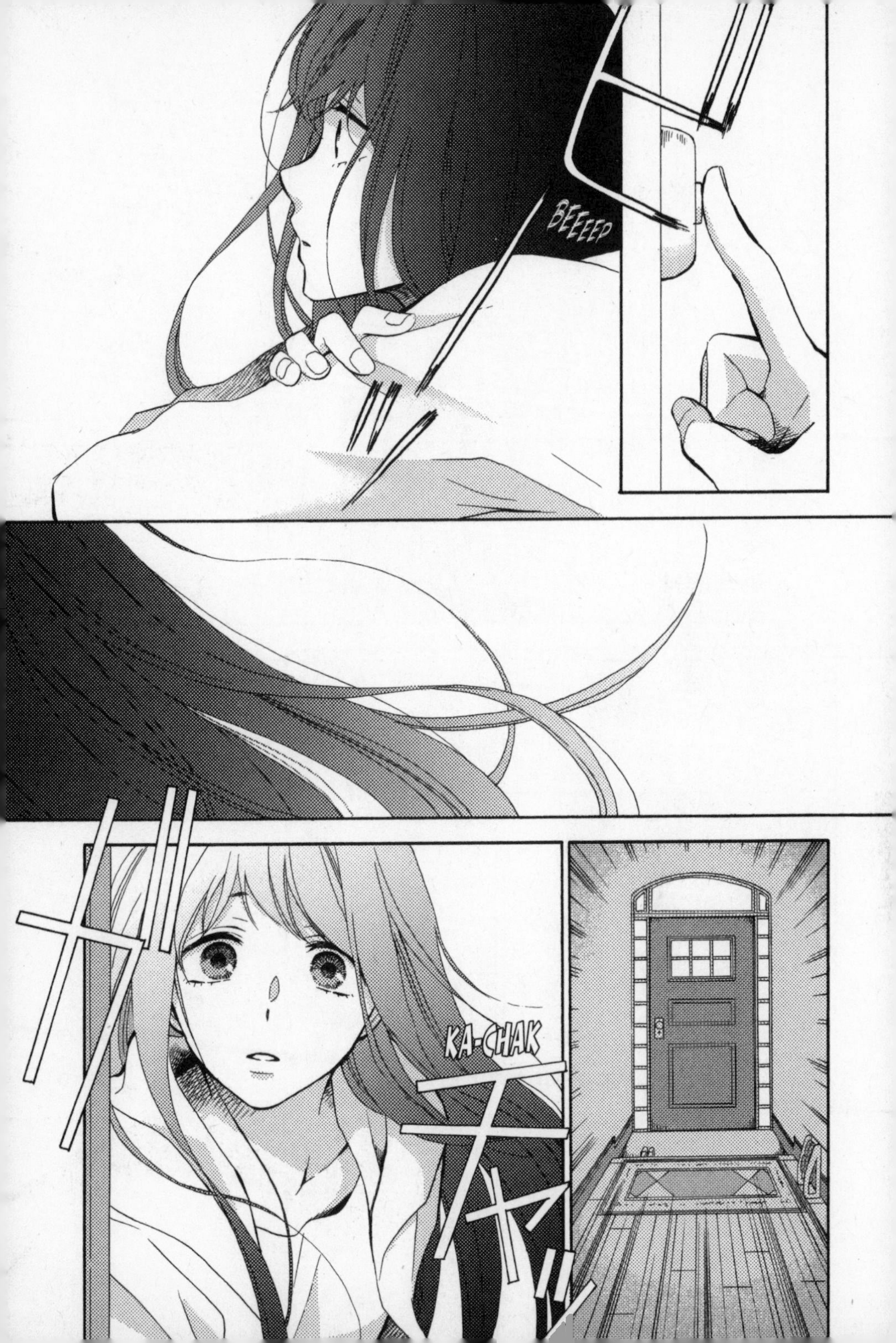
BEEEEP
KA-CHAK

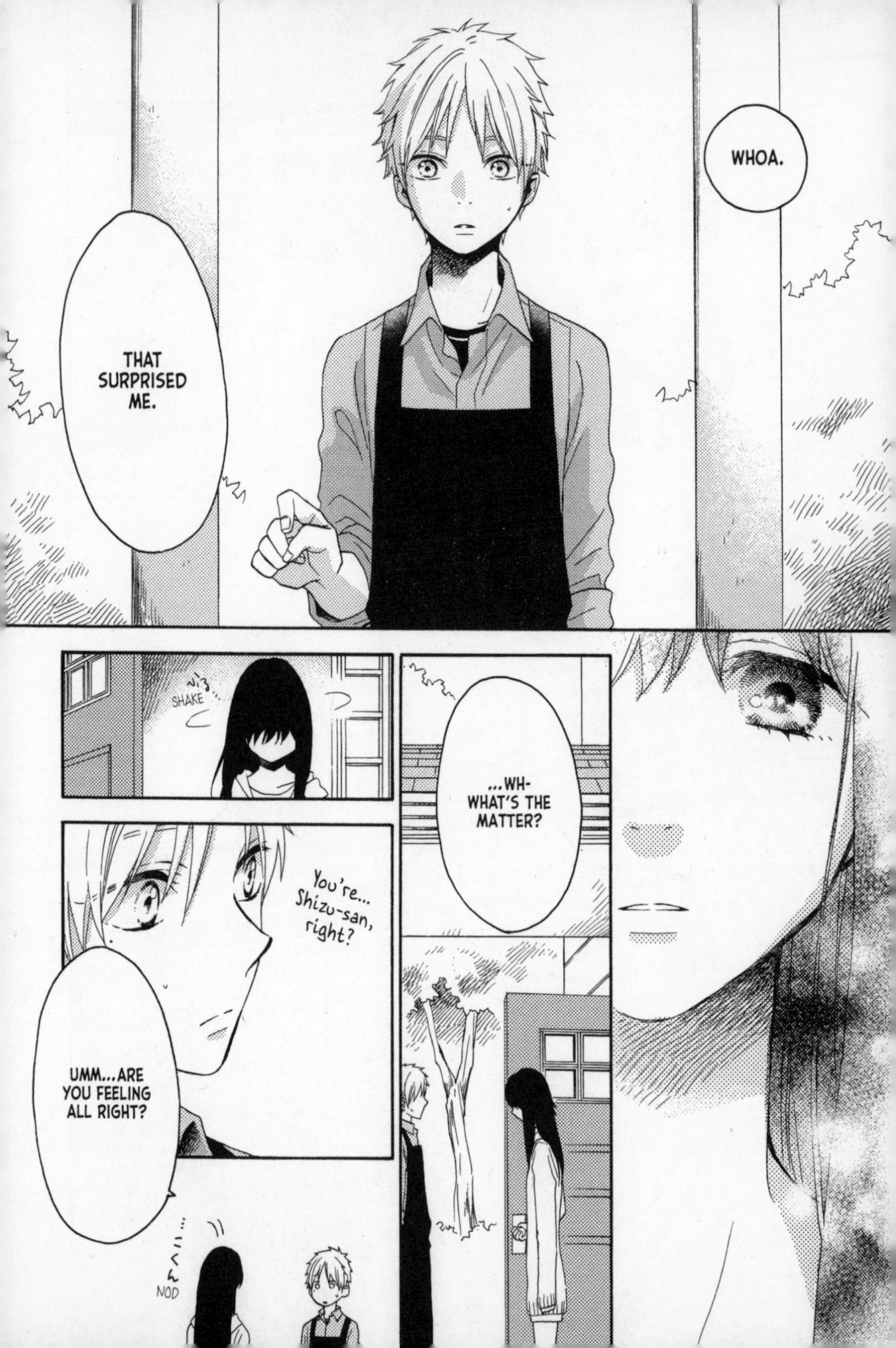

WHOA.
THAT SURPRISED ME.
...WH- WHAT'S THE MATTER?
SHAKE
You're... Shizu-san, right?
UMM...ARE YOU FEELING ALL RIGHT?
NOD

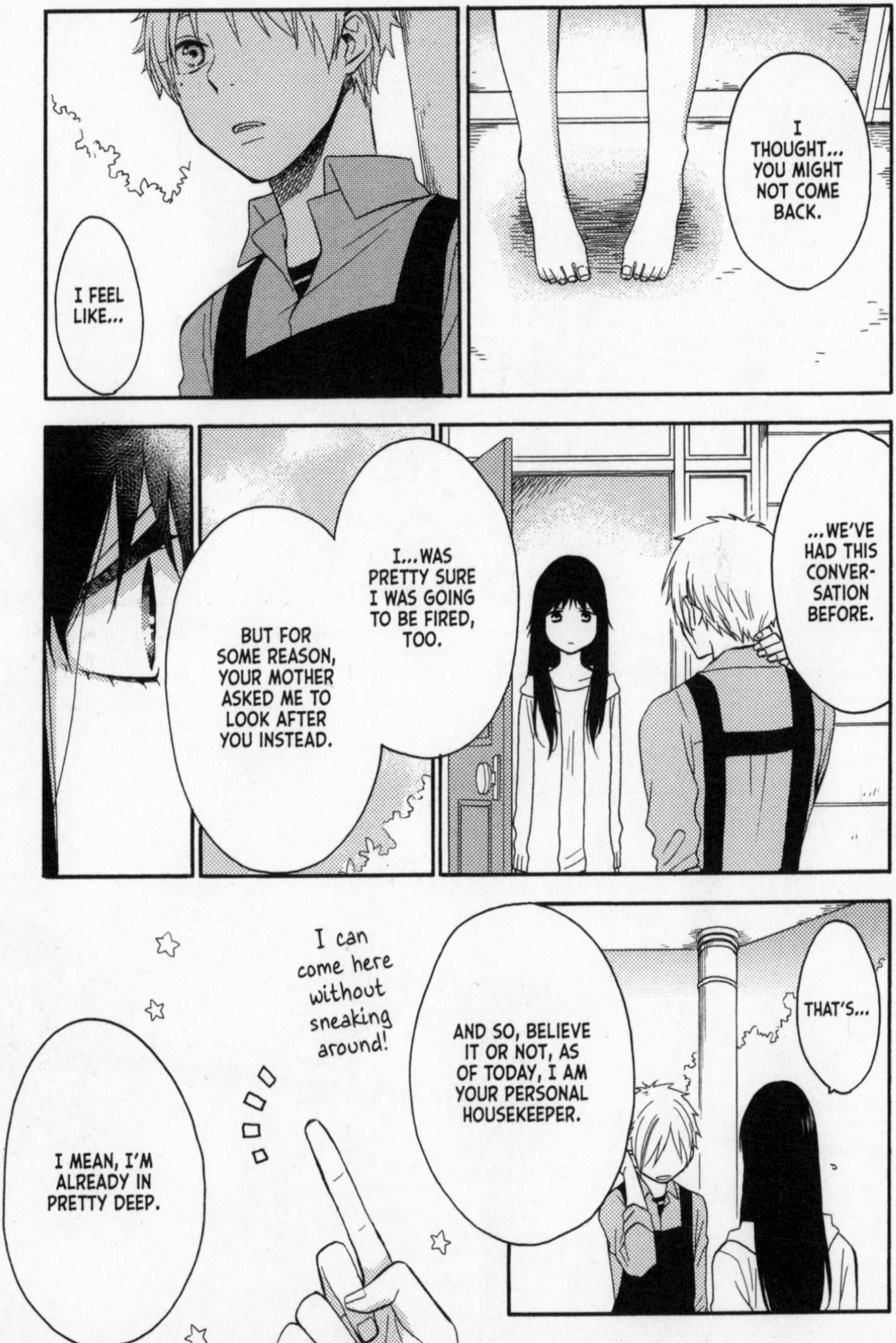
I THOUGHT... YOU MIGHT NOT COME BACK.
I FEEL LIKE...
...WE'VE HAD THIS CONVER-SATION BEFORE.
I...WAS PRETTY SURE I WAS GOING TO BE FIRED, TOO.
BUT FOR SOME REASON, YOUR MOTHER ASKED ME TO LOOK AFTER YOU INSTEAD.
THAT'S...
AND SO, BELIEVE IT OR NOT, AS OF TODAY, I AM YOUR PERSONAL HOUSEKEEPER.
I can come here without sneaking around!
I MEAN, I'M ALREADY IN PRETTY DEEP.

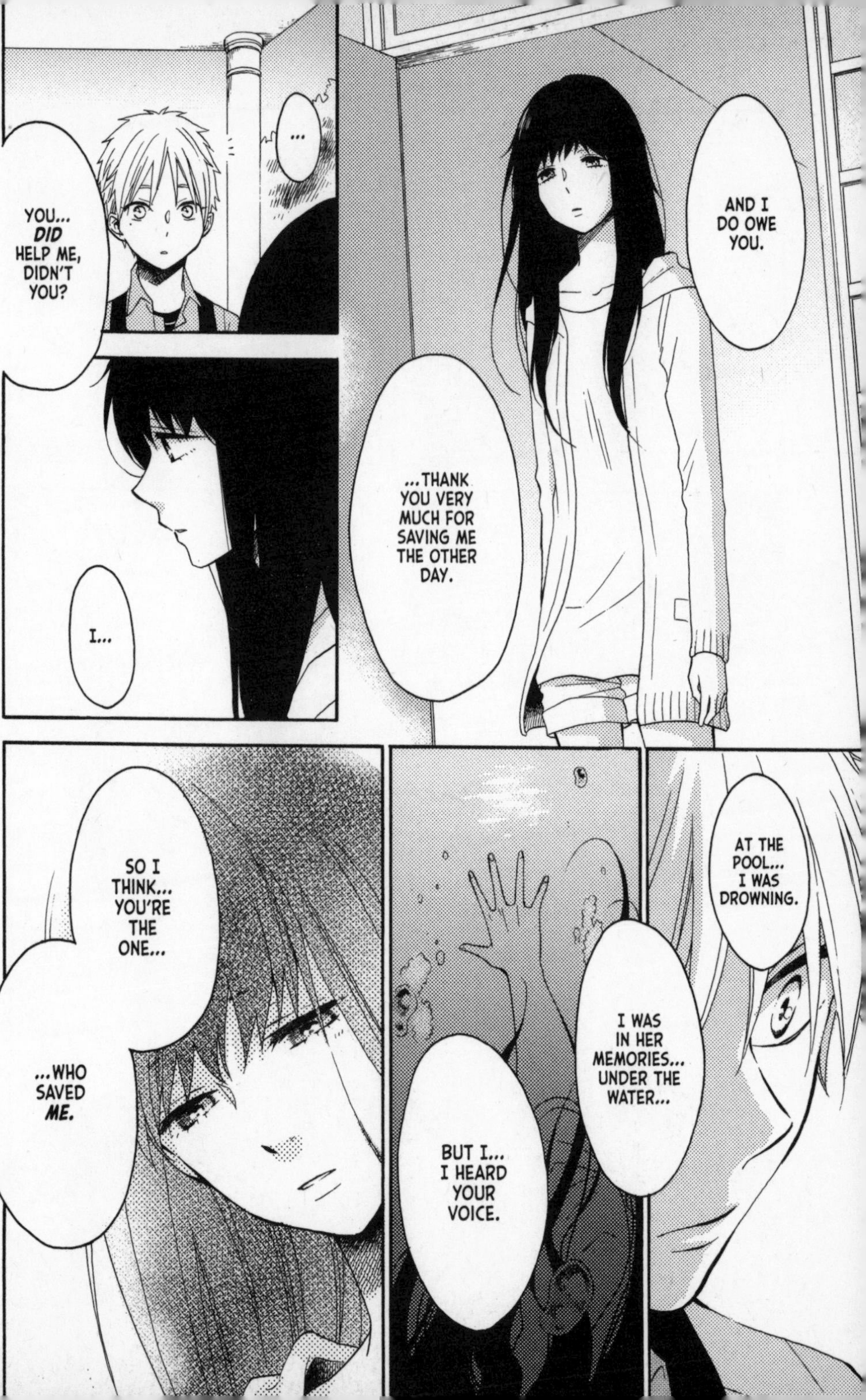
AND I DO OWE YOU.
...THANK YOU VERY MUCH FOR SAVING ME THE OTHER DAY.
...
YOU... *DID* HELP ME, DIDN'T YOU?
I...
AT THE POOL... I WAS DROWNING.
I WAS IN HER MEMORIES... UNDER THE WATER...
BUT I... I HEARD YOUR VOICE.
SO I THINK... YOU'RE THE ONE...
...WHO SAVED *ME.*

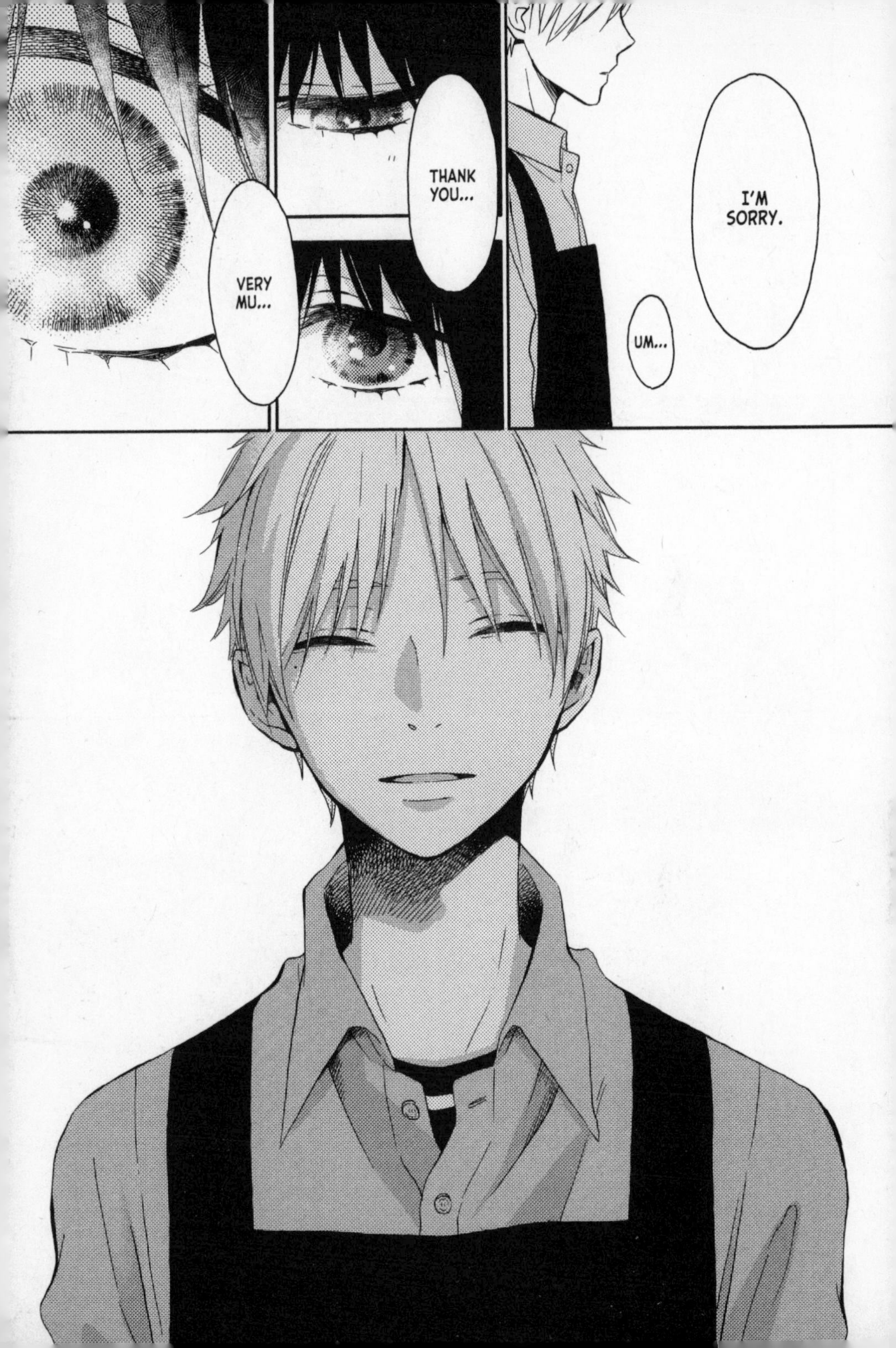
I'M SORRY.
UM...
THANK YOU...
VERY MU...

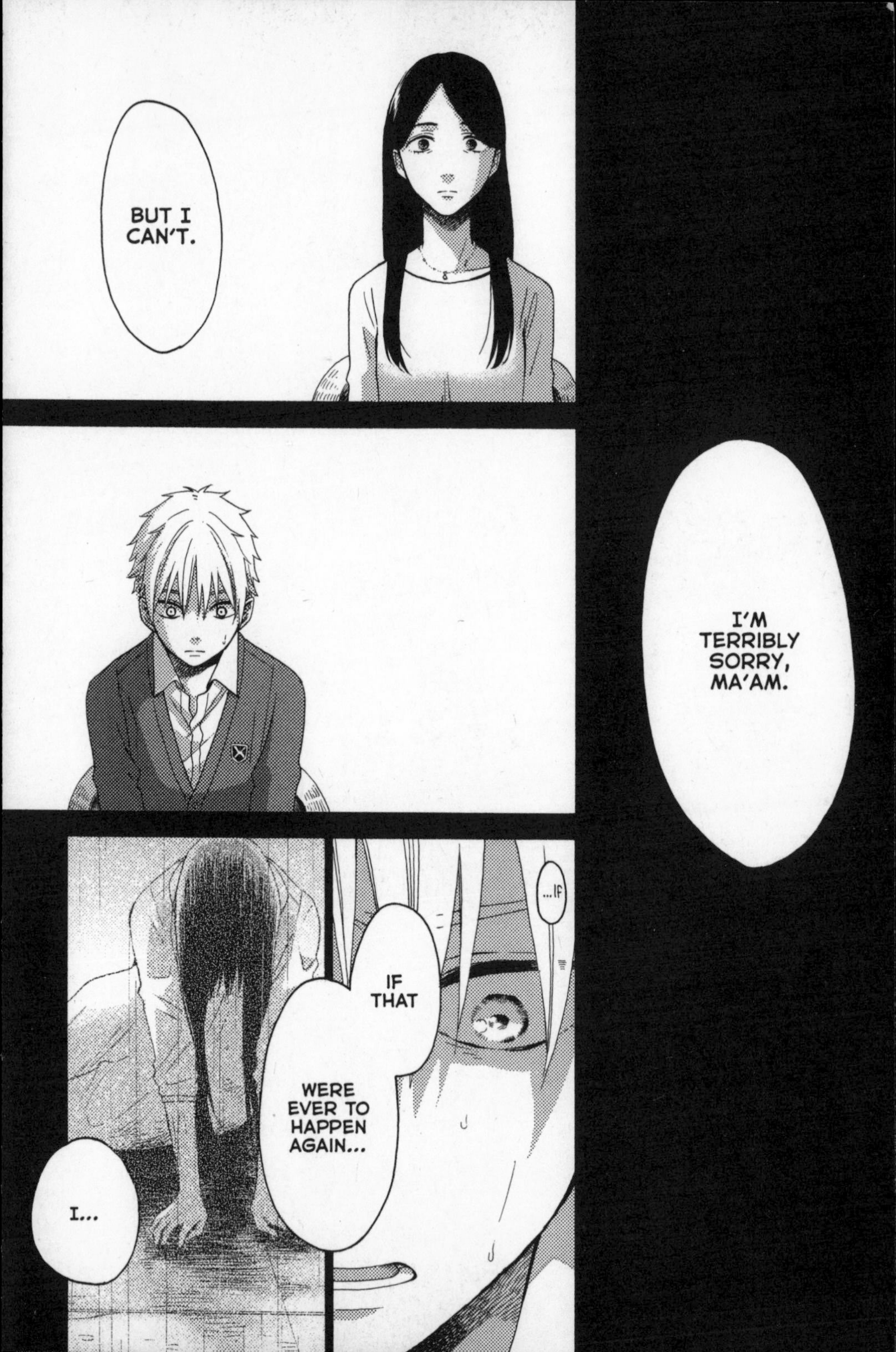
I'M TERRIBLY SORRY, MA'AM.
BUT I CAN'T.
...IF
IF THAT
WERE EVER TO HAPPEN AGAIN...
I...

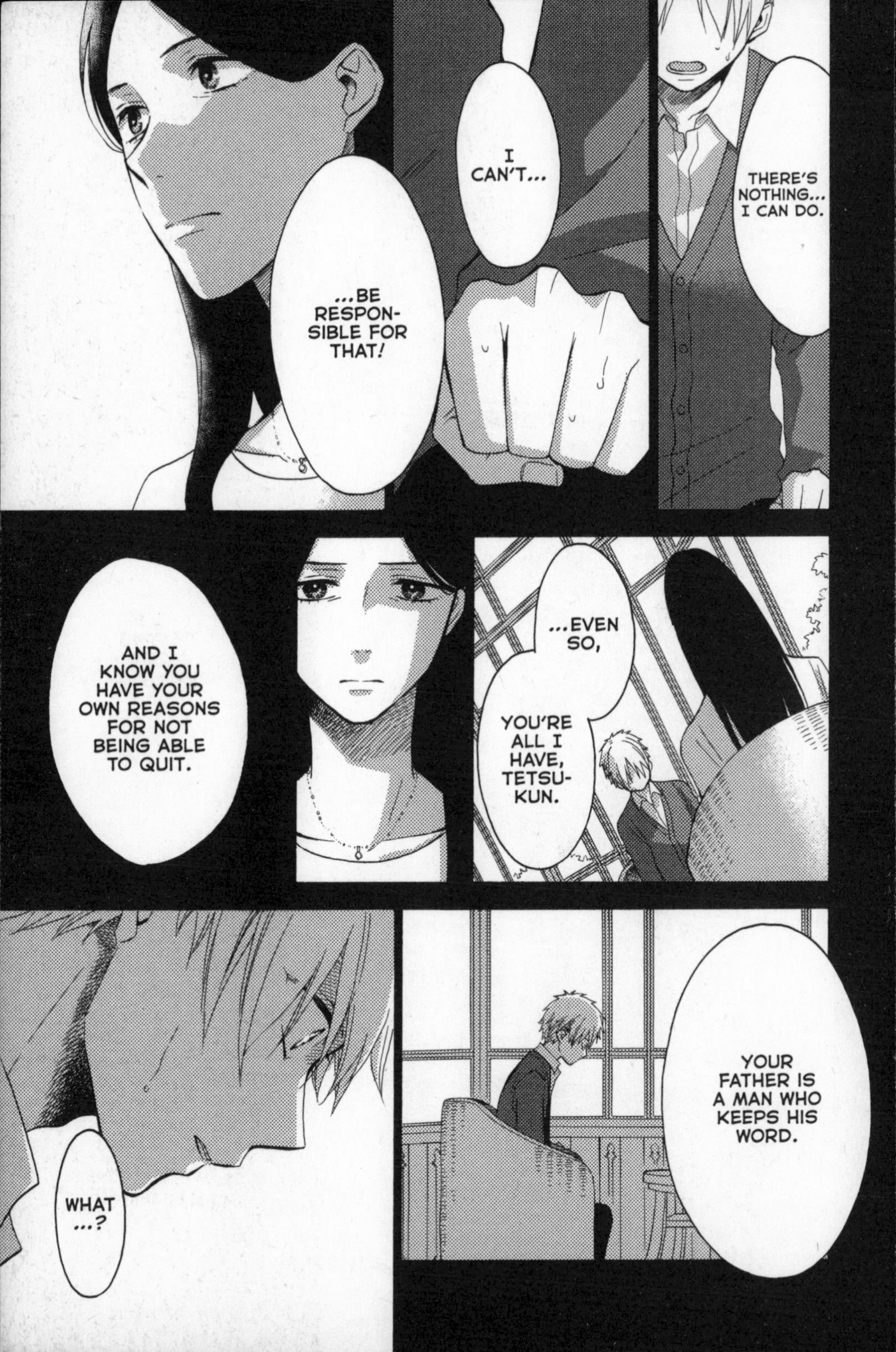
THERE'S NOTHING... I CAN DO.
I CAN'T...
...BE RESPONSIBLE FOR THAT!
...EVEN SO,
YOU'RE ALL I HAVE, TETSU-KUN.
AND I KNOW YOU HAVE YOUR OWN REASONS FOR NOT BEING ABLE TO QUIT.
YOUR FATHER IS A MAN WHO KEEPS HIS WORD.
WHAT...?

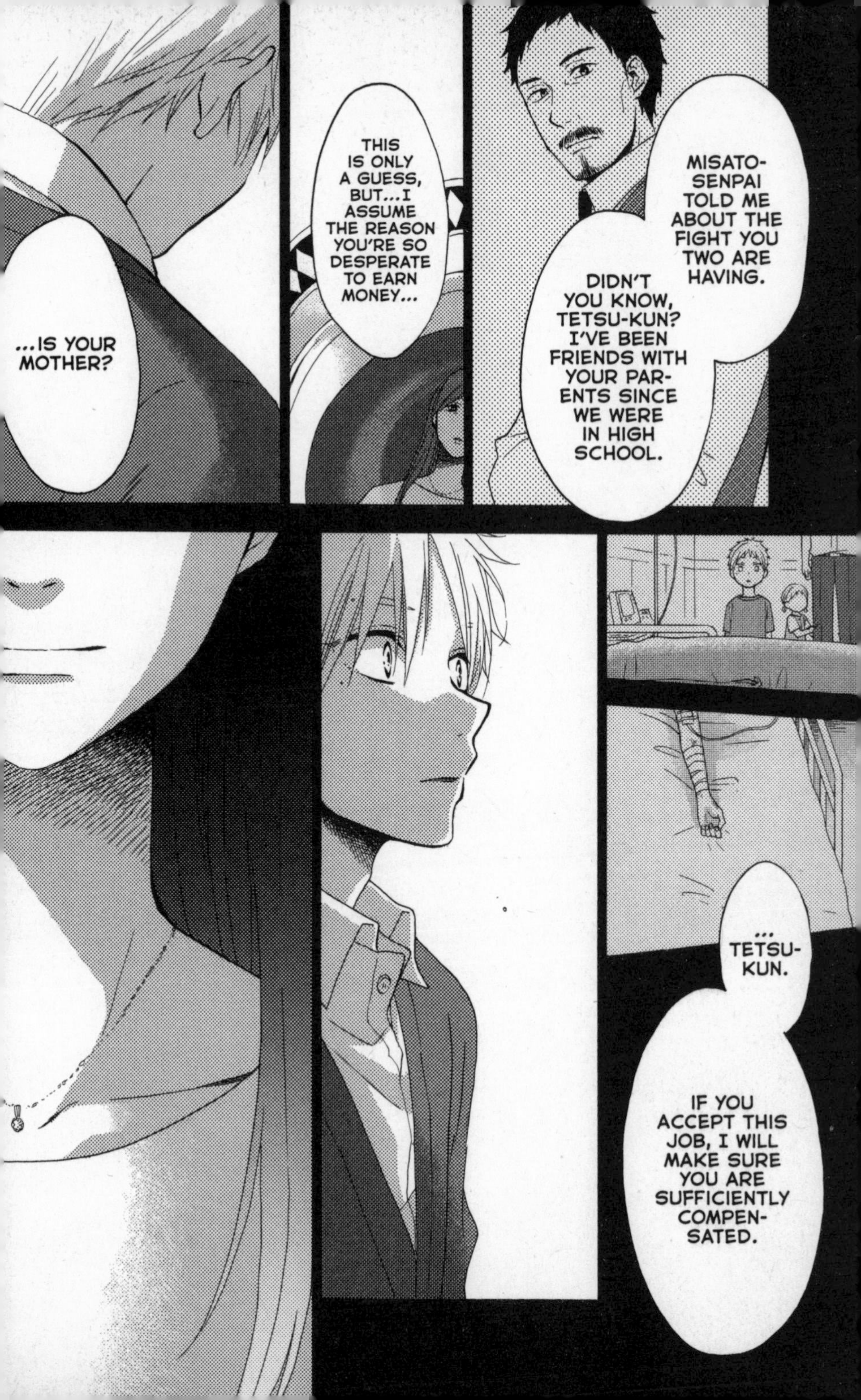
MISATO-SENPAI TOLD ME ABOUT THE FIGHT YOU TWO ARE HAVING.
DIDN'T YOU KNOW, TETSU-KUN? I'VE BEEN FRIENDS WITH YOUR PARENTS SINCE WE WERE IN HIGH SCHOOL.
THIS IS ONLY A GUESS, BUT...I ASSUME THE REASON YOU'RE SO DESPERATE TO EARN MONEY...
...IS YOUR MOTHER?
...TETSU-KUN.
IF YOU ACCEPT THIS JOB, I WILL MAKE SURE YOU ARE SUFFICIENTLY COMPENSATED.

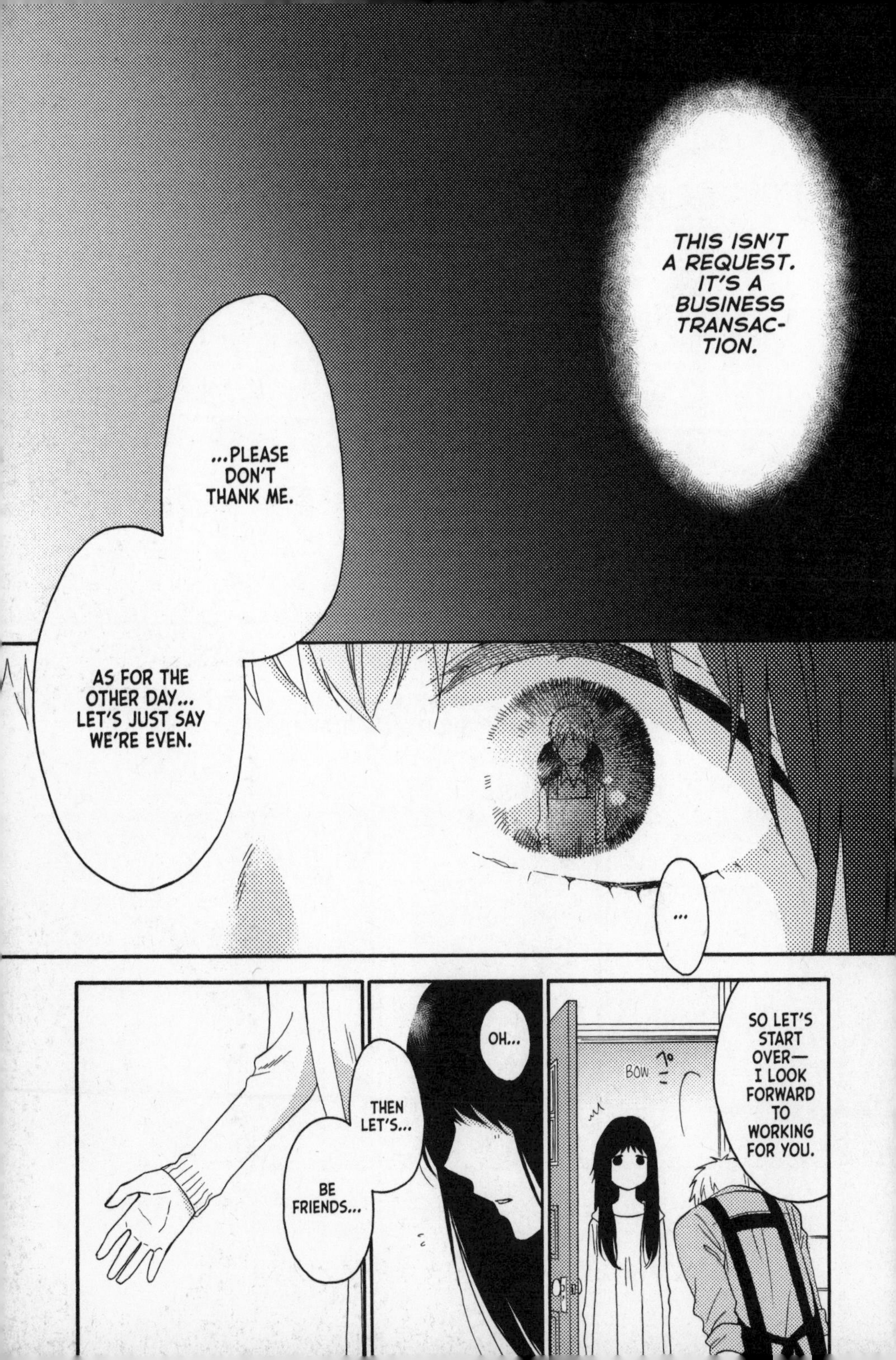
THIS ISN'T A REQUEST. IT'S A BUSINESS TRANSACTION.
...PLEASE DON'T THANK ME.
AS FOR THE OTHER DAY... LET'S JUST SAY WE'RE EVEN.
...
SO LET'S START OVER— I LOOK FORWARD TO WORKING FOR YOU.
BOW
OH...
THEN LET'S...
BE FRIENDS...

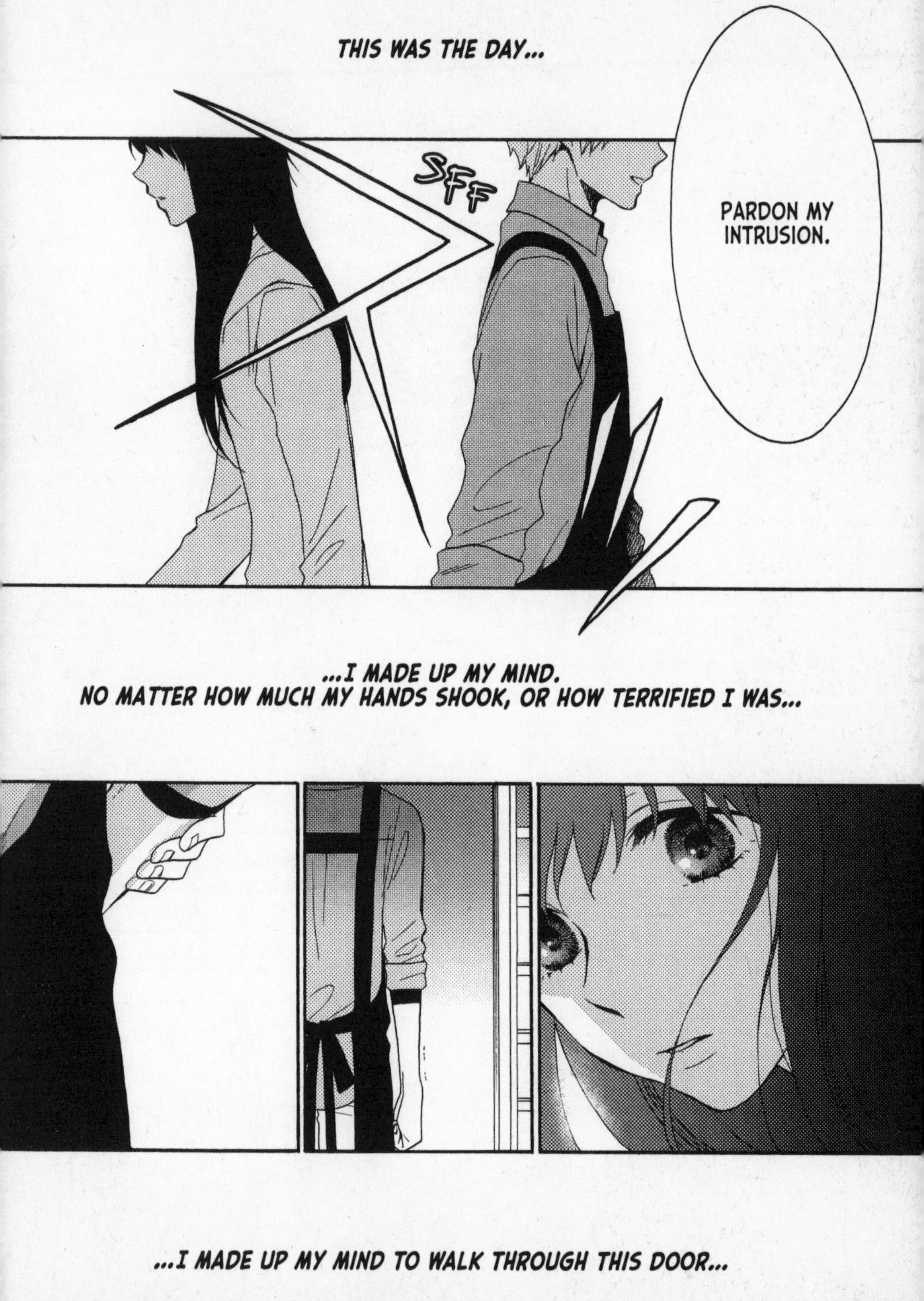
PARDON MY INTRUSION.
THIS WAS THE DAY...
SFF
...I MADE UP MY MIND.
NO MATTER HOW MUCH MY HANDS SHOOK, OR HOW TERRIFIED I WAS...
...I MADE UP MY MIND TO WALK THROUGH THIS DOOR...

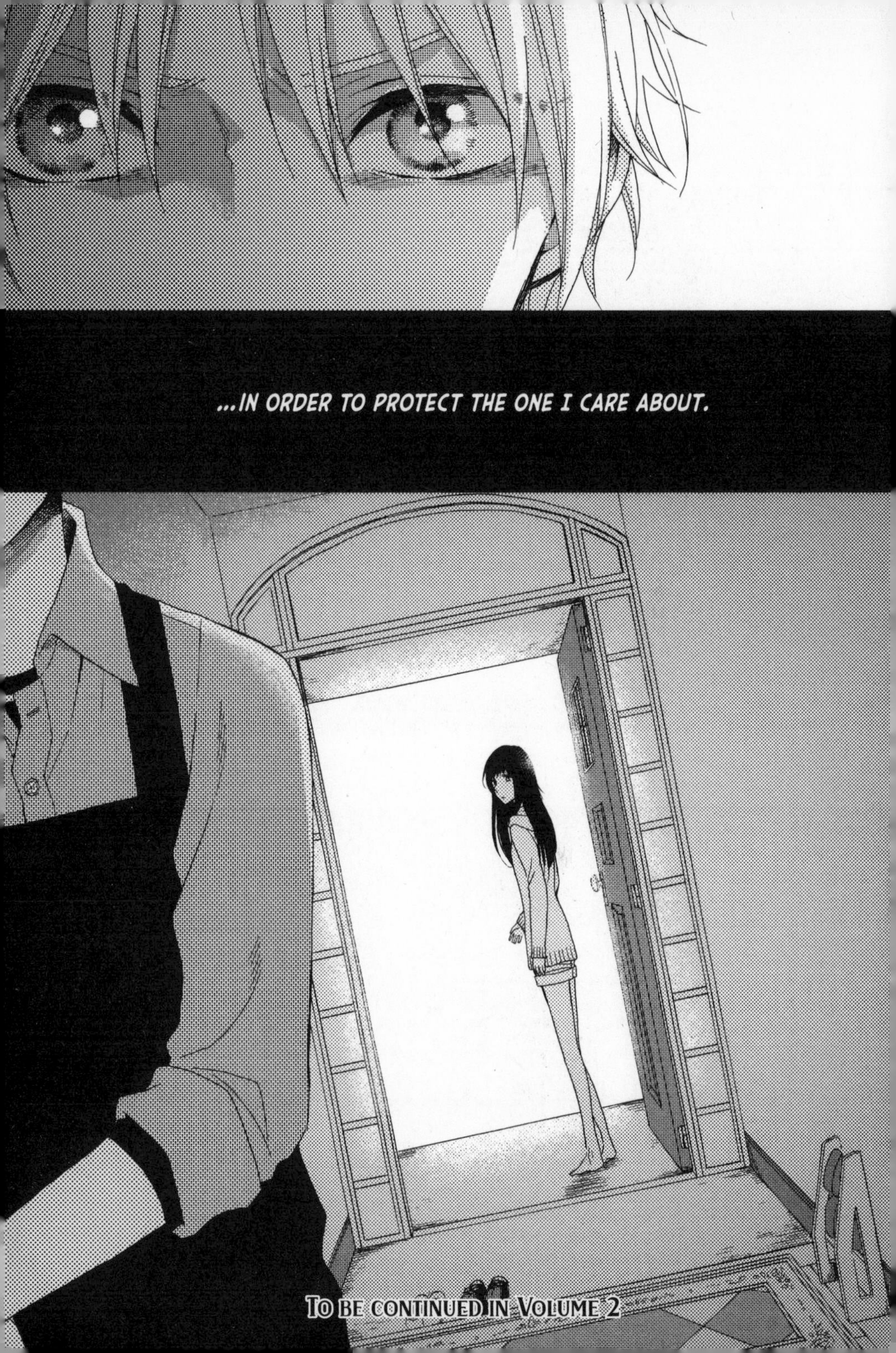
...IN ORDER TO PROTECT THE ONE I CARE ABOUT.
TO BE CONTINUED IN VOLUME 2

Bonus
Sleeping Beauty

Thank you for reading this far!

FAMILY RULES

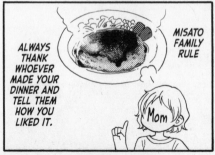

MISATO FAMILY RULE
ALWAYS THANK WHOEVER MADE YOUR DINNER AND TELL THEM HOW YOU LIKED IT.
Mom
THANKS FOR DINNER, YOU STUBBORN PUNK!
Taking it to the sink.
IT TASTED GREAT, AS USUAL, YOU FOOL!!
FATHER-SON FIGHT IN PROGRESS
SCREW YOU! LISTEN TO ME FOR ONCE, YOU DAMN GEEZER!
Pouring the post-dinner tea
BLUP BLUP
I'M GLAD YOU LIKED IT!!!
Your demi-glace was the best!
Well maybe I'll make it again!
SLURP
...WHAT IS GOING ON?

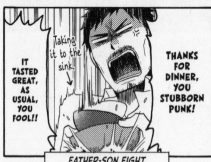

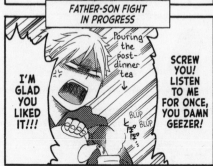

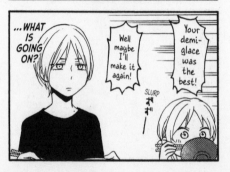

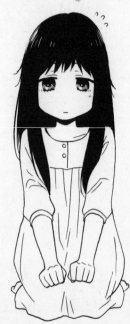

WHO EVEN CARES ANYMORE

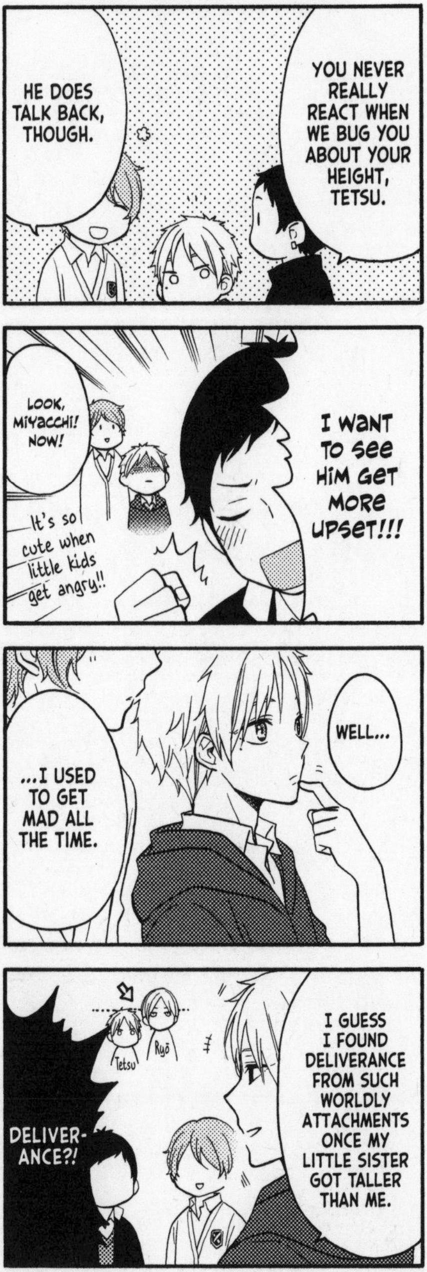
YOU NEVER REALLY REACT WHEN WE BUG YOU ABOUT YOUR HEIGHT, TETSU.
HE DOES TALK BACK, THOUGH.
I WANT TO SEE HIM GET MORE UPSET!!!
LOOK, MIYACCHI! NOW!
It's so cute when little kids get angry!!
WELL...
...I USED TO GET MAD ALL THE TIME.
I GUESS I FOUND DELIVERANCE FROM SUCH WORLDLY ATTACHMENTS ONCE MY LITTLE SISTER GOT TALLER THAN ME.
Ryō
Tetsu
DELIVER-ANCE?!

SALT IN THE WOUND

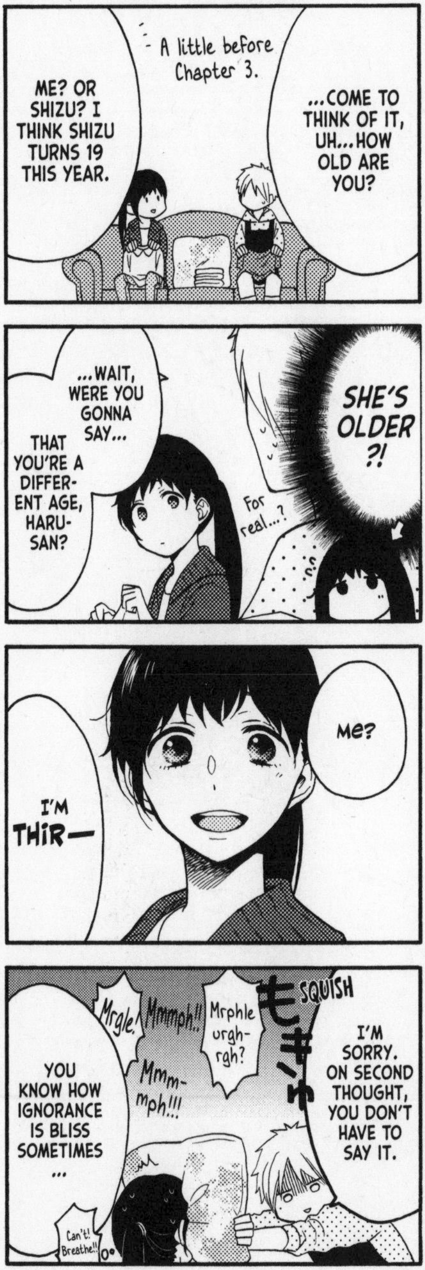
...COME TO THINK OF IT, UH...HOW OLD ARE YOU?
A little before Chapter 3.
ME? OR SHIZU? I THINK SHIZU TURNS 19 THIS YEAR.
SHE'S OLDER?!
For real...?
...WAIT, WERE YOU GONNA SAY...
THAT YOU'RE A DIFFERENT AGE, HARU-SAN?
ME?
I'M THIR—
SQUISH
I'M SORRY. ON SECOND THOUGHT, YOU DON'T HAVE TO SAY IT.
Mrphle urgh-rgh?
Mmmph!!
Mrgle.
Mmm-mph!!!
YOU KNOW HOW IGNORANCE IS BLISS SOMETIMES...
Can't! Breathe!!

Wake Up, Sleeping Beauty
Height Chart ☆

☆ SPECIAL THANKS TO ☆ ☆

My editor Y-san
Ōga-san
Kyoko-san
Oikawa-san
My family, friends, and
former colleagues who are
always supporting me.

THANKS TO THE HELP OF MANY PEOPLE, I HAVE NOW
RELEASED MY SECOND GRAPHIC NOVEL. I WANT TO
KEEP WORKING HARD UNTIL IT'S OVER, SO I CAN
REPAY YOU ALL WITH MY MANGA.

A FEW WORDS ABOUT UNDER THE COVER.
BASICALLY, I DRAW SHORT COMICS FOR UNDER THE
SLIPCOVER, WITH THE IDEA THAT YOU'LL READ THEM
AFTER YOU'VE READ THE BOOK. SO IF YOU LIKE, GO
AHEAD AND READ THEM WHEN YOU'VE FINISHED.
[EDITOR'S NOTE: WE'VE INCLUDED THESE ON THE
NEXT PAGES FOR OUR ENGLISH READERS!]

WELL, I HOPE TO SEE YOU AGAIN IN VOLUME TWO!

Megumi Morino

2015.4.13

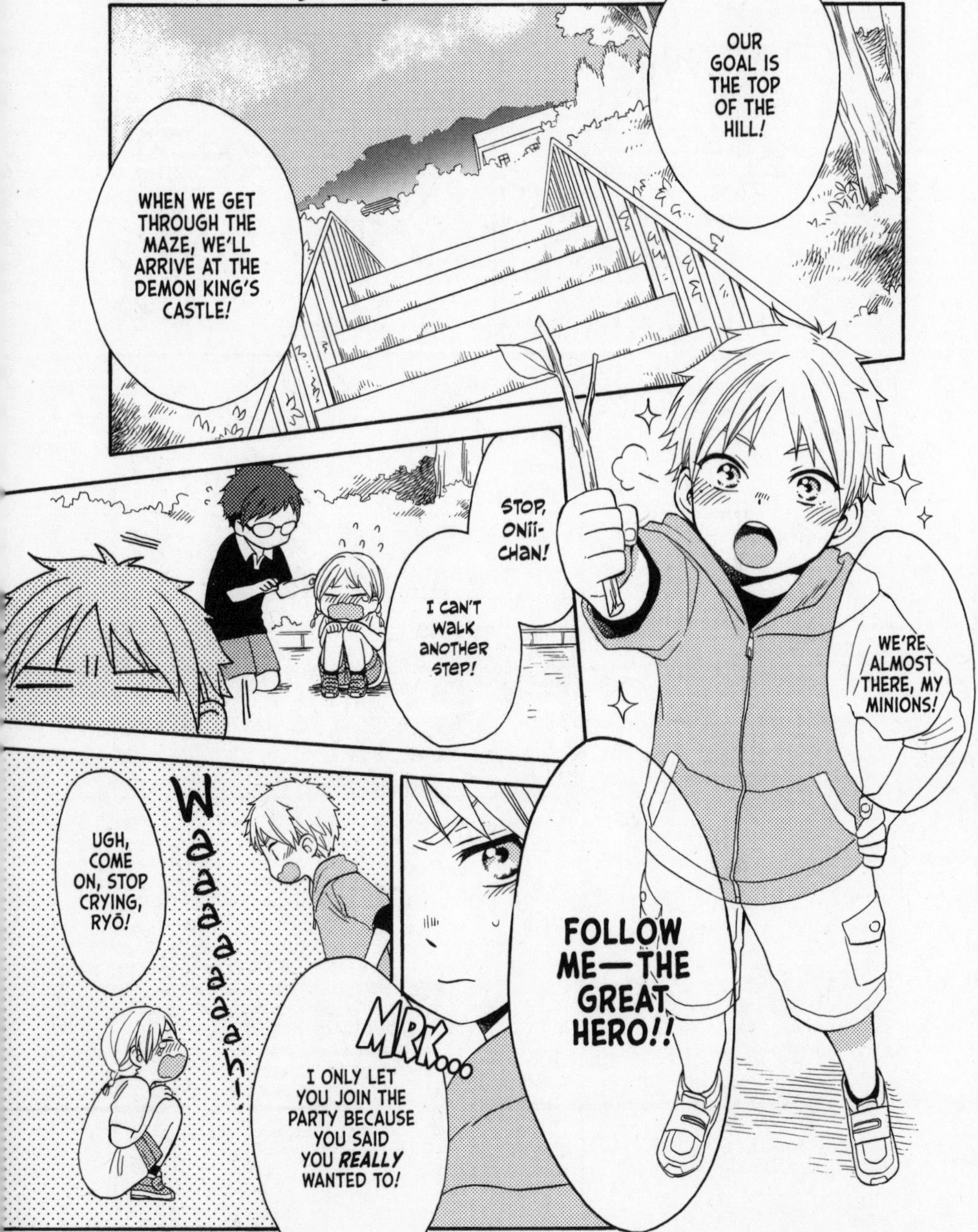
OUR GOAL IS THE TOP OF THE HILL!
WHEN WE GET THROUGH THE MAZE, WE'LL ARRIVE AT THE DEMON KING'S CASTLE!
WE'RE ALMOST THERE, MY MINIONS!
FOLLOW ME—THE GREAT HERO!!
STOP, ONII-CHAN!
I CAN'T WALK ANOTHER STEP!
MRK...
I ONLY LET YOU JOIN THE PARTY BECAUSE YOU SAID YOU ***REALLY*** WANTED TO!
Waaaaaaaah!
UGH, COME ON, STOP CRYING, RYŌ!

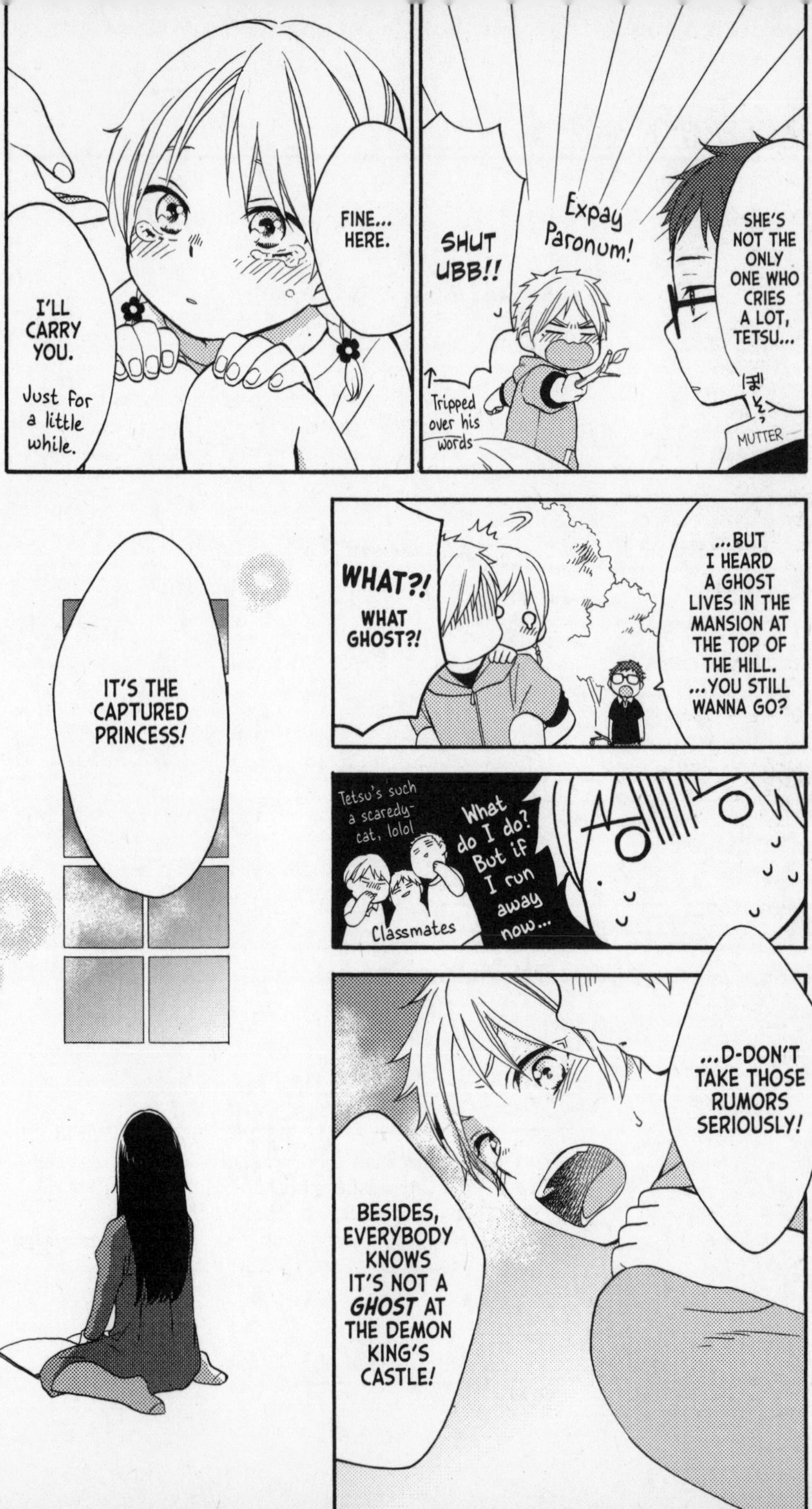
SHE'S NOT THE ONLY ONE WHO CRIES A LOT, TETSU...
MUTTER
Expay Paronum!
SHUT UBB!!
Tripped over his words
FINE... HERE.
I'LL CARRY YOU.
Just for a little while.
...BUT I HEARD A GHOST LIVES IN THE MANSION AT THE TOP OF THE HILL. ...YOU STILL WANNA GO?
WHAT?! WHAT GHOST?!
What do I do? But if I run away now...
Tetsu's such a scaredy-cat, lolol
Classmates
...D-DON'T TAKE THOSE RUMORS SERIOUSLY!
BESIDES, EVERYBODY KNOWS IT'S NOT A GHOST AT THE DEMON KING'S CASTLE!
IT'S THE CAPTURED PRINCESS!

TRANSLATION NOTES

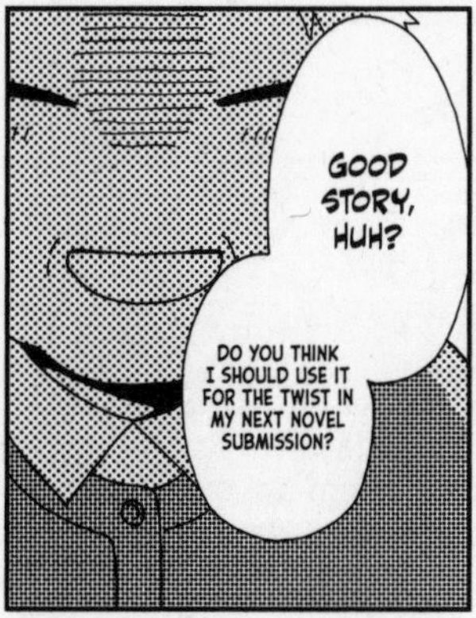
GOOD STORY, HUH?
DO YOU THINK I SHOULD USE IT FOR THE TWIST IN MY NEXT NOVEL SUBMISSION?

Novel submission, page 8
Kumada-san has not made it big as an author yet, so she gets her stories out there by submitting them to publishing companies. In Japan, some publishers have regular competitions in which amateur authors can submit their writing. The best stories will be published, and the authors may be given a contract.

Dust cloth for the new semester, page 19
In Japan, students are expected to help keep their classrooms clean, and not just by being considerate and not leaving trash on the floor—they are expected to sweep, dust, etc. The school provides most of the cleaning supplies, but students are asked to bring their own dust cloths.

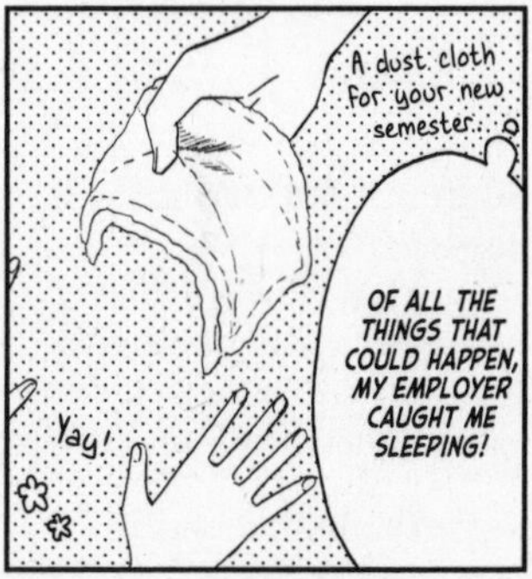
A dust cloth for your new semester...
OF ALL THE THINGS THAT COULD HAPPEN, MY EMPLOYER CAUGHT ME SLEEPING!
Yay!

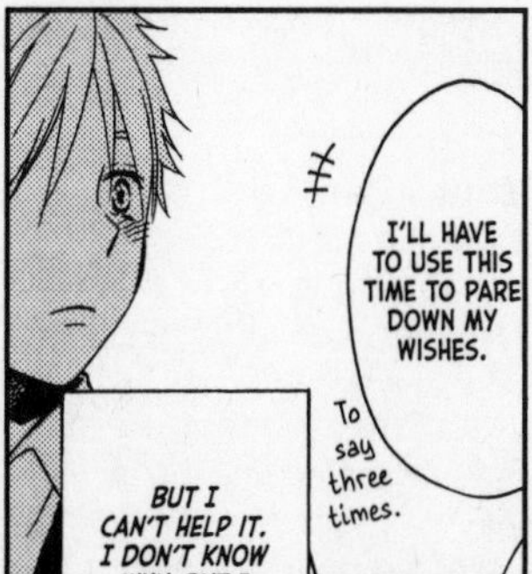
I'LL HAVE TO USE THIS TIME TO PARE DOWN MY WISHES.
To say three times.
BUT I CAN'T HELP IT. I DON'T KNOW WHY, BUT I CAN'T RESIST THAT SMILE.
Okay, so we'll meet up at one in the morning!
Do you have a cell phone?
Nope!

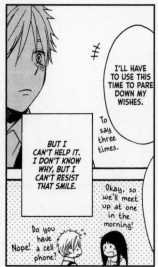

Pare down my wishes, page 38
In Japan, the rules for wishing on a shooting star are to repeat the wish three times while the star is still falling. If the wisher succeeds, the wish will come true. Here, it is unclear whether Shizu has a long list of wishes to pare down, or if the idea is to come up with the shortest way to recite one or two wishes.

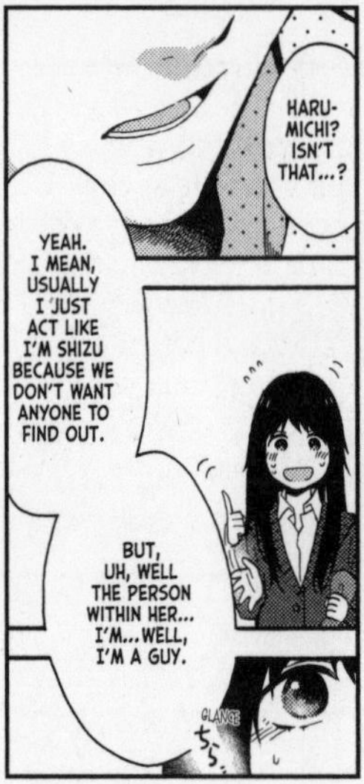
HARUMICHI? ISN'T THAT...?
YEAH. I MEAN, USUALLY I JUST ACT LIKE I'M SHIZU BECAUSE WE DON'T WANT ANYONE TO FIND OUT.
BUT, UH, WELL THE PERSON WITHIN HER... I'M...WELL, I'M A GUY.
GLANCE

Harumichi? Isn't that…?, page 80

Tetsu is realizing that there are two things about Harumichi that defy his expectations. First, Harumichi is a masculine name. Second, what he really commented on in the Japanese text was Harumichi's choice of the first person pronoun. While English only has one variety of first-person singular pronouns, Japanese has a few different ones, chosen based on formality and even gender. Although women can use pronouns like the *ore* Harumichi uses here, the societal assumption is that anyone who calls themselves *ore* is male.

Sōmen noodles in April, page 81

Sōmen is a noodle dish served with a light dipping sauce, usually eaten cold in the summer. Tetsu makes the out-of-season dish because he lacked ingredients to make anything else.

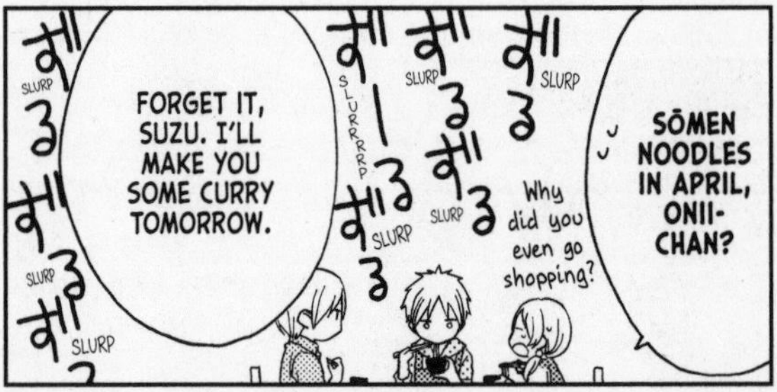
SŌMEN NOODLES IN APRIL, ONII-CHAN?
Why did you even go shopping?
SLURP
SLURP
SLURP
SLURRRRP
SLURP
FORGET IT, SUZU. I'LL MAKE YOU SOME CURRY TOMORROW.
SLURP
SLURP
SLURP

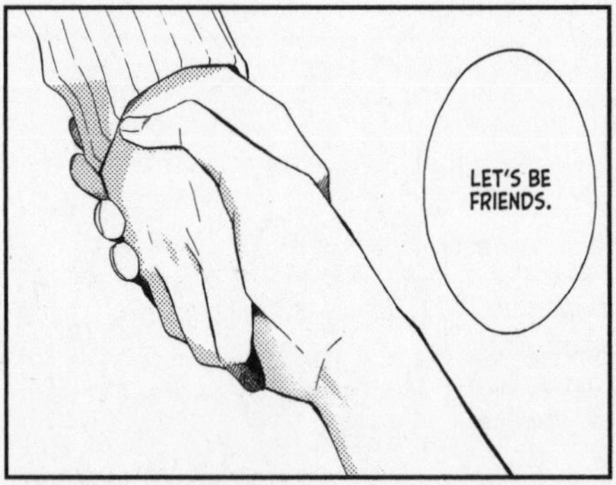
LET'S BE FRIENDS.

Let's be friends, page 98

There's a ritual expression in Japanese that comes in varying levels of politeness, but its unabbreviated form is usually *yoroshiku onegai shimasu,* which translates roughly to, "I hope you treat me (or this endeavor) well." It can be used when meeting someone for the first time; when people are about to work on a project together; when someone is about to start working for someone; or even in a fighting game when characters are about to fight each other. In this case, since the endeavor is one of friendship, it is translated as, "Let's be friends."

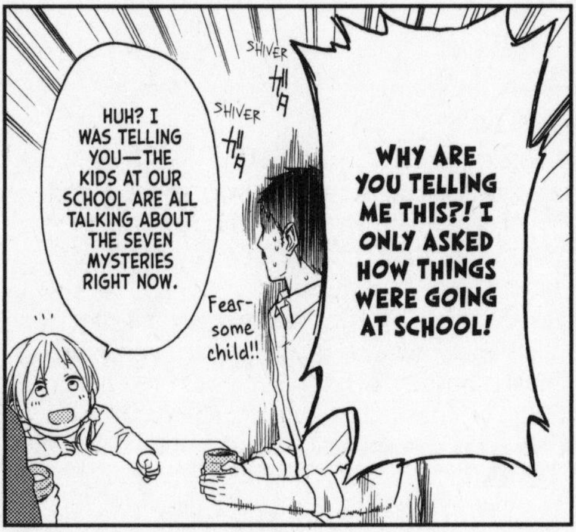
WHY ARE YOU TELLING ME THIS?! I ONLY ASKED HOW THINGS WERE GOING AT SCHOOL!
SHIVER
SHIVER
HUH? I WAS TELLING YOU—THE KIDS AT OUR SCHOOL ARE ALL TALKING ABOUT THE SEVEN MYSTERIES RIGHT NOW.
Fear-some child!!

Seven Mysteries, page 106
Also translated as "Seven Wonders" or "Seven Horrors," the word *nana-fushigi* refers to the seven inexplicable occurences that take place in one location. Many schools have their own set of them. They often refer to things such as a statue that moves, or mysterious noises in the hall at night believed to be the moaning of a spirit, etc.

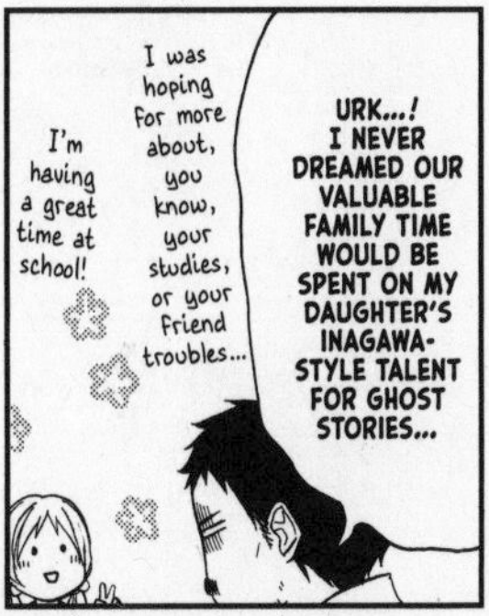
URK...! I NEVER DREAMED OUR VALUABLE FAMILY TIME WOULD BE SPENT ON MY DAUGHTER'S INAGAWA-STYLE TALENT FOR GHOST STORIES...
I was hoping for more about, you know, your studies, or your friend troubles...
I'm having a great time at school!

Inagawa-style talent for ghost stories, page 106
Junji Inagawa is a Japanese actor who has become famous for his excellent ghost stories narrations.

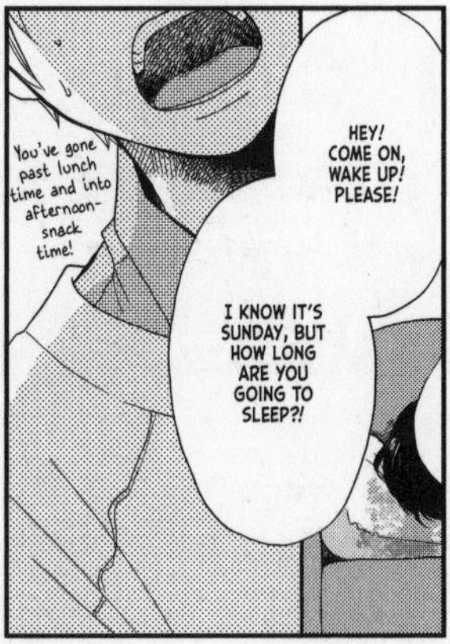
HEY! COME ON, WAKE UP! PLEASE!
I KNOW IT'S SUNDAY, BUT HOW LONG ARE YOU GOING TO SLEEP?!
You've gone past lunch time and into afternoon-snack time!

Past lunch and into snack time, page 115
In Japan, the word for snack is *oyatsu,* which comes from *yatsudoki,* the eighth hour, which in modern times is between two and four o'clock.

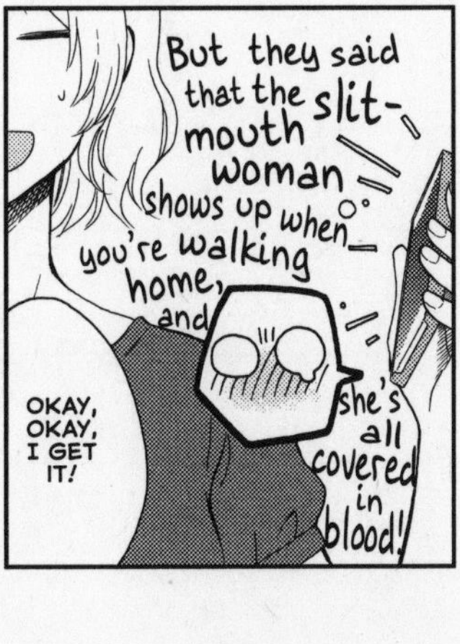
But they said that the slit-mouth woman shows up when you're walking home, and she's all covered in blood!
OKAY, OKAY, I GET IT!

Slit-mouth woman, page 143
Slit-Mouth Woman, or *Kuchi-Saké Onna,* is an urban legend from Japan about a masked woman who will stop people on their way home and ask them if they think she's pretty. If her victims tell her she's not pretty, she'll kill them, but if they say she is, she will remove her mask to reveal a mouth that has been slit open from ear-to-ear and ask if they still think she's pretty. If they say yes, she'll slit their mouth to match hers.

Japan's most powerful spirit medium delves into the ghost world's greatest mysteries!

Story by Kyo Shirodaira, famed author of mystery fiction and creator of *Spiral, Blast of Tempest,* and *The Record of a Fallen Vampire.*

Both touched by spirits called yôkai, Kotoko and Kurô have gained unique superhuman powers. But to gain her powers Kotoko has given up an eye and a leg, and Kurô's personal life is in shambles. So when Kotoko suggests they team up to deal with renegades from the spirit world, Kurô doesn't have many other choices, but Kotoko might just have a few ulterior motives...

IN/SPECTRE

STORY BY KYO SHIRODAIRA
ART BY CHASHIBA KATASE

Based on the critically acclaimed classic horror manga

The first new *Parasyte* manga in over 20 years!

NEO ParaSyte f

BY ASUMIKO NAKAMURA, EMA TOYAMA, MIKI RINNO, LALAKO KOJIMA, KAORI YUKI, BANKO KUZE, YUUKI OBATA, KASHIO, YUI KUROE, ASIA WATANABE, MIKIMAKI, HIKARU SURUGA, HAJIME SHINJO, RENJURO KINDAICHI, AND YURI NARUSHIMA

A collection of chilling new *Parasyte* stories from Japan's top shojo artists!

Parasites: shape-shifting aliens whose only purpose is to assimilate with and consume the human race... but do these monsters have a different side? A parasite becomes a prince to save his romance-obsessed female host from a dangerous stalker. Another hosts a cooking show, in which the real monsters are revealed. These and 13 more stories, from some of the greatest shojo manga artists alive today, together make up a chilling, funny, and entertaining tribute to one of manga's horror classics!

KC KODANSHA COMICS

KODANSHA COMICS

"I'm pleasantly surprised to find modern shojo using cross-dressing as a dramatic device to deliver social commentary... Recommended."

-Otaku USA Magazine

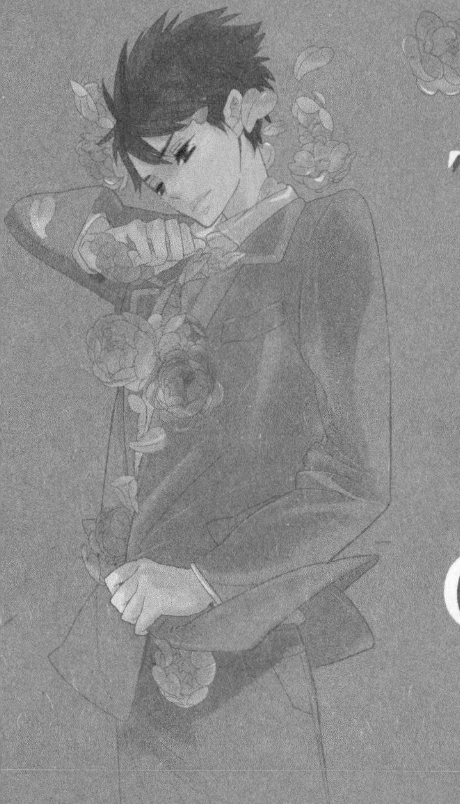

The prince in his dark days

By Hico Yamanaka

A drunkard for a father, a household of poverty... For 17-year-old Atsuko, misfortune is all she knows and believes in. Until one day, a chance encounter with Itaru–the wealthy heir of a huge corporation–changes everything. The two look identical, uncannily so. When Itaru curiously goes missing, Atsuko is roped into being his stand-in. There, in his shoes, Atsuko must parade like a prince in a palace. She encounters many new experiences, but at what cost...?

FIRE FORCE

By Atsushi Ohkubo

The city of Tokyo is plagued by a deadly phenomenon: spontaneous human combustion! Luckily, a special team is there to quench the inferno: The Fire Force! The fire soldiers at Special Fire Cathedral 8 are about to get a unique addition. Enter Shinra, a boy who possesses the power to run at the speed of a rocket, leaving behind the famous "devil's footprints" (and destroying his shoes in the process). Can Shinra and his colleagues discover the source of this strange epidemic before the city burns to ashes?

A Kodansha Comics Trade Paperback Original.

Wake Up, Sleeping Beauty volume 1 copyright © 2015 Megumi Morino
English translation copyright © 2017 Megumi Morino

Published in the United States by Kodansha Comics,
an imprint of Kodansha USA Publishing, LLC, New York.

Publication rights for this English edition arranged through Kodansha Ltd., Tokyo.

First published in Japan in 2015 by Kodansha Ltd., Tokyo,
as Ohayou, Ibarahime volume 1.

Cover Design: Tomohiro Kusume (arcoinc)

ISBN 978-1-63236-519-4

Printed in the United States of America.

www.kodanshacomics.com

9 8 7 6 5 4 3 2 1

Translation: Alethea and Athena Nibley
Lettering: Lys Blakeslee
Editing: Haruko Hashimoto
Kodansha Comics Edition Cover Design: Phil Balsman